Parents and Children in the Mid-Victorian Novel

Madeleine Wood

Parents and Children in the Mid-Victorian Novel

Traumatic Encounters and the Formation of Family

palgrave
macmillan

Madeleine Wood
Children's Services
NSPCC
London, UK

ISBN 978-3-030-45471-5 ISBN 978-3-030-45469-2 (eBook)
https://doi.org/10.1007/978-3-030-45469-2

Cover image: © Ian Dagnall Computing/Alamy Stock Photo, 'Peace Concluded' by John Everett Millais, 1856.

This Palgrave Macmillan imprint is published by the registered company Springer Nature Switzerland AG
The registered company address is: Gewerbestrasse 11, 6330 Cham, Switzerland

For my Dad

Preface

> [...] *when some of our fellows were wounded in India, they came home bringing bullets inside them. They did not talk of them, and they were stout and hearty, and looked as well, perhaps, as you or I; but every change in the weather, however slight, every variation of the atmosphere, however trifling, brought back the old agony of their wounds as sharp as ever they had felt it on the battle-field. I've had my wound, Bob; I carry the bullet still, and I shall carry it into my coffin.*
>
> Mary Elizabeth Braddon, *Lady Audley's Secret* (1862), 1:98.

Explaining his torment and grief on hearing news of his wife's death, George Talboys presents Robert Audley with a metaphor: the pain that he feels is like a war wound; it recurs, invisibly pushing him towards a predetermined fate. This fate structures the novel: the sensational action hinges on George's disappearance and the revelation that his wife Lucy, now married to another man, tried to murder him. Through George, Mary Elizabeth Braddon formulates psychological trauma with startling specificity, clarity and eloquence; and yet at the point of writing, psychological trauma was not found in the medical lexicon.

This study explores trauma in a dual time frame: the mid-Victorian period and the later emergence of psychoanalysis. I argue that the mid-Victorian novel anticipates later psychoanalytic concepts of trauma, thereby exceeding the parameters of contemporary medical discourse. This is not simply a comparative reading: I argue it is the historical conditions of the mid-century period that lead to this new literary emphasis and pave the way for the emergence of psychoanalysis in Vienna at the *fin de siècle*. In arguing this, it is precisely metaphors such as George Talboys's that are at stake. The novelists examined here construct complex narrative and thematic structures: traumatisation is represented through symbolic patterning and recurring scenes, inseparable from mid-Victorian narrative discourse, mimesis and the development of experimental realisms. *Traumatic Encounters* is not a chronological account of the relationship between Freudian psychoanalysis and literature; I explore the narrative modes of novel and case history in order to shed light on nineteenth-century representations of family.

* * *

I interpret the medical category of trauma as a historical construction, rather than as a transhistorical truth; however, this observation does not lessen the psychological import of traumatic experience, nor indeed its individual and cultural realities. Nevertheless, one of the fundamental problems with the category of trauma as it has evolved in the late twentieth- and early twenty-first centuries is the assumption that somehow we all know what a traumatic event *is*. The mid-twentieth century bore witness to Auschwitz, Hiroshima and Nagasaki: devastation on a seemingly unprecedented scale. Philosophers, psychologists and historians have rightly focused on the threat posed to memory and subjectivity when threatened by total nullification, with the debate circling around testimony and bearing witness. However, this discussion cuts in different directions: on the one hand, philosophers examine the possibility of *being* in the modern world; on the other, clinicians examine memory as a neurobiological process. While noting the importance of the latter, the memory debates are not the focus of this project. Although, as Bessel van der Kolk argues in *Psychological Trauma* (1987), there may be particular events that have specific neurobiological consequences for the way in which we process memory, it would be unwise to adopt such an universalising and ahistorical model.[1] The fact that, to date, neuroscientific studies still show that some traumas can be recalled, while others cannot, illustrates the false

[1] Van der Kolk's diagnostic approach leads him to assert 'closer examination makes it clear that the human response to overwhelming and uncontrollable life events is remarkably consistent' (1987, 2). According to van der Kolk and van der Hart (1995), a trauma is 'a frightening event outside of ordinary human experience' (172) which disrupts the operation of 'ordinary memory' (ibid., 162): 'Memories and feelings connected with the

dichotomy that underpins much of twentieth-century trauma studies in which memory is opposed to fantasy and the event is opposed to subjective experience. The complex nexus of psychological experience remains unaccounted for.[2]

Sigmund Freud developed the concept of psychical reality to try and negotiate these problems, brought to light in his early psychoanalytic cases in the 1890s. Throughout his case histories, we see the ongoing tension between external and interior reality. Fantasy bridges this: by arguing that the memory process involves psychological investment, Freud highlights the inseparability of fantasy and subjectivity. Psychical reality means 'everything in the psyche that takes on the force of reality for the subject'; 'Phantasies, even if they are not based on real events, now come to have the same pathogenic effect [as memory] for the subject' (Laplanche and Pontalis 1988, 363). Fantasy, though, whether conscious or unconscious, is not simply *opposed* to empirical reality: it is the mode in which we engage (or indeed perhaps attempt to disengage) with our reality.

For Freud, psychological symptoms emerge in response to the outside world, through phantasmatic investment. Crucially, this does not negate the possible reality of traumatic events. Looking at *Studies on Hysteria*, we see that trauma is not just extraordinary and horrific, it is also the quotidian. A kiss, misplaced and unwanted, leads to a reprimand that plays on Lucy R's mind unconsciously; the unexpected sight of her dead sister in her coffin haunts Frau Emmy von N. Freud does not separate these

trauma are forgotten and return as intrusive recollections, feeling states (such as overwhelming anxiety and panic unwarranted by current experience), fugues, delusions, states of depersonalization, and finally in behavioral reenactments' (van der Kolk 1987, 185). Van der Kolk (2005) later developed his concept of 'developmental trauma', differentiating this from post-traumatic stress disorder. Developmental trauma is by definition 'interpersonal' and involves the child's 'care-giving system' (402): it is a trauma presented through a relationship, possibly involving 'maltreatment' (ibid.) This idea of trauma is much closer to what we see in the Victorian novels; however, van der Kolk does not consider the child's process of meaning making, fantasy or symbolisation in any detail.

[2] Some strands of social work theory have considered the relationship between the traumatic event/series of events and the meaning attributed to the event by the subject. Nancy Boyd Webb presents a 'tripartite assessment' model which comprises, 'Nature of the traumatic event', 'factors in the support system/recovery environment' and 'factors affecting individual response' (Boyd Webb 2015, 25). Boyd Webb cites Anna Freud's comments on the 'specific meaning' of traumatic events (7). However, 'meaning' is a sub-theme in Boyd Webb's tripartite assessment, rather than a determining factor in itself, and fantasy is not theorised within her discussion.

normal, but painful moments, from the sexual abuse seen in Katharina's case; in so doing, he reminds us that each individual experience of traumatisation requires in-depth reading.

Freud reads trauma as a temporal and spatial structure: as a series of scenes. Each secondary or auxiliary scene relates symbolically in some way to the primal scene: the trauma is reframed, replayed. The scenographic model likewise underpins Freud's analyses of fantasy in essays such as 'Screen Memories' (1899); 'Childhood Memories and Screen Memories' (1901); 'Delusions and Dreams in Jensen's *Gradiva*' (1907); 'Creative Writers and Daydreaming' (1908) and 'A Child is Being Beaten' (1915). John Fletcher's important book *Freud and the Scene of Trauma* (2013) explores the placement of trauma in Freud's thought in intricate detail, constructing a nuanced critique. Fletcher argues 'that it is Freud's mapping of trauma *as a scene*, the elaboration of a *scenography* of trauma, that is central to both his clinical interpretation of his patients' symptoms and his construction of successive theoretical models and concepts to explain the power of such scenes in his patients' lives' (xiii).

So why should any of this be of relevance to the mid-Victorian novel? Something specific happens in this historical moment: we see a psychological and narratological model emerge in which cross-generational relationships are presented as formative and traumatising for the protagonists. Each of the novels investigated in this study hinges upon (usually multiple) traumatic and familial events, which become the source of character, plot and desirousness. The 'trauma' is not something that lies outside of the self; it is formative for the protagonist's subjectivity. Nearly fifty years before the introduction of trauma as a psychological category at the *fin de siècle*, authors show their protagonists coming into being in a state of psychological damage. The—extended and frequently non-biological—parent-child relationship operates as a prism through which the novelists explore the wider social forces that play upon the protagonists. This is not simply a device. The mid-Victorian novelists extend contemporary medical and philosophical understanding by representing the psychological dynamism of the parent-child relationship. Moreover, this relationship is consistently shown to be in the process of being extended, disrupted, deferred or cancelled out. There is nothing static or nuclear about the families we see in the mid-Victorian novel.

Literary critics have not been slow to analyse the psychological dimensions of the Victorian novel. In *Shock, Memory and the Unconscious in Victorian Fiction*, Jill Matus draws an important link between prototypical theories of trauma and Victorian literature, placing her textual readings in the context of contemporary theories of shock. Her research builds upon the influential work of Sally Shuttleworth and Jenny Bourne Taylor, both of whom create important interdisciplinary readings of Victorian fiction in relation to contemporary psychological discourses. Matus's authoritative work presents an account of the development of psychological and materialist theories of the mind from the early nineteenth century onwards. In line with Shuttleworth and Taylor, Matus describes psychology as a 'newly forming discipline' at the mid-century (Matus 2009, 26).

The Victorian idea of shock mediates between the concept of moral insanity and *fin-de-siècle* theories of hysteria and trauma. Matus charts the uneven development of shock through the work of nineteenth-century materialists including William Carpenter, Henry Maudsley and Herbert Spencer. She examines physiological discourses surrounding the nervous system: altered states of consciousness or split consciousness, memory and belatedness. Her study shows that literary authors were active in theorising the relation between body and mind. In her analysis of Dickens's short story 'The Signalman', Matus writes, 'If he lost his voice in the Staplehurst accident, he found it later in articulating, in this story of ghostly clairvoyance and hindsight, the characteristics of trauma barely broached in the medical discourse of nervous shock during the 1860s' (104). Like Matus, I argue that mid-nineteenth-century literary texts formed, as well as reflected, new ways of thinking about the mind; however, unlike Matus, I argue that the representation of trauma and psychological belatedness emerges specifically through the mid-Victorian novel's representation of the bourgeois home, and within a cross-generational schema. In Chapter 3, I argue that Dickens's awareness of traumatic psychological experience predates his railway accident in 1865, and can be charted back to his writing of the mid-late 1840s: *Dombey and Son* and the 'autobiographical fragment'.

As Matus rightly argues, the 'The term "trauma" emerged in the late nineteenth century when the label for a physical wound came to be associated with a mental state. A precondition of that shift was that the mind had to be conceived of as physical, material and physiological—and therefore vulnerable—like the body' (7).[3] Examining the technological context

[3] It is the idea of the mind's vulnerability to wounding that underpins George Talboys's metaphor, with which I opened. Braddon self-consciously places her narrative in the context of an alienating Victorian modernity (II.6, 205), and while *Lady Audley's Secret*

of medical theory in the 1880s, Paul Lerner and Mark S. Micale highlight Herbert Page's work on railway injuries 'without apparent mechanical lesion' (2001, 12), and Sir James Paget's theory of 'neuromimesis': 'purely functional, fear-induced disorders that closely imitated neurological diseases' (ibid).[4] William James used 'trauma' with this new meaning in English for the first time in 1894 and disseminated European theories to an Anglo-American audience (Matus 2009, 87, 89); Jean-Martin Charcot, Pierre Janet, Hermann Oppenheim, Josef Breuer and Freud were the key figures. Freud, then, participated in a disputatious Anglo-American and European field of study, concerned with both physical and mental trauma and hysteria. Charcot's elaboration of a theoretical connection between trauma and hysteria was central to the further development of trauma as a psychological category. Fletcher explains, Charcot 'extended the hysteria diagnosis to include the post-traumatic nervous derangements caused by physical traumas, such as workplace accidents, and the new high-speed means of travel' (Fletcher 2013, 19): traumas occurred when the victim suffered a strong emotional or shock response in an unprepared, hypnoid state (20). Charcot's emphasis on altered states of consciousness, and their relation to the creation and experience of trauma, influenced Janet, Breuer and Freud.[5] Janet's 1889 work *L'Automatisme psychologique* explored the relationship between altered states

does not prioritise the parental in quite the same manner as the novels examined here, it is grounded in a *cross-generational* problem. Sir Michael Audley is a figure of the past, while the younger generation, including his second wife, are products of Victorian modernity.

[4] Fletcher charts the importance of J. Russell Reynolds's work on 'morbid idealisation', published in 1869 (13), linking this back to Sir Benjamin Brodie's earlier work (Fletcher 2013, 13–14). In the third edition of *Pathological and Surgical Observations on the Diseases of the Joints* (1834), Brodie outlines an inorganic form of pain and inflammation, which he names 'local hysterical affection' (115). He places the emphasis on hysterical young women with a 'morbid condition of the nerves' (115), primarily suggesting that these women are in need of exercise and clean living. Brodie does not analyse the women's psychological state in any depth, referring to the chronic pain itself as the 'subject of her complaints' (116).

[5] Paul Lerner argues that Oppenheim's separation of traumatic neurosis from hysteria, set out in his monograph, *Die traumatischen Neurosen* (1889), has too often been interpreted as an affirmation of a purely somatic theory of trauma. Lerner points out that the placement of affect is also central to Oppenheim's theory. Discussing his category of traumatic neurosis, Oppenheim writes, 'In the genesis of this illness, physical trauma is only partially responsible. An important—and in many cases the major role—is played by the psyche: terror, emotional shock' (qtd. in Lerner and Micale 2001, 145).

of consciousness, the split self, sense-perception and divided memory systems. It was reviewed and critiqued by William James in his 1890 article, 'The Hidden Self'.

In his early writings, Freud presents himself as the diligent pupil of his favoured teachers, Breuer and Charcot. Despite a powerful homage to Janet's work on split consciousness and hysteria in the 1893 'Preliminary Communication' (Breuer and Freud 2001, 12), his relationship with the latter was more complex. Breuer's theoretical chapter in *Studies on Hysteria* makes frequent polite references to Janet; however, there were significant divergences. Refuting Janet's idea that hysteria is a sign of weakness, Breuer states 'In complete opposition to Janet's views, I believe that in a great many cases what underlies dissociation is an *excess* of efficiency' (233). The distinction between the germinal psychoanalytic unconscious and Janet's idea of split consciousness is beautifully implied by Breuer with a Classical reference and metaphor: 'In our cases the part of the mind which is split off is "thrust into darkness", as the Titans are imprisoned in the crater of Etna, and can shake the earth but can never emerge into the light of day' (229). Freud's early texts, 'The Neuro-Psychoses of Defence' (1894) and 'Heredity and the Aetiology of the Neuroses' (1896), critiqued the role Janet attributed to split consciousness, and instead asserted the importance of defensive repression and premature seduction, respectively—neither of which were concepts employed by Janet. The cracks had appeared quickly, then, and became embarrassingly public at the 1913 International Congress of Medicine where Janet criticised psychoanalysis for its unoriginality, claiming 'priority' for 'having discovered the cathartic cure of neuroses' (Ellenberger 1981, 344).

Intersected by a complex web of theory without being defined by it, the mid-Victorian novel substantively intervenes into the emerging psychological field of the mid-nineteenth century. By presenting family relationships as decisive for our psychological state as well as our social identity, the authors pushed beyond the contemporary scientific models available to them. In so doing, they are uncannily prescient: the use of traumatisation as structuration, plotting and character development anticipated Freud's *fin-de-siècle*manoeuvres. This correspondence is more than a hermeneutic lens: I contend that it was the changing historical conditions of the mid-century that led to the representation of the parent-child relationship as both formative and traumatising. If, as

Carolyn Dever (1998) argues, mid-Victorian literature created the prototypes for Freudian psychoanalysis, there are strong historical reasons why this was the case: Freud's theories were formulated through his work with the bourgeois families of Vienna and his own self-analysis.[6] Trev Lynn Broughton and Helen Rogers (2007) maintain that 'there is still no adequate theoretical framework, psychoanalytic or psychological, with which to comprehend the psychic consequences of living within the complex, sprawling family networks fostered by the contingencies of Victorian life' (19).[7] I disagree. An 'adequate theoretical framework' may be much closer than we realise. By creating a dialogue between lesser-known psychoanalytic theories of trauma and the mid-Victorian novel, we realise that the novels themselves *actively* formulate interpretative frameworks. The everyday traumatisation we see at work in the novels' representation of the parent-child relationship is inextricable from the orphanhood, abuse, financial crimes and secrets that emerge from the 'sprawling family networks fostered by the contingencies of Victorian life'.

London, UK Madeleine Wood

Works Cited

Literary Texts

Braddon, Mary Elizabeth. 1862. *Lady Audley's Secret*. 3 vols. London: Tinsley Bros.

Breuer, Josef and Sigmund Freud. 2001. *Studies on Hysteria*. *SE* 2.

Brodie, Benjamin. 1834. *Pathological Diseases of the Joints*. 3rd ed. Washington: Duff Green.

Broughton, Trev Lynn and Helen Rogers, eds. 2007. *Gender and Fatherhood in the Nineteenth Century*. Basingstoke: Palgrave Macmillan.

[6] In his self-analysis, Freud came to the conclusion that his father had abused his brother and 'several younger sisters' (qtd. in Fletcher 2013, 94). Fletcher writes, 'The figure of the father drops away over the next two years in the letters to Fleiss of 1898-9' (106); however, the seductive adult (in Freud's own case, his nurse) remained a feature of his thought throughout the late 1890s.

[7] Broughton and Rogers draw on Barbara Caine's remarks on the Strachey family in *Bombay to Bloomsbury* (84).

Dever, Carolyn. 1998. *Death and the Mother from Dickens to Freud: Victorian Fictions and the Anxiety of Origins*. Cambridge: Cambridge University Press.
Dickens, Charles. 1974. *Dombey and Son*. Edited by Alan Horsman. Oxford: Clarendon Press.
———. 2009. 'The Signalman'. In *Ghost Stories*, 303–320. London: CRW Publishers.

Primary Psychoanalytic Texts

Abbreviations

Breuer, Josef and Sigmund Freud. 2001. *Studies on Hysteria*. *SE* 2.
Freud, Sigmund.
———. 'A Child is Being Beaten'. *SE* 17:175–204.
———. 'Childhood Memories and Screen Memories'. In *The Psychopathology of Everyday Life*. *SE* 6:43–52.
———. 'Creative Writers and Daydreaming'. *SE* 9:141–154.
———. 'Delusions and Dreams in Jensen's *Gradiva*'. *SE* 9:3–96.
———. 'Heredity and the Aetiology of the Neuroses'. *SE 3*:141–156.
———. 'The Neuro-Psychoses of Defence'. *SE 3*:43–61.
———. 'Screen Memories'. *SE* 3:301–322.
Laplanche, Jean and Jean Bertrand Pontalis. 1988. *The Language of Psychoanalysis*. Translated by Donald Nicholson Smith. London: Karnac.

Secondary Texts

Brodie, Benjamin. 1834. *Pathological Diseases of the Joints*. 3rd edition. Washington: Duff Green.
Broughton, Trev Lynn and Helen Rogers, eds. 2007. *Gender and Fatherhood in the Nineteenth Century*. Basingstoke: Palgrave Macmillan.
Ellenberger, Henri. 1981. *The Discovery of the Unconscious: The History and Evolution of Dynamic Psychology*. New York: Basic Books.
Fletcher, John. 2013. *Freud and the Scene of Trauma*. New York: Fordham University Press.
James, William. 1890. 'The Hidden Self'. *Scribner's Magazine*. Vol. 7: 361–373. Online at https://babel.hathitrust.org/cgi/pt?id=coo.31924097557262&view=1up&seq=369&q1=William%20James.
Janet, Pierre. 1889. *L'Automatisme psychologique: Essai de psychologie expérimentale sur les formes inferieures de l'activité humaine*. Paris: Félix Alcan.
van der Kolk, Bessel A. 2005. 'Developmental Trauma: Toward a Rational Diagnosis for Children with Complex Trauma Histories'. *Psychiatric Annals* 35, no. 5: 402–408.

———. ed. 1987. *Psychological Trauma*. Arlington, VA: American Psychiatric Press.

Lerner, Paul and Mark S. Micale, eds. 2001. *Traumatic Pasts: History, Psychiatry, and Trauma in the Modern Age, 1870–1930*. Cambridge: Cambridge University Press.

Matus, Jill. 2009. *Shock, Memory and the Unconscious in Victorian Fiction*. Cambridge: Cambridge University Press.

Oppenheim, Hermann. 1892 [1889]. *Die traumatischen Neurosen nach den in der Nervenklinik der Charité in den letzten 5 Jahren gesammelten Beobachtungen*. Berlin: Hirschwald.

van der Kolk, Bessel A. and Onno van der Hart. 1995. 'The Intrusive Past: The Flexibility of Memory and the Engraving of Trauma'. In *Trauma: Explorations in Memory*, edited by Cathy Caruth. Baltimore: John Hopkins University Press.

Webb, Nancy Boyd. 2015. 'Family and Community Contexts of Children and Adolescents Facing Crisis or Trauma'. In *Play Therapy with Children and Adolescents in Crisis*, 4th ed., edited by Nancy Boyd. 3–21. New York, NY: The Guildford Press.

Acknowledgements

Traumatic Encounters: Parents and Children in the Mid-Victorian Novel is the product of many years work on psychoanalysis and the mid-Victorian novel, starting its life in embryonic form in my Ph.D. thesis, *Victorian Familial Enigmas: Inheritance and Influence*, in which I read novels by Charles Dickens and Wilkie Collins through a psychoanalytic lens. My postgraduate study was undertaken at the University of Warwick from 2004 to 2009. The Arts and Humanities Research Council funded both my M.A. and Ph.D.: it would not have been possible for me to enter the academy without this opportunity, for which I am sincerely grateful.

This book represents the culmination of my career in Victorian literary scholarship; in the final stages of revision, I worked as a social worker in Child Protection, and at the time of manuscript submission, I am now a Children's Services Practitioner at the NSPCC. I do not represent the views, policy or research of the NSPCC in this publication, and the book was not produced or contracted within the period of my work for the NSPCC. I am, however, grateful to the organisation, where I am fortunate to work in a team of highly dedicated and skilled practitioners.

Traumatic Encounters bears witness to a series of intellectual encounters and strands of thought, which led me to recognise the importance of my textual analyses for a historical understanding of the Victorian period; it took shape in the context of my own development as a nineteenth-century literary scholar and later, in my move out of the academy into social work practice with children. Working directly with children who have experienced trauma, as I do now, I realise again the importance of the theories and texts I analyse here; literature can widen our field of vision, enabling new ways of being in the work.

I arrived at Warwick University in 2004 as an M.A. student, knowing that I wanted to research psychoanalysis and childhood, and on my first day, met John Fletcher, who supervised me from my Masters degree onwards. *Traumatic Encounters* would not exist without John. He developed my thinking on childhood by focusing my attention on trauma and its shifting presence in psychoanalytic theory and literature—encouraging me to note and analyse 'scenographies'. This idea underpinned everything that followed. I feel privileged to have worked with John; he is the most meticulous scholar I know, and he has consistently encouraged me always to push for a similar rigour in my own thinking. He provided important pointers on the book manuscript, particularly in his detailed responses to Chapters 1 and 2. I am more grateful to John than I can say—he has been a generous and supportive presence in my life since I was 24 years old.

On a similar note, I would not have survived the idiosyncratic business of junior academic life without the support of my Ph.D. examiner, Cora Kaplan, who helped me in numerous ways following my *viva*. From writing me references for job applications, to reading my research and writing, and at other times, simply cheering me up, Cora was unfailingly kind. Her advice to me in my *viva* provided the basis for the extensive development of my research as I moved from thesis to book. While I know it will embarrass her to read this, Cora exemplifies the very best of what senior academics can be in their work with junior colleagues, and I wish to thank her.

The book has an uncanny power of its own, taking me back to my earlier professional self. I hold fond memories of the eight years I spent in the Department of English and Comparative Literary Studies at the University of Warwick, studying and teaching, and would like to thank the staff I worked alongside, especially my Ph.D. mentor, Emma Francis. I'd like to thank Elizabeth Ludlow for her encouragement and constant generosity of spirit. Thank you to John Bowen (University of York) for continuing to support me after examining my Ph.D. thesis.

There were many productive academic relationships which facilitated the development of this book from 2012 onward; from my time at Brunel, I'd like to thank Jessica Cox, Claire O'Callaghan and Emma Butcher; thanks to Josephine McDonagh and Adelene Buckland from Kings College London. Thank you to Margaret Reynolds and Catherine

Maxwell from Queen Mary University of London, and also to David Colclough, for his kindness and support with my post-academic applications. I am very grateful to John O. Jordan for his reassurance and encouragement about my use of Jean Laplanche when we met in 2012.

I would like to thank all of my students, from Warwick, Brunel, Kings College London, Queen Mary University of London and several summer schools in Oxford. I loved my teaching—and I feel privileged to have shared my love of literature and its possibilities in the classroom. *Traumatic Encounters* would not have been written without that inspiration and excitement.

But I could not have finished this book without the love, dedication and immense patience of my mum, Sarah Poynting. I'd also like to mention my brother, Ed Wood, his wife, Katie Allen, Isaac and Lois, and my little sister, Phoebe. I am also blessed to have friends who love and care about me, without whom the completion of this project would not have been possible. I could list twenty names, but I will focus on those four who, over many years, have repeatedly taken proactive steps to support me through hard times—Rebecca Komene, Joe Hill, Ruth Keeling, Will Roberts—I can't thank you enough. The family is not just a biological structure, as the Victorian novel so rightly shows; with that in mind, I am also grateful for my dog, Malachi, lovingly present since 2009.

This book has a sadness hidden at its heart, as my father, Nick Wood, died in 2007, while I was halfway through my Ph.D. Writing became a work of mourning, a way of making sense of my own family as well as others, a process of reparation. This book, like the thesis which preceded it, is dedicated to him.

My analysis of *Dombey and Son* was first published by *Dickens Studies Annual* (43: 2012) as, 'Whispers and Shadows: Traumatic Echoes in Paul Dombey's Life, Death and Afterlife'. A small portion of my writing on *Armadale* was previously located in 'Female Narrative Energy in the Writings of Dead White Males: Dickens, Collins and Freud', contained in *Cross-Gendered Literary Voices: Appropriating, Resisting, Embracing* (2012). The collection was edited by Rina Kim and Claire Westall and published by Palgrave.

Contents

CHAPTER 1

Introduction

The category of trauma relies on origins but—as psychoanalysis and trauma studies repeatedly show—origins tend to recede from view. In order to understand the literary representation of parents and children in the mid-Victorian novel, we must place the enquiry within a dynamic historical context: the consolidation of bourgeois ideology from 1832 onwards and the anxieties concerning home emerging in the 1840s. However, in so doing, I do not imply that 1832 constitutes a decisive wound. The pathologisation of the parent-child relationship occurred through a complex network of historical and literary conditions propelled by bourgeois ideologies of home, nationhood and gender. Mid-Victorian novelists (contemporary with Karl Marx, without following him) actively formulate the relationship between ideology and (un)consciousness, and they do so within a cross-generational schema. The elder generation does not just psychologically damage the younger; they perform, consciously or unconsciously, an ideological inscription.

The way in which bourgeois ideologies are maintained through fantasy is a recurring concern for this study. Drawing on Marx and Fredrich Engels, Slavoj Žižek (1989) writes, 'What they do not know is that their social reality itself, their activity, is guided by an illusion, by a fetishistic inversion. What they overlook, what they misrecognize, is not the reality but the illusion which is structuring their reality, their real social activity'. He clarifies this: 'And this overlooked, unconscious illusion is what may be called the *ideological fantasy*' (32–33). Žižek provides two helpful

M. Wood, *Parents and Children in the Mid-Victorian Novel*,
https://doi.org/10.1007/978-3-030-45469-2_1

examples of such illusions: first, that money is the literal 'embodiment of wealth'; and second, that the Law is universal (31–32). Žižek claims that even if we know these are fantasies, we act *as if* they are true, thus reinforcing the ideological structure of bourgeois capitalism.[1] I argue that the mid-Victorian novel perpetuates the ideological fantasy of home as sanctified and private (and separate from the marketplace), while simultaneously revealing this to be a damaging fetish. There is nothing stable about this process, however, as the textual analyses show.

Traumatic Encounters does not focus on childhood in isolation, but on the dynamic relationships between parents and children. However, this development is predicated upon the earlier 'discovery' of childhood. The mid-Victorian novel shows us that we are always children to our own parents—childhood is not simply a lost realm, being someone's 'child' is a structural position in the family. Jacqueline Rose's *The Case of Peter Pan* (1992 [1984]) identifies the 'impossible relations between adult and child' (1). In elaborating this thesis, Rose reads children's literature in the context of eighteenth- and nineteenth-century thinkers, John Locke, Jean-Jacques Rousseau and Sigmund Freud. Rose analyses Peter Pan in detail, considering the commercialisation of the child. Rose wrote the preface to the second edition of *The Case of Peter Pan* in 1992 in the context of heightened media attention and awareness of childhood sexual abuse. Sexual abuse is not the explicit focus for this study (most notably because it is not the specific focus for the mid-Victorian novels I analyse); however, it cannot be excluded from the wider conversation concerning cross-generational trauma.[2] I look at this from the psychoanalytic perspective in this chapter. Now, in the context of internet pornography and its regulation, and the shocking revelations of the Jimmy Savile case in Britain (from 2012 onwards), the definition and protection of childhood become ever more pertinent.[3] The Serious

[1] Žižek's emphasis on performativity comes from Louis Althusser whom I discuss later in the chapter.

[2] I use the term 'cross-generational trauma' in preference to 'transgenerational' or 'intergenerational' trauma throughout the monograph. In so doing, I hold in mind the multiple forms in which traumatisation can occur. The term 'intergenerational' is generally used to indicate something operating between two generations, while 'transgenerational' usually means the passing down of historical trauma; however, 'cross-generational' retains both possibilities.

[3] Jean Laplanche (2011) warns against the creation of new 'Monsters', arguing that our understanding of adult-child relationships *requires* the conceptual dimension of the

Crime Act 2015 criminalised coercive and controlling behaviour in intimate relationships and the family, showing the ways in which the anxieties expressed in the mid-Victorian novel continue to resonate in twenty-first century Britain. Since the Children Act 1989 (CA 1989), the state's involvement in family life has been grounded by Section 1 CA 1989, the 'Paramountcy Principle', which insists that the 'child's welfare shall be the court's paramount consideration'. This principle, without the supporting legislation, is found throughout the mid-Victorian novel.[4]

Creation of Childhood

The mid-Victorians inherited a complex set of eighteenth-century intellectual legacies concerning childhood. Eighteenth-century empiricist thought brought about a paradigmatic shift: the insistence that each child is born as a *tabula rasa* necessitated a detailed consideration of the processes by which minds are formed. For Locke, childhood therefore emerged as a conceptual necessity; education became a philosophical question, though his educational treatise, *Some Thoughts Concerning Education*, treats the topic in a matter-of-fact fashion: unlike Rousseau, he does not create a philosophical *Bildungsroman*. Instead, Locke reflects pragmatically upon parenting and pedagogy, with some startlingly progressive formulations. He insists that 'childish actions' and play should be permitted to be 'free and unrestrained' (2007, 43); he argues that children should learn actively, through 'practice', rather than 'rules' (45): he writes, '*Praise should be given in public, blame in private*' (43).[5] Most significantly, he seeks to construct a nuclear family, despite the lived reality of middle- and upper-middle-class life: 'Next, to make them in love with the company of their parents, they should receive all their good things there, and from their hands. The servants should be hindered

repressed sexual unconscious (130): we must think about how to understand adults as well as protecting children.

[4] I worked for ten years in the academy before retraining as a social worker in child protection, and spending 18 months in a frontline Local Authority service. I am now a Children's Services Practitioner at the NSPCC, working in a team specialising in the assessment and support of children who have been affected by sexual abuse. It was my study of the Victorian period that led me to change career following the completion of this monograph.

[5] This is a significant precursor to the public and private divide so central to Victorian society, and satirised by Dickens in *Great Expectations* through Wemmick.

from making court to them' (49). Embedded within this Enlightenment philosophy, then, we have a class-based codification of family. Moreover, Locke is concerned with the parent-child relationship as the focus for emotion, moral influence and pedagogy. He does, however, see it as the parent's duty to rule the child with 'fear and awe' in their early years, and to soften with time (33). He argues in favour of home schooling for girls and boys since children are 'susceptible of vicious impressions' (50). Throughout, it is moral authority that is privileged, rather than systems of punishment or reward (37): 'the great work of a governor is to fashion the carriage, and form the mind; to settle in his pupil good habits, and the principles of virtue and wisdom; to give him, by little and little, a view of mankind' (75).

Rousseau's *Emile: On Education* presents itself as a grave and urgent departure from previous works, including Locke's. In the Preface, he writes, 'Childhood is unknown. Starting from the false idea one has of it, the farther one goes, the more one loses one's way' (1979, Book I, 32). Criticising contemporary thinkers, he adds: 'They are always seeking for the man in the child without thinking of what he is before being a man'. Rousseau designates childhood as inherently different from adulthood. The child is 'natural man', governed by instinct and sensation rather than reason, which is developed later through experience, defined as the coalescing of sensations into ideas, and ideas into reason (Book II, 203). Rousseau's emphasis on experience and practice is not simply opposed to Locke's educational treatise, or to empiricism more widely. Like Locke, he is concerned with the family. He appeals to maternal love in the Preface, but quickly moves on to consider the degeneracy of mothers in mid-eighteenth-century France: 'No mother, no child. Between them the duties are reciprocal, and if they are ill-fulfilled on one side, they will be neglected on the other' (46). His representation of the mutual influence of parents and children has much in common with the debates concerning familial responsibility found throughout the mid-Victorian novel.

The text poses an imaginative encounter between adult and child that sets the foundation for Romantic and Victorian literature. Like Locke, Rousseau is concerned with the child's entrance into a social realm; however, where Locke saw the governor's duty as 'to settle in his pupil good habits', Rousseau argued the child should be kept away from the corrupting force of civilisation until youth, fostering the child's identity as 'natural man'. Rose writes, 'For Rousseau, education has the same function of giving back to culture the nature it had destroyed [...] Nature is not something which can be retrieved, it has to be *added*' (1992, 44). The child's governor is not an authority figure in the conventional sense, but someone who manipulates the environment around the child to develop their autonomy. Throughout *Emile*, Rousseau makes a powerful argument concerning free will: it exists where necessity operates as the only check on our behaviour. In *Emile* which, we must remember, is a philosophical treatise and not a parenting manual, childhood is driven by an elaborate theatrics: the governor defines each situation without the child's knowledge, giving the illusory impression that Emile is confronting natural law rather than adult authority. This theatricality resonates with how childhood is mobilised in Victorian literature, specifically in the *Bildungsroman*.

Rousseau argues that the parent should not make moral demands upon the child: morality is associated with the social contract, which is a contract between adults. In a witty parody of a conversation between the governor and child, Rousseau highlights the circularity of attempting to enforce a moral norm upon a child:

> Master. You must not do that.
> Child. And why must I not do it?
> Master. Because it is bad to do.
> Child. Bad to do? What is bad to do?
> Master. What you are forbidden to do.
> Child. What is bad about doing what I am forbidden to do?
> Master. You will be punished for having disobeyed.
> Child. I shall fix it so that nothing is known about it.
> Master. You will be spied upon.
> Child. I shall hide.
> Master. You will be questioned.
> Child. I shall lie.
> Master. You must not lie.
> Child. Why must I not lie?
> Master. Because it is bad to do, etc. (Book II, 90)

He goes on: 'Childhood has its ways of seeing, thinking and feeling which are proper to it. Nothing is less sensible than to substitute ours for theirs, and I would like as little to insist that a ten-year-old boy be five feet tall as that he possess judgement. Actually, what would reason do for him at that age? It is the bridle of strength, and the child does not need this bridle' (ibid.). We find a comparable insistence on the child's 'way of seeing' throughout the mid-Victorian period. In *Hard Times* (1854), arguing against the growing dominance of utilitarian thought, Dickens represents the importance of maintaining the child's 'fancy' in an industrialised and alienating modern world, an argument that can be coherently traced back to Rousseau who, despite writing before industrialisation, formulates modern existence in terms of alienation and disenfranchisement. Post-Rousseau, childhood appears progressively different from adulthood, something to be protected and yearned for; at the same time, it was the source of profound psychological and social anxiety—as it is now.

By the Romantic period, there were two overlapping but non-identical lines of thought concerning childhood. On the one hand, the child represents what is lost and irrevocable; on the other, childhood is seen as a distinct period to be governed and controlled. Authors with radically dissimilar views repeatedly stressed the importance of childhood as the path to reason or enlightenment. For Rousseau, this entry into reasoned thought should be delayed as long as possible. When this retardation ceases to be viable, the youth's entrance into the civil realm must be meticulously monitored and controlled: he is carefully initiated into the social contract.

The British Romantic poets inherited much from Rousseau, and all the novelists addressed in this study are, in their turn, heavily influenced by and refer to Romanticism. George Augustus Sala's piece for *Household Words*, 'Little Children' (1853), illustrates the continuing importance of Wordsworth and Locke to the mid-Victorian moment: Sala appropriates Wordsworth's famous formulation, 'the child is father to the man', and a Lockean concept of the child as a 'blank sheet of paper' (289; 291) in order to reaffirm the essential goodness of children (292): children are born loving (293). The wider corpus of William Blake's poetry was first disseminated in Alexander Gilchrist's *Life of William Blake* (1863), and in 1868, Algernon Swinburne wrote an important critical analysis of the poet. Juliet Barker's (2010 [1994]) biography of the Brontës shows the influence of Romanticism upon the family's writings. Romanticism is not something that stands outside of the Victorian period, and it could be argued that it functions by *Nachträglichkeit*—by deferred effect. Late Romantics were also early Victorians: Thomas De Quincey continued to write and publish until his death in 1859, including an important new edition of *Confessions of an English Opium Eater* (1856).

Wordsworth, like Rousseau, was interested in the dramatic encounters between adults and children, and poses this in epistemological terms.

In 'We are seven', Wordsworth subtly undermines the enlightened adult perspective. The poetic speaker approaches a little girl playing by her woodland cottage. He idealises her: she has a 'rustic, woodland air', 'Her hair was thick with many a curl' and 'Her beauty made me glad'. He asks her how many brothers and sisters she has, and in the subsequent debate, the speaker attempts to enforce a reasoned view of death as absence upon the child. The little girl repeatedly refuses his view, reaffirming 'we are seven' despite the death of two of her siblings, and absence of two more at sea. The little girl's refusal to accept that her family is irrelevant because they are not physically present is an ethical speech act: her statement is performative. Families do not cease to be family when they die. Moreover, her use of the plural pronoun creates a sense of communal belonging, reminding us that the adult speaker—in contrast—is wandering and alone.

This poem is significant in the wider context of *Traumatic Encounters* because the adult makes a demand on the child that she cannot fulfil *on his terms*: it is comparable to the parodic conversation between the governor and Emile presented by Rousseau. The girl's so-called frozen [...] innocence (Richardson 1994, 72) is actually a measured and thoughtful acceptance of her siblings' changed position, but on her own terms. She is aware they have gone away, and her wish to sing at their graves is no more fanciful than the speaker's assertion that they are in heaven. The seemingly enlightened speaker refuses her vision: '"But they are dead; those two are dead!/ Their spirits are in heaven!"/ 'Twas throwing words away;' (ll.65–67). In this simple ballad, Wordsworth presents two opposing visions of the world, two competing epistemologies: similar conflicts underpin the adult-child encounters found in psychoanalysis. The poem ends without resolving the dialectical play of thought.

The full complexity of Wordsworth's thoughts concerning childhood came to fruition in his poetic *Bildungsroman*, *The Prelude*, which operates within a dual time frame; finally published in 1850, *The Prelude* is—practically speaking—a mid-Victorian text. However, the unpublished 1805 thirteen-book *Prelude* encompasses the vast majority of the material found in the 1850 edition, and as Shuttleworth (2010) notes, sections of the text had been published much earlier (7). In Book I, Wordsworth presents his childhood in Rousseauian terms: a 'naked savage' in the landscape (I.304). However, in contrast to *Emile*, Wordsworth prioritises the child's power of imagination and explores how this imagination is elicited through encounters with the sublimity of the natural world. He, even more profoundly than Rousseau, presents the child as free: necessary checks come only from nature in the childhood section of Book I. This does, though, follow the opening section in which the adult Wordsworth bemoans his loss of freedom and productivity.[6]

Rousseau's representation of the governor's theatrics in *Emile* would seem irrelevant here: however, Wordsworth's orchestration of his early life in the Lake District—the writing of his own *Bildungsroman*—is also theatrical and effaces the presence of adult authority. He creates a series of *mises-en-scène* in which the child's coming into being is shown. The scene on the lake poses an energetic encounter between the child and the natural world: 'the huge cliff/Rose up between me and the stars, and still,/With measured motion, like a living thing/Strode after me' (I.409–412 [1805 text]). Wordsworth represents this as uncanny, intrusive: it is the 'trouble of my dreams' (I.427). However, he swiftly repositions the scene within a wider philosophical reflection on how the human soul is built through an encounter with the 'eternity of thought,/That gives to forms and images a breath' (I.429–430); such moments provide the foundation for a powerful poetic subjectivity, 'A grandeur in the beatings of the heart' (I.441). There is a tension here: at the moment of his fear, the natural world appears to hold the power, rebuking Wordsworth for 'lustily' (I.401) rowing on the 'silent lake' (I.402); however, this is subsequently reframed in elevated and Neoplatonic terms.

In Book II, Wordsworth moves *The Prelude* into a different philosophical context by problematising Locke's idea that the mind is like a 'cabinet' (II.228) into which our sensations are neatly ordered. Attempting to resolve this problem, Wordsworth presents the mother-child dyad as formative:

> Blest the infant babe
> (For with my best conjectures I would trace
> The progress of our being), blest the babe
> Nursed in his mother's arms, the babe who sleeps
> Upon his mother's breast, who when his soul
> Claims manifest kindred with an earthly soul,

[6]As John Fletcher rightly pointed out when reading this monograph in manuscript form, Wordsworth turns to the natural world as a way of overcoming his writer's block: the return to origins is, in his words, 'highly idealised' and does not involve returning to his parents. I am grateful to John for his detailed response to this portion of the argument, which encouraged me to tease out the dynamics of Wordsworth's 'primal scenes' in more detail through the concept of the uncanny.

Does gather passion from his mother's eye! (II.237–243)

Despite his critique of Locke, Wordsworth's thought is not simply opposed to empiricism: it is the child's openness to the world, and his encounters with it—whether represented by mother, river, or mountain—which is decisive for the development of reason as well as poetic sensibility. Here, the infant's being—his 'soul'—recognises itself in the mother's soul. The baby lays claim to his mother, and she enlivens his being: 'Such feelings pass into his torpid life/Like an awakening breeze' (II.245–246). This is a potent rethinking of the way in which experience shapes us: subjectivity is always intersubjective. Sensations, feelings, are transformed as they are passed from mother to child. Intersubjectivity is likewise central to the mid-Victorian novel: however, the novels repeatedly present these primary relationships in a state of traumatic rupture.

Childhood Memory

Wordsworth and Thomas De Quincey explore the nature of memory through their concepts of 'spots of time' and the 'palimpsest', ideas which reverberate throughout the mid-Victorian novel: both theories address childhood, and the fraught relation between adult and child. This focus is a continuation of earlier philosophical concerns: in an *Essay Concerning Human Understanding*, Locke argued that identity is co-extensive with memory; memory is the foundation of selfhood.[7] Memory was likewise important to Rousseau, suggesting that Emile could not remember or memorise in the same way as an adult because his mind had not yet begun to form the 'ideas' necessary for the functioning of long-term memory. During childhood, Emile begins to group sensations into simple ideas, and these simple ideas later form complex ideas, enabling the development of reason as a young adult (Book II, 203). Wordsworth's representation of childhood is inseparable from his theory of memory; almost a hundred years before Freud wrote 'Screen Memories' (1899) and 'Childhood Memories and Screen Memories' (1901), Wordsworth

[7] In *A Treatise of Human Nature* (1739–1740) sceptic empiricist David Hume problematises this: to have 'an idea of self', we would need to have a continuous 'impression' that gave rise to that idea; for Hume, no such continuous impression is possible (164).

presented the childhood scene at the heart of subjective being. He theorises the dynamic of memory: his 'spots of time' bridge, without closing up, the gap between child and adult.

Although 'Lines written a few miles above Tintern Abbey' (*Lyrical Ballads*, 1798) does not address childhood per se, Wordsworth carefully formulates the relation between past, present and future in the poem. Wordsworth reflects on the ongoing enrichment the vision of the Abbey has given him in memory: 'These forms of beauty have not been to me/As is a landscape to a blind man's eye:' (ll.24–25); 'I have owed to them,/In hours of weariness, sensations sweet/Felt in the blood, and felt along the heart' (ll.27–29). The poet posits the revivifying effect of memory; however, standing again in the landscape, he refers to 'recognitions dim and faint' (l.61) and he stands in 'sad perplexity' (l.62). The impossibility of memory bringing the past back *as itself* drives the poem: the insurmountable separation between adult and youth renders any simple continuity untenable. Wordsworth presents his youthful self as closer to nature: 'For nature then [...] To me was all in all' (ll.74–77): the mountain and the wood were 'An appetite: a feeling and a love' (l.83). He writes, with an aching sense of pathos and resignation: 'I cannot paint/ What then I was' (ll.78–9). Memory is a vivifying force for the poet, but nevertheless it blurs into elegy, it reverberates with something that can never *be*. It is impossible to bring this moment into the present-tense: 'That time is past,/And all its aching joys are now no more,/ And all its dizzy raptures' (ll.86–88). At the same time, Wordsworth presents the 'recompense' (l.91) of adulthood: the poet hears 'The still, sad music of humanity'; he can recognise 'A motion and a spirit, that impels/All thinking things, all objects of all thought/And rolls through all things' (ll.103–105).

Wordsworth drives *The Prelude* through his concept of memory and presents his nomenclature here: 'There are in our existence spots of time/Which with distinct pre-eminence retain/A vivifying virtue' (XI.257–259). Childhood scenes have greater potential to fulfil this function:

> Such moments, worthy of all gratitude,
> Are scattered everywhere, taking their date
> From our first childhood – in our childhood even
> Perhaps are most conspicuous. (XI.273–276)

The disjunction between the child's and the adult's engagement with the world underwrites, rather than undermines, the efficacy of the spots of time. It is the poet's exposure to this difference that refreshes him. Spots of time emerge most powerfully from the early years when 'We have had deepest feeling that the mind/Is lord and master, and that outward sense/Is but the obedient servant of her will' (XI.270–272). The child's feeling of omnipotence imprints upon the self, but through delay and deferral.[8] However, the scenes that Wordsworth presents here feel far more unsettling than his theorisation would imply: in the wake of his father's death, the young Wordsworth looks out from the 'crag' (I.370) towards 'the one blasted tree,/And the bleak music of that old stone wall' (I.377–378). This moment lacks the dynamism of the childhood scenes in Book I of *The Prelude*, and through pathetic fallacy, the adult Wordsworth implies (without admitting) a melancholy return to his bereavement.

Wordsworth's model of selfhood is complex, pushing far beyond Locke's, and creates a conceptual foundation for mid-Victorian literature. 'Ode: Intimations of Immortality from Recollections of Early Childhood' (renamed in 1815, first published as 'Ode' in 1807) opens by presenting childhood as a lost visionary time: 'The things which I have seen I now can see no more' (l.9). In drawing on Plato's allegory, Wordsworth implies that in growing up, the boy will enter the cave; he is no longer visionary: 'Heaven lies about us in our infancy!/Shades of the prison-house begin to close/Upon the growing Boy' (ll.66–68). However, the melancholy tone alters when Wordsworth considers the 'benedictions' left by these earliest experiences:

> O joy! that in our embers
> Is something that doth live,
> That Nature yet remembers
> What was so fugitive!
> The thought of our past years in me doth breed
> Perpetual benedictions [...] (ll.132–137)

Wordsworth displaces the subject of memory: it is Nature, not he, who can bear witness to these vanished scenes. And yet this 'Nature' does

[8] In 'The Uncanny' (1919), Freud argues that experiences producing this feeling of omnipotence in adulthood are experienced as uncanny because they remind us of a part of early life which has been repressed.

seem to belong to him in some way. It bridges thought—represented earlier in the poem by the pansy—and our bodily existence. The use of the shared pronoun 'our' is significant: it is not his own, unmediated experience, which provides benediction, but his intellectual understanding of childhood as concept and sense of communal being[9]: '*We* will grieve not, rather find/Strength in what remains behind' (ll.182–183) [my emphasis]). The 'embers' may still ignite. Wordsworth's formulation of childhood is crucial to the mid-Victorians; moreover, his temporal model provides an antecedent for the representation of familial 'trauma' we see in the novels. For Wordsworth, as we see in 'Tintern Abbey', the past cannot return as itself, and while the alienating effects of this disjunction haunt the poet, it is also the source of redemptive inspiration and communal being. In the mid-Victorian novel, the past also returns in differential form, but it is often the source of shock, dissociation and compulsion. This does not mean that redemption is discarded; nostalgia is uncannily located *within* traumatic narratives. The past returns, but the Victorians' dark refractions of Wordsworth's 'spots of time' do not represent the child's omnipotence, but rather subjection to the adult world, a possibility raised by Wordsworth through the account of his father's death in Book XI of *The Prelude*.

Late Romantic, early Victorian, and opium addict, Thomas De Quincey also produced a paradigmatic model of memory; and like Wordsworth, this was by thinking through the distance between adult and child self. In *Suspiria de Profundis*, parts of which were first published in *Blackwood's Edinburgh Magazine* in 1845, De Quincey presented the idea of the palimpsest.[10] For the benefit of his uneducated 'female reader', he explained that a palimpsest is 'a membrane or roll cleansed of its manuscript by reiterated successions' (139), before making his argument concerning memory:

[9]This poem can be heard echoing in Dickens's writings. Wordsworth represents the sea as death; Dickens uses this idea to structure *Dombey and Son* (ll.165–170). Children are closer to immortality, but this means that they are also closer to death. The danger and threat correlated with childhood is brought to the surface in Dickens's appropriation of the image.

[10]The publication of this text predates all of the novels under consideration in this study.

> What else than a natural and mighty palimpsest is the human brain? Such a palimpsest is my brain; such a palimpsest, O reader! is yours. Everlasting layers of ideas, images, feelings, have fallen upon your brain softly as light. Each succession has seemed to bury all that went before. And yet in reality not one has been extinguished. (144)

Josephine McDonagh (1987) argues that the idea of the palimpsest is a troubling one: 'A model that both erases and retains the past, the palimpsest always disrupts a sense of temporality; and the kind of history facilitated by its retentive function is at once restorative and violating' (214). Like the 'spot of time', the palimpsest has darker possibilities: the retention or reappearance of distressing, traumatic, experiences. De Quincey links the palimpsest to the formative power of childhood experience, arguing that that 'into all the *elementary* feelings of man, children look with a more searching gaze than adults' (127), an insistence on the primary impressionability of childhood likewise demonstrated by the mid-Victorian novel.

De Quincey's account of his early childhood memories is comparable to Freud's concept of screen memory. Multiple conflicts are fused within the luminous fragments that precede the teleological sequence of memory, which only begins after his sister Jane's death. De Quincey connects Jane's death to the recent 'sufferings' (98) caused to her by her nurse, who had treated her 'harshly, if not brutally' (97). The terrifying vision of the nurse after Jane's death is formative and primal: attempting to avoid the nurse's face, De Quincey recounts, 'The feeling which fell upon me was a shuddering awe, as upon a first glimpse of the truth that I was in a world of evil and strife' (98). Unlike Wordsworth, he does not represent the child's imagined mastery of the world; on the contrary, memory comes from subjection; he is a 'powerless infant' (98). The little De Quincey is not exposed to the natural sublime, but to a human grotesque. Edmund Burke (1764) writes, 'Ugliness I imagine likewise to be consistent enough with an idea of the sublime. But I would by no means insinuate that ugliness of itself is a sublime idea, unless united with such qualities as excite a strong terror' (226). That terror is undoubtedly present when De Quincey is in the servant's presence: he experiences a sublime 'shuddering awe'. An enigma is propelled towards the boy, and from that point on 'the character of [his] thoughts' was 'changed greatly' (98). The little boy's consciousness begins here: the emergence of his subjectivity is intimately associated with an ugly sublime (an idea also linked to his use of opium); his sense of a persecutory adult world; and the mourning of his second sister Elizabeth, the sight of whom in her coffin puts him into a trance-like state (106).

Childhood and Mid-Victorian Psychology

In the 'Rat Man' case history ('Notes upon a Case of Obsessional Neurosis', 1909), Freud made a now famous assertion: 'the unconscious, I explained, *was* the infantile; it was that part of the self which had become separated off from it in infancy' (177). This idea undoubtedly resonates with Romanticism, but mid-Victorian psychologists did not position childhood in the same privileged position. Despite this, the mind's permeability to the influence of the other was a concern, and this permeability is felt in the traumatic encounters we see in the novels. Shuttleworth presents the 1840s as the key decade in the development of childhood psychology, and it is also a crucial decade for my project.[11]

Henri Ellenberger charts the rise of dynamic psychiatry through two overlapping discourses and praxes: mesmerism and hypnosis. Ellenberger illustrates how the social conditions grounding the encounter between mesmerist and patient defined eighteenth-century theoretical formulations and the efficacy of the praxes, establishing this argument through his discussion of the Marquis de Puységur and his patient, Victor Race: Puységur hypnotised Race in 1784 (Ellenberger 1981, 45). Ellenberger argues that Victor, the working-class man, creates—through and within the second consciousness that appears when he is in a somnambulist state—an identification with his social superior. This identification is played out through the appearance of an enhanced, and previously hidden, personality. The idea that hidden consciousness

[11] Shuttleworth (2010) highlights the lack of proto-Freudian insight in mid-century medical discourse. Discussing Jean-Étienne Esquirol's and James Cowell Prichard's identification of 'insanity' in childhood she writes, 'We are not in the domain of Freud here; there is no attempt to analyse the family dynamics that could lead a child to hate her mother or stepmother' (25). However, as Shuttleworth shows, the idea that parental mistreatment could lead to wayward childhood behaviour is found in Thomas Mayo's *Elements of the Human Mind* (1838): giving an account of a previously violent and controllable boy, Mayo writes that 'My pupil had been treated with affection, he had been tenderly entreated to conduct himself well, he had been threatened, he had been scolded, he had been punished; *but he had never been praised*' (qtd. in Shuttleworth, 27). This observation seems basic compared to the model of parent-child and governor-child relationships we are offered by Locke and Rousseau.

appears through a dynamic and unequal encounter with another therefore predates the mid-Victorian novel and undoubtedly forms part of its conceptual groundwork.

Mid-Victorian novelists frequently refer to mesmerism, approaching it through John Elliotson, its most high profile medical proponent in the British context.[12] Elliotson was an acknowledged influence on both Dickens and Collins, and as a mesmerist, he affirmed the radical openness of the subject to the influence of another. Sidelined from the medical community, Elliotson's journal *Zoist* was produced to counter the scepticism about mesmerism found in the mainstream medical community. In 'Instances of Double States of Consciousness Independent of Mesmerism' published in *Zoist* in July 1846, Elliotson describes cases of double consciousness amongst children and adults. In the article, he demonstrates his concern for children and young people who are wrongfully accused of being naughty or criminal when they are experiencing psychological disorder. Coming before the first publication of *The Journal of Mental Pathology and Psychological Medicine* in 1848, Elliotson's emphasis on altered states of consciousness in children is even more notable. Through his account of a case in Bavaria, he draws together two potentially separate issues: criminal accountability in children and the mentally ill; his concerns with the medical and legal categorisation of children's behaviour positions him at the forefront of developing psychological understanding. Despite being ridiculed by many in the medical profession, Elliotson was recuperated by literary authors, including Dickens, Collins and Harriet Martineau. His ideas were disseminated within the periodical press, as well as in his own specialist journal. The question of how to bear witness is posed throughout Elliotson's article; his theories provide a clear antecedent to *fin-de-siècle* and twentieth-century trauma theory, despite the fact he does not attempt to identify a psychological event underlying double consciousness.[13]

[12] Matus (2009) cites Elliotson's mesmeric theory at various points throughout her monograph, pointing out, however, that Dickens does not simply reproduce Elliotson's theories in *The Mystery of Edwin Drood* (117).

[13] William Hamilton's earlier concept of hidden knowledge-systems—his second stage of latency—is comparable, although not identical to, John Elliotson's theory of double consciousness. However, Hamilton's most radical proposition is found in the theorisation of his third degree of latency; his insistence that what is unconscious defines our conscious actions: 'I do not hesitate to maintain, that what we are conscious of is constructed out of what we are not conscious of—that our whole knowledge, in fact, is made up of the

Forbes Winslow established *The Journal of Mental Pathology and Psychological Medicine* in 1848 (Shuttleworth 2010, 28). However, to put this in perspective, by this point, *Wuthering Heights*, *Jane Eyre* (1847) and *Dombey and Son* had already been published (the latter was serialised between October 1846 to April 1848).[14] The journal therefore arose in a pre-existing *literary* context in which childhood was prioritised, and an asymmetrical cross-generational relationship was presented as decisive, not only for pathological states, but also for subjectivity and identity. The articles on childhood insanity included in the journal seem unsubtle in comparison with the novels published around this date. Shuttleworth (2010) writes, 'The picture thus builds up of children as beings liable to uncontrolled passion which can manifest itself in homicidal impulses, and subject to hallucinations from an early age, with faulty parenting and inherited tendencies as the two primary forms of causation' (29). She highlights the influence of the literature on Winslow's journal, which distinguished it from more established medical publications such as *The Lancet* (ibid., 32), citing Winslow's ambivalent panegyric of Dickens: 'No man exercises, for good or evil, so overwhelming an influence upon the national mind and character' (32).

The idea of moral influence was central to Winslow's thought. Moral management was inseparable from the developing psychological discourses of the 1840s and the 1845 Lunacy Act, in which (through the Lunacy Commission) the building and inspection of asylums became a legal imperative. From the publication of *An Inquiry Concerning the Indications of Insanity: With Suggestions for the Better Protection and Care of the Insane* (1830) onwards, John Conolly argued that insanity could be cured with effective guidance and control: in his eyes, the asylum was a humanitarian institution, which should protect rather than punish (487). At the same time, in Winslow's journal the nursery became a possible asylum in the making, requiring control and surveillance (Shuttleworth 2010, 30).

The dominance of physiological thought at the mid-century cuts in two directions. On the one hand, as Matus shows, the proto-traumatic idea of shock was seized upon by contemporary writers and redeployed

unknown and the incognisable' (Hamilton 1998, 82). Hamilton's lectures were presented in 1836 and published posthumously in 1859 (Shuttleworth and Taylor 1998, 80).

[14] Shuttleworth (2010) clarifies that Winslow's article 'On the Incubation of Insanity' (1846) was written after the serialisation of *Dombey and Son* began (31).

with immense subtlety. On the other, the novelists' exploration of traumatisation worked *against* a strictly materialist model and was heavily influenced by Romanticism. The fifth edition of William Carpenter's *Principles of Human Physiology* (1855) reformulated unconsciousness in materialist terms. In a drastically expanded section dealing with the nervous system and operation of the mind, Carpenter argued that 'Unconscious Cerebration' (589), or brain action analogous to thought, occurs without our knowledge in the Cerebrum: these 'reflex actions' (588–589) can 'evolve intellectual products when their contents are transferred to the Sensorium' (589). However, the potential radicalism of this is qualified by Carpenter's over-emphasis on willpower. In the Preface to *Principles of Mental Physiology* (1875 [1874]), Carpenter sets out his conceptual framework through the ideas of automatism and 'Will' (x). He later writes that 'by concentrating the Mental gaze (so to speak) upon any object that may be within its reach, [the will] can make use of this to bring in other objects by associative suggestion. And moreover, it can virtually determine what shall not be regarded by the Mind' (26). Unconsciousness is represented here as willed choice. Despite this, Carpenter acknowledges that some of us find it easier to control our mental processes than others, describing those with less will as 'Automata' (27): 'puppets to be pulled by suggesting strings, capable of being played upon by everyone who has have made himself master of our springs of action' (ibid.).

All of the novelists examined here are concerned with the state of will in the wake of traumatisation. Significantly, Collins represents the dissociation engendered by the mechanisation of thought in both *No Name* and *Armadale*. However, he treats this idea differently from Carpenter: mechanisation—the loss of autonomy—is frequently the result of too much will, rather than too little. Despite this, Collins and Carpenter can be drawn together through the idea of psychological influence. Carpenter argues that the mind lacking in will is at the mercy of outside suggestions; it is permeable. In both *No Name* and *Armadale,* we witness the distressing consequences of inheriting someone else's obtrusive wilfulness. Mid-Victorian discourses of monomania, developed by James Prichard in *A Treatise on Insanity and other Disorders Affecting the Mind* (1837 [1835]), are also relevant in this context: in monomania, even a rational mind can become possessed by one overriding idea: 'under the influence of some particular illusion' (16). The category of monomania unquestionably influenced the representation of obsession and compulsion in the literature of the period; the novels show how 'a particular illusion' held by the parents can lead to traumatisation in the children.[15] In so doing, however, they push beyond the parameters of Prichard's theory and formulate something new.

Unlike Freud, Carpenter did not consider the unconscious as the internal other; instead, he uses the symbol of the rider and horse to describe the relationship between the conscious mind and unconscious physiological processes (24). The horse provides the dynamism, but the rider has overall control. Carpenter's position is a development of eighteenth-century empiricism, but the idea is refigured in physiological terms. Significantly for us, however, Carpenter (1875) connects the mind's openness to others with childhood:

> the Emotional state seems often to be determined by circumstances of which the individual has no Ideational consciousness, and especially by the emotional states of those by whom he is surrounded; a mode of influence which acts with peculiar potency on the minds of Children, and which is a most important element in their moral education. (540–541)

This idea of the child's susceptibility to emotional, and unconscious, influences is an extension of earlier Victorian arguments regarding the moral management of the child; however, the fact that Carpenter figures this in terms of the child's unconscious openness to the adult other is provocative. In the fifth edition of *Principles of Human Physiology* (1855), Carpenter had not quite reached this point, but he does insist upon the formative impact of childhood in establishing nervo-muscular habits (486), and ideational associations (541, 855). Nevertheless, it is important to point out that this edition was published after many of the novels examined here: the novelists pre-empt Carpenter's insistence on the formative impact of children's physical and mental experience (set out in 1855), and the child's unconscious openness to the other (set out in 1874). With this in mind, we need to consider the changing historical conditions of the mid-nineteenth century, which the novels reflect upon and address.

[15] Prichard does not address this possibility in *A Treatise on Insanity*.

Family and Ideology

Thomas Carlyle's *Signs of the Times* (1829) represents a paradigm shift in nineteenth-century thought; although Carlyle was concerned with tracing the present moment, he presages the concerns of the mid-Victorian period. His formulation of alienation predates Marx's by more than ten years. Carlyle argues that the times are 'mechanical' (64): 'There is no end to machinery. Even the horse is stripped of his harness, and finds a fleet fire-horse yoked in his stead. Nay, we have an artist that hatches chickens by steam; the very brood-hen is to be superseded!' (ibid.). Carlyle traces this problem in both philosophical and practical terms, identifying Locke as the father of nineteenth-century materialism (68). His analysis of reification and alienation is not explicitly connected to the family; however, his Shakespearean insistence that 'The time is sick and out of joint' (84) points us back towards *Hamlet*, and the spectral father who insists on his son healing the wounds of the past. Carlyle's reference to the 'brood-hen' connects the means of production with the means of reproduction, reminding us of the impact of technology upon 'natural' processes, including parenthood. His insistence on the sickness of the age lurks everywhere in the mid-Victorian novel, and perhaps no more so than in *Bleak House* with its apocalyptic present-tense narration. Carlyle uses parents and children as both metaphor and metonym to indicate a radical breach between past and present—the old traditions and modernity: 'There is a deep-lying struggle in the whole fabric of society; a boundless grinding collision of the New with the Old. The French Revolution, as is now visible enough, was not the parent of this mighty movement, but its offspring' (84). Carlyle, no friend to Revolution, implies that class conflict, the destruction of the old order, produces a traumatised and traumatising 'offspring'.

I interpret the parent-child relation as a cross-generational structure, not as a singular biological fact. This approach has historical, conceptual and literary justification: foster families and extended families were a consistent feature of the period; rates of maternal mortality in childbirth meant that second marriages, such as Mr. Dombey's, were commonplace; low life expectancy increased the possibility of remarriage before the introduction of divorce reform. Jane Gallop (1984) reminds us that bourgeois families were defined by the presence of extra-familial outsiders, such as nurses, governesses and servants (145). Rachel Bowlby (2007) reinforces these points, arguing that the nuclear family was a twentieth-century phenomenon (10). However, this does not lessen the ideological weight placed upon parental roles in the writings of, say, Locke, Rousseau and Wordsworth. There is a tension between the social condition of the family—its lived conditions—and the moral and emotional pressure placed upon the ideal. We can relate this back to ideological fantasy: frequently, the novels, or the protagonists within the novels, work to deny or efface the extended condition of family and perpetuate a fantasised nuclear model, occluding economic realities in the process. This is by no means an even or stable process. Dickens's novels prioritise the parental demand; however, these demands operate across an extended structure, frequently encompassing 'parental' figures from different classes.

What is apparent through an analysis of the mid-Victorian novel is that the closed off nature of the family is purely illusory. The mid-Victorian novel enacts a tension: a gesture towards closure which is disrupted by a repudiated other. This disruption becomes the focus for the movement of plot. Dickens's novels invoke this imaginary state, but always in a process of interruption or deferral. The family is an ideological structure, which is perpetuated by a fetishistic fantasy of home. Knowingness concerning the compromised nature of home is present throughout the mid-century, and yet the novels function by actively participating in the fantasy. Even *Wuthering Heights* ultimately presents a couple and a home that we are encouraged to buy into. Nelly is demoted to servant (rather than foster-sister as she was in the childhood section), Heathcliff is dead, and the strangely liminal Lockwood saunters back to the south. The penetrability of the family (and the threat posed by social outcasts/outsiders) is key: bourgeois hegemony is a site of anxiety, even in the midst of its affirmation. In the mid-Victorian novel, these movements are consistently found in the same text: family is the source of a fundamental ambivalence.

High levels of infant mortality meant that death was inextricable from the Victorian idea of childhood as Dickens's 'A Child's Dream of A Star' makes abundantly clear (*Household Words*, 1850). In this short sketch, the main character loses his sister, his infant brother, his mother and his daughter in turn. Each dies and departs to a shining star where they await the arrival of the boy/man. To our twenty-first-century 'first world' eyes, not accustomed to confronting the loss of children, the sketch feels desperately sad, albeit recuperated by Dickens's maudlin sentimentalising. However, more interestingly, the short piece performs a kind of traumatic substitutability; each loss somehow replays the primary loss of the boy's sister in early childhood. This links the piece back to De Quincey's account of his childhood and presages the case of Frau Emmy von N. in Freud's *Studies on Hysteria*.

Parent-child relationships in the mid-Victorian period are characterised by haunting, absence, excess and substitutability. They must therefore be decentred and analysed in relation to wider structures. What is at stake is the cross-generational transmission of trauma (secrets, illegitimacy, transgression, death or loss) in addition to money, property and ideology. The older generation attempts to author the younger, but this is not restricted to biological relationships, nor indeed to two generations of the same family. Further, the sanctity of the parent-child relationship is problematised by the appearance of familial outsiders (including Heathcliff, Miss Wade, Biler, Anne Catherick, Captain Wragge and Lydia Gwilt) whose dangerous textual knowledge refracts back onto our understanding of the novels' seemingly more intimate relationships. The extent to which the novels 'close up' around the threat embodied by such characters, alternatively embracing or rejecting the disruption and alterity they bring, is examined in the textual analyses of later chapters. The anxiety concerning the parent-child relationship is inextricable from the social and legal changes feeding the novels. The Victorian novel's emphasis on family fantasy speaks to wider nineteenth-century issues: expansion of Empire, inheritance, class conflict, and female subjugation and politicisation.

Reading the mid-Victorian moment demands an intersectional approach: on a basic level, an awareness of the historical gender-class matrix. However, even this is a dangerous simplification, as the growth of global trade and Imperial expansion meant that race and nationhood were inseparable from the formulation of gender and class. Leonore Davidoff and Catherine Hall (2002) reveal the inseparability of family and capitalist enterprise in the early nineteenth century, arguing further that it was this inseparability that led to the construction of separate sphere ideology. The anxiety concerning family is connected to the expansion of capitalist enterprise and the ramifications of this in class-gendered terms. Novelists think very self-consciously about the tension between the family as an economic institution, and the ideology of family and home that occludes, while depending upon, its economic status. The expansion of the law's regulatory powers throughout the nineteenth century is also fundamental, as Davidoff and Hall point out (199). The increasing intervention of law in the home is central to the novels; the idealisation of home is inextricable from fears concerning its permeability, and this is conceived of in legal terms.

Thomas Malthus attempted to delineate, even delimit, the family in terms of biological connections and their contingent responsibilities in *An Essay on the Principles of Population* (1798) and used this delineation in order to refute societal responsibility for poverty. Responsibility is purely individual: poverty is effectively self-willed. In the third edition (1809), he writes: 'If he [the father] cannot support his children they must starve; and if he marry in the face of a fair probability that he shall not be able to support his children, he is guilty of all the evils which he thus brings upon himself, his wife, and his off-spring' (334). This concept of the undeserving poor casts a long shadow across the Victorian period, and in combination with Utilitarian thinking, propelled the 1834 Poor Law. Workhouses were given the impossible and inhumane remit to deal with the lack of adequate employment, denied by officials at the time (Englander 1998, 23); with mental and physical deficiency; and even with orphan children. This shift from the provision of outdoor aid to the establishment of the workhouse was widely criticised and protested against, operating as a point of political mobilisation and radicalism. For instance, Chartism should be contextualised by the 1832 Reform Act (which failed to enfranchise the working classes) and the 1834 Poor Law. On a smaller scale, Patrick Brontë was closely involved in protests against the Poor Law in the 1830s (Barker 2010, 312), although there is no evidence that his children involved themselves in such actions. Elizabeth Gaskell was concerned with ideas of the deserving and the undeserving poor, finding her most radical voice in *North and South* (1855). Dickens's anti-Malthusian and anti-Utilitarian sentiment is perpetuated throughout his writings. In *Great Expectations*, Jaggers becomes the unexpected mouthpiece of Dickens:

> Put the case that pretty nigh all the children he saw in his daily business life, he had reason to look upon as so much spawn, to develop into the fish that were to come to his net – to be prosecuted, defended, forsworn, made orphans, be-devilled somehow. (III.12, 410)

The Poor Law was the motive force for Dickens's second novel *Oliver Twist* (1838), but he was still thinking of it when writing his last complete novel, *Our Mutual Friend* (1865): Betty Higden goes on the tramp to avoid the workhouse. His presentation of Oliver as a middle-class boy, who escapes from the workhouse to the eventual sanctuary of the bourgeois home, is an inverted nightmare. Utter financial collapse could leave the lower-middle classes equally vulnerable to the workhouse. As the son of a debtor, an inhabitant of the Marshalsea no less (a fact which haunts the 'autobiographical fragment'), Dickens is particularly alert to this danger, which Oliver represents in allegorical form.

In *Wuthering Heights*, Emily Brontë represents a seemingly enclosed and historical world in order to explore the effects of change upon a community in detail. The shift to modernity is played out within the confines of Wuthering Heights. Narrating Cathy and Heathcliff's childhood history, Nelly Dean relates how the servants would sit in the 'house' (the central living and kitchen area) with the family. When Mr. Earnshaw dies, and Hindley brings home Frances, this practice is stopped, and a new separation is created between family and servants. The novel enacts a shift between the earlier (and now obsolete) meaning of the 'Family' to denote the whole household including the servants, and the use of the word to define a set of relationships within people of the same class and bloodline. In *Pamela*, Samuel Richardson uses the word in its older sense (1740).[16]

By the mid-nineteenth century, family takes on a more rigid definition, one in which the servants are ostensibly placed outside. However, the mid-Victorian novel demonstrates the necessary incompleteness of this process. In *Jane Eyre*, Bessie plays a formative role in Jane's childhood, singing the folkloric songs that haunt her narrative. Jane's role as governess unsettles the boundaries between those included and those excluded from the family group.[17] This builds upon the Brontë sisters' own experiences: both Anne and Charlotte suffered from the social liminality of the governess's role; however, it is worth bearing in mind that

[16] Nancy Armstrong (1987) discusses *Pamela*'s significance in terms of the 'politics of the domesticating culture' (5–6).

[17] Mary Poovey (1989) suggests that Victorian literature's focus on family depoliticises social concerns: analysing *Jane Eyre*, she argues that 'The effect of making Jane's dependence a function of family and personality is to individualise her problems so as to detach them from her position of governess' (137). However, Poovey elides the fact that Victorian social values and economics were constructed through the middle-class family: an individual's exclusion from this structure *was* political. By making Jane's dependence 'a function of family', Charlotte Brontë does not negate the possibility of political analysis. The 'psychologizing gesture' (137) Poovey identifies is not simply a literary motif.

the presence of a governess impacted upon the entire family. Barker relates how Mary and Elizabeth Robinson continued to write to Anne in confidence long after her departure (616).

The mid-Victorian novels examined here are poised precisely in relation to a transitional legal process in which adult-child relationships were reconceived. The 1839 Infant Custody act, for which social reformer Caroline Norton successfully campaigned, meant that mothers could petition for custody of children aged seven and under, and request access rights for older children. This remained the sole custody legislation until 1873, when mothers' rights for custody were extended until the child was sixteen. Anne Brontë's *The Tenant of Wildfell Hall* (1848) demonstrates the inequities of the wider situation at the mid-century, since Helen's actions would have been proscribed in law both before and after the Act was passed in 1839. Helen saves her young son, Arthur, from the destructive influence of her alcoholic and womanising husband by running away and making her living as an artist. Contemporary reviews criticised the novel, one anonymous reviewer writing Brontë had a 'morbid love of the coarse' (Allott 1974, 250). While most of the novels addressed in this study do not directly refer to custody legislation, they are grounded in conflicts between paternal and maternal authority in an extended sense: *The Mill on the Floss*, for instance, poses such conflict through Mrs. Tulliver's formidable family. Conflicts are played out psychologically, through the fraught formation of the child's subjectivity. In Charlotte Brontë's *Shirley* (1849), Mrs. Pryor lays claim to her estranged daughter: 'from *my* veins issued the tide which flows in *yours*; that you are *mine* – my daughter – my own child' (III.1, 361). In *North and South*, the estrangement between Margaret and Mrs. Hale is healed through Margaret opening herself up to her mother's grief concerning Frederick, the beloved first-born. From 1873 onwards, maternal rights were enshrined in law, and motherhood's negated status, arguably, abated. This fact, coupled with the passing of the first Married Woman's Property Act in 1870, created a different kind of literary climate, and one in which traumatisation was conceived of in new ways. The 'New Woman' appeared in a socio-political climate that had *begun* to endorse female emancipation.[18]

[18] Another important shift came with the 1878 Matrimonial Causes Act, which protected women and their children from domestic violence. Widening the issue, in my conclusion I consider how Thomas Hardy's representation of inheritance from the 1870s onwards differs from the mid-century treatment of the theme.

In considering the relationship between gender and the law, we need to pause upon the 1857 Matrimonial Causes Act. The nature of divorce law meant that the legal profession could actively intervene in the supposedly private sphere of the home. Further, the 1857 Act famously concretised sexual double standards by not permitting women to sue for divorce on the basis of a husband's adultery alone. The flaws in this legislation also meant that George Lewes and Marian Evans could not marry, since Lewes had ostensibly condoned his wife's adultery. The ambivalence concerning marriage is felt throughout sensation fiction of the 1860s. *No Name* creates a powerful critique of the institution as a whole, rendered in Gothicised and parodic terms. Dickens's *Hard Times* presents a powerful case for divorce reform through Stephen, even if when Dickens separated from Catherine, he handled things very differently. Presenting his now infamous letter concerning the failure of his marriage to the *London Times* and *Household Words*, Dickens complicated the boundary between public and private in shockingly modern form by presenting a statement to his adoring readers:

> Some domestic trouble of mine, of long-standing, on which I will make no further remark than that it claims to be respected, as being of a sacredly private nature, has lately been brought to an arrangement, which involves no anger or ill-will of any kind, and the whole origin, progress, and surrounding circumstances of which have been, throughout, within the knowledge of my children. (Slater 2009, 454)

The final claim, 'within the knowledge of my children', is provocative bearing in mind the concerns of the current study. Dickens rhetorically implies that his children's knowledge is equivalent to their consent and approval. To be fair to Dickens, this—almost monstrous—proposition could be challenged by any of his novels, which present psychologically acute accounts of how children (literal and adult) could be affected by potentially compromising knowledge. Bearing in mind that Dickens's separation was propelled by his relationship with Ellen Ternan, his reference to his children's knowledge makes uncomfortable reading. The necessary transgression of the boundary between public and private spheres is inherent in the establishing of these categories, as Dickens's marital crisis reveals. The foremost writer of home was a public figure, and Dickens's home was under pressure to conform privately in line with the standards that he established publicly. This movement between public and private performance—startlingly apparent in Dickens's case—can be seen as a wider Victorian paradigm, and one that Dickens questions and ironises in his novels.

What I want to emphasise is the manner in which the state (as well as the press) could be seen to intervene in the life of its citizens.[19] Louis Althusser's treatment of subjectivity in his theory of interpellation is of direct relevance to my textual readings. In 'Ideology and Ideological State Apparatuses', Althusser argues that we are subjects in the sense we are subjected to state ideology, presenting this in allegorical form as the 'hail' of the police (1971, 163 and *n*.18). Judith Butler's appropriation of Althusser's theory in *Bodies that Matter* (Butler 1993) helpfully develops this. Butler emphasises the excessive quality of the 'call', arguing that 'the performative, the call by the law which seeks to produce a lawful subject, produces a set of consequences that exceed and confound what appears to be the disciplining intention motivating the law' (122). Butler is concerned with the bodily and psychological ramifications of this (en)gendering: without recourse to theoretical terminology, the mid-Victorian novel shares the exact same concern.[20]

Authors in the mid-nineteenth century actively formulated the relationship between the social address—the 'hail' of the police—and distortions of *consciousness*. In so doing, they push beyond any available medical framework. In Carlyle's *Past and Present* (1843), the workhouse becomes symptomatic of a wider 'enchantment', the devastating force of a mechanised age: 'Do not look at us. We sit enchanted here, we know not why. The Sun shines and the Earth calls; and, by the governing Powers and Impotences of this England, we are forbidden to obey' (260). Carlyle's representation of the entrancement or dissociation bound up in the historical moment directly impacts upon the mid-Victorian novel. In *Past and Present*, Carlyle links the entranced Condition of England to the working-class body. He focalises the issue through the suffering body of a little boy, at the mercy of cannibalistic parents:

[19] This is central to D. A. Miller's Foucauldian readings in *The Novel and the Police* (1988); however, my focus on fantasy and unconsciousness distinguishes my readings from his.

[20] Butler later draws on Jean Laplanche's general theory of seduction in order to conceive the relation between gender and the enigmatic message of the other (Butler 2014, 118–133).

> The Stockport Mother and Father think and hint: Our poor little starveling Tom, who cries all day for victuals, who will see only evil and not good in this world: if he were out of misery at once; he well dead, and the rest of us perhaps kept alive? It is thought, and hinted; at last it is done. And now Tom being killed, and all spent and eaten, Is it poor little starveling Jack that must go, or poor little starveling Will? – What a committee of ways and means! (262)

The reference to the 'committee of ways and means' is heavily weighted. Despite Carlyle's presentation of working-class inhumanity, he implies the culpability of bourgeois state organisation: governance by 'committee'. It is certainly no coincidence that the literary pathologisation of parents and children burgeoned in the 'hungry' 1840s. For Carlyle, the literal and spiritual hunger of an entire class becomes correlated with persecutory parental force.[21] In the mid-Victorian novel, the idea that parents prey on children is repeatedly found and forms part of a wider social critique. The child (even the grown-up child) is a symptom of a dangerous modern world, and the elder generation threatens the younger—frequently in spite of themselves. In *No Name*, Mr. Vanstone's failure to enact his will before his death, and save his illegitimate daughters from destitution, haunts Magdalen. Little Dorrit is physically shrunk by her father's selfishness. Heathcliff is taken from the streets of Liverpool, the bustling centre of the slave trade, speaking a language no one understands, and is thrust into a strange, isolated, community with devastating effect. Even the queenly Margaret Hale must reconcile herself to the changing conditions of her existence: this reconciliation is physical, ethical, social and emotional.

Traumas are played out in a changing global context. The French Revolution and the Napoleonic Wars continued to play into the mid-century consciousness; if mid-century bourgeois dominance had been enabled by the consolidation of the middle classes after the Napoleonic wars, then international affairs could impact negatively upon this dominance. In *Wuthering Heights* and *Shirley,* international conflict is shown to penetrate, and perhaps even define, the home. In *A Tale of Two Cities*, Dickens represents the French Revolution in terms of family trauma;

[21] Carolyn Steedman points out that from 1800 to 1900 children constituted 30–40% of the population and could therefore be considered 'part of the perishing and dangerous classes' (1995, 117).

vengeful revolutionary fervour is traced back to the rape of Madame Defarge's sister. This manoeuvre could be read as neutralising the novel's political protest (and in many ways it does); however, at the same time, Dickens hints at something else. Political injustice *is* personal. Dr. Manette's episodes of dissociation are the symptom of a political wound: the result of his long incarceration in the Bastille. This trauma is subsequently enacted—through a compulsion to repeat—within the home. In *A Tale of Two Cities*, Dickens makes manifest a wider mid-century thought. Home cannot be safe from socio-political forces, since these produce the ideology of home. Writing to Austen Layard in 1855, Dickens emphasised the intimacy of social injustice: the 'alienation of the people from their own public affairs' was 'smouldering'; 'it is extremely like the general mind of France before the breaking out of the first Revolution, and is in danger of being turned by any one of a thousand accidents – a bad harvest – the last straw too much of aristocratic insolence or incapacity – a defeat abroad – a mere chance at home – into such a Devil of a conflagration as has never been beheld since' (2012, 294). Trauma is intimate and social: 'accidents' are not simply accidental; they relate to the dissemination of power: 'aristocratic insolence or incapacity', or 'a mere chance at home'. The authors analysed in *Traumatic Encounters* repeatedly present and problematise the relationship between the home and the marketplace, and this problem is (partially) healed from *within* the parent-child relationship. In *Dombey and Son*, writing directly after the repeal of the Corn Laws in 1846, Dickens frames alienation and trauma within the context of free-market capitalism.

The introduction of the transatlantic steamship crossing in 1838 enabled the continuing growth of emigration from Britain and Ireland, and the devastating problems in trade, crop harvests and the Irish potato famine pushed many to make the journey to the United States or Canada. Gaskell and Charlotte Brontë present emigration as a possible solution for the disenfranchised in *Mary Barton*, *Shirley* and *Villette*, a disenfranchisement predicated on the condition of the family home, as well as wider social factors. These novels participate in a wider ideological moment, which began earlier. In *Roughing it in the Bush* (1852), Susanna Moodie insists that the public (including herself) were (mis)sold emigration: 'In 1830, the great tide of emigration flowed westward. Canada became the great landmark for the rich in hope and poor in purse. Public newspapers and private letters teemed with the unheard-of advantages to be derived from a settlement in this highly favoured region' (xvi). Dickens's satiric treatment of emigration in *Martin Chuzzlewit* (1844) was based on his own trip to America in 1842 and his writing of *American Notes* (1842): the former unambiguously serves to reinvest the English home, Martin's return starting a process of family restitution and healing. Emigration directly impacted upon the Brontës: Patrick Brontë was an entirely self-made man, having migrated to Britain from a working-class family in Ireland.[22] While emigration alone cannot account for the conceptual shift played out in the novels, it is nevertheless one of the global factors at work, as well as in the authors' personal contexts.[23] Robert Young writes that the English were 'No longer defined solely by their historical and ethnic origins [...] now recast as a transnational brotherhood united by race and language. They became a globalized race' (2007, 108). However, if this is the case, then it was by no means unilateral or simple: the home is repeatedly reinvested, even sanctified, in the same publications that insist upon its transportability. *Household Words* is a case in point here: the *Household Words Narrative* for 1850 reported assiduously on the campaign to transport orphan girls to America, as well as the activities of The Female Emigration Society (*Household Words Narrative*, August 1850, 180). At the same time, Dickens's novels of this same period present the home as an uncanny and haunted space, but one—seemingly—in which the majority of his heroines are doomed to remain.

Analysis of the mid-nineteenth-century pathologisation of the family is of importance to the field of Victorian studies; however, this analysis also points us towards more nuanced ways of thinking about the traumas which make us who we are. The family appears as both traumatising and enabling for the individual, and the process of traumatisation performs an ideological inscription. The authors respond to and perpetuate mid-nineteenth-century bourgeois dominance, and as we shall see, ideological struggles are focalised through the family. Emily and Charlotte Brontë, Charles Dickens, Wilkie Collins, Elizabeth Gaskell and George Eliot all represent dissociation as a potential corollary of traumatic experience; however, none of the authors represent this as an objective process

[22] Carlyle lambasted the influx of Irish immigrants into Britain in characteristically racist terms in 'Chartism' (1839): 'There abides he, in his squalor and unreason, in his falsity and drunken violence, as the ready-made nucleus of degradation and disorder' (19).

[23] Josephine McDonagh (2013) analyses the significance of migration and global connectivity in her readings of Charlotte Brontë and George Eliot.

lying outside of subjectivity; dissociation is bound up in the nature of the trauma, and what it *means* for the individual and the family. Social structures ground the possibility and parameters of traumatisation, and the historical event underpinning traumatisation in the mid-Victorian novel is the ascendancy of the bourgeois family itself. Parental demands are represented as formative for the child's identity, while being potentially traumatising. Each of the novels places gendered conflict at the heart of the narratives: identity is constructed in response to maternal and paternal modes of authority. Further, as I go on to show, the convoluted plots of mid-Victorian novels are grounded by the notion (both openly and covertly) that families share in the construction of fantasy.

Works Cited

Literary Texts

Brontë, Anne. 1996. *The Tenant of Wildfell Hall.* Edited by Stevie Davies. London: Penguin.

Brontë, Charlotte. 2008. *Jane Eyre.* Edited by Margaret Smith. Oxford: Oxford University Press.

———. 2008. *Shirley.* Edited by Herbert Rosengarten and Margaret Smith. Oxford: Oxford University Press.

———. 2008. *Villette.* Edited by Margaret Smith. Oxford: Oxford University Press.

Brontë, Emily. 2008. *Wuthering Heights.* Edited by Ian Jack. Oxford: Oxford University Press.

Carlyle, Thomas. 1971. *Selected Writings.* Edited by Alan Shelston. Harmondsworth: Penguin.

———. 1971. 'Chartism'. In *Selected Writings.* Edited by Alan Shelston, 149–232. Harmondsworth: Penguin.

———. 1971. *Past and Present.* In *Selected Writings.* Edited by Alan Shelston, 257–312. Harmondsworth: Penguin.

———. 1971. *Signs of the Times.* In *Selected Writings.* Edited by Alan Shelston, 59–86. Harmondsworth: Penguin.

Collins, Wilkie. 1995. *Armadale.* Edited by John Sutherland. London: Penguin.

———. 1986. *No Name.* Edited by Virginia Blain. Oxford: Oxford University Press.

De Quincey, Thomas. 1996. Confessions of an English Opium Eater. In *Confessions of an English Opium Eater and Other Writings*, edited by Grevel Lindop, 1–80. Oxford: Oxford University Press.

———. 1996. *Suspiria de Profundis*. In *Confessions of an English Opium Eater and Other Writings*, edited by Grevel Lindop, 87–182. Oxford: Oxford University Press.

Dickens, Charles. 1850. 'A Child's Dream of a Star'. *Household Words* 1, no. 2 (6 April): 25–26.

———. 1966. *Oliver Twist: Or the Parish Boy's Progress*. Edited by Kathleen Tillotson. Oxford: Clarendon Press.

———. 1972. *The Mystery of Edwin Drood*. Edited by Margaret Cardwell. Oxford: Oxford University Press.

———. 1974. *Dombey and Son*. Edited by Alan Horsman. Oxford: Clarendon Press.

———. 1979. *Little Dorrit*. Edited by Harvey Peter Sucksmith. Oxford: Clarendon Press.

———. 1982. *Martin Chuzzlewit*. Edited by Margaret Cardwell. Oxford: Clarendon Press.

———. 1993. *Great Expectations*. Edited by Margaret Cardwell. Oxford: Clarendon Press.

———. 1998. *Hard Times*. Edited by Paul Schlicke. Oxford: Oxford University Press.

———. 2004. *American Notes*. Edited by Patricia Ingham. London: Penguin.

———. 2008. *A Tale of Two Cities*. Edited by Andrew Sanders. Oxford: Oxford University Press.

———. 2008. *Bleak House*. Edited by Stephen Gill. Oxford: Oxford University Press.

———. 2008. *Our Mutual Friend*. Edited by Michael Cotsell. Oxford: Oxford University Press.

———. 2012. *The Selected Letters of Charles Dickens*. Edited by Jenny Hartley. Oxford: Oxford University Press.

Dickens, Charles, ed. *The Household Narrative of Current Events (for the year 1850) Being a Monthly Supplement to Household Words, Conducted by Charles Dickens*. 27 March 1850; 30 March 1850; 28 July 1850. Dickens Journals Online. http://www.djo.org.uk/household-narrative-of-current-events/year-1850.

Eliot, George. 1981. *The Mill on the Floss*. Edited by George Haight. Oxford: Oxford University Press.

Gaskell, Elizabeth. 1996. *Mary Barton*. Edited by Macdonald Daly. London: Penguin.

———. 2008. *North and South*. Edited by Angus Easson. Oxford: Oxford University Press.

Moodie, Susanna. 2005. *Roughing it in the Bush*. New York: Cosimo Classics.

Richardson, Samuel. 2008. *Pamela*. Edited by Thomas Keymer and Alice Wakely. Oxford: Oxford University Press.

Sala, George. 1853. 'Little Children'. *Household Words* 8, no. 192 (26 November): 289–293.

Shakespeare, William. 2008. *The Norton Shakespeare*. Edited by Stephen Greenblatt. London and New York: W. W. Norton.

Swinburne, Algernon. 1868. *William Blake: A Critical Essay*. London: John Camden Hotten. http://www.gutenberg.org/files/35995/35995-h/35995-h.htm.

Wordsworth, William. 1984. *The Major Works*. Edited by Stephen Gill. Oxford: Oxford University Press.

———. 1995. *The Prelude: The Four Texts*. Edited by Jonathan Wordsworth. London: Penguin.

Primary Psychoanalytic Texts

Abbreviations

Breuer, Josef and Sigmund Freud. 2001. *Studies on Hysteria*. *SE* 2.

SE: *The Standard Edition of the Complete Psychological Works of Sigmund Freud*. 2001. Translated from the German under the general editorship of James Strachey, in collaboration with Anna Freud and assisted by Alix Strachey and Allan Tyson. London: Vintage.

Freud, Sigmund.

———. 'Childhood Memories and Screen Memories'. In *The Psychopathology of Everyday Life*. *SE* 6:43–52.

———. 'Screen Memories'. *SE* 3:301–322.

———. 'The Unconscious'. *SE* 14:161–215.

———. 'The Uncanny'. *SE* 17:217–256.

———. 'Notes upon a Case of Obsessional Neurosis'. *SE* 10:153–318.

———. *Two Case Histories: 'Little Hans'* and *The 'Rat Man'*. *SE* 10.

Laplanche, Jean. 2011. *Freud and the Sexual*. Edited by John Fletcher. Translated by John Fletcher, Jonathan House, and Nicholas Ray. London: International Psychoanalytic Books.

Secondary Texts

Allott, Miriam, ed. 1974. *The Brontës: The Critical Heritage*. London and New York: Routledge.

Althusser, Louis. 1971. 'Ideology and Ideological State Apparatuses'. In *Lenin and Philosophy, and Other Essays*. Translated by Ben Brewster. London: New Left Books.

Armstrong, Nancy. 1987. *Desire and Domestic Fiction: A Political History of the Novel*. New York and Oxford: Oxford University Press.

Barker, Juliet. 2010 [1994]. *The Brontës*. London: Abacus.

Bowlby, Rachel. 2007a. *Freudian Mythologies: Greek Tragedy and Modern Identities.* Oxford: Oxford University Press.
Burke, Edmund. 1764. *A Philosophical Enquiry into the Origins of Our Ideas of the Sublime and the Beautiful*, 4th ed. London.
Butler, Judith. 1993. *Bodies That Matter: On the Discursive Limits of Sex.* New York and London: Routledge.
———. 2014. 'Seduction, Gender and the Drive'. In *Seduction and Enigmas: Laplanche, Theory, Culture*, edited by John Fletcher and Nicholas Ray, and translated by Nicholas Ray, 118–134. London: Laurence and Wishart.
Carpenter, William. 1855. *Principles of Human Physiology: With Their Chief Applications to Psychology, Pathology, Therapeutics, Hygiene and Forensic Medicine.* 5th ed. London: John Churchill.
———. 1875 [1874]. *Principles of Mental Physiology: With Their Applications to the Training and Discipline of the Mind and the Study of Morbid Conditions.* New York: D. Appleton and Co.
Conolly, John. 1830. *An Inquiry Concerning the Indications of Insanity: With Suggestions for the Better Protection and Care of the Insane.* London: John Taylor.
Davidoff, Leonore and Catherine Hall. 2002. *Family Fortunes: Men and Women of the English Middle Class 1780–1850.* Rev. ed. London: Routledge.
Ellenberger, Henri. 1981. *The Discovery of the Unconscious: The History and Evolution of Dynamic Psychology.* New York: Basic Books.
Elliotson, John. 1846. 'Instances of Double States of Consciousness Independent of Mesmerism'. *The Zoist: A Journal of Cerebral Physiology & Mesmerism* 14 (July): 157–187.
Englander, David. 1998. *Poverty and Poor Law Reform in Nineteenth-Century Britain, 1834–1914: From Chadwick to Booth.* London: Longman.
Gallop, Jane. 1984. *Feminism and Psychoanalysis: The Daughter's Seduction.* Ithaca: Cornell University Press.
Gilchrist, Alexander. 1863. *Life of William Blake, 'Pictor Ignotus', with Selections from His Poems and Other Writings.* London and Cambridge: Macmillan.
Hamilton, William. 1998. 'Three Degrees of Mental Latency'. In *Embodied Selves: An Anthology of Psychological Texts 1830–1890*, edited by Sally Shuttleworth and Jenny Bourne Taylor, 80–82. Oxford: Oxford University Press.
Hume, David. 2007. *A Treatise of Human Nature*, edited by David Fate Norton and Mary J. Norton. The Clarendon Edition of the Works of David Hume. Vol. 1. Oxford: Clarendon Press.
Locke, John. 2007. *Some Thoughts Concerning Education.* Edited by John William Adamson. Mineola, NY: Dover Publications, Inc.
———. 2014. *Essay Concerning Human Understanding.* Ware: Wordsworth Editions.

Malthus, Thomas. 1809. *An Essay on the Principle of Population: Or, A View of Its Past and Present Effects on Human Happiness with an Inquiry into Our Prospects Respecting the Future Removal or Migration of the Evils Which It Occasions.* Vol. 1. Washington City: Roger Chew Wrightman.

Matus, Jill. 2009. *Shock, Memory and the Unconscious in Victorian Fiction.* Cambridge: Cambridge University Press.

McDonagh, Josephine. 1987. 'Writings on the Mind: Thomas De Quincey and the Importance of the Palimpsest in Nineteenth-Century Thought'. *Prose Studies* 10, no. 2 (September): 207–224.

———. 2013. 'Rethinking Provincialism in Mid-Nineteenth-Century Fiction: *Our Village* to *Villette*'. *Victorian Studies* 55, No. 3 (Spring): 399–424.

Miller, D. A. 1988. *The Novel and the Police.* Berkeley: University of California Press.

Poovey, Mary. 1989. *Uneven Development: The Ideological Work of Gender in Mid-Victorian England.* London: Virago.

Prichard, James. 1837 [1835]. *A Treatise on Insanity and Other Disorders Affecting the Mind.* Philadelphia: E. L. Carey & A. Hart.

Richardson, Alan. 1994. *Literature, Education, and Romanticism: Reading as Social Practice, 1780–1832.* Cambridge: Cambridge University Press.

Rose, Jacqueline. 1992 [1984]. *The Case of Peter Pan: Or the Impossibility of Children's Fiction.* Philadelphia: Pennsylvania University Press.

Rousseau, Jean Jacques. 1979. *Emile: On Education.* Translated by Allan Bloom. New York: Basic Books.

Shuttleworth, Sally. 2010. *The Mind of the Child: Child Development in Literature, Science and Medicine, 1840–1900.* Oxford: Oxford University Press.

Shuttleworth, Sally and Jenny Bourne Taylor, eds. 1998. *Embodied Selves: An Anthology of Psychological Texts 1830-1890.* Oxford: Oxford University Press.

Slater, Michael. 2009. *Charles Dickens.* New Haven: Yale University Press.

Steedman, Carolyn. 1995. *Strange Dislocations: Childhood and the Idea of Human Interiority.* London: Virago.

Swinburne, Algernon. 1868. *William Blake: A Critical Essay.* London: John Camden Hotten. http://www.gutenberg.org/files/35995/35995-h/35995-h.htm.

Young, Robert. 2007. *The Idea of English Ethnicity.* Oxford: Wiley Blackwell.

Žižek, Slavoj. 1989. *The Sublime Object of Ideology.* London: Verso.

CHAPTER 2

A Crisis in Relations: Psychic Wounds, Fantasy, and the Construction of Family

The mid-Victorian novel shows that we do not have to name a concept directly in order to represent it: the representation of familial 'trauma' in the mid-century novel sets the groundwork for later debates about identity and the family. The novels do not simply perpetuate a pre-existing medical discourse. By placing ideas of memory and fantasy, dissociation and fragmentation, the compulsion to repeat, and healing centre stage, each of the novelists presents and enacts a newly pathologising mode of reading the family. The knowingness, or self-consciousness, with which the novelists treat this theme is marked. The mid-Victorian novel's pathologisation of the family must be recognised as a crucial aspect of the developing discourse of 'trauma', before and after the letter. Most significantly, the novels encourage us to see trauma not as an unspeakable, unrepresentable, Thing which happens to us, but as a fundamental aspect of the way in which we come into being. In order to make this shift theoretically, we would need to recognise the traumatic potential in the everyday, as Freud did startlingly in 'A Project for a Scientific Psychology' (1950 [1895]) and *Studies on Hysteria* (1893–1895), and as Jean Laplanche does through his 'general theory of seduction'. The fact that something has been wounding does not necessarily make it unusual, as mid-Victorian authors repeatedly imply. Theory and literature have a shared emphasis on the cross-generational nature of trauma, and the novels illuminate key concerns within psychoanalytic debate. This proposition connects my study to Carolyn Dever's *Death and the Mother from*

M. Wood, *Parents and Children in the Mid-Victorian Novel*,
https://doi.org/10.1007/978-3-030-45469-2_2

Dickens to Freud: Victorian Fiction and the Anxiety of Origins (1998). Like Dever, I argue that our understanding of psychoanalytic thought can be enriched by an examination of Victorian prototypes: unlike Dever (who focuses specifically on the figure of the dead mother), I relate this to the wider concept of cross-generational trauma.

This chapter does not attempt to resolve all of the complexities of psychoanalytic and post-psychoanalytic trauma theory; such a project is clearly beyond the scope of a comparative literary study. Instead, I explore Freud briefly in conjunction with lesser-known psychoanalytic theorists in order to reconsider the way in which trauma emerges in a cross-generational schema, and the implications this has for our understanding of literary narrative and the family itself. As Dever rightly argues, mid-Victorian thematics provide a prototype for 'the narrative mode through which Freud structures normative psychoanalytic development' (3). However, in contrast to Dever, I do not read the psychoanalytic plot as unavoidably 'narcissistic' (3). By exploring the shifting representations of trauma in Freud's writings, a new kind of critical conversation can take place between text and theory. By taking our lead from the novels, the complexity of cross-generational relationships in Freudian and post-Freudian thought can be more readily appreciated. Despite the seemingly unilateral fashion in which Freud presents the Oedipus complex as the normative fantasy structure (first named in 'A Special Type of Choice of Object Made by Men' [1910]), the intricacies of his writing consistently belie this unilateralism. Freud's shifting theorisation of trauma was inseparable from his developing concept of fantasy, and this entails a more nuanced and dynamic model than a simplified 'desire for the mother, and jealousy of the father'. Laplanche and Jean-Bertrand Pontalis (1988) reinforce this, pointing out that 'It is the different types of relation between the three points of the triangle which – at least as much as any particular parental image – are destined to be internalised' (286). By working in dialogic fashion between literature and theory, we can reaffirm the productive potentialities in Freud's thought, exploited by later theorists such as Laplanche, Nicolas Abraham and Maria Torok, Éric Toubiana, and Anne Ancelin Schützenberger. The mid-Victorian novel therefore informs my reading of psychoanalytic theory, and vice versa. In this chapter, I establish this dialogue through a reconsideration of the status of trauma and fantasy within psychoanalytic thought.

Freud, Trauma and Primal Phantasy

Freud's theorisation of the family moved in fits and starts throughout his career and cannot be easily separated from his development of meta-psychology. The parent-child relationship is not simply a structure; it is a process, involving multiple acts of psychological investment (and disinvestment), both conscious and unconscious. Fantasy moves across the family group. The mid-Victorian novel represents gendered conflicts between maternal and paternal figures as formative for the child, and this can be illuminated by Freud's idea of primal phantasy.

Notably, while Josef Breuer and Freud do not explicitly set out to analyse the emergence of familial trauma in *Studies on Hysteria*, symptomologies are repeatedly set in the context of complex family networks. In the 'Preliminary Communication' (first published in 1893), the authors presented a model of traumatic hysteria that continued to resonate throughout Freud's career, despite his theoretical shifts and conceptual inconsistencies. Childhood is briefly prioritised as the originary source of traumatisation: 'Quite frequently it is some event in childhood that sets up a more or less severe symptom which persists during the years that follow' (Breuer and Freud 2001, 4). This idea is borne out by the case histories, despite the lack of emphasis placed upon it by the two authors. The event is formulated within an affective model of the mind: Breuer and Freud write that, 'Any experience which calls up distressing affects – such as those of fright, anxiety, shame or physical pain – may operate as a trauma of this kind' (6). In a traumatic event, the affect called up is not discharged and is converted into a symptomology. While Breuer consistently reasserts the significance of 'hypnoid states' for the lack of discharge, Freud's contributions present an increasing emphasis on defensive repression. Memory is critical in this model. It is in the 'Preliminary Communication' that we find the now famous assertion that '*Hysterics mainly suffer from reminiscences*' (7). The status of memory is productively complicated throughout *Studies*: the trauma is not forgotten in any straightforward way. Instead, the authors argue that the memory becomes detached from associative connections, which may, in their turn, be repressed from consciousness (12):

> [...] the memory of the trauma – acts like a foreign body which long after its entry must continue to be seen as an agent that is still at work; (6)

Breuer and Freud write that the memories are 'not at the patient's disposal' (9); as I show in my textual analyses, a comparable idea is at work in mid-Victorian treatments of memory.

Multiple factors define the theorisation of traumatic aetiology in the 'Preliminary Communication' (6), and it is only in 'Miss Lucy R.'s' history that Freud self-consciously constructs a 'scenographic' model of trauma. However, his first case history, 'Frau Emmy von N.', undoubtedly presents a scenic model located in a dazzling sequence of family traumatisation, despite Freud's lack of theoretical reflection on the fact. Like Thomas De Quincey in *Suspiria de Profundis*, Frau Emmy's memory appears to be precipitated by frightful and vivid childhood scenes. Moreover, like De Quincey, at the heart of her scenography, there is a dead sister: 'Then I was frightened again when I was seven and I unexpectedly saw my sister in her coffin' (De Quincey 1996a, 52). This sequence is reinforced for Emmy: 'when I was eight and my brother terrified me so often by dressing up in sheets like a ghost; and again when I was nine and I saw my aunt in her coffin and her jaw suddenly dropped' (Breuer and Freud 2001, 52). In each of these scenes, death is sudden, intrusive, and the child cannot make sense of it.

Notably, Freud conceives the case in social terms; discussing Emmy's fear of madness, he writes, 'Her fear of asylums and their inmates went back to a whole series of unhappy events in her family and to stories poured into her listening ears by a stupid servant-girl' (Breuer and Freud 2001, 87–88). The family's legacies are mediated via the working-class figure, paralleling numerous mid-Victorian novels.[1] This speaks to a specifically bourgeois anxiety: the home, while purporting to represent the safe enclosure of domestic values, is actually a permeable and diverse space. The fact that the 'stupid servant-girl' controls the dissemination of Emmy's family's history is important. A tension emerges between the authorised and the pirated family history, a problem found throughout the mid-Victorian novel.

There are explicit cases of cross-generational trauma presented in *Studies*. Paternal abuse defines Katharina's history, albeit censored by Freud in his claim that the perpetrator was Katharina's uncle by marriage (Freud's self-censorship is revealed in a later footnote). Freud again portrays a father as an uncle in his brief account of Rosalia's history:

[1] We could think of Lydia Gwilt in Wilkie Collins's *Armadale* (1866); Uriah Heep in Charles Dickens's *David Copperfield* (1850), for instance.

here, although 'uncle' is not sexually abusive towards the young woman, he is presented as a violent household tyrant, with a predilection for servant girls (170). In case we were in any danger of forgetting, Freud's self-censorship underscores the status of these case histories as *text*—as constructed narratives. The male author's writing of the woman's story is shown to be fraught with complications throughout *Studies on Hysteria*, and the power dynamics are far from simple. The manner in which female figures complicate the seemingly masculine act of vocalisation or narrativisation is likewise critical for my analyses of the mid-Victorian novel.

Freud introduced the primal scene of trauma in Miss Lucy R.'s case, although it is not named here as such. Lucy, an English governess living with two children and their father, presents Freud with a strange hysterical symptom: she experiences the perpetual smell of burnt pudding. In the first stage of his analysis, Freud discovers that this smell was present when Lucy received a letter from her mother asking her to return home. As Freud writes, the smell 'was intimately associated with an experience—a little scene—in which opposing affects had been in conflict with each other' (115). However, he expresses dissatisfaction with this solution: Lucy's conflict (extrapolated thus far) had not been repressed and therefore lacked pathogenic potential (116). Delving further back, Freud connects this scene in the nursery back to two earlier moments that revealed Lucy's problematic status in the house. In the first and earliest scene, Lucy's male employer vehemently reprimanded her for allowing a lady visiting the house to kiss the children 'on the mouth' (120); in the second scene, an elderly male visitor tries to kiss the children, and the father 'shouts' at him to prevent it (119); at this, Lucy feels a 'stab at my heart' (120), the confrontation bringing back the shame and disappointment of the earlier scene (120). Freud argues that the primary 'traumatic moment' (123) engenders auxiliary scenes, through a series of correlatives, symbolic and contiguous. The later scene in the nursery produced the symptom by bringing the affective conflict to the fore: Lucy's desire to escape the house and her ambivalence towards her male employer.

Freud's hermeneutic technique is underpinned by his conviction that psychological meaning is relational, built up by echoes, repetitions and parallelisms. It is a structuralist analysis, and the richness of Freud's own writing consistently belies the simplicity of his conclusion that Lucy is in love with her employer. As Fletcher claims, the three scenes Freud identifies only make sense in the context of Lucy's earlier promise to the children's dying mother that she would 'take their mother's place with them' (Breuer and Freud 2001, 115; Fletcher 2013, 50). This promise creates a conflict between Lucy's feeling of obligation to the children, as a devoted mother figure, and her wish to leave the house to join her own mother. This earlier deathbed scene, while never repressed from consciousness, intersects with the 'traumatic moment' and the later auxiliary scenes Freud identifies. This structural problem points towards the fundamental duality of Lucy's desire: loyalty towards the dead (and living) mother is offset by desire for the father. Fletcher writes, 'This conflict might be described as a conflict between two sequences or scenographies: that bearing on the mother and that bearing on the father' (50).

The case illustrates how each individual inhabits plural subject positions, which—in Lucy's case—conflict with one another. Lucy's multiple roles as daughter, governess, surrogate mother and potential wife become untenable. Further, her employer's fear of his friends kissing his children 'on the mouth' places a profound question mark over the appropriate parameters governing adult-child relationships. This issue is echoed in Freud's brief history of Emma, set out several months after the publication of *Studies on Hysteria*, in 'A Project for a Scientific Psychology' (1895). The 'Project' was put aside quite rapidly by Freud and only published posthumously; it reframes the theorisation of hysteric conversion in reference to neurology, while presenting a psychological model.[2] In both *Studies* and the 'Project', Freud presents the idea that 'hysterical patients are subject to a *compulsion* which is exercised by *excessively intense* ideas' ('Project', 347). In the 'Project', this is theorised through reference to the structure of the brain, the manner in which external 'stimuli' operate upon the neurones (303). While these hypotheses may seem far removed from the concerns of the mid-Victorian novel, Freud illustrates his economic model through an analysis of cross-generational trauma.

'Emma' was Emma Eckstein, the young woman Wilhelm Fliess operated on with such devastating effect in 1895 when he left half a metre of gauze in her nasal cavity, and who subsequently went on to become the first female psychoanalyst in 1897 (Masson 1985, 116–118; Appignanesi and Forrester 1994, 138). Her botched operation continued to haunt Freud, forming part of the backdrop for his specimen dream, Irma's Injection (*Interpretation of Dreams,* 106–118). In the 'Project',

[2] Fletcher (2013) charts Freud's move away from Charcot and neurology in 1893, his theoretical detachment of hysteria from the anatomy of the nervous system (28).

Freud uses one element of her complex case to theorise trauma. Having a phobia of going into shops alone, Emma presents Freud with a scene from when she was twelve. Walking into a shop, she left in a panic because she believed that the shop workers were laughing at her clothes. Freud focuses on various incongruous details in his analysis: most notably, the fact that one of the shop assistants had 'pleased her sexually' ('Project', 353). Through analysis, this scene links back to a much earlier—*seemingly forgotten*—childhood moment in which a shopkeeper had 'grabbed at [Emma's] genitals through her clothes' (354). Freud traces the symbolic and contiguous correlatives between the first scene in the sweet shop and the scene which engendered the phobia. Despite the brevity of the case, and the comparative paucity of his narrative technique, Freud reads the two scenes with precision, highlighting details such as the laughing face of the shop assistant, and the importance of clothes to the two scenes. Through this reading, Freud argues that the earlier childhood scene is activated in a deferred—*Nachträglich*—fashion. This temporal mechanism was first named *Nachträglichkeit* in a letter to Fliess in 1897.[3]

Nachträglichkeit, translated by James Strachey as 'deferred action', and by Laplanche as both *après coup* and 'afterwardsness' ('Notes on Afterwardsness', 1999c) provides the temporal structure for Emma's trauma:

> […] it is highly noteworthy that it [the sexual release] was not linked to the assault when this was experienced. Here we have the case of a memory arousing an affect which it did not arouse as an experience, because in the meantime the change [brought about] in puberty had made possible a different understanding of what was remembered.
>
> Now this case is typical of repression in hysteria. We invariably find that a memory is repressed which has only become a trauma by *deferred action* […]. (Freud 'Project', 356)

In an editorial gloss to this passage, Strachey argues that Freud's proposition concerning belatedness would be undermined by his subsequent 'discovery' of childhood sexuality located in *The Interpretation of Dreams*, *Fragment of an Analysis of a Case of Hysteria* (1905 [1901]), and fully extrapolated in *Three Essays on the Theory of Sexuality* (1905). However,

[3]Freud's letter to Wilhelm Fliess of 14 November 1897 ('Letter 75').

this is clearly not the case: afterwardsness defines Emma's case regardless of the theoretical status of childhood sexuality; as a young child, she is involved in an event beyond her comprehension and subjected to an intrusive, violating act. Moreover, at no point in his writings does Freud try to suggest that a child's experience of sexuality is the same as an adult's.

In William Wordsworth's poem 'We are seven', discussed in Chapter 1, the poetic speaker makes a demand upon the child which she cannot fulfil on his terms. Emma's case—one of sexual abuse—likewise poses an epistemological problem, bound up in the compromising encounter between adults and children, although the violence of the scene of course pushes beyond the difficulty posed by the poem. The uneasy sexualisation of adult-child relationships lurks throughout the mid-Victorian novel: we could think of Good Mother Brown's manhandling of Florence Dombey; Magdalen Vanstone's eroticised relation to her father and his past; Mrs. Havisham's damaging projection onto Estella. Moreover, the mid-Victorian novelists found their realist enterprise on a comparable sense of afterwardsness.

The childhood abuse returns to haunt Emma in (barely) disguised form. With this in mind, it is perhaps surprising that Freud does not dwell upon the fact that the eight-year-old Emma returned to the sweet shop again after the initial assault, writing only:

> She now reproached herself for having gone there the second time, as though she had wanted in that way to provoke the assault. In fact a state of 'oppressive bad conscience' is to be traced back to this experience. (354)

This state of 'oppressive bad conscience' is not theorised within the context of Emma's phobia. However, by creating a dialogue between the *Studies* and Emma's case, a new vision of early-period Freud can emerge; not only concerned with the literal scene of paternal seduction,[4] but also with the wider dynamism of childhood experience: the asymmetrical encounter between adult and child. Laplanche predicates his general theory of seduction on a similar premise.

Cross-generational trauma is foregrounded at distinct points in Freud's early writings. While retaining the factual basis of the hysterical patient's

[4] In 'The Aetiology of Hysteria' (1896) Freud argued that paternal seduction was the underlying cause of hysteria.

traumatic acting out (and the 'truth' of the abuse explored in 'The Aetiology of Hysteria' [1896]), Freud began to imply an alternative mode of reality in his letter to Wilhelm Fliess dated 2 May 1897:

> Everything goes back to the reproduction of scenes, some of which can be arrived at directly, but others always by way of phantasies set up in front of them. The phantasies are derived from things that have been *heard* but understood *subsequently* and all their material is, of course, genuine.[5] ('Letter 61', 247)

While this could simply be read as an affirmation of childhood abuse, it does in fact open up possibilities for theorising a more complex relationship between event and fantasy, and therefore adult-child relationships. There is an ambiguity in the nature of the originary 'material' which can be 'genuine', but which may not represent the empirical 'truth' of an event. 'Psychical reality' is implied here without being theorised. In his early writings, Freud formulates memory as both a construction and as a trace; he does not neglect the fact that childhood memory can represent external as well as psychical realities. Thinking back to Emma's case, the first childhood memory is apparently not repressed or forgotten until the third scene (when she is twelve), at which point the phobia emerges. This ambiguity is not a failing in Freud's account, but a productive complication. In a letter to Fliess dated 6 December 1896, Freud argues that the temporal dynamic of memory must be seen in the plural: 'subjected from time to time to a *re-arrangement* in accordance with fresh circumstances – to a *re-transcription* [...] memory is present not once but several times over [...] laid down in numerous species of indications' ('Letter 52', 233). Memory cannot photograph experience; memory—as we experience it—is defined by cathexis: or, in simpler terms, by the way in which we 'invest' memory traces with libido, with desire.

In Freud's early examinations of the topic, he argues that the strangely luminous memories of childhood can stand in for a plethora of early experiences: due to displacement, the subject represents significant events to herself through a process comparable to metonym. Freud compares this to 'shams', which 'are not made of gold [...] but have laid beside something

[5] 'Letter 69' shows Freud's seeming abandonment of his paternal seduction theory and is dated 21 September 1897 (259–260).

that is gold' ('Screen Memories', 307). For example, rather than remembering the formative loss of his nurse and his mother's confinement with his younger sister, Freud remembers a scene in which he demands that his older half-brother opens a cupboard ('Childhood Memories and Screen Memories', 50–51).

In 'Screen Memories' (1899) and 'Childhood Memories and Screen Memories' (part of *The Psychopathology of Everyday Life* [1901]), Freud argues that the 'tendentious' production of memory is temporal as well as symbolic, outlining two modes ('Childhood Memories and Screen Memories', 44). First, the 'retroactive' memory involves the displacement of adult fantasy into childhood memory.[6] Second, the memory that 'pushes forward' involves a later memory, standing in place of 'screened-off' childhood experience: this is Emma's predicament in the 'Project'—the scene from when she was twelve screens the earlier scene of abuse.

Freud claims that in our childhood memories, we can see ourselves, not from a first-person perspective, but in the third person, as a character ('Childhood Memory and Screen Memory', 47). Despite emphasising the importance of fantasy to the production of memory in the earlier essay ('Screen Memories', 1899), Freud retains the possibility here that traces of authentic visual perception feed into the most unlikely of screen memories; memories instead become 'well adapted to represent' fantasy ('Screen Memories', 315). In the later essay, Freud writes that 'we are forced to suspect that in the so-called earliest childhood memories we possess not the genuine memory-trace but a later revision of it, a revision which may have been subjected to the influences of a variety of later psychical forces' ('Childhood Memories', 47–48). Looking at these two texts together, it should be stressed that a screen memory is not simply a false memory. The key feature of Freud's early hypotheses is his emphasis on psychical time: there is a *negotiation*, the seeking of a 'compromise' ('Screen Memories', 308). Freud's theorising also involves compromise; although Freud repeatedly considers the retrogressive production of memory (see, 'Screen

[6] In *David Copperfield*, Dickens represents the storm leading to the deaths of Steerforth and Ham in similar terms: David writes, 'I now approach an event in my life, so indelible, so awful, so bound by the infinite variety of ties to all that preceded it, in these pages, that, from the beginning of my narrative, I have seen it growing larger and larger as I advanced, like a great tower in a plain, and *throwing its fore-cast shadow even on the incidents of my childish days*' (ch. 55, 765 [my emphasis]).

Memories', 322), the idea that the past is *formative* and the source of repetition is likewise present, albeit less persistently: 'Some of these screen memories dealing with events later in life owe their importance to a connection with experiences in early youth which have remained suppressed' (ibid., 320).

Freud's supposed *volte-face* on the all-pervasiveness of paternal abuse[7] did not eradicate the presence or importance of cross-generational trauma in his writings. Fletcher (2013) demonstrates this by tracing the 'oscillation' (107) of seduction in Freud's letters to Fliess, showing that within three months of abandoning the theory of paternal seduction, Freud was thinking about the reality of seduction once more (105). Freud clearly remained open to the possibility that adult abuse was real and led to mental disturbance. However, at the same time, he recognised that the fragmentary 'memories' which his patients produced did not necessarily represent an empirical reality that could simply be excavated. Moreover, paternal seduction does not encompass the vicissitudes of cross-generational traumatisation in *Studies on Hysteria* or the 'Project'. Even here, traumatic hysteria is inextricable from identity formation—it is not just about illness. While Freud's traumatic model was undoubtedly stifled in *The Interpretation of Dreams* and the *Three Essays on Sexuality* as a result of his focus upon the primary processes and infantile sexuality, the 'event' of seduction was never lost from his writings. In the *Three Essays*, Freud unexpectedly comes to the defence of his paternal seduction essay, 'The Aetiology of Hysteria' (190). Freud's development of the primal phantasy in 'A Case of Paranoia Running Counter to the Psychoanalytic Theory of the Disease' fulfilled the latent potential of his earlier writings.

In the latter essay, Freud analyses a young woman's paranoiac delusion of being overheard while having sex with her lover in order to posit a normative childhood fantasy—the scene of parental sex, in which the child is the hidden watcher or listener. This primal phantasy is constructed through the real and imagined interplay of desires between the two parents and the listening or watching child: a form of psychical reality irreducible to a single consciousness. The case reveals the mobility of subject positions in Freud's model of fantasy: in the case, 'she herself *became* her

[7] This reversal has been the focus for much of the criticism of Freud as clinician and theorist, notably from Jeffrey Masson in *Assault on Truth* (1984).

mother' (269). P. Ikonen and E. Rechardt (1984) reinforce the intersubjectivity of the primal phantasy: as they rightly point out, in order to come into being the subject must be both included and excluded from certain structures. To be somebody one has to be included, but to avoid being turned into someone else one must also be excluded (65). The female patient in 'A Case of Paranoia' is torn between her unconscious sense of obligation towards her mother (and the female colleague who comes to represent her mother) and the desire for her lover.

Importantly, Freud does not limit 'primal phantasies' solely to the scene of parental sex in this essay, but also names 'seduction' and 'castration' as 'primal phantasies' ('Case of Paranoia', 269). Primal phantasy is, by definition, a temporal structure, produced—as Fletcher (2013) shows (223)—through afterwardsness. However, Freud is also concerned with primal phantasy as a topographical structure—a *mise-en-scène* in which competing desires are posed. What is notable here for my reading of both Freud and the mid-Victorian novel is that all these fantasies involve *cross-generational* scenes: a traumatic encounter between child and adult. Moreover, a comparable idea underpins the mid-Victorian narrative.

The operation of identification and desire explored in a 'Case of Paranoia' is critical—not only to our understanding of the primal phantasy as the scene of parental sex, seduction or castration—but also to the primal scene of trauma. In my readings of the novels, I retain the potential slippage between the primal scene of trauma, the traumatic event (set out in *Studies* and the 'Project') and the 'primal phantasy'. Retaining the crossovers and blurring between these two concepts allows a dynamic model of trauma to emerge, in which the subject's identification with the primary moment—whether the event *or* the fantasy—is formative not only for symptom formation, but also for the formation of identity. In a significant theoretical intervention, Ruth Leys (2007) considers the possibility of the subject's primary identification with the scene of trauma (8–9); this mimetic theory 'posits a moment of terrorized identification with the aggressor' (9). In this model, the 'victim's perceptual and cognitive apparatus' are deeply impacted by the psychic violence of the scene: the trauma may not become 'part of the ordinary memory system' owing to a 'kind of post-hypnotic forgetting' (8). As Leys points out, this proposition raises issues concerning the status of survivors' testimony (9).

This theory is positioned in opposition to the 'antimimetic' model that conceives trauma as an 'external' violence perpetuated against a 'passive' subject'. Within the humanities, Cathy Caruth is the foremost figure proponent of the 'antimimetic' position. Accepting Bessel van der Kolk's neurobiological hypotheses uncritically, Caruth argues that the traumatic event lies outside the subject's experience; the event is registered in the neurones, but remains inaccessible to language and symbolisation (van der Kolk and van der Hart 1995; Caruth 1995; LaCapra 2001, 107).[8] In stark contrast to Freud in the 'Project' and *Studies on Hysteria*, Caruth (1996a) describes trauma as an 'unpleasurable event that has not been given psychic meaning in any way' (30).

The mimetic theory of trauma is an important characteristic of Freud's most famous case history: *From the History of an Infantile Neurosis* (1918 [1914]), otherwise known as the Wolf Man history. The Wolf Man was the pseudonym of Sergei Konstantinovich Pankeyev who, at the time of seeing Freud, was a deeply troubled young Russian aristocrat, living a strangely dislocated cosmopolitan life, moving between various sanatoria (Pankeyev 1989a). Crucially, the case is based upon the movement between two ideas: the primal scene of trauma as an empirical reality and the primal *phantasy* of parental sex as the origin of the subject's entrance into the Oedipus complex. Freud plays with the blurring between these two concepts in his ongoing debate with Karl Jung. Much to Freud's irritation and fascination, Jung rejected the idea of infantile sexuality, arguing that sexual fantasies relating to childhood were *all* retrospectively constructed. This tension is enacted within the process of Freud's writing while he shifts (nervously) between seemingly contradictory positions. Using Sergei's famous childhood dream of the six or seven white wolves in the tree as his source material, Freud constructs the infinitesimal details of the childhood primal scene with an almost obsessive attentiveness. However, despite Freud's circling around this singular event, the childhood history is grounded in a whole series of sexualised scenes, which are traversed and complicated by the process of fantasy, without simply being 'false'. This places the history within a similar conceptual space to Freud's early essays 'Screen Memories', and 'Childhood Memories and Screen Memories'.

Freud separates Sergei's childhood complexes into two main phases: the first characterised by his naughtiness and sexualisation, contemporary with his sister Anna's attempted seduction; the second characterised by

[8]Van der Kolk's theory relies on a distinction between 'narrative memory' and 'traumatic memory', a distinction I critique in my reading of Dickens in Chapter 4.

his obsessional neurosis, and coming after the wolf dream, which operates as the traumatic event. Much of Freud's analysis therefore hinges on the search for the empirical reality hiding behind the dream and the movement into the second phase. It is within this context that Freud constructs the scene of the parents having sex—'*a tergo*' (37)—on a hot summer evening, observed by the toddler in his cot. Freud argues that the dream operates as the auxiliary scene, reactivating the complex established in the 'primal scene' through afterwardsness. While Freud's construction of the primal scene is problematic (strangely replaying the Wolf Man's obsessional neurosis perhaps), his urge to move between dream and reality indicates the dynamism of fantasy: something established consciously can be partially repressed and continue to operate both consciously and unconsciously.

The haunting repetition of scenes powerfully resonates with the mid-Victorian novels I examine; however, the Wolf Man's case also reads like a modernist novella: James Strachey observes that Freud is forced to develop a series of sophisticated narrative strategies in order to deal with the complexity of his material, exhibiting 'extraordinary literary skill' (6). It is, at the same time, a detective story, with Freud attempting to reconstruct the crime through the complex layering of clues. Sergei recounts Freud's love of Arthur Conan Doyle's Sherlock Holmes, reflecting: 'The fact that circumstantial evidence is useful in psychoanalysis when reconstructing a childhood history may explain Freud's interest in this type of literature' Pankeyev 1989b, 146). Writing his own *Memoirs*, Sergei bemoaned the fact they were taking on the character of 'a short family novel' (Gardiner 1989, 342), later remarking to Muriel Gardiner that he attempted to eschew the novelistic and give 'preference to the epic element, rather than the sentimental or theatrical' (343). The Wolf Man's history and Sergei's life provide us with an exemplary case of what is at stake when plotting a life. Sergei refuses to make his tragic history the matter of Dickensian sentiment or Dostoyevskian psychological torment—authors he refers to in his *Memoirs*.[9]

[9] The childhood chapter, written last shortly before Sergei's death, is stark, giving us little information about his feelings, but providing a fascinating first-hand account of life in an extended aristocratic family on a Russian estate before the Revolution. Sergei's *Memoirs*, begun after Freud's death, self-consciously build up to the event which took on all traumatic importance from his middle age onwards: the suicide of his wife Therese in 1938.

Reading across Freud's texts, fantasy emerges in a specific temporal model: past, present and fantasy are conjoined. Drawing together the play of the child, the creative work and the analysand's transference, Freud argues that each is governed by the reactivation of an infantile wish, or the repetition of a structuring desire ('Creative Writers', 139). The temporal model of fantasy, which provides the theoretical backbone for such texts as 'A Child is Being Beaten' (1919), 'Leonardo da Vinci and a Memory of his Childhood' (1910), and 'Creative Writers and Daydreaming' (1908), relies on repetition. Repetition likewise defines the Wolf Man case: however we respond to Freud's interpretation, it seems undeniable that Sergei continued to play out scenarios going back to early childhood.[10] In *Beyond the Pleasure Principle* (1920), Freud brought the idea of repetition to the forefront of meta-psychology in his formulation of the death drive.

The structure of *Beyond the Pleasure Principle* itself deserves attention. Freud begins by posing a question: why should shell-shocked soldiers return to the scene of their trauma in their dreams? He suggests that they are 'fixated' to their trauma, not because they think about it too much, but precisely because they are 'more concerned with *not* thinking of it' (13). But with this provocative comment hanging in the air, he makes a potentially frustrating announcement: 'I propose to leave the dark and dismal subject of the traumatic neurosis and pass on to examine the method of working employed by the mental apparatus in one of its earliest *normal* activities – I mean in children's play' (14). The text is rightly renowned for what follows: Freud's analysis of his grandson's game, of '*fort-da*' (gone/there):

> What he did was to hold the reel by the string and very skilfully throw it over the edge of his curtained cot, so that it disappeared into it, at the same time uttering his expressive 'o-o-o-o'. He then pulled the reel out of the cot again by the string and hailed its reappearance with a joyful '*da*' ['there']. This, then, was the complete game – disappearance and return. (15)

In the first stage of his analysis, Freud suggests that Ernst plays at throwing his mother away with a cotton reel in order to create a sense

[10]This point should be widened to include his entire family. Psychological illness was rife: his sister, father and wife all committed suicide.

of his mastery over her absence and presence, going on to write: 'The interpretation of the game then became obvious. It was related to the child's great cultural achievement – the instinctual renunciation (that is, the renunciation of instinctual satisfaction) which he had made in allowing his mother to go away without protesting' (15). Deploying his characteristic rhetoric, Freud pulls back here to acknowledge that there is something missing from this interpretation. The desire for mastery alone could not override the pleasure principle. In this shift of focus from the *extraordinary* war neuroses to the *ordinary* familial scene, Freud implies the all-pervasiveness of the compulsion to repeat, a compulsion associated with trauma. The *mise-en-scène* of trauma is presented as the domestic space.[11] With a dramatic chapter break, and the question concerning Ernst's game hanging in the air, Freud moves on to consider the consulting room, the scene of analysis.

It is this shift that brings together various elements of theory addressed in my discussion of Freud. By the time he wrote *Beyond the Pleasure Principle*, Freud could not attribute the compulsion to repeat to the search for 'libidinal satisfaction' or 'as a simple attempt to overcome unpleasant experiences': instead, he posits a primary 'daemonic' 'force'—a drive 'independent of the pleasure principle and apt to enter into opposition to it' (Laplanche and Pontalis 1988, 98).[12] This shift—rhetorical and exploratory—is performed through the consecutive analyses of the child's game, *fort/da*, and clinical transference. By introducing a primal drive responsible for the compulsion to repeat, Freud expands the concept of trauma and reframes traumatisation as an aspect of normative childhood development:

> The child's sexual researches, on which limits are imposed by his physical development, lead to no satisfactory conclusion; hence such later complaints as 'I can't accomplish anything; I can't succeed in anything'. The tie of affection, which binds the child as a rule to the parent of the opposite sex, succumbs to disappointment, to a vain expectation of satisfaction or to jealousy over the birth of a new baby – unmistakable proof of the infidelity of the object of the child's affections.

[11] This places the reader comfortably, smoothing the ground for the audacious conceptual chapters that follow, culminating in Freud's elaboration of drive theory, and the famous statement that '*the aim of all life is death*' (38).

[12] 'The Uncanny' (1919) is an important antecedent to *Beyond the Pleasure Principle*.

> [...] Patients repeat all of these unwanted situations and painful emotions in the transference and revive them with the greatest ingenuity. (21)

Freud proposes that the quotidian conditions of childhood function as traumas that are repeated within the transference: 'Loss of love and failure leave behind them a permanent injury to self-regard in the form of a narcissistic scar' (20). He suggests that dreams attempt to 'bind' the penetrative excitation that breaks in through these wounds; however, this process is also propelled by the deathly compulsion to repeat—much like Ernst's game (36). What is most important for us here is that traumatic repetition can be seen as a process in which 'unboundedness' is displayed with 'daemonic' force as the 'compulsion to repeat' (35), *and* as an indicator of the possibility of binding (or working-through):

> the compulsion to repeat the events of his childhood in the transference evidently disregards the pleasure principle in every way. The patient behaves in a purely infantile fashion and thus shows us that the repressed memory-traces of his primaeval experiences are not present in him in a bound state and are indeed in a sense incapable of obeying the secondary process. It is to this fact of not being bound, moreover, that they owe their capacity for forming, in conjunction with the residues of the previous day, a wishful phantasy that emerges in a dream. (36)

The majority of psychoanalytic theorists, with the notable exception of Laplanche, do not adequately address Freud's early trauma theory in conjunction with *Beyond the Pleasure Principle*. Freud clearly responds to the subject matter of his bourgeois patients and his own family life; however, as we have seen, this has conceptual rationale. Childhood is the site of traumatisation whether it be through the loss of a parent (played out and anticipated by Ernst), or through the triangulation of desire represented by primal phantasy. In his development of the general theory of seduction, Laplanche draws on these elements of Freud and places the cross-generational relationship at the heart of subjective development, arguing that this relationship is inherently traumatic: an idea likewise presented by the mid-Victorian authors considered in this study. Complex fantasies, responsible for forming *and* threatening personal identity, are constructed in response to primary traumatic events.

Laplanche and the 'Compromised Message'

Jean Laplanche's project emerged from and challenged Jacques Lacan's dominance in the 1960s through an attentive return to Freud's writings. Laplanche charts the presence of Freud's radicalism, but as well what he terms the 'going astray' ('Unfinished Copernican Revolution', 60): the return of conservative theoretical paradigms. His reading of Freud is predicated upon the idea that the subject's fundamental openness to the other is primary, and that this decentring of the self constitutes Freud's radicalism. Laplanche argues that the elements of Freud's thought positing the openness of the subject to the other are 'Copernican'; conversely, 'Ptolemaic' moments prioritise the ego as a cohesive, 'even self-begetting', entity. However, as Laplanche clarifies, this theoretical dualism is unavoidable—the 'going astray' is built into the structure of psychoanalytic thought itself: 'I have tried to show, [...] the movement by which, on the basis of an initial Copernicanism (of the little human's orbiting round the sexual adult), man closed in on himself, in a Ptolemaic system' ('A Short Treatise on the Unconscious', 109). The subject's primary openness can only ever be part of the story; the ego must also be constructed through the translation of the adult message (ibid.). Laplanche's argument builds upon numerous potentialities in Freud's writing; in 'The Unconscious' (1915), Freud notes that 'It is a very remarkable thing that the *Ucs* of one human being can react upon that of another, without passing through the *Cs*. This deserves closer investigation [...] but, descriptively speaking the fact is incontestable' (198–199).

Laplanche's intervention is valuable in a discussion of mid-Victorian fiction as by creating this dialogue we see that the novels similarly represent the primary openness of the child to the adult world, and the traumatising effects of this openness. Each of the novels is concerned with drawing ethical parameters around the parent-child relationship: in the novels, moral feeling is formed by negotiating these fraught and disrupted relationships. In *North and South,* for example, Margaret re-orientates herself outwards into the conflicted community of industrial Manchester in order to heal the wounds caused by her broken family. Laplanche argues that traumatisation is the basis for identity formation. Trauma is not the extraordinary—it is the everyday. In Laplanche's theory, adult gestures, words, and sounds, are heavily loaded: never neutral—never controllable; they are laden. We 'say' far more than we realise with every look. Laplanche's theory implies that every parental[13] gesture—whether verbal or non-verbal—takes on the status of an address. Laplanche (2011) names this the 'compromised message' (or 'enigmatic signifier') because it is compromised by the adult's *unconscious*: 'an interference or 'noise' comes to inhabit this communication like a parasite, an interference that initially proceeds from one side only, and that is the side of the adult' (21). In a state of hyperawareness, but lack of comprehension, the child attempts to translate the compromised message: it operates as a 'signified to the subject' ('Reference to the Unconscious', 102).

Laplanche argues that this process is formative for subjectivity and the development of the infant's unconscious. The necessarily partial nature of the baby's metabolising process leads to the first repression and the formation of the unconscious: the repressed part of the message remains an active force. In this context we can remember Thomas De Quincey's memory of the servant's face discussed in Chapter 1: 'The feeling which fell upon me was a shuddering awe, as upon a first glimpse of the truth that I was in a world of evil and strife' (*Suspiria de Profundis*, 98). In this psychological self-fashioning, De Quincey represents this moment as providing the dynamism for an apparently teleological sequence of memorisation: in other words, it functions as the starting point for narrative. For my purposes, it does not matter whether or not De Quincey presents his own case truthfully or accurately. What is significant is his formulation of the primal moment as *intrusive*—coming from the outside: an aggressive and threatening gaze is directed towards the young boy, and somehow he must decode it. His inability to translate the woman's threatening demeanour is critical: it is only a 'glimpse' into a new world. The novels present protagonists engaged on quests for self-definition in which they must translate and exorcise parental stories and legacies.

In reconstructing a Freudian paradigm hinging upon the child's reception of the adult other's 'enigmatic' and 'compromised' message, Laplanche's narrative directly echoes the mid-Victorian novelistic plot, as well as De Quincey's tantalising reference in *Suspiria de Profundis*. This nineteenth-century plotting is not incidental: Laplanche prioritises Freud's *fin-de-siècle* thought by taking Emma's brief case history as the definitive *mise-en-scène* for his theory in 'Reference to the Unconscious'.

[13] This is not just the biological parent—but all the carers and adults around the child.

Despite this nineteenth-century underpinning, to date Laplanche's theories have not been substantially deployed in Victorian literary criticism. In *Supposing Bleak House*, John O. Jordan does use Laplanche's idea of the primal scene and compromised message to analyse the haunting of Esther's narrative, and the burial of the mother-daughter story. Jordan does not, however, extend this analysis to create a larger conceptual model: the tone of *Supposing Bleak House* remains playful and reflective, rather than strongly argumentative.

Laplanche draws upon potentialities found within Freud's thought in order to construct his general theory of seduction, one such potentiality being found in Freud's *Three Essays on the Theory of Sexuality*. The *Three Essays* represent a key moment in the history of psychoanalysis, not least because they operate as a point of convergence for Freud's own competing theoretical models concerning infantile sexuality. Laplanche discusses the 'disruptive', 'traumatising' qualities of this hybrid, palimpsestic text in *Freud and the Sexual* drawing the reader's attention to the 'strange' and 'baroque' content of Freud's first edition, published in 1905 (249–250). Later editions of the *Three Essays* foreground a heteronormative developmental model which plays out in small amendments throughout, but is most clearly illustrated by Freud's addition of new sections in 1915: '[5] The Sexual Researches of Children' (194), in which castration and penis envy play a central part; and '[6] The Phases of Development of the Sexual Organisation' (197). However, in contrast, the first edition tends to prioritise autoeroticism and its provocation through erotogenic zones. Significantly, Freud proposes that the mother eroticises the infant's body by creating these zones, the most obvious being the mouth through breast-feeding:

> The satisfaction of the erotogenic zone is associated, in the first instance, with the satisfaction of the need for nourishment. To begin with, sexual activity attaches itself to functions serving the purpose of self-preservation and does not become independent of them until later. No-one who has seen a baby sinking back satiated from the breast and falling asleep with flushed cheeks and a blissful smile can escape the reflection that this picture persists as a prototype of the expression of sexual satisfaction later in life. (181–182)

The drive leans on the bodily function (whether feeding or excretion),[14] so that the function itself becomes an erotically dynamic process: the locus and source of desire. The mother's care, her 'washing and rubbing' (187), creates a template for the child's later sexual activity. In *Freud and the Sexual* Laplanche draws upon this in order to theorise the compromised message: he argues that parental nurturance maps unconscious sexual signification onto the infant's body; once implanted, this becomes libidinally invested and phantasmatic. This is a two-phase schema; the adult's implantation is followed by the infant's 'translation, binding and repression' (Fletcher 1999, 16). The remainder left after the infant's first attempt at translation is the repressed kernel of the unconscious, the 'source object of the drive'. The initial implantation functions through afterwardsness: the infant's retrospective attempt to translate and bind the primary implantation.

In order to explore the general theory of seduction and think through its relevance to the mid-Victorian novel, it is helpful to return to Laplanche's lecture series, 'Reference to the Unconscious' and 'The Problematic of the Id', presented at University of Paris, between 8 November 1977 and 7 February 1979, and published as *Problématiques IV: L'inconscient et le ça* (published in English as *The Unconscious and the Id* in 1999). In addition, I use Laplanche's analysis of Freud's 'A Child is Being Beaten' to explore the relation between translation and fantasy, along with ideas presented by Dominique Scarfone, who works on Laplanchean premises. This overview does not pretend to be comprehensive; I wish to highlight how Freudian theory can be reinvigorated through Laplanche's intervention, and the significance of this process for our reading of mid-Victorian literary paradigms and the ethics of the parent-child relationship.

In theorising the unconscious, Laplanche works from, and against, Lacan's claim that '*l'inconscient est structuré comme un langage*'. As Laplanche shows through an attentive return to Lacan's mathematical formulae, accepting his analogy with algebra means accepting that the unconscious has a *pre-determined* symbolic structure (the Symbolic with a capital S), and this fails to take account of the disruption produced by

[14] In a process named *Anlehnung* by Freud, and translated by Strachey's coinage *anaclisis*.

the passage of language into the unconscious, caused by the child's fragmentary process of translation. It is worth quoting Laplanche at length here:

> it is, to say the least, problematic to bring in the notion of the 'signified', whether in the sense of a code [...]; or, on the other hand, in the sense of a communication – that is to say, not necessarily a 'contents' with a clearly defined meaning, but in the sense of a message, albeit vague and above all enigmatic, but addressed *to the other.* In the unconscious, is there yet a signified, a message to communicate and to deliver? Well, I think we need to hold onto this, which reopens our discussion in our attempt to come up with a definition of language: the unconscious is a phenomenon of meaning, but without any communicative finality. ('Reference to the Unconscious', 102)

It is on this basis that Laplanche turns to the 'seduction theory, which is shown marvellously clearly, with a truly mythical luminosity, by a clinical example' (103)—that of Emma.

Laplanche argues that in the first childhood scene in the sweet shop: 'something is ***signified*** to the child, "signified to the subject", but remains in her as a sequence that is absolutely not comprehended. There is certainly "a" sexual signified in view, but what is left behind is only a thing or a sequence of things, of thing-presentations' (103–104). Laplanche moves to consider Emma's second visit to the shop:

> She 'goes back there' not only because sexual excitement already exists for her, but in order to find the trauma again, and to try to rediscover precisely the enigmatic signified, this 'signified to the subject' which has not been delivered, in spite of an act which itself bears signification. (104)

I'll return to this shortly, but first I want to emphasise that Laplanche uses Emma's case as an *allegory* for a much earlier scenario: the birth of the unconscious in the infant:

> Let us say, taking as our guide this sequence of scenes, that the signified is first of all a sexual, enigmatic signified, which cannot be assimilated at first by the baby who receives it. It certainly has a relation with what is called, a little too quickly, the 'desire of the mother'. Clearly, the desire of the mother is shown in the way she takes care of the child, but it is not revealed there. It is at once conveyed and hidden, in the care, the

> handling, in what is given attention, in attitudes. In the most schematic terms, it is symbolised by the breast, or at least, in the unconscious. It will be taken up in the form of a certain number of representational elements (*Vorstellungsrepräsentanz*) as the breast. You can see how it is over-hasty and facile to say that the unconscious *is* 'the discourse of the other' [as Lacan claimed]. The child's unconscious is not directly the discourse of the other, nor even the desire of the other. (105)

Freud's account of Emma Eckstein's history is uncharacteristically stark and primarily functions in order to establish the idea of *Nachträglichkeit*. It is this narrative style that enables Laplanche to reconfigure the case as myth, representing the belated temporal structure of trauma underpinning infantile development: 'The disqualified "message" conveys nothing except its energy. In the same way, the first scene in Emma's case conveys nothing but the fact that it is traumatising, with no knowledge of what constitutes this traumatisation – and moreover, that is why Emma goes back' (106).

Employing a case in which an actual abuse does take place makes the transposition of the history into the theoretical schema of seduction more heavily loaded: the general theory of seduction is concerned with the unconscious enigmas lurking within the adult message, rather than physical abuse. Like Freud (in texts such as 'A Case of Paranoia'), Laplanche uses a pathological example in order to extrapolate a normative scenario. Unlike Freud, Laplanche does not reflect in depth upon the pathological situation in itself: by which I mean, he does not consider the abusive excess that defines Emma's case. These two aspects are not mutually incompatible, since adult sexual desire is foreign to, and different from, children. However, Laplanche does not consider the violence of the event—to quote Freud, 'the shop keeper grabbed at her genitals through her clothes' ('Project', 354).

Emma herself is lost in the mythic reading—like Eurydice she is sent back to the underworld when we turn to look at her. In order to make more sense of Emma's experience, we would also need to think about the difficulty of a child translating a message that is not enigmatic *enough*: a problem found in all the novels under consideration, and the specific source of the vampiric fathers in *No Name* and *Armadale*. In a lecture addressed to the Association des psychiatres français in 2002, published in English in *Freud and the Sexual* (2011), Laplanche gestures towards this issue in the context of intergenerational abuse and raises the possibility that there are some messages which involve a 'radical failure of translation' (130): 'Is there a message when it is something that thus imposes a translation that is nothing other than the message itself? Or when the message is paradoxical perhaps?' (131). This question connects Laplanche's later work to the ethical considerations of the mid-Victorian novel as well as the 'urgent', 'shocking' (131), twenty-first century context: he ends by considering, 'When he [the recipient of the message] fails to translate them, in what ways is he possessed by them?' (131).

Returning to 'Reference to the Unconscious', Laplanche does not pause on the 'oppressive bad conscience' Emma felt after her second visit to the shop ('Project', 354). In the original account of the case, Freud interprets this as stemming from her guilt; by returning it was 'as though she had wanted to provoke the assault' (354). This 'as though' is critical: Freud implies a fault line in Emma's thought process.[15] Twentieth- and twenty-first century accounts show that children who are sexually abused frequently blame themselves for the abuse. This assumption of guilt could be read as an internalisation of the abuser's violating 'message'. Laplanche's distinction between 'hollowed-out' and 'filled-in' clinical transference is helpful here. 'Filled-in' transference involves translations of the parental message made in childhood. These are immobile representations, imagos, scenarios and repetitions that the analysand projects onto the analyst. 'Hollowed-out' transference instead maintains the open relation to the enigmatic other we bear in very early infanthood (see, 'Transference: its Provocation by the Analyst'). In an important intervention, Dominique Scarfone extends this hypothesis to the *transmission* of the compromised message itself, differentiating between normative and psychotic transmission. In the normative 'hollowed' scenario, an enigma and an accompanying 'compromise-formation', which 'translates for the infant', are transmitted. But, in psychotic transmission, a *prohibition* of translation is transmitted with the message, and the translating mechanism of the child is undermined as a consequence; this leads to the 'intromission' of a filled-in superego, persecuting and corrosive of reality (69–76).[16] This superego operates as a kind of vampiric other within the

[15] In his later text, *Life and Death in Psychoanalysis* (1976 [1970]), Laplanche briefly notes the 'bad conscience' and argues that in the second scene Emma attempts a 'seduction' (39).

[16] Laplanche points towards this possibility in 'Implantation, Intromission': 'I have no doubt that a process related to intromission also has its role in the formation of the

child—intrusive and unwelcome—the source of guilt and recrimination against the self.

Of course these reflections must remain entirely speculative in relation to the real little girl hidden within Emma's case and Emma Eckstein's life, but nevertheless, Scarfone's extension of Laplanche's theory allows the violence of the story to be sensitively addressed: opening up the possibility that in acts of sexual abuse some kind of prohibition against translating the experience is transmitted. It is worth noting that while none of the mid-Victorian novels I analyse address direct sexual abuse per se, they represent states of psychological breakdown in the wake of persecutory cross-generational traumas (whether intergenerational or transgenerational). These traumas are not asexual: they are intimately related to the protagonists' assumption of sexual and gendered identities. What brings Laplanchean theory and the mid-Victorian novel together is the shared emphasis on the parameters of the cross-generational relationship.[17]

It is worth teasing out how Laplanche situates fantasy in his general theory of seduction. In a co-authored piece, 'Fantasy and the Origins of Sexuality', Laplanche and Jean-Bertrand Pontalis insist upon the parity between unconscious fantasy and conscious daydreams:

> The hysterical fantasies which 'have important connections with the causation of the neurotic symptoms' (we must be dealing with unconscious fantasies) have as 'common source and normal prototype what are called the daydreams of youth.' In fact it is conscious fantasy itself which may be repressed and thus become pathogenic. (20)

The same issue is at work in 'A Child is Being Beaten', in which Freud analyses masochistic fantasies in children. The beating fantasy is grounded in Freud's triadic temporal model discussed earlier in the chapter. The first scene involves the child subject watching their sibling being beaten (past event); the second is a repressed wish that the subject themselves would be beaten (present wish); and the third is the conscious masturbatory thought of 'a child is being beaten' (fantasy future). In 'Interpretation

superego, a foreign body that cannot be metabolised' (136). I return to this later in the chapter when discussing Éric Toubiana.

[17] Laplanche's concern with the ethical dimensions of the issue becomes clear in *Freud and the Sexual*. It is worth noting that he sees the category of the message as essential for understanding both victim and perpetrator (157–158).

between Determinism and Hermeneutics', Laplanche readdresses Freud's essay to show how translation operates in the formation of this fantasy. Laplanche argues that the first scene propels an enigmatic message from the parent towards the watching child, while the two subsequent scenes involve a process of translation, or 'metabolisation', a process that remains incomplete, and complicated by the child's fixation on the primal scene:

> there can be no linear causality between the parental unconscious on the one hand and what the child does with these on the other. All the Lacanian formulae on the unconscious as 'discourse of the other', or the child as a 'symptom of the parents', disregard the break, the profound reshaping, which occurs between the two, and which may be likened to a metabolism that breaks down food into its constituent parts and assembles them into a completely different entity. (160)

As Laplanche reminds us in 'Reference to the Unconscious', all fantasies are 'scenarios involving relations between bodies' (137). However, the placement of the subject within the fantasy is far from stable. Laplanche argues that the location of fantasy can change through repression, without the content undergoing significant modification. As he shows in his analysis of the beating fantasy, it is the subject's placement within the fantasy structure that changes; or, to put it in narrative terms, the focalisation employed ('Interpretation between Determinism and Hermeneutics', 155)—the eyes we see through, the consciousness functioning as lens. In fantasy, we can enter a scene as a point of view, as a spectator, rather than an active participant: I discuss this later in relation to Emily Brontë's *Wuthering Heights* and Dickens's 'autobiographical fragment'. Laplanche argues (with others such as Dominick LaCapra) that phantasmatic investment occurs in the conscious *and* unconscious: it is therefore a category that can help us move beyond the ideological schism between purposeful concealment and 'genuine' forgetting. LaCapra (1985) states that 'even an actual event must be the object of phantasmatic investment to become pathogenic' (16).

Mourning and Working-Through

Mid-Victorian literature created the prototypes for the psychological theories that followed in the early twentieth century: the novels show the ambivalence, stoppages and fantasised responses at work in mourning.

In the nineteenth century, there were highly delineated cultural practices determining how grief should be performed, and the responsibilities this placed upon the mourner. The aesthetics of mourning are presented throughout the literature of the period, taking in practices such as funereal processions, clothing, and the personal and communal expression of sentiment. The politics of mourning are likewise ever-present—such as the making and reading of wills, the conditions placed upon economic inheritance. The popularity of Alfred Tennyson's *In Memoriam*, published in 1850, and the death of Prince Albert in 1861, underscored the pre-existing importance of mourning practices to the period. The question of how to voice grief is repeatedly returned to in the mid-Victorian novel. As my textual readings show, the aesthetics and politics of mourning are varied, but nevertheless each novel is grounded within such an aesthetic, emerging from the traumatic rendering of parent-child relationships.

Freud's 'Mourning and Melancholia' is more than an account of grief; it is a critical moment in the development of his meta-psychology. And yet, to see these two facets of the work as opposed undermines the profundity of what Freud achieves in the essay. 'Mourning and Melancholia' (published in 1917 and written in 1915) is the corollary to 'On Narcissism: An Introduction', published in 1914. The two essays theorise the construction of the ego as an internal 'thing'.[18] In 'On Narcissism', Freud writes that 'we are bound to suppose that a unity comparable to the ego cannot exist in the individual from the start; the ego has to be developed' (76–77). Freud represents the ego as an object that is developed through an internal investment of libido. Reading across 'Mourning and Melancholia', 'On Narcissism' and 'The Uncanny' (1919), it is clear that the conscious self—by which I mean the totality that for convenience I call 'Me'—is alienable. It has to be maintained through investment, a process that starts in infanthood and is therefore impacted on by our parents. The ego has the potential to be fractured or wounded: it is Me—and yet I can never simply "be there". In 'On Narcissism', Freud not only discusses primary infantile narcissism, but also discusses how the subject invests their 'ego ideal' through secondary narcissism (94–95). As the term suggests, the ego ideal is that version of ourselves with which we feel compelled to conform.

[18]'Mourning and Melancholia' and 'On Narcissism' signal Freud's move towards his second topography, comprising superego, ego and id, elaborated and named fully in *The Ego and the Id* (1923).

The ego, then, is not a pre-given entity and can therefore be threatened from outside or inside. As the novels also intimate, this danger comes to the fore when dealing with loss. Freud writes:

> It is well worth notice that, although mourning involves grave departures from the normal attitude to life, it never occurs us to regard it as a pathological condition and to refer it to medical treatment. We rely on its being overcome after a certain lapse of time, and we look upon any interference with it as useless or even harmful. ('Mourning and Melancholia', 243–244)

This passage shows that 'grave departures from the normal' are—paradoxically—the norm, and this is born out by the mid-Victorian novel's attitude towards loss. In the novels, the boundary between mourning and pathological melancholia frequently becomes blurred. Freud differentiates mourning and melancholia through one distinguishing feature: in melancholia, the loss of the other becomes a loss of self. Grieving subjects berate themselves for their own failures: 'The disturbance of self-regard is absent in mourning; but otherwise the features are the same' (244). Melancholia, then, is the nightmarish version of mourning in which the ego is palpably threatened. Freud theorises that in a normative mourning process we invest, and then disinvest, the connections surrounding the lost object. This is a fraught process:

> Reality-testing has shown that the loved object no longer exists, and it proceeds to demand that the libido shall be withdrawn from its attachments to that object. This demand arouses understandable opposition – it is a matter of general observation that people never willingly abandon a libidinal position, not even, indeed, when a substitute is already beckoning to them. This opposition can be so intense that a turning away from reality takes place and a clinging to the object through a hallucinatory wishful psychosis. Normally, respect for reality gains the day. Nevertheless, its orders cannot be obeyed at once. They are carried out bit by bit, at great expense of time and cathectic energy, and in the meantime the existence of the lost object is psychically prolonged. (244–245)

Even in a normative scenario, anguish is heightened before it can be worked through. Mourning involves the creation, or replaying, of a phantasmatic *mise-en-scène*: the 'hallucinatory wishful psychosis' that denies loss. But if mourning itself is already so dangerous, so illusory, how can melancholia be distinguished from it? Freud argues that melancholia arises as a response to losses where there has been a 'conflict due to ambivalence' (256).[19] Melancholia apparently arises, then, because of a problem in the original object relation. It is worth quoting Freud at length to make sense of this idea, so central to his essay and to my readings of the novels:

> An object-choice, an attachment of the libido to a particular person, had at one time existed; then, owing to a real slight or disappointment coming from this loved person, the object-relationship was shattered. The result was not the normal one of a withdrawal of the libido from this object and a displacement of it on to a normal one, but something different, for whose coming-about various conditions seemed to be necessary. The object-cathexis proved to have little power of resistance and was brought to an end. But the free libido was not displaced on to another object; it was withdrawn into the ego. There, however, it was not employed in any unspecified way, but served to establish an *identification* of the ego with the abandoned object. Thus, the shadow of the object fell upon the ego, and the latter could henceforth be judged by a special agency, as though it were an object, the forsaken object. In this way, an object-loss was transformed into an ego-loss and the conflict between the ego and the loved person into a cleavage between the critical activity of the ego and the ego as altered by identification. (248–249)

We identify with what we have lost—and perhaps with what we never had. Freud presents this as a romantic drama: disappointed, abandoned and alone, we take in the thing that we love into our own self. Freud formulates the ego's identification through his new concept of narcissism, writing that 'The narcissistic identification with the object then becomes a substitute for the erotic cathexis' (249):

> It represents, of course, a *regression* from one type of object-choice to original narcissism. [...] The ego wants to incorporate this object into itself, and, in accordance with the oral or cannibalistic phase of libidinal development in which it is, it wants to do so by devouring it. (249–250)

[19] Earlier in the essay, Freud writes—rather unconvincingly—that melancholia is 'in some way related to an object-loss which is withdrawn from consciousness, in contradistinction to mourning, in which there is nothing about the loss which is unconscious' (245). This latter point feels rather unlike Freud. In a psychoanalytic framework, it is difficult to imagine loss or bereavement without unconscious elements, nor indeed, imagine an object relation that does not participate in some ambivalence.

We take in the other in the hope of preserving them, but instead we devour ourselves. The ego is 'consumed' (246): eaten away. (Dickens presents a corresponding idea in *Dombey and Son* through Florence.) In so doing, we perform our loyalty—our subservience—to the loved one. The superego, unnamed here, but nevertheless clearly formulated, watches superciliously over the process; the 'critical agency' looking in on our altered self, as if the latter were an unwelcome intruder. The melancholic subject's loud berating of herself is a displaced criticism of the 'incapable' other with whom she now identifies (248).

For Freud, melancholia is more than a pathological response to loss; it is part of the wider dynamic of how we respond to others. As a result of this, there is ambivalence at work in 'Mourning and Melancholia': on the one hand, the healthy response to loss is to transfer our love from one object to another; on the other, the essay openly associates melancholia with female goodness. In a moralising moment, Freud claims that a 'good' woman will be more liable to fall into a melancholic state than a 'worthless' one:

> A good, capable, conscientious woman will speak no better of herself after she develops melancholia than one who is in fact worthless; *indeed, the former is perhaps more likely to fall ill of the disease than the latter*, of whom we too should have nothing good to say. (247 [my emphasis])

This passage appears to have little to do with Freud's sophisticated discussion of ambivalence, which shortly follows it. In the quotation above, melancholia surfaces as a female concern, apparently a sign of women's morality. Freud's rather pompously dismisses the 'worthless' woman and refers to the justified criticism of this woman by 'we', the community. He implies that the good woman is not only moral, but she also refuses to transfer her sexual gifts from one person to another, instead becoming unwell. Further, it appears by extension that the virtuous woman does not (or cannot?) openly criticise her 'incapable' (248) love object unless she develops a pathological identification with him.[20] Yet again, Freud writes a kind of double text: on the one hand, the essay presents his elegant

[20] This could be productively compared to Ruth Leys's discussion of mimetic trauma—the survivor's identification with the aggressor. It would be interesting to deploy Freud's thinking around the melancholic subject's identification with the lost love object to reconsider relationships characterised by abuse; in frontline social work practice, it is possible to observe the way in which women can identify with men who have been violent and

meta-psychological model; on the other, there is a sense of a *roman à clef*. His later description of the melancholic subject as a 'great nuisance' appears to bespeak a sense of personal grievance (248).

Despite the elegance of his formulations and writing, Freud effaces the reality of loss in 'Mourning and Melancholia'. What is lacking here, in Laplanche's terms, is the 'Copernican' sense of the subject's openness to the loved other, the other as someone who speaks and acts. Laplanche comments upon the essay:

> [For Freud] the dead person, for his part, is really dead. There is no danger, no otherness to be sensed, except by pure projection. A category is lacking here in Freud, but it is not that of the 'symbolic', it is that of the message or the signifier, which is something quite different. [...] A signifier remains a signifier, even if it is set down thousands of years ago, and found in the desert or in a pyramid. It could even be said thus to gain in otherness, as the other who emitted or wrote it is no longer there to support it, to be its guarantor or interpreter. ('Time and the Other', 248)

Laplanche's eloquent statement is in tune with a mid-Victorian sensibility. The passage quoted above echoes Charles Dickens's famous observation in a speech of 1869:

> It was suggested by Mr. Babbage, in his ninth "Bridgewater Treatise," that a mere spoken word - a single articulated syllable thrown into the air - may go on reverberating through illimitable space for ever and for ever, seeing that there is no rim against which it can strike - no boundary at which it can possibly arrive. (1869 online)

All of the novels examined in *Traumatic Encounters* imply that the dead send messages; however, this is not supernatural, or certainly not in any simple fashion. The relationship between the dead and the living is conceived of in nuanced psychological terms, coalescing around the problematic status of inheritance. This lacuna in Freud is tackled by Toubiana in *L'héritage et sa psychopathologie* (1988).[21] Written under the direction of Laplanche, Toubiana gives an account of the specific

abusive towards them, and this perpetuates the woman's susceptibility to entering into such relationships.

[21] To date, the full text has not been translated into English; Toubiana's work on Julius Caesar is reproduced in *Seduction and Enigmas: Laplanche, Theory, Culture* (2014),

pathologies engendered by the act of inheritance. He frames this enterprise as an investigation of the '*psychopathologie de la vie quotidienne*' ('psychopathology of everyday life') (2). The monograph situates this in relation to legal discourse, drawing heavily on the French Civil Code, as well as *Julius Caesar* and *King Lear*. The Oedipus complex and mourning are accorded a key status.

Toubiana opens his monograph with the statement: '*L'héritage est une des meilleures photos de famille qui soit*'; 'Inheritance is one of the best family photos there can be'. Going on to explain:

> *L'héritage est une photographie; à l'inverse du cinéma, la photo fige le mouvement même si elle laisse imaginer un avant et un après du temps de la pose. Chacun y a sa place et personne n'est prêt à oublier la sienne ni celle des autres.* (1)
>
> Inheritance is a photograph; in contrast with cinema, the photo freezes movement, even if it leaves to the imagination a before and an after time of the pose. Each person has their place there, and no one is ready to forget their own, or the place of the others.

Conflicts and desires are fixed within a familial scene. The act of inheritance—the bequest—operates as a kind of primal scene. Toubiana's writing implies a theatrics of inheritance, and this resonates with the presentation of inheritance in the mid-Victorian novel. The novels use the disruption caused by financial legacies to create a historical and present-day snapshot of the family, while using the inheritance plot to propel the narrative forwards. Like a screen memory, inheritance draws together past and present (and indeed future) in a brightly lit moment. But it is more complex than that, because the bequest creates a shadow: the 'undead' presence of the deceased. The French Civil Code states that in *'La Saisine'* (the legal process which governs inheritance) '*le mort saisit le vif*', or 'the dead seizes the living'. Toubiana connects the legal phrase to Freud's description of melancholia: 'the shadow of the object fell upon the ego'. In Toubiana's model, inheritance engenders an almost violent introjection or incorporation of the dead, in which the agency appears to be placed within the lost object rather than in the subject. He argues that a prototype for this 'incorporation' of the object occurs

translated by Nicholas Ray. The direct and indirect translations that follow from *L'héritage et sa psychopathologie* are my own.

in the early moments of ego-formation through the development of the superego: the work of melancholia therefore repeats something primal.[22] The asymmetrical encounter that led to the development of the superego is internally replayed after the death of the object, and the ego is eaten away (through the cannibalistic logic of melancholia which first devoured the lost object).[23]

In his analysis of *Julius Caesar*, Toubiana focuses on the concept of *emprise*, or 'influence' (translated by Nicholas Ray as 'mastery' [2014, 176]). The nuances of the French term *emprise* imply not only an influence on people, but also a hold: *emprise* is perpetuated after death through inheritance. Toubiana reads Caesar as the all-powerful father who refuses to enunciate his own death and therefore haunts his symbolic 'sons', specifically Brutus, as a vampire (54). Hidden behind the political discourse Toubiana identifies the *mise-en-scène* of the drives: sexual domination is the hidden aspect of *emprise*. Paternal vampires are central to *No Name* and *Armadale*, although in Dickens's novels, it is more often the maternal figure who emerges as an uncanny revenant. Both Elizabeth Gaskell and George Eliot subtly work against the Gothicism of loss, in order to emphasise the ethical process of working-through.

It is worth taking stock at this point. In Laplanche's general theory of seduction, the enigmatic message 'implanted' by the other operates as the provocative force in the development of the child's unconscious: it is the result of otherness, without being reducible to the Other. Through his concept of 'intromission', Laplanche theorises a more violating process through which the superego is produced: in contrast to implantation, intromission 'blocks' metabolisation, creating the superego as a 'foreign body' ('Implantation', 136). Dominique Scarfone, John Fletcher and Toubiana follow Laplanche in granting agency to the other, rather than to the subject in these primary moments. In doing so, Scarfone and Fletcher adopt Laplanche's term 'intromission', while Toubiana relies on Freud's theory of melancholia.

[22] This builds on Freud's idea of the 'special agency' that watches the ego in 'Mourning and Melancholia', and his formulation of the superego in The Ego and the Id (1923).

[23] Fletcher, taking his cue from Laplanche's 'Implantation, Intromission' (cited earlier in this chapter), critiques Toubiana's deployment of melancholia in relation to the development of the super-ego, arguing that the latter is a result of a violating *intromission*, rather than incorporation, in which the agency remains fiercely with the other, thus leading to a 'psychotic enclave'.

Fletcher (2002) reads E.T.A. Hoffmann's *The Sandman* in terms of intromission, writing that the Sandman is both 'paternal legacy and psychotic enclave' (134). Scarfone thinks about these issues in relation to the transmission of a message that prohibits or forecloses the child's process of translation (notably in the novels, we repeatedly witness the consequences of a message which is not enigmatic *enough*). Toubiana explores a similar moment by considering the act of inheritance: the continuing operation of the dead's *emprise* and how that compares to the development of the superego. These variant perspectives raise the possibility of a different kind of unconscious, one that is not only provoked, but also inhabited by the other person. Julia Kristeva's theorisation of melancholia and Nicolas Abraham and Maria Torok's concept of the psychic crypt address this possibility in different ways.

Kristeva argues that clinical depression, or melancholy as she also terms it, is the result of a primary problem: the failure to mourn the inevitable loss of the Maternal Thing (the primal mother of the earliest infant-mother dyad, preceding the constitution of subject and object). For Kristeva (1989), this mourning occurs in language: having acknowledged the loss of the Thing, we rediscover our *mothers* in language through the following negation: '"I have not lost her (that is the negation), I can recover her in language"' (43). However, the depressed subject cannot do this. Instead, she disavows the negation of the loss of the Thing, remaining 'painfully riveted' to the Thing, thus creating 'a *psychic inside* thus constituted once and for all as distressed and inaccessible' (63). Kristeva argues that this situation leads to a 'loss of meaning' (42): symbolic language cannot access this 'psychic inside', which remains the preserve of the semiotic (63). Kristeva's case histories in *Black Sun* present women with unconscious fantasies concerning their mothers which are primary or primal, leading to linguistic dissociation and psychological fragmentation (76): they cannot *speak* to or from their loss. In Chapter 3, I address this in relation to Caroline Helstone in *Shirley*.[24]

[24] Kristeva outlines the subject's entrance into the symbolic in *Revolution in Poetic Language* (1974). She theorises that our first modes of signification are located in the bodily space associated with the earliest mother-child dyad, naming this the semiotic. Preceding 'the establishment of the sign' and the constitution of a 'knowing' subject, the semiotic is intimately connected to the bodily drives, to the body of the Mother, a '*psychosomatic* modality of the signifying process' (36, 38). The constitution of subject and object (and therefore the possibility of symbolic representation) follows the 'break' engendered by the '*thetic* phase' (40).

Both Abraham and Torok's and Kristeva's theories are predicated upon the idea of entombment—something, someone, is taken in and buried. Abraham and Torok's theory of the crypt differs from Kristeva's representation of melancholia by presenting an alternative psychic topography: a different kind of space. They build on Freud's concept of melancholia, but represent a substantive intervention into the psychoanalytic field. In a series of essays, published in English as *The Shell and the Kernel*, the two psychoanalysts address interpersonal traumatisation. They argue that being subjected to trauma carves out a pathological and damaging space within the ego, named the crypt. The crypt is a burial place, which encloses inadmissible material. In his foreword to *The Wolf Man's Magic Word*, Jacques Derrida writes, 'No crypt presents itself. The grounds [*lieux*] are so disposed as to disguise and to hide: something, always a body in some way' (xiv). It is distinct from the dynamic unconscious found in Freud's first topography, and the biologised *id* of his second: it is not formed by repression, neither is it endogenous. The crypt contains a 'memory they buried without legal burial place: The memory is of an idyll, experienced with a valued object and yet for some reason unspeakable' ('The Lost Object', 141).

Abraham and Torok's wider theorisations rely on the idea that a secret belonging *to the other* can be transmitted and encrypted. Abraham clarifies this:

> The phantom is a formation of the unconscious that has never been conscious – for good reason. It passes – in a way yet to be determined – from the parent's unconscious into the child's [...] it works like a ventriloquist, like a stranger within the subject's own mental topography. ('Notes on the Phantom', 173)

The phantom has not been subject to Freud's process of defensive repression; in receiving the phantom of the other's secret, the child has received a 'gap in the unconscious, an unknown unrecognised knowledge' (Abraham and Torok 'The Lost Object', 140). The miniature case histories found in *The Shell and the Kernel*, such as 'The Man of Milk and His Fetish', read like modernist short stories.[25] Language appears dislocated: signifiers create structures that (partially) occlude primal scenes of trauma.

[25] Derrida (1976) likewise observes that the '*The Wolf Man's Magic Word* reads like a novel, a poem, a myth, a drama' (xxv).

The silencing of shared trauma—critical to the concept of the phantom—leads to a situation where language acts out. Like Freud, Abraham and Torok are concerned with excavating hidden narrative. Abraham claims that 'entire libraries of enigmas in literature would yield up their key, were we but to reconsider the "supernatural element" responsible for them: to be precise, the appearance of a Specter' ('The Phantom of Hamlet', 188). Abraham and Torok insist on the linguistic basis of traumatisation; the centrality of the 'secret' in the creation of psychic topographies: 'it is precisely a matter of words [...] whose covert existence is certified by their manifest absence' ('Topography of Reality', 159–160). Nicholas Rand writes that 'The phantom represents the interpersonal and transgenerational consequences of silence' (168).

Abraham and Torok's book-length rereading of the Wolf Man's case, *The Wolf Man's Magic Word*, operates as the corollary to the theoretical framework presented in *The Shell and the Kernel*. The authors analyse traumatisation linguistically, arguing that Sergei's shifts between different languages point towards something effaced and yet ever returning: a 'cryptonymic' secret (21). Abraham and Torok define 'cryptonyms' as 'words that hide' through a process of 'semantic displacement' (18), not a '*metonym of things* but a *metonymy of words*' (19).[26]

Reading the Wolf dream through a compelling symptomology of linguistic displacement (or cryptonymy), working across English and Russian, leads Abraham and Torok to posit an alternative primal scene in which the father and sister engaged in a sexual act which Sergei witnessed, and from which he felt excluded: 'his impossible desire to occupy one or the other place in the scene he saw, his genuine "primal scene"' (40).[27] They argue that the dream-text encodes an argument between Sergei's English nursery maid and his mother, in which the mother denies her son could have witnessed the event.[28] This leaves the boy in an impossible position: 'Had he not been contaminated by the mother's fear, he

[26] To be precise, cryptonymy, as a figure, is defined in the following terms: the 'word' is replaced 'by the synonym of its alloseme' (19).

[27] For my purposes here, it is not necessarily important whether Abraham and Torok correctly decipher this, the most opaque and yet somehow most blatant, of Freud's case histories. Rather, I want to think about the potential for these ideas in relation to the constructed traumas presented by the mid-Victorian novel.

[28] The English governess appears in Freud's account through the Wolf Man's childhood screen memory of her eroticised teasing.

would not have allowed himself to be treated like a liar and be made to gag on the truth' (38). Derrida explores the constructed situation in his foreword to the book:

> The Wolf Man would have had to have incorporated within him, in his Self, his older sister: his sister as seduced by the father and trying to repeat the same scene with her brother. And by the same token, the Wolf Man, the brother, would also have had to have incorporated the father's place, the paternal penis confused with his own. The violence of the mute forces that would thus be setting up the crypt does not end with the trauma of a single unbearable and condemned seduction scene – condemned to remain mute, but also condemned as a building is condemned, by official order of the court. (xv)

In this view, Sergei is in an intolerable position: unconsciously caught by the continuing prohibitions that scaffold the crypt, and the desire that plays out around the prohibition. The trauma is not found in a single unrepeatable and unspoken scene, but in duration—a state of condemnation: the 'violence of the mute forces' are continually 'setting up the crypt'. There is therefore, as Derrida argues, an 'impossible or refused mourning' (xxi) for the sister which defines the enclaved space:

> The special difficulty of the Wolf Man's analysis was due to the fact that his position as 'witness for the prosecution' put him in a paradoxical situation: He knew that he was the object of his parents' fears. By espousing their apprehension of him, he must have been, to some extent, afraid of himself [...]. (Abraham and Torok 1976, 40)

Sergei's 'hieroglyphic' (Derrida, xxiv) linguistic code, at work in his dreams and fantasies, is interpreted as a way of bearing witness to the scene and maintaining the crypt. In his *Memoirs*, Sergei describes his mourning for his sister, Anna, after her suicide as 'unconscious' in direct opposition to his mourning for his wife. Recounting the period following Anna's death, he states that '[his] thoughts and feelings seemed to be paralysed' (24). Sergei gives only a brief account of Anna's death and funeral; however, he narrates in some detail the tragic early death of Lermontov, 'the second greatest poet of Russia' (31) and the pilgrimage he undertakes to the poet's grave in the Caucasus, notably, where Anna herself had committed suicide. Sergei's conscious mourning of the poet appears to displace the *work of mourning* for his sister, which has been rendered impossible by, in his own words, his 'melancholy', 'unconscious identification' with Anna (26).

Abraham and Torok's emphasis on witnessing brings us back, at the conclusion of this chapter, to a fundamental debate within twentieth-century theory: the question of bearing witness to trauma. On one side of the debate, Caruth (1996b) argues that 'trauma is not locatable in the simple violent or original event in an individual's past, but rather in the way that its very unassimilated nature – the way it was precisely *not known* in the first instance – returns to haunt the survivor later on' (4). In contrast to Freud, van der Kolk and Caruth present trauma as a state of haunting emerging from a single and singular event empty of 'psychic meaning' ('Traumatic Departures', 30). As Ruth Leys shows in *Trauma: A Genealogy*, both Caruth and van der Kolk represent traumatic memories as intrusive histories: by definition truthful, *literal*, and yet unknown: outside representation (229). Trauma is, in Caruth's terms, an 'interruption of a representational mode' (Caruth 1996b, 115, n.6; also quoted in Leys 2000, 267).

Leys (2000) performs a meticulous and powerful critique of this position, examining the shaky evidential base in relation to van der Kolk's neurobiological propositions, and Caruth's overreliance on Paul de Man's deconstructive thinking. If we were to accept Abraham and Torok's reading (and writing) of Sergei Konstantinovich Pankeyev even tentatively, not as a confirmed diagnosis, but as a means of thinking through traumatic mechanisms, Caruth's theorising of the traumatic memory as the 'real' appears even more problematic.[29] The play of language through and within the Wolf Man's trauma, clear in Freud's case history and Sergei's *Memoirs*, implies the complex fantasised responses that coalesce around traumatisation. However we choose to read Sergei and his experiences, his trauma appears located in the temporal structure produced in a sequence of almost dizzying *representations,* not in the intrusion of an unmediated history. Further, his psychic drama does not result from unknowingness in any straightforward way;

[29] Dominick LaCapra (2001) also critiques these theoretical manoeuvres, showing how Caruth appropriates van der Kolk's neurobiological hypothesis concerning the 'incomprehensible or unreadable' nature of the traumatic experience located in the right side of the brain (physically separated from the language centres in the left side of the brain), in order to put a form of deconstructive thinking into play influenced by Paul de Man (107*fn*): in this view, the trauma is the inaccessible 'real' or 'literal'.

bearing in mind his sister's sexual precocity, her suicide, and his father's psychological breakdowns and suicide, it seems like he 'knows' far too much. In Abraham and Torok's interpretation, Sergei creates hidden linguistic structures through which his real witnessing is expressed, while remaining necessarily silent. Abraham and Torok's reading of case relies on the idea that the walls of the crypt are erected and maintained to prevent material being assimilated (a theory presented in 'The Lost Object', 141): this requires psychical force.

While accepting the limitations of Caruth's quasi-neurobiological model, the ethical imperative that underpins her theorisation of bearing witness resonates strongly with the presentation of ethics in the mid-Victorian novel. Deploying Caruth, Judith Greenberg (1998) argues that 'Translating the trauma into language or narration demands a negotiation of "indirect telling", or 'a reliance upon echoes' (320):

> Echo's story in particular frames a doubly frustrating condition of trauma: first, the inability to originate or control speech (the inaccessibility of the original event and the impossibility to narrate it), and then, the isolation or rejection that occurs after the fragments Echo finally finds to utter go unattended. (332)

For both Caruth and Greenberg, the ability (or inability) to bear witness or testimony is central. Caruth uses the metaphor of a voice crying out from the wound, taken from Tasso's story of Tancred and Clorinda, to argue that trauma is always bound up with an encounter with the other: it is 'the story of the way in which one's own trauma is tied up with the trauma of another, the way in which trauma may lead, therefore, to the encounter with an other, through the very possibility and surprise of listening to another's wound' (8). This ethical imperative can be found throughout the mid-Victorian novel, in which it becomes a gendered concern. As I have argued elsewhere, women take on a privileged role in relation to male mourning (Wood 2012). In *Fragment of an Analysis of a Case of Hysteria*, Dora is the provocative source of Freud's writing, and the object of a powerful and destabilising counter-transference. Her voice is both enabled and silenced by the history (20). I connect Freud's authorial investment in Dora with the gendering of mourning processes in *Little Dorrit* and *Armadale;* in the novels, it is the women's voices, their ability and desire to speak, or to remain silent, which determine the modes of mourning played out in the texts, and the narrative resolution: they are 'talismans and keepers of secrets: centres of narrative energy through which the characters and the texts themselves orientate' (17). In Freud's 'The Theme of the Three Caskets', and in the mid-Victorian novel, this function is inextricable from women's symbolic association with motherhood. In order to mourn loss, male characters (including Freud) endow their beloveds with maternal—generative and destructive—power.

Anne Ancelin Schützenberger's group therapy bridges systemic family therapy and Freudian psychoanalysis. Drawing on ideas from the Palo Alto group, anthropologist Gregory Bateson's ecological theory, systems theory, Jacob Moreno's psychodramatic practice and psychoanalytic theory, Schützenberger conceives the family as a dynamic topographical system. In Schützenberger's praxis with terminally ill patients, group therapy members each create a 'genosociogram' from memory. The genosociogram is a family map, documenting affective bonds and events and incorporating several generations, setting out the symbolic and biological family structure (1998, 10–11). The genosociogram is similar to the genogram used by systemic family therapists such as John Burnham (Burnham 1986, 25–44)[30]; however, unlike the genogram, it also represents *unconscious* allegiances, debts and gifts passed across the generations: 'contextual transgenerational psycho-genealogy' (Schützenberger 1998, 62). Schützenberger's research illuminates the 'anniversary syndrome':

> [...] every time I worked with a new patient, I sought "repetitions", "invisible and unconscious family loyalties" and unconscious identifications with a key person in the family history, loved or unloved. And I found the links to key people: cancers occurring at the same age that a mother, grandfather, motherly aunt, or godmother had died from a cancer or in an accident. (60)

A comparable idea is found in *Dombey and Son*; Paul Dombey's death is always-already happening: it is the seemingly inevitable sequel to Fanny Dombey's deathbed scene. Widening the issue, Dickens died on the fifth anniversary of the Staplehurst railway disaster, an event which, as

[30] It is significant that systemic practice is now a key component of social work training (in Children's Services) in many local authorities.

Michael Slater notes, 'he had never really recovered' (2009, 613).[31] The genosociogram not only helps medical professionals make decisions concerning treatment, but also enables clients to perform a work of mourning, becoming author of their own family novel. Schützenberger argues that the genosociogram illuminates the way in which we operate within conscious and unconscious family topographies, which determine not only who we are, but also and how we think, feel and act: what we do, and what happens to us, in our lives. This topographical idea underpins my understanding of the mid-Victorian novel. My textual analyses demonstrate how echoes and repetitions determine the plotting across extended and highly convoluted family groups. For Schützenberger, the way in which the family topography determines the individual's bodily identity is central; in the mid-Victorian novel, as in *The Ancestor Syndrome*, these two aspects are intimately connected. The mid-Victorian novelistic plot anticipates Schützenberger's genosociogram by more than a hundred years.

Works Cited

Literary Texts

Collins, Wilkie. 1986. *No Name*. Edited by Virginia Blain. Oxford: Oxford University Press.

———. 1995. *Armadale*. Edited by John Sutherland. London: Penguin.

De Quincey, Thomas. 1996a. *Confessions of an English Opium Eater*. In *Confessions of an English Opium Eater and Other Writings*, edited by Grevel Lindop, 1–80. Oxford: Oxford University Press.

———. 1996b. *Suspiria de Profundis*. In *Confessions of an English Opium Eater and Other Writings*, edited by Grevel Lindop, 87–182. Oxford: Oxford University Press.

Dickens, Charles. 1974. *Dombey and Son*. Edited by Alan Horsman. Oxford: Clarendon Press.

———. 1979. *Little Dorrit*. Edited by Harvey Peter Sucksmith. Oxford: Clarendon Press.

[31] Dickens experienced indications of post-traumatic shock, 'nervous dread' (Slater 2009, 551) and 'railway shaking' (585). Dickens later wrote that it was his work attempting to alleviate suffering 'for hours amongst the dead and the dying' (Slater 2009, 536) which so heavily impacted upon him. Dying on the 9 June 1870, Dickens perhaps demonstrated an unconscious identification with the many people he saw die on the 9 June 1865.

———. 1981. *David Copperfield*. Edited by Nina Burgis. Oxford: Clarendon Press.

———. 1993. *Great Expectations*. Edited by Margaret Cardwell. Oxford: Clarendon Press.

———. *Speeches: Literary and Social*. http://www.gutenberg.org/files/824/824-h/824-h.htm.

Pankeyev, Sergei. 1989a. *The Memoirs of the Wolf Man*. In *The Wolf-Man and Sigmund Freud*. Edited and translated by Muriel Gardiner, 3–132. London: Karnac Books.

———. 1989b. 'My Recollections of Sigmund Freud'. In *The Wolf-Man and Sigmund Freud*, edited and translated by Muriel Gardiner, 135–152. London: Karnac Books.

Tennyson, Alfred. 2007. *In Memoriam A. H. H.* In *Selected Poems*, edited by Christopher Ricks, 96–198. London: Penguin.

Wordsworth, William. 1984. *The Major Works*, edited by Stephen Gill. Oxford: Oxford University Press.

Primary Psychoanalytic Texts

Abbreviations

SE: *The Standard Edition of the Complete Psychological Works of Sigmund Freud*. 2001. Translated from the German under the general editorship of James Strachey, in collaboration with Anna Freud and assisted by Alix Strachey and Allan Tyson. London: Vintage.

Abraham, Nicolas and Maria Torok. 1976. *The Wolf Man's Magic Word: A Cryptonymy*. Translated by Nicholas Rand. Minneapolis: University of Minnesota Press.

———. 1994. *The Shell and the Kernel: Renewals of Psychoanalysis*. Edited and translated by Nicholas Rand, 187–205. Chicago: University of Chicago Press.

Breuer, Josef and Sigmund Freud. 2001. *Studies on Hysteria*. *SE* 2.

Freud, Sigmund.

———. 'The Aetiology of Hysteria'. *SE* 3:191–221.

———. *Beyond the Pleasure Principle*. *SE* 18:3–64.

———. 'A Case of Paranoia Running Counter to the Psychoanalytic Theory of the Disease'. *SE* 14:261–272.

———. 'A Child is Being Beaten'. *SE* 17:175–204.

———. 'Childhood Memories and Screen Memories'. In *The Psychopathology of Everyday Life*. *SE* 6:43–52.

———. 'Creative Writers and Daydreaming'. *SE* 9:141–154.

———. *The Ego and the Id*. *SE* 19:3–63.

———. *Fragment of an Analysis of a Case of Hysteria*. *SE* 7:3–122.

———. *From the History of an Infantile Neurosis*. *SE* 17:3–122.

———. *The Interpretation of Dreams. SE* 4 and 5.
———. 'Leonardo da Vinci and a Memory of his Childhood'. *SE* 11:63–137.
———. 'Letter 52'. *SE* 1:233–239.
———. 'Letter 69'. *SE* 1:259–260.
———. 'Letter 75'. *SE* 1:268.
———. 'Mourning and Melancholia'. *SE* 14:237–260.
———. 'Notes Upon a Case of Obsessional Neurosis'. *SE* 10: 153–318.
———. 'On Narcissism: An Introduction'. *SE* 14:67–104.
———. 'A Project for a Scientific Psychology'. *SE* 1:283–397.
———. 'Screen Memories'. *SE* 3:301–322.
———. 'A Special Type of Choice of Object Made by Men (Contributions to the Psychology of Love I)'. *SE* 11:163–176.
———. 'The Theme of the Three Caskets'. *SE* 12:289–301.
———. *Three Essays on the Theory of Sexuality. SE* 7:125–245.
———. 'The Uncanny'. *SE* 17:217–256.
———. 'The Unconscious'. *SE* 14:161–215.
Gardiner, Muriel, ed. 1989. *The Wolf-Man and Sigmund Freud.* London: Karnac.
Kristeva, Julia. 1989. *Black Sun: Depression and Melancholia.* Translated by Leon S. Roudiez. New York: Columbia University Press.
———. 2002. *Revolution in Poetic Language.* In *The Portable Kristeva*, edited and translated by Kelly Oliver, 27–70. New York: Columbia University Press.
Laplanche, Jean. 1976. *Life and Death in Psychoanalysis.* Translated by Jeffrey Mehlman. Baltimore: Johns Hopkins University Press.
———. 1999a. *Essays on Otherness.* Edited by John Fletcher. Translated by Luke Thurston, Philip Slotkin and Leslie Hill. London: Routledge.
———.1999b. 'Implantation, Intromission'. In *Essays on Otherness*, 133–137.
———. 1999c. 'Notes on Afterwardsness'. In *Essays on Otherness*, 260–265.
———. 1999d. 'Reference to the Unconscious'. In *The Unconscious and the Id*, translated by Luke Thurston and Lindsay Watson, 1–121. London: Rebus Press.
———. 1999e. 'A Short Treatise on the Unconscious'. In *Essays on Otherness*, 84–116.
———. 1999f. 'Time and the Other'. In *Essays on Otherness*, 238–263.
———. 1999g. 'Transference: Its Provocation by the Analyst'. In *Essays on Otherness*, 214–233.
———. 1999h. 'The Unfinished Copernican Revolution'. In *Essays on Otherness*, 52–83.
———. 2011. *Freud and the Sexual.* Edited by John Fletcher. Translated by John Fletcher, Jonathan House and Nicholas Ray. London: International Psychoanalytic Books.

Laplanche, Jean and Jean Bertrand Pontalis. 1986. 'Fantasy and the Origins of Sexuality'. In *Formations of Fantasy*, edited by Victor Burgin, James Donald and Cora Kaplan, 5–34. London: Methuen.
———. 1988. *The Language of Psychoanalysis*. Translated by Donald Nicholson Smith. London: Karnac.
Schützenberger, Anne Ancelin. 1998. *The Ancestor Syndrome: Transgenerational Psychotherapy and Hidden Links in the Family Tree*. Translated by Anne Trager. London: Routledge.
Toubiana, Éric. 1988. *L'Héritage et sa Psychopathologie*. Paris: Presses Universitaires de France.
———. 2014. 'The Ides of March: From Mastery to Vampirism'. In *Seduction and Enigmas: Laplanche, Theory, Culture*, edited by John Fletcher and Nicholas Ray, and translated by Nicholas Ray, 176–208. London: Laurence and Wishart.

Secondary Texts

Appignanesi, Lisa and John Forrester. 1994. *Freud's Women*. London: Phoenix.
Burnham, John. 1986. *Family Therapy*. London: Tavistock Publishing.
Caruth, Cathy. 1995. Introduction to Part II, 'Recapturing the Past'. In *Trauma: Explorations in Memory*, 151–157. Baltimore: Johns Hopkins University Press.
———. 1996a. 'Traumatic Departures: Survival and History in Freud'. In *Trauma and Self*, edited by Charles B. Strozier and Michael Flynn, 29–44. London: Rowman & Littlefield.
———. 1996b. *Unclaimed Experience: Trauma, Narrative, History*. Baltimore: Johns Hopkins University Press.
Derrida, Jacques. 1976. Foreword: *Fors*: The Anglish Words of Nicholas Abraham and Maria Torok. In *The Wolf Man's Magic Word: A Cryptonymy*, translated by Nicholas Rand, xi–xlviii. Minneapolis: Minneapolis University Press.
Dever, Carolyn. 1998. *Death and the Mother from Dickens to Freud: Victorian Fictions and the Anxiety of Origins*. Cambridge: Cambridge University Press.
Fletcher, John. 1999. 'Introduction: Psychoanalysis and the Question of the Other'. In *Essays on Otherness*, by Jean Laplanche, 1–51. London: Routledge.
———. 2002. 'Freud, Hoffmann and the Death-Work'. *Angelaki* 7, no. 2: 125–141.
———. 2013. *Freud and the Scene of Trauma*. New York: Fordham University Press.
Gardiner, Muriel, ed. 1989. *The Wolf-Man and Sigmund Freud*. London: Karnac.
Gaskell, Elizabeth. 2008. *North and South*. Edited by Angus Easson. Oxford: Oxford University Press.

Greenberg, Judith. 1998. 'The Echo of Trauma and the Trauma of Echo'. *American Imago* 55, no. 3: 319–347.

Ikonen, P. and E. Rechardt. 1984. 'On the Universal Nature of Primal Scene Fantasies'. *International Journal of Psychoanalysis* 65, no. 1: 63–72.

Jordan, John O. 2011. *Supposing Bleak House*. Virginia: Virginia University Press.

van der Kolk, Bessel A. and Onno van der Hart. 1995. 'The Intrusive Past: The Flexibility of Memory and the Engraving of Trauma'. In *Trauma: Explorations in Memory*, edited by Cathy Caruth. Baltimore: John Hopkins University Press.

LaCapra, Dominick. 1985. *History and Psychoanalysis*. Minneapolis: Minnesota University Press.

———. 2001. *Writing History, Writing Trauma*. Baltimore: Johns Hopkins University Press.

Leys, Ruth. 2000. *Trauma: A Genealogy*. Chicago: University of Chicago Press.

———. 2007. *From Guilt to Shame: Auschwitz and After*. Princeton: Princeton University Press.

Masson, J. M., 1984. *The Assault on Truth: Freud's Suppression of the Seduction Theory*. New York: Farrar, Straus and Giroux.

———. trans. and ed. 1985. *The Complete Letters of Sigmund Freud to Wilhelm Fliess, 1887–1904*. Cambridge MA: Harvard University Press.

Scarfone, Dominique. 2003. '"It was *not* my Mother": From Seduction to Negation'. *New Formations* 48: 69–76.

Schützenberger, Anne Ancelin. 1988. *The Ancestor Syndrome: Transgenerational Psychotherapy and Hidden Links in the Family Tree*. Translated by Anne Trager. London: Routledge.

Slater, Michael. 2009. *Charles Dickens*. New Haven: Yale University Press.

Wood, Madeleine. 2012. 'Female Narrative Energy in the Writings of Dead White Males: Dickens, Collins and Freud'. In *Cross-Gendered Literary Voices: Appropriating, Resisting*, Embracing, edited by Rina Kim and Claire Westall, 15–35. Basingstoke: Palgrave Macmillan.

CHAPTER 3

Emily and Charlotte Brontë—Childhood Passions and Pathologies: *Wuthering Heights* and *Shirley*

In this chapter, I draw together one of the most highly regarded of the Brontës' novels with one of the least: *Wuthering Heights* (1847) and *Shirley* (1849). I show how cross-generational traumatisation propels both novels, despite their radically different styles. In *Shirley*, Charlotte Brontë directly addresses her sisters' writings (notably *Wuthering Heights* and *Agnes Grey* [1847]) through intertextual echoes; she creates a fragmented, hybrid novel, which pulls between heart-wrenching anguish, and a mythic, yet elegiac, process of healing and reparation. Both novels are positioned self-consciously within the process of history: family trauma is inseparable from the ambivalence concerning the past and modernity.

Elizabeth Gaskell's influential biography, *The Life of Charlotte Brontë* (1857), establishes the image of the Brontë sisters in the rural wilds of Yorkshire, at the mercy of a brutal unpredictable father, and a drunken debauched brother: Gaskell, following Charlotte's Brontë, represents a family removed from Victorian modernity.[1] However, as Juliet Barker's meticulous biography shows, Haworth was not a remote outpost, but part of a thriving industrial community: 'What is more, the time of

[1] As both Barker (2010, 654–655) and Lucasta Miller (2001, 24–25) point out, Charlotte Brontë herself was directly responsible for the mythologizing of the family: in a 'Biographical Notice of Ellis and Acton Bell' (written after her sisters' deaths as a preface to the 1850 edition of their works) she presents them as products of a rude, untutored, world—seemingly identical with the world of *Wuthering Heights*.

M. Wood, *Parents and Children in the Mid-Victorian Novel*,
https://doi.org/10.1007/978-3-030-45469-2_3

Patrick Brontë's ministry there, from 1820 to 1861, saw some of the fastest growth and biggest changes that were to take place in Haworth and the surrounding area' (2010 [1994], 105). The damaging effects of the Brontë myth can be readily appreciated when reading Anne Brontë's *The Tenant of Wildfell Hall* (1848). Enclosure and isolation are not mythic, but the direct result of Helen's abusive marriage to Arthur Huntingdon. The novel sits coherently within the late 1840s context discussed in Chapter 1; the family home is shown to be a dangerous and threatening space in which female autonomy is prohibited. Helen's marriage to Gilbert Markham involves the restitution of familial as well as romantic bonds.

In all of the Brontë sisters' writings, the relationship between the romantic and familial is inextricable; however, there is not necessarily anything more incestuous at work than in the rest of mid-Victorian fiction. In the mid century the idea of companionate marriage became dominant: families were not just a matter of birth, but about romantic choices *and* marital alliances; the conceptualisation of romantic love frequently occurs within a familial context. In the writings of the Brontë sisters, the female heroine, orphaned or alienated from her birth family, finds 'kin' in the figure of her lover, alerting us to the crisis within the parental (or indeed non-parental) home itself.

The tumultuous shift to nineteenth-century global modernity provides the backdrop for both *Wuthering Heights* and *Shirley*. Opening in 1801, *Wuthering Heights* points towards the Act of Union between Britain and Ireland, which came into effect on 1 January of that year. By 1801, the war with France had been raging for nine years, and the Treaty of Amiens 1802 was still to come. The narrative begins on the brink of peace, but a peace that was itself short-lived. Looking back twenty-five years to the beginning of the story in Cathy and Heathcliff's childhood takes us to 1776 when the Thirteen Colonies ceded from Britain to become the United States of America following the beginning of the Revolutionary War in 1775. Heathcliff is representative of these wider global contexts; Emily Brontë's purposefully vague presentation of his origins means that he can stand in for, or imply, numerous conflicted national and global events. In *Shirley*, the ongoing economic problems caused by the war with France directly impacts upon the world of the novel: the French Revolution leads to the fall of the Gérard-Moore house and Robert's obdurate attitude towards the Luddite rebellion. This pushes Caroline to illness and the brink of death when he rejects her love and his kinship with her. In both novels, the home is not sacrosanct: national and global political forces interpellate it.

The Primacy of the Child: The Ghostly Encounters of *Wuthering Heights*

Wuthering Heights is founded on an unknowable trauma, which repeats and haunts, circulating beyond the limits of Cathy and Heathcliff's story. Lockwood's reading of Cathy's diary and his ghostly encounters at Wuthering Heights present him with an enigma that he is compelled to translate. Standing in the place of the reader, Lockwood attempts to decipher, excavate and exhume the 'secret' that drives the novel: generations of critics have followed in his footsteps.[2] Brontë's representation of secrecy relies on its dynamic movement rather than its empirical content: there is something passed from the elder generation to the younger—an action or gesture—motioning between exile, intrusion and return. Of all the novels I analyse, *Wuthering Heights* is the most obviously traumatic: it presents the violent aftermath of something that remains intangible, and which problematises bearing witness. However, despite this intangibility, a more specific dynamic of trauma is presented, and this is grounded in a cross-generational model. The novel is structured around exclusion: characters are repeatedly placed on the periphery of a desired scene. This problem can be charted back to Mr. Earnshaw, although it pushes beyond the confines of the novel through Heathcliff's mysterious history.

Wuthering Heights, in Gothic fashion, explores the destabilising and transgressive nature of fantasy—culminating in Heathcliff's exhumation of Cathy.[3] This gruesome moment in the text renders Heathcliff a more pathos-ridden and tragic figure. Like Antigone (Sophocles 1984), he is concerned with the burial of the dead.[4] Brontë is alert to the various forms of fantasy; the narrative moves between dreams, hallucinations, conscious daydreaming, folklore and storytelling. Fantasy is not just a personal concern; it operates across the extended family structure (including Lockwood) and moves between different perspective points. In the Wolf Man case, Sergei's dream provided Freud—paradoxically perhaps—with his empirical source material. In Freud's interpretation,

[2] J. Hillis Miller (1982) writes, 'The act of interpretation always leaves something over, something just at the edge of theoretical vision which that vision does not encompass' (52).

[3] I follow Mr. Earnshaw and Heathcliff's practice by referring to the elder Catherine as 'Cathy'. I refer to her daughter as 'Catherine'.

[4] Steve Lukits (2008) also makes this comparison.

the dream operates as the second scene in the traumatic structure, which activates the affective complex set up, but not consciously felt in the earlier constructed moment: the primal scene in which little Sergei sees his parents having sex. The placement of the dream within Freud's case history resonates with Brontë's use of fantasy in *Wuthering Heights*. Lockwood's dream of the chapel, in which he inhabits Cathy's and/or Heathcliff's point of view, allows for a plural first-person account to emerge, which counterpoints Nelly's witnessing. The dream operates as the first scene in a traumatic sequence, which reactivates the earlier scenes through afterwardsness. Through Cathy, Brontë insists upon the permeable membrane between dreams and waking realities: 'I've dreamt in my life dreams that have stayed with me ever after, and changed my ideas; they've gone through and through me, like wine through water, and altered the colour of my mind' (I.9, 70).

Windows and Messages

Exclusion is repeatedly enacted and inscribed: scenes of violence at windows occur throughout *Wuthering Heights*. In chronological rather than narrative terms, the scene at Thrushcross Grange is the first. Looking through the window, Heathcliff and Cathy see a 'splendid' scene from which they are excluded: as Heathcliff tells Nelly, 'Old Mr. and Mrs. Linton were not there. Edgar and his sister had it entirely to themselves; shouldn't they have been happy? We should have thought ourselves in heaven!' (I.6, 41–42). When Cathy is welcomed into the house, her foot bleeding from the bulldog's bite, Heathcliff is excluded. Mr Linton—in his single line of dialogue—reiterates the problem of Heathcliff's origins: 'Oho! I declare he is that strange acquisition my late neighbour made in his journey to Liverpool – a little Lascar, or an American or Spanish castaway'. Heathcliff refuses to leave the house without Cathy, and is 'dragged [...] into the garden'. Undeterred Heathcliff 'resumed my station as spy; because, if Catherine had wished to return, I intended shattering their great glass panes to a million fragments unless they let her out' (I.6, 44). The pathetic ferocity of Heathcliff's desire to break through the barrier between himself and Cathy establishes the pattern of their relationship. The 'great glass panes' of the window contrast with the old-fashioned casements at *Wuthering Heights*; the latter appear more permeable, Nelly telling Lockwood it is possible to leave the house through Cathy's bedroom window. The reference to the glass not only points towards the Lintons' status (Window Tax was not repealed until 1851), but also relates to a confrontation with identity: Heathcliff's own and Cathy's. Shortly afterwards Nelly shows Heathcliff his reflection in the looking glass, and is told, 'Don't get the expression of a vicious cur that appears to know the kicks it gets are its desert, and yet hates all the world, as well as the kicker, for what it suffers' (I.7, 50). Nelly's language wryly refers us back to the little dog, passionately pulled to and fro by Edgar and Isabella. Later, in delirium, Cathy looks in the mirror and does not recognise herself. The reflective surface of glass operates figuratively to conceive how identity is constructed in relation to others. It is in this moment at Thrushcross Grange that Heathcliff's exile becomes fact. Cathy is no longer exiled with Heathcliff; she is accepted by the bourgeois world represented by the Lintons and aspired to by Hindley. She takes on sign value. In order to analyse this further, we need to look at the novel's frame; Cathy's diary deals with events contemporaneous with this scene, stopping short of their final rebellion against Hindley's authority.

The novel, in epic mode, begins *in medias res.* Lockwood's narration begins precisely, with a date: 1801. In his first diary entry, we get a glimpse of Lockwood's history, which is subsequently subsumed by the family tragedy that he is exposed to. As we shall see, displacement defines the two families in *Wuthering Heights*, and this process is also at work in relation to Lockwood. Reading across the novel, it becomes clear that he bears a striking resemblance to Linton: effete and gentlemanly, newly arrived from the south, Lockwood likewise fails to thrive in the harsh Yorkshire landscape. Lockwood has the potential to be a figure of pathos. Like most of the children—literal and adult—in the novel, his relationship with the elder generation is strained: 'my dear mother used to say I should never have a comfortable home, and only last summer I proved myself perfectly unworthy of one' (I.1, 3). The anecdote following this is bathetic but intriguing. Lazing at a seaside resort, Lockwood's passionate love for a young woman, a 'fascinating [...] goddess' (3), disappears when she expresses her feelings for him: she 'looked a return—the sweetest of all imaginable looks—and what did I do? I confess it with shame—shrunk icily into myself, like a snail' (4). This anecdote refracts back onto both his waking experiences at Wuthering Heights and his dreaming. Catherine and Cathy undoubtedly provoke Lockwood's interest and his openness to the family's trauma, but this is inseparable from his fascination with

Heathcliff. Lockwood's powerful identification with his host leads him to return to the Heights for the second time:

> [...] possibly some people might suspect him of a degree of under-bred pride – I have a sympathetic chord within that tells me it is nothing of the sort; I know, by instinct, his reserve springs from an aversion to showy displays of feeling – to manifestations of mutual kindliness. He'll love and hate, equally under cover, and esteem it a species of impertinence to be loved or hated again – No, I'm running on too fast – I bestow my own attributes over-liberally on him. (3)

Lockwood's projection onto Heathcliff means that he misreads him: in adulthood, Heathcliff's loves and hates are rarely 'under cover'. There is, however, a lurking truth despite this. Heathcliff undoubtedly finds it impertinent to be loved—*again*. His concept of love is singular and unique. Homosocial desire defines and disrupts Lockwood's interpretation of Heathcliff, providing the dynamism for his 'reading'. Lockwood tries to become a character in the family's drama, but as the frame narrator, he can only ever exist on the margins or periphery—the reader or critic, annotating and editing someone else's story. At the same time, this process involves an act of translation; Lockwood attempts to process the enigmatic messages he receives at the Heights. His desire to hear Nelly's story is, by his own account, slightly out of character (I.4, 28). His own loves and hates remain 'under cover' through his self-willed act of projection onto the Yorkshire family and, conversely, by unwillingly receiving the family's trauma.

The idea of writing on the margins directly links Lockwood to Cathy. Cathy annotates her books and also the margin of the house: the window ledge. This reveals the tension between masculine and feminine control over the story, and male and female property rights (brought to the fore after Edgar Linton's death). Cathy's signature is like an author's mark, and yet nevertheless, in the primal scene of dreaming she is placed outside of the house that represents the novel; Brontë presents female authorship as spectral. This chapter presents a *mise-en-âbyme*: deepening levels of text draw Lockwood into a dreamlike state. Lying in 'vapid listlessness' awaiting sleep, Lockwood rereads the names scratched upon the window ledge:

> I leant my head against the window, and continued spelling over Catherine Earnshaw – Heathcliff – Linton, till my eyes closed; but they had not rested five minutes when a glare of white letters started from the dark, as vivid as spectres – the air swarmed with Catherines; and rousing myself to dispel the obtrusive name, I discovered my candle wick reclining on one of the antique volumes, and perfuming the place with an odour of roasted calf-skin. (15)

Catherine Earnshaw is reduced to the two male names—Heathcliff and Linton—and it is only in sleep that 'Catherine' returns to Lockwood. Her name forces itself back in, just as later her ghost demands entry into the house. But it is the word, rather than the girl, which first haunts him. The names, and the ambiguity concerning identity bound up with them, transmit an enigma towards Lockwood, which provokes a further act of reading. The 'roasted calfskin' is visceral; there is a sense of bodily threat. Feeling 'ill at ease' and nauseated by the smell of burning leather, he flicks through Cathy's books in the hope of exorcising all the 'Catherines'. Lockwood cannot, however, extricate himself from Cathy's story. Despite this, Lockwood's attention is not held until he reaches the caricature of Joseph: 'An immediate interest kindled within me for the unknown Catherine, and I began, forthwith, to decypher her faded hieroglyphics' (16). It is the male figure who prompts Lockwood's reading and rouses his interest in Cathy herself. This is perpetuated in his attitude towards Heathcliff and the younger Catherine; later, when encouraging Nelly's story, Lockwood reflects, '"I'll turn the talk to my landlord's family!" [...] "A good subject to start – and that pretty girl-widow, I should like to know her history; whether she be a native of the country, or, as is more probable, an exotic that the surly indigenae will not recognise as kin"' (I.4, 28). Catherine's story is indexed via Heathcliff's.

Cathy's diary propels an enigma towards Lockwood concerning the family, herself, and Heathcliff, which he attempts to resolve: unconsciously in dreaming, and consciously by inviting Nelly Dean's 'gossip' (I.4, 28). The diary, or at least Lockwood's reading of it, begins *in medias res* with the statement: 'An awful Sunday. I wish my father were back again. Hindley is a detestable substitute' (16). It is only when Cathy quotes Joseph that we realise that this refers to Mr. Earnshaw's death: 'T' maister nobbut just buried [...] and yah darr be laiking! shame on ye!' (17). Cathy elides the loss, but it is nevertheless felt everywhere in her diary. Her voice, summoned up in writing, trails out while bemoaning

Heathcliff's fate: 'He [Hindley] has been blaming our father (how dared he?) for treating H. too liberally; and swears he will reduce him to his right place –' (18). A break in the text follows, forcing the reader to share Lockwood's shift of attention. With Lockwood falling asleep, his eyes lose focus: the main text pushes against Cathy's marginal annotations: 'my eye wandered from manuscript to print' (18); 'half consciously, worrying my brain to guess what Jabes Branderham would make of his subject' (18). Cathy's diary provokes Lockwood's chapel dream, but the dream does not simply recast Lockwood *as* Cathy. The dream draws together printed text and marginal annotations. The dream is shown to continue—in distorted form—Lockwood's waking thoughts by providing an answer to his question concerning Branderham's sermon. The dream therefore also responds to Cathy's words regarding Hindley and Heathcliff: 'he will reduce him to his right place' (18). In proto-Freudian fashion, Lockwood's identity is displaced in the chapel dream, disrupted by Cathy's lingering voice and her despair at Heathcliff's exclusion. The dreamer is Lockwood, and yet not Lockwood.

Berated by Joseph for not carrying a cudgel, Lockwood reflects, 'I considered it absurd that I should need such a weapon to gain admittance into my own residence' (18). At that moment the dream consciousness changes:

> Then, a new idea flashed across me. I was not going there; we were journeying to hear the famous Jabes Branderham preach [...] and either Joseph, the preacher, or I had committed the 'First of the Seventy-First,' and were to be publicly exposed and excommunicated. (18)

Heathcliff is the hidden protagonist here. Lockwood's reading of Cathy's diary trails off at a question concerning Heathcliff's position in the household, and the dream is haunted by this same question. At the same time, these thoughts of exclusion echo Lockwood's own feeling of rejection when he tried to enter Wuthering Heights earlier that day, while pre-empting the appearance of the ghostly Cathy in the second dream. The proto-Freudianism of this 'dreamwork' is startling; the archaic childhood past and the present moment are drawn together through the motif of entering the house: through a wishful fantasy. This situation is complicated by the fact that Lockwood does not dream of his own childhood: his story is usurped—'cuckoo' fashion—by Heathcliff and Cathy. The dreaming subject is not singular, but condensed (in Freud's terms):

a compound figure comprising Lockwood, Heathcliff and Cathy. The lengthy sermon in Lockwood's dream repeats the account given by Cathy in her diary, in which she, Heathcliff, and the ploughboy are made to sit and listen to Joseph for three hours (16). Listening to Branderham in his dream, Lockwood acts out Cathy's childhood frustration: 'How I writhed, and yawned, and nodded, and revived! How I pinched and pricked myself, and rubbed my eyes, and stood up, and sat down again' (19). The chapel dream culminates in a collective act of violence against the outsider:

> With that concluding word, the whole assembly, exalting their pilgrim's staves, rushed round me in a body, and I, having no weapon to raise in self-defence, commenced grappling with Joseph, my nearest and most ferocious assailant, for his. In the confluence of the multitude, several clubs crossed; blows, aimed at me, fell on other sconces. Presently the whole chapel resounded with rappings and counter-rappings. Every man's hand was against his neighbour; (20)

Communal violence against the outsider is also violence meted out *to* the community: 'Every man's hand was against his neighbour'. The dream's message pre-empts the story told by Nelly. This ethical warning is borne out by Nelly's account, if not by Nelly herself: in attacking the—supposedly—foreign threat, the community reveals its own fragility. The chapel dream takes on significance through the operation of afterwardsness. We realise that we—and Lockwood—are not only hearing echoes, but also producing them. The readers receive a 'compromised message', which we attempt to translate. The devastating consequences of Hindley's exiling of Heathcliff are everywhere felt, even if we cannot yet understand them.

Through the diary, Cathy's voice intrudes upon the unwilling Lockwood, and he becomes open to the other's trauma. When Heathcliff appears in the bedroom, Lockwood assesses him with a cool, medicalised, gaze. He notices that his own unexpected appearance 'startled him like an electric shock' (I.3, 21); Heathcliff was 'crushing his nails into his palms, and grinding his teeth to subdue the maxillary convulsions' (22). 'I guessed, however, by his irregular and intercepted breathing, that he struggled to vanquish an access of violent emotion' (23). Traumatisation racks the body: Heathcliff's near-delirium echoes Cathy's prior to her death. Watched by Lockwood, Heathcliff 'wrenched open the lattice, bursting, as he pulled at it, into an uncontrollable passion of tears':

> There was such anguish in the gush of grief that accompanied this raving, that my compassion made me overlook its folly, and I drew off, half angry to have listened at all, and vexed at having related my ridiculous nightmare, since it produced that agony; though *why*, was beyond my comprehension. (24)

The cool detachment is unsettled; Lockwood is emotionally involved. The irony of this is obvious: the withdrawn and 'snail-like' Lockwood is, by his own account, incapable of responding to other people's emotions: an enclosed narcissist, projecting onto others without opening himself up to their feelings. At Wuthering Heights, the family's trauma infects him, and he is caught within a maelstrom of feeling, albeit at second hand. Brontë shows identification to be unsettlingly close to desire: Lockwood's professed desires are heterosexual, but his processes of identification relate to men. If we read identification as a modality of desire, then Lockwood is not as impotent as he may first appear. He moves from narcissistic self-concern (demonstrated through his initial identification with Heathcliff, as well as his history with the young woman at the seaside) to a traumatic openness to the other (demonstrated by his unwilling encounter with Cathy). These two aspects converge when he witnesses Heathcliff's desolation and feels 'compassion'.

Excommunication

Nelly's account of Cathy and Heathcliff's childhood presents a slanted perspective into the past. Nelly is both internal and external to the drama: while Lockwood clearly interprets her as lying outside of the family, the childhood portions of the novel indicate otherwise. Nelly describes herself as Hindley's 'foster sister' (I.8, 58), and Dr. Kenneth reminds her that she and Hindley are exactly the same age: 'He's barely twenty-seven, it seems; that's your own age; who would have thought you were born in one year!' (II.3, 164). Notably, the strongest grief shown by Nelly within the novel follows Hindley's death: 'I [...] wept as for a blood relation' (164). Like Cathy and Heathcliff, Hindley and Nelly wandered the moor together in play: she finds their childhood hiding place, 'still full of snail shells and pebbles' (I.11, 96): the material relic of a sibling bond disrupted by class difference. These details remind us that there are other stories waiting to be told in *Wuthering Heights*: a *newly* created class schism, related to Hindley's attempted assumption of a gentlemanly status, and placed within the context of the industrial revolution, underwrites the novel.

It is clear from these details that Nelly's mother breastfed Hindley while nursing her own infant daughter. It is never explained who nursed Cathy. Nelly dry nurses Hareton and Catherine. Extended family structures define the novel, but these structures are a source of anxiety. Heathcliff's entrance into the house reveals this; however, Nelly occupies a comparable place to Heathcliff in the family—inside, and yet not safely contained or controlled:

> Before I came to live here, she commenced, [...] I was almost always at Wuthering Heights; because my mother had nursed Mr. Hindley Earnshaw, that was Hareton's father, and I got used to playing with the children – I ran errands too, and helped to make hay, and hung about the farm ready for anything that anybody would set me to. (I.4, 30)

Describing Mr. Earnshaw's departure to Liverpool, Nelly explains that she heard everything he said to Hindley and Cathy, 'for I sat eating my porridge with them' (30), adding, 'He did not forget me, for he had a kind heart, though he was rather severe sometimes. He promised me a pocketful of apples and pears, and then he kissed his children good bye and set off' (30–31). Nelly occupies a strangely liminal place in this scene; she sits with the children, but is not kissed goodbye. Nelly and Heathcliff are of the family and external to it: Nelly uses this position in order to influence the plot (most dramatically at Thrushcross Grange); Heathcliff strikes directly at the economic foundation of the Earnshaws. Nelly's power is bound up with her voice: what she chooses to tell and to whom. In this context, we can remember the decisive role of the 'stupid servant girl' in Frau Emmy's history in *Studies on Hysteria*: trauma is bound up with class-based anxiety.

Heathcliff's entrance into the family reveals their violence, he does not create it: pre-existing ferocity is brought to the surface and redeployed onto the foreign stranger. Much later Nelly discusses Cathy's condition with Dr. Kenneth, saying, 'you are acquainted with the Earnshaws' violent dispositions' (I.12, 114). When Cathy first meets the unnamed boy, she 'showed her humour by grinning and spitting at the stupid little thing, earning for her pains a sound blow from her father to teach her cleaner manners' (I.4, 32). The father's 'sound blow' onto the six-year-old little girl should not be accepted unquestioningly; the mid-Victorian middle classes did not advocate an impulsively aggressive style of parenting. Nelly bullies and pinches Heathcliff and abandons him on the stairs hoping that he will run away of his own accord: 'I put it on the landing of the stairs, hoping it might be gone on the morrow [...] I was obliged to confess, and in recompense for my cowardice and inhumanity was sent out of the house' (32):

> This was Heathcliff's first introduction to the family: on coming back a few days afterwards, for I did not consider my banishment perpetual, I found they had christened him 'Heathcliff': it was the name of a son who had died in childhood, and it has served him ever since for both Christian and surname. (32)

If, as Nelly claims, Heathcliff's history is a 'cuckoo's' (30), then this is thrust upon him. He takes the place of the dead son because he is placed in the nest, not because he forces his way in.[5] Mr. Earnshaw's compassion towards Heathcliff is offset by the cruelty of everyone else in the household (and indeed Earnshaw's roughness towards own children). Hindley is by far the softest presence, weeping over his broken fiddle, although it is also Hindley who emerges as Heathcliff's chief adversary shortly afterwards (32). As we also see in Charles Dickens's and Wilkie Collins's novels, there is an originary conflict between the parents that determines the younger generation: 'Mrs. Earnshaw was ready to fling it [Heathcliff] out of doors: she did fly up – asking how he could fashion to bring that gipsy brat into the house, when they had their own bairns to feed, and to fend for? What he meant to do with it, and whether he was mad?' (31). Brontë carefully delineates each motion here; the description is theatrical—like a stage direction. The use of indirect (bordering upon free indirect) discourse brings Mrs. Earnshaw's verbal violence into the present-tense of the narration, equating it with her curtailed physical action—she was 'ready to fling it'. She scolds her husband, while 'half dead with fatigue' he tells his tale: 'seeing it starving, and houseless, and as good as dumb, in the streets of Liverpool' he brings the little boy home (31). There are no extraneous words expended; the reference to Heathcliff's 'dumbness' reminds us of the power bound up in (English) speech. Nelly relates how Mr. Earnshaw 'took to [Heathcliff] strangely, believing all he said (for that matter, he said precious little, and generally

[5] It is not clear here whether this son was older or younger than Hindley.

the truth,) and petting him up far above Cathy, who was too mischievous and wayward for a favourite' (32). In Nelly's account, Mr. Earnshaw operates as the fulcrum and focal point for the children's loves and hatreds. Nelly's memories of Mr. Earnshaw and her concern with his legacy impact upon her behaviour to Heathcliff after Cathy's return from Thrushcross Grange:

> I went on to think about his fondness for Heathcliff, and his dread lest he should suffer neglect after death had removed him; and that naturally led me to consider the poor lad's situation now, and from singing I changed my mind to crying. It struck me soon, however, there would be more sense in endeavouring to repair some of his wrongs than shedding tears over them – I got up and walked into the court to seek him. (I.7, 48)

When Heathcliff threatens Hindley, it is by appealing to the father's authority: 'I'll tell how you boasted that you would turn me out of doors as soon as he died, and see whether he will not turn you out directly' (I.4, 33). While Hindley and Heathcliff compete over Mr. Earnshaw's favours, Cathy and Mr. Earnshaw compete over Heathcliff: Cathy delights in displaying her power over him (36).

In Freud's model of primal phantasy, there are actors and an audience: children watch or listen to something which is beyond their comprehension, but from which they feel excluded. As earlier suggested, *Wuthering Heights* presents numerous scenes defined by exclusion: Cathy presents us with an early example in her diary when she mocks Hindley and Frances's loving caresses and speech as 'foolish palaver that we should be ashamed of' (I.3, 17). Heathcliff presents a comparable scene in more pathetic terms: discussing his and Cathy's desire to see Thrushcross Grange, he says, 'we thought we would just go and see whether the Lintons passed their Sunday evenings standing shivering in corners, while their father and mother sat eating and drinking, and singing and laughing, and burning their eyes out before the fire. Do you think they do?' (I.6, 41). Exclusion is mobile: passed from person to person. Heathcliff, Hindley, Cathy, Edgar and Isabella are all alternately placed at the periphery of a desired scene. Eavesdropping and spying are therefore decisive. When Heathcliff leaves the Heights he does so because he overhears Cathy's saying that it would be degrading to marry him (I.9, 71). The parents establish this pattern of exclusion.

The confrontation between Mr. and Mrs. Earnshaw is played out over the body of Heathcliff; despite her failure to expel him, Mrs. Earnshaw continues to wish Heathcliff gone (I.4, 32). The mother and indeed the very possibility of maternal love are written out of *Wuthering Heights*. Nelly gives the impression that Heathcliff's entrance into the family hastens Mrs. Earnshaw's death, writing, it 'happened in less than two years after' (32). Although Mr. Earnshaw seems at first a compassionate man and kindly father, he swiftly appears punitive and threatening to all but Heathcliff: Nelly tells us that 'suspected slights of his authority nearly threw him into fits' (35). In his illness, he becomes a brutal despot; however, his pre-existing capacity for violence is shown by the 'sound blow' he gave Cathy. Mrs. Earnshaw is defined solely by her disgust for Heathcliff. The family is split in two: aligned on one side, Mr. Earnshaw, Cathy and Heathcliff; on the other side, Mrs. Earnshaw, Hindley and Nelly. Joseph stands alone, loyal to no one except his master. This situation is complicated by Mr. Earnshaw's treatment of Cathy:

> After behaving as badly as possible all day, she sometimes came fondling to make it up at night.
>
> "Nay, Cathy," the old man would say, "I cannot love thee; thou'rt worse than thy brother. Go, say thy prayers child, and ask God's pardon. I doubt thy mother and I must rue that we ever reared thee!"
>
> That made her cry, at first; and then, being repulsed continually hardened her, and she laughed if I told her to say she was sorry for her faults, and beg to be forgiven. (I.5, 36–37)

Mr. Earnshaw's rejection of Cathy is a traumatic exclusion, or excommunication, which is felt throughout the novel through afterwardsness. To appropriate Cathy's language, it is felt like a dream, 'gone through and through': 'like wine through water' (I.9, 70). The rejection of Cathy affects our understanding of Lockwood's second dream: Cathy may not be physically cast out in her lifetime, but her father emotionally rebuffs her. Her continuing love for him is clear; in the moments before his death, she 'kissed his hand and said she would sing him to sleep' (I.5, 37). After he dies, she is isolated, and despite finding friendship with the Lintons, she finds kin only in Heathcliff. The absolutism of her identification with Heathcliff protects her from the impact of her father's rejection. Later confessing to Nelly, she says 'My great miseries in this world have been Heathcliff's miseries, and I watched and felt each from the beginning; my great thought in living is himself' (I.9, 72–73). Her concern for Heathcliff's exclusion *consciously* supersedes the thought of her own; however, as we will see, the sense of her own negation returns to her in dream and delirium. Heathcliff's trauma—his suppression after Mr. Earnshaw's death—is the visible scene; Cathy's is hidden behind or beneath it. Their mutual identification is indexed via Mr. Earnshaw, despite the fact that Heathcliff was loved, and Cathy—according to Mr. Earnshaw himself—was not.

Mr. Earnshaw's death redraws the battle lines around the pre-existing conflict. Nelly eavesdrops upon Cathy and Heathcliff and hears them comforting themselves with images of heaven:

> The little souls were comforting each other with better thoughts than I could have hit on; no parson in the world ever pictured Heaven so beautifully as they did, in their innocent talk; and, while I sobbed, and listened, I could not help wishing we were all there safe together. (I.5, 38)

It is interesting that this happens off stage. We do not ever see—through Nelly—the children mourning Mr. Earnshaw, and neither does Cathy's diary suggest a state of mourning. It is Hindley—the 'detestable substitute' father—who is the cause of Cathy's tears, Cathy evasively noting 'I wish my father were back again' (I.3, 16). The rights (and rites) due to the dead coalesce around the literal placement of body and spirit.[6] Cathy and Heathcliff's pathetic vision of heaven is inseparable from Cathy's later premonition of her own exile:

> I was only going to say that heaven did not seem to be my home; and I broke my heart with weeping to come back to earth; and the angels were so angry that they flung me out, into the middle of the heath and on the top of Wuthering Heights; where I woke sobbing for joy. (I.9, 71)

Through her father's rejection, and her vision of heaven after his death, Brontë implies that Cathy's spirit will not rest with his. They will not be 'all there safe together' as Nelly hopes. The joyfulness of Cathy's exile

[6] Linton and Catherine argue over their 'perfect idea of heaven's happiness'. Linton wishes to lie indolently on the heath, and Cathy imagines herself 'rocking in a rustling tree' (II.10, 218).

from heaven is questioned by Lockwood's second dream: 'melancholy', 'ice-cold' and sobbing, the little ghost Cathy cries, 'I'm come home, I'd lost my way on the moor!'; 'It's twenty years,' mourned the voice, 'twenty years, I've been a waif for twenty years!' (I.3, 20–21). Exile is only acceptable when it is shared: without Heathcliff, Cathy is abject.

Familial and theological modes of exclusion are interrelated. Brontë suggests that the family and the saved are defined, even produced, through violent processes of abjection, which cast out those deemed to be unacceptable. However, in theological terms, the spectral is a liminal category that unsettles these categorisations: the spectre is neither saved nor damned and therefore has radical potential, to resist if not to act.[7] Heathcliff and Cathy both emerge as figures of resistance. Analysing *Wuthering Heights* in terms of cross-generational trauma reveals the superb nuance of Brontë's emotional and psychological understanding. Medical discourse did not tackle the relationship between desire and identity until the *fin de siècle*. *Wuthering Heights* shows love produced and felt within the context of traumatisation. Heathcliff and Cathy's love attempts to heal the damage caused by the family's division—to make reparation; however, it is also a symptom of this same damage and is potentially deadly. Brontë's presentation of the natural world reflects this. On the night of Mr. Earnshaw's death 'A high wind blustered round the house, and roared in the chimney' (I.5, 37). The night that Heathcliff first leaves the house, 'the storm came rattling over the Heights in full fury. There was a violent wind, as well as thunder, and either one of the other split a tree off at the corner of the building' (I.9, 75). When Cathy is delirious at Thrushcross Grange, she hears 'that wind sounding in the firs by the lattice' (I.12, 110). Lying in Cathy's bed, Lockwood hears a 'gusty wind' and the 'driving of the snow' (I.3, 20). Exclusion or excommunication has dynamism: it moves, haunts—wuthers.

Silence and Delirium

The repeated violence found at windows generates a symbolic structure for the novel as a whole. A secret—relating to a primal scene in which a

[7] The Brontës had read James Hogg's *Private Memoirs and Confessions of a Justified Sinner*, and Branwell, Charlotte and Emily were directly influenced by it (Barker 2010, 241). The complexity of Emily Brontë's narrative discourse, and the centrality of exhumation, can be traced back to Hogg's novel.

body intrudes where it should not be, or is not wanted—moves through the novel like 'wine through water'. However, there is not a hidden event within *Wuthering Heights* which could be excavated; a fantasy structure repeats, but its origin is displaced and deferred (as in the Wolf Man's history). In Freud's analysis of childhood beating fantasies, the content is always the same, but the protagonists and the point of view shift. *Wuthering Heights* works on a similar premise: excommunication moves through the text as character after character is exiled in turn. Heathcliff, Cathy, Hindley and Isabella all attempt to prevent their own exile, but only succeed in passing it on, or reinscribing it. By circling around a primal scene that always seems to signify more than it means—the body intruding where it should not be, or is not wanted—*Wuthering Heights* deals in the unsaid and the unsayable.

Laplanche describes fantasy as the 'relations between bodies' ('Reference to the Unconscious', 137), and this is certainly borne out by *Wuthering Heights*: we sense a hidden desire, or an unstated problem, fuelling this. Brontë creates subtextual depth by allowing questions to remain unanswered, most notably concerning Heathcliff's origins and his three-year absence. However, it is critical that the unsaid *remains* unsaid. Like Henry James in *The Turn of the Screw*, Brontë sets traps for the reader. *Wuthering Heights* is an experimental text, which consistently draws attention to its own construction: the gaps and silences are therefore heavily weighted. The novel poses a powerful question: what happens when secrets are never brought out into the open? What if the law of revelation, insisted upon by Wilkie Collins in *No Name*, fails? What does it mean to *know* that there's something you *do not* know? Abraham and Torok's formulation of the secret is helpful here:

> All secrets are shared at the start. Hence the 'crime' under consideration cannot be a solitary one, since it was turned into a secret. The 'crime' points to an accomplice, the locus of undue enjoyment, as well as to others who are excluded and, by dint of this same enjoyment, eliminated. In the absence of a concept of infringement, the 'crime' would entail no secret. ('Topography of Reality', 158)

This passage helps to illuminate Brontë's enterprise in *Wuthering Heights*. The conflict between Mr. and Mrs. Earnshaw converges on the disputed body of Heathcliff, but both parents remain enigmatic to the reader: we cannot understand the strength of Mrs. Earnshaw's aversion to Heathcliff, nor the aggressiveness of Mr. Earnshaw's love. Heathcliff's origins are unknown, but without the parents' response, this in itself would not necessarily be a problem. The intersubjective trauma is decisive: the reaction to Heathcliff, which exposes something unseen, and unknown, about the family itself. There is a secret here—but that is not to say that we can detect its content. The impossibility of articulation, 'dumbness', is equated with the foreign 'gibberish' that Heathcliff speaks when he enters the house (I.4, 31). Brontë is therefore able to signal far outside the context of the novel itself, pointing obliquely to the violence of eighteenth-century colonialism, the slave trade, revolution and war. There are global traumas on the periphery of the novel, but if they are activated, it is within the familial *mise-en-scène*.

Nelly tells Lockwood that Heathcliff 'was not insolent to his benefactor; he was simply insensible, though knowing perfectly the hold he had on his heart, and conscious he had only to speak and all the house would be obliged to bend to his wishes' (33). The 'hold' that Heathcliff has upon Mr. Earnshaw's heart is inseparable from his voice. Heathcliff's 'dumbness' in the streets of Liverpool elicits Mr. Earnshaw's compassion, and his subsequent truthfulness ensures his love. To speak is to tug at the father's heart and force others to 'bend'. Brontë implies that speech, for Heathcliff, is bound up with the revelation of a shared secret. Mr. Earnshaw believes every word Heathcliff speaks to be true, and Nelly supports this judgement parenthetically to Lockwood (32). When Mr. Earnshaw's health and mental state deteriorate, it is the manner in which the rest of the family speak to Heathcliff which causes his anger: 'he was painfully jealous lest a word should be spoken amiss to him, seeming to have got into his head the notion that, because he liked Heathcliff, all hated, and longed to do him an ill-turn' (I.5, 35). Conversely, we are told that Mrs. Earnshaw 'never put in a word on [Heathcliff's] behalf, when she saw him wronged' (32). It is the family's speech—and their silence—which is the focal point for the drama. Speech and silence are presented as decisive actions.[8] Mr. Earnshaw ostensibly prevents his family from expressing their feelings towards Heathcliff in order to protect him: however, the passage above implies that it is his own feeling that is the source of anxiety.

[8] Nanette Auerhahn and Dori Laub's (1998) analysis of Holocaust survivors' children shows that the parent's obsessive retellings can be just as elliptical and effacing as silence, while silence itself can be as burdened as speech.

Brontë shows that speech is bound up with feeling: it is not a closed system of linguistic markers. It is of the body—it throbs. Silence, whether it is chosen, or whether it is inflicted upon us, is not only an absence of sound, it is a physical experience and a moral choice. While silence is initially empowering for Heathcliff, it becomes inhibiting after Mr. Earnshaw's death. When Hindley separates Cathy and Heathcliff after their intrusion at Thrushcross Grange, it is the latter's right to speak to Cathy that is targeted: 'Heathcliff received no flogging, but he was told that the first word he spoke to Miss Catherine should ensure a dismissal' (I.6, 45). The construction of this sentence creates an equivalence between the flogging and the enforced silence. The lack of communication between the two guarantees Heathcliff's exile: he is excommunicated. Their love becomes inarticulate and stuttering:

> 'What good do I get – What do you talk about? You might be dumb or a baby for anything you say to amuse me, or for anything you do, either!'
>
> 'You never told me before that I talked too little, or that you disliked my company, Cathy!' exclaimed Heathcliff in much agitation.
>
> 'It is no company at all, when people know nothing and say nothing,' she muttered. (I.8, 61)

Cathy's rebuke reframes Heathcliff as the foreign stranger who entered the house many years before. However, she is not immune to the influence of Hindley's actions and the paternal problem they point back to. When she speaks to Nelly about her feelings for Heathcliff, she has to do so in occluded terms: 'It's my secret; but if you will not mock at me, I'll explain it; I can't do it distinctly – but I'll give you a feeling of how I feel' (I.9, 70). She explains her love for Heathcliff through her dream of being exiled from heaven, which leads her to say: 'he's more myself than I am. Whatever our souls are made of, his and mine are the same, and Linton's is as different as a moonbeam from lightning, or frost from fire' (71). Their love is forged in exile and cannot be articulated outside of trauma's compulsion to repeat.

Steven Vine (1999) reads spectrality and entombment in *Wuthering Heights* through Abraham and Torok's theory of the phantom and the crypt. He creates a compelling argument, suggesting that Cathy and Heathcliff fail to mourn for one another, and this defines their mutual identification as well as their tragedy. Following Stevie Davies, Vine argues that 'the text's cryptic incorporations and inclusions compulsively enclose or contain one identity within another in an unsettling play of textual phantoms, with the result that the novel unfolds nothing less than a poetics of haunting' (172). Read in this manner, Cathy and Heathcliff appear like Russian dolls: 'She "is" Heathcliff insofar as, this side of death, she is the living crypt that encloses him, while he is the "hidden ghost"[9] [...] that has its home in her' (182). However, problematically, Vine does not put this in the context of the cross-generational story. In a footnote he writes, 'strictly speaking the ghost or phantom in Abraham and Torok belongs to "a parental unconscious". Here, I use the words "ghost" and "phantom" in what Derrida calls "the wider sense ... of the inhabitant of a crypt belonging in the Self"' (186). Taking Jacques Derrida's sense here means that the generational context of Cathy and Heathcliff's desire is effaced, and the dynamism of Abraham and Torok's formulation, which relies on the idea that a secret belonging to the other is *transmitted*, is lost. A comparable dynamism underpins the plotting and psychology of the mid-Victorian novel. The literary phantom is more than an internal other, it is a symptom of cross-generational "trauma": the inheritance of secrets and lies. There is a refusal of mourning in *Wuthering Heights*, but the family's primary conflict and Mr. Earnshaw's death lie at the heart of this.[10] Heathcliff's exile supersedes the father's death, and the latter is never directly mourned despite the agony Cathy and Heathcliff feel: 'And they both set up a heart-breaking cry' (I.5, 37).

Brontë draws together physical and psychological woundedness. When Mr. Earnshaw presents Heathcliff to his wife, he complains of his long journey, concluding 'And at the end of it, to be flighted to death!' (I.4, 31): Heathcliff's appearance is shocking in the medical sense of the term and seems to precipitate a deathly process. As we have seen, Mrs. Earnshaw dies two years after Heathcliff's arrival, and Mr. Earnshaw's health 'suddenly' fails, claiming that the family 'disagreements' are 'in his sinking frame' (35). Hindley, Cathy and Heathcliff all push themselves towards death. There is a 'death drive' at work in the family: a compulsion to repeat: exile and death—exile and death, which comes from the elder generation. The contrary desire is for articulation: for an end to ex*communication*. But the two mechanisms are intricately intertwined;

[9]'Hidden ghost' is a quotation from Emily Brontë's 'The Prisoner', published in 1846 (1992, 166). Brontë heavily edited this poem prior to publication to conceal the original Gondal narrative (Barker 2010, 568).

[10]Vine hints at this traumatic loss only once (1999, 182–183).

trauma is of body and mind, and for Cathy, articulation comes within delirium at Thrushcross Grange. She cannot work through her loss, only act it out. The illness that kills her is a repetition of an earlier episode: recounting her second delirium, Nelly says, 'the changes in her moods, began to alarm me terribly; and brought to my recollection her former illness, and the doctor's injunction that she should not be crossed' (I.12, 108). When Heathcliff first leaves Wuthering Heights in 1780, Cathy is struck down with fever. Although Nelly leaves open the possibility that she is made ill through exposure, it is clear that her fever is caused by the shock of Heathcliff leaving: 'she burst into uncontrollable grief; and the remainder of her words were inarticulate' (I.9, 77). Tellingly, when Nelly rebukes her for Heathcliff's absence, Cathy refuses to hold any communication with her for 'several months' (I.9, 78). Silence is correlated with both a failure and refusal of mourning: 'Then the doctor had said that she would not bear crossing much, she ought to have her own way; and it was nothing less than murder, in her eyes, for any one to presume and contradict her' (I.9, 78). Cathy attempts to preserve herself and Heathcliff in silence. But she is irretrievably damaged by his departure. When Heathcliff returns Thrushcross Grange, she tells Nelly: 'The event of this evening have reconciled me to God and humanity! I had risen in angry rebellion against providence – Oh, I've endured very, very bitter misery, Nelly!' (I.10, 88). Once more Brontë uses the window as a symbol for a boundary or crossing: Edgar and Cathy sit 'together in a window' when Heathcliff is announced as 'A person from Gimmerton' (83). The reunion is mediated via others: conversations between Cathy and Heathcliff prior to Cathy's illness deal primarily with Isabella's love for Heathcliff. It is in illness and delirium that Cathy speaks *to* and *of* Heathcliff, and in so doing, she returns to childhood scenes.

Nelly plays a crucial role in Cathy's delirium: she bears witness to Cathy's traumatisation but is incapable of feeling compassion towards her, and this directly impacts on Cathy's health. (Indeed it could be argued that by refusing to tell Edgar about his wife's deteriorating condition, Nelly is responsible for Cathy's death.) Nelly's cruelty contrasts with Lockwood's 'compassion' towards Heathcliff's impassioned grief. When Cathy speaks, just as when she was fifteen and confessing her secret to Nelly, she does so to someone who is incapable of hearing her: Nelly interrupts: 'Give over with this baby work!' (I.12, 108). Cathy's description of the lapwing chicks dying in their nest figures the novel as a whole:

> Bonny bird; wheeling over our heads in the middle of the moor. It wanted to get to its nest, for the clouds touched the swells, and it felt rain coming. This feather was picked up from the heath, the bird was not shot – we saw its nest in the winter full of little skeletons. Heathcliff set a trap over it, and the old ones dare not come. I made him promise he'd never shoot a lapwing, after that, and he didn't. (108)

If we were in any doubt whether or not *Wuthering Heights* is a novel about childhood traumatisation, then this passage would reveal it to us in beautifully haunting and resonant form. Cathy's account feels elliptical: we are not sure whether she is presenting a chronological account. It feels like one of Freud's screen memories, a luminous moment compacting past and present with deep figurative importance. Despite Cathy's claim that the lapwing was not shot, the end of the passage leaves us uncertain of the parent bird's fate. Heathcliff's trap seems to prevent the adult lapwings returning to their young, and this foreshadows his destructive actions towards the younger generation. However, the elisions, temporal dualism and symbolism complicate a one-dimensional reading.[11] As we know from Nelly's earlier reference to his cuckoo history, Heathcliff is also placed in the nest: he is one of the starved frozen young. After Mr. Earnshaw's death, Heathcliff is trapped within a family that has become a place of danger: in his own words, 'standing shivering in corners, while [...] father and mother sat eating and drinking' (I.6, 41).[12] The grotesquery and pathos of the 'little skeletons' reminds us that wounded children populate *Wuthering Heights*.

The rich mythology and literary history surrounding lapwings enrich our understanding of this moment. In his 1825 volume of customs and proverbs, Robert Nares writes: 'The bird is said, and I believe truly, to draw pursuers from her nest by crying in other places' (436).[13] The 'bonny bird' 'wheeling' over Cathy and Heathcliff's heads may be heroically luring them away from her chicks. However, the mythology and folklore complicate this, since lapwings are repeatedly associated with deceit. Shakespeare uses the lapwing's cry as a figure for duplicitous

[11] The two forms of violence—shooting and trapping—likewise confuse matters.

[12] Here, he is thinking of Hindley and Frances as the surrogate father and mother, in contrast to Edgar and Isabella's parents.

[13] Strangely, when the nest is directly threatened, the lapwing feigns vulnerability, dragging a wing upon the ground to distract the predator from the young.

speech in *The Comedy of Errors*: 'Far from her nest the lapwing cries away / My heart prays for him, though my tongue do curse' (4.2.26–27). In *The Assembly of Foules*, Geoffrey Chaucer writes of 'the false lapwynge, ful of trecherye' (l.347). In Book 6 of John Dryden's translation of Ovid's *Metamorphoses*, Tereus, the rapist of Philomela, is transformed into a 'lapwing'.[14] Interestingly, Dryden presents the lapwing as despotic and imperious, qualities associated with Mr. Earnshaw in the childhood section of *Wuthering Heights*, and later with Hindley and Heathcliff. The fact that Tereus's crime was sexual casts a strange shadow over Brontë's symbolism. The lapwing is an ingenious loving parent, *and* a disingenuous crested predator. Cathy's reference to the 'old ones' is eerie: the phrase sounds mythic and threatening. Brontë creates a double text. Heathcliff's 'trap' appears both protective and violent: perhaps we are supposed to read him as the bird 'ful of trecherye' who can *save* the young from the elder generation.[15] Hareton's continued loyalty towards Heathcliff reinforces this possibility. Cathy's hallucinatory memory of the lapwings forms part of the novel's wider fantasy structure; circling around exile and troubled articulation: 'Far from her nest the lapwing cries away' (*Comedy of Errors*, 4.2.27).

Cathy's despair can only be articulated through an altered state of consciousness, in which, as we have seen, the temporality of the novel

[14] Published after Dryden's death in 1717 under the editorship of Sir Samuel Garth, and with additional translations from Addison, Pope and others. It was reissued in the early nineteenth century:

> 'Tereus, through grief, and haste to be reveng'd,
> Shares the like fate, and to a bird is chang'd:
> Fix'd on his head, the crested plumes appear,
> Long is his beak, and sharpen'd like a spear;
> Thus arm'd, his looks his inward mind display,
> And, to a lapwing turn'd, he fans his way'. (Dryden et al. 1826, VI.1044–1049)

Patrick Brontë owned a copy of Dryden's *The Works of Virgil*, in which his children had doodled on the margins (Thormählen 2014, 98), while Alexander Pope's translation of the *Iliad* is referenced in the siblings' juvenilia (Barker 2010, 172). There is therefore a healthy probability (if not a confirmed fact) that Dryden's translation of Ovid would have formed part of the family's reading.

[15] The threat from the elder generation conceptually links Brontë's literary enterprise with Freud's case histories in *Studies on Hysteria*, particularly those of Rosalia and Katharina, and Emma from 'A Project for a Scientific Psychology' (discussed in Chapter 2).

is disrupted. She imagines herself back at Wuthering Heights and is conscious of an anomalous presence: 'there are two candles on the table making the black press shine like jet'; 'It *does* appear odd – I see a face in it!' (I.12, 109). This reaches forwards to Lockwood's timeframe, as well as backwards to her own childhood. She cannot see her mirrored image as her self and instead sees a stranger reflected in the (imagined) black press: 'Oh! Nelly, the room is haunted! I'm afraid of being alone!'; Nelly responds 'It was *yourself*, Mrs. Linton'. Cathy is haunted, but she is also spectral:

> 'Oh, dear! I thought I was at home,' she signed. 'I thought I was lying in my chamber at Wuthering Heights. Because I'm weak, my brain got confused, and I screamed unconsciously. Don't say anything; but stay with me. I dread sleeping, my dreams appal me'. (109)

The language here indicates the precision of Brontë's 'traumatic' model and the self-consciousness with which it is created. Cathy's anguish draws her back to the childhood scenes that drive the novel. This passage is critical to my reading, so I quote at length here:

> I'll tell you what I thought, and what has kept recurring and recurring till I feared for my reason – I thought as I lay there with my head against that table leg, and my eyes dimly discerning the grey square of the window, that I was enclosed in the oak-panelled bed at home; and my heart ached with some great grief which, just waking, I could not recollect – I pondered, and worried myself to discover what it could be; and most strangely, the whole last seven years of my life grew a blank! I did not recall that they had been at all. I was a child; my father was just buried, and my misery arose from the separation that Hindley had ordered between me and Heathcliff – I was laid alone, for the first time, and rousing from a dismal doze after a night of weeping – I lifted my hand to push the panels aside, it struck the table-top! I swept it along the carpet, and then, memory burst in – my late anguish was swallowed in a paroxysm of despair – I cannot say why I felt so wildly wretched – it must have been temporary derangement, for there is scarcely cause – But supposing at twelve years old I had been wrenched from the Heights, and every early association, and my all in all, as Heathcliff was at that time, and been converted at a stroke into Mrs. Linton, the lady of Thrushcross Grange, and the wife of a stranger; an exile, and outcast, thenceforth, from what had been my world – You may fancy a glimpse of the abyss where I grovelled! (110–111)

Brontë represents Cathy's dissociation with acuity. Cathy's melancholy (her failure to mourn her father, her self and Heathcliff) disrupts her memory, and she is taken back to the source of her trauma: her exile from Heathcliff and, I argue, the veiled effects of her father's rejection of her. Cathy's trauma is figured here as medical shock with the capacity to make her ill, and disrupt memory, but it is also the foundation for her self and her self in Heathcliff: her 'all in all'. We learn that Heathcliff had slept in the same bed as Cathy up until this moment: 'I was laid alone for the first time'. At the very point her father is buried, she is denied the comfort of her only friend: the image of her lying alone prefigures Heathcliff's anguish concerning her burial and his placement next to her. Looking over the moor at the candle in the window of her old bedroom, she considers her own death: 'I'll not lie there by myself; they may bury me twelve feet deep, and throw the church down over me, but I won't rest till you are with me ... I never will!' (111–112). Read in dialogue with the passage quoted above, Cathy echoes the pathos-ridden voice of her own childhood self, 'weeping' in the dark because 'I was laid alone'. Her language pre-empts Heathcliff's language after her death: 'Be with me always – take any form – drive me mad! only *do* not leave me in this abyss, where I cannot find you! Oh, God! it is unutterable! I *cannot* live without my life! I *cannot* live without my soul!' (II.2, 148).

Brontë presents, *avant la lettre*, a poetics of trauma. The injury to Cathy's hand described in the passage above points backwards (or forwards in chronological terms) to Lockwood's second dream in which he pushes her hand violently down upon the window frame. It also pre-empts the details of Heathcliff's death. The 'despair' and confusion that follow upon her state of waking mean that Cathy becomes the little Cathy Linton from Lockwood's dream—lost and exiled from her family: as Nelly observes 'Catherine was no better than a wailing child!' (I.12, 110). Cathy and Heathcliff's love is defined by a deathly compulsion to repeat:

> 'I wish I could hold you,' she continued bitterly, 'till we were both dead! I shouldn't care what you suffered. I care nothing for your sufferings. Why shouldn't you suffer! I do! Will you forget me – will you be happy when I am in the earth? Will you say twenty years hence, 'That's the grave of Catherine Earnshaw. I loved her long ago, and was wretched to lose her; but it is past'. (II.1, 140)

Heathcliff, with justification, replies 'Do you reflect that all those words will be branded in my memory, and eating deeper eternally, after you have left me? You know you lie to say I have killed you; and Catherine, you know that I could as soon forget you, as my existence!'. Nelly relates the 'strange and fearful picture' of the two lovers to Cathy's earlier conviction that 'Heaven would be a land of exile to her'. Brontë reminds us, through Nelly, that this distressing scene forms part of a larger sequence of traumatisation.

Exorcism?

Wuthering Heights shifts between mythic and historical forms: it is epic in its tragic dimensions: Aeschylus's *Oresteia* and Sophocles's Theban dramas are echoed in this localised story of violence, revenge and restoration. At the same time, Nelly's voice—overpowering without controlling Lockwood's narration—grounds the story in a sense of the actual and historical. Bearing witness is shown to be heavily loaded: at key points in the narrative we see Nelly's actions impact upon the course of the drama; her gaze and interpretation are flawed. The voicing of the trauma operates alongside the resolution of the trauma: the two threads are parallel in time, if not in space, and the relationship between the two remains unclear. Does telling the family's story have a curative function, and if so, for whom?

Wuthering Heights intertwines cause and effect. Through Lockwood, we hear traumatic echoes before we are able to decipher them. The second generation's story is interwoven with Heathcliff and Cathy's until Isabella's flight to the south of England, at which point Nelly skips over several years in her narration. The displacements defining the younger generation do not undermine the traumatic reading of the text, but rather demonstrate the psychological nuance of the novel as a whole. The haunting that defines Cathy and Heathcliff is not re-enacted without alteration in the second. Lockwood experiences the trauma instead: the *mise-en-scène* is not transmitted simply by virtue of blood; for Lockwood, it requires a powerful identification to open up his self to the trauma of the other. Lockwood's similarity to Linton is noteworthy in this context. Before his death, Linton suffers far more psychologically than Hareton and Catherine, despite his physical cosseting. When Catherine runs home (escaping through her mother's window no less) to speak to Nelly, Heathcliff pursues her, using Linton's vulnerability to lure her back to the Heights:

> my presence is as potent on his nerves as a ghost; and I fancy he sees me often, though I am not near. Hareton says he wakes and shrieks in the night by the hour together; and calls you to protect him from me; and, whether you like your precious mate or not, you must come – (II.15, 254)

Linton's illness and decline appears inevitable; the Linton family's congenital physical weakness is coupled with a hauntedness transmitted by Heathcliff. Linton enacts the psychological and physical violence of his parents' marriage in his own flesh. After Linton's death, woundedness in the younger generation becomes correlated with economic loss rather than mental disorder through Catherine and Hareton's story.

Heathcliff and Hindley are determined by Mr. Earnshaw's paternal legacy: the two young men act out an inverted form of the Prodigal Son parable (Luke 15:11–32), both leaving the Heights for exactly three years. However, rather than being joyously reunited with a worthy father, such a reunion is impossible. Hindley and Heathcliff instead become the father, or head of the household, upon their return and re-enact Mr. Earnshaw's authoritative violence in their own paternal roles. Hindley's love for Hareton combines the loving and hateful aspects of Mr. Earnshaw's paternal feelings in hyperbolic and terrifying form: as a little boy, Hareton 'encountering either his wild-beast's fondness or his madman's rage – for in one he ran a chance of being squeezed and kissed to death, and in the other of being flung into the fire, or dashed against the wall –' (I.9, 65). Heathcliff is a violent man, but arguably no more so than Hindley or Mr. Earnshaw. In fact all the fathers, with the exception of Edgar, appear 'wolfish' (I.10, 90) at different moments. However, unlike the other two men, Heathcliff appears as a parodic caricature of masculinity: the brutal man who looks ironically in, and offers a commentary on, his own violence. The reader's shock results from the calm *laissez-faire* manner in which he treats this violence; speaking of Isabella, he reflects: 'if I lived alone with that mawkish, waxen face; the most ordinary would be painting on its white the colours of the rainbow, and turning the blue eyes black, every day or two' (I.10, 94). Explaining his hanging of Isabella's puppy, he comments that 'no brutality disgusted her – I suppose she has an innate admiration of it, if only her precious person were secure from injury!' (I.14, 133). Heathcliff *and* Brontë satirise the Byronic hero, even while Brontë underscores his appeal. In so doing, of course, she echoes Byron's parodic treatment of himself.

Hareton is most compromised during his father's lifetime, as Nelly's first visit to the Heights after Cathy's marriage to Edgar shows. Despite Nelly's attempt to fix Hareton's phrase, 'Devil Daddy' upon Heathcliff, the little boy's subsequent conversation is ambiguous:

> 'Ah! and the devil teaches you to swear at Daddy?' I observed.
> 'Aye – nay,' he drawled.
> 'Who then?'
> 'Heathcliff'.
> I asked if he liked Mr. Heathcliff?
> 'Aye!' he answered again.
> Desiring to have his reasons for liking him, I could only gather the sentences – 'I known't – he pays Dad back what he gies to me – he curses Daddy for cursing me – He says I mun do as I will'. (I.11, 97–98)

Hareton's faltering language explains much that follows. He perceives Heathcliff as a protector: 'he curses Daddy for cursing me'. Again, speech and violence are made equivalent. Heathcliff undoubtedly brutalises Hareton;[16] however, if we are to believe the little boy, he also protects him from the worse of Hindley's excesses. Prior to his departure from the Heights in 1780, Heathcliff unwittingly saves the infant Hareton when Hindley drops him from the top of the staircase. Seemingly against his will, Heathcliff continues to save Hareton: he cannot bring himself to damage him in any real sense; he does not prevent Catherine teaching him to read, and neither does he prevent their burgeoning love affair: 'he wondered how [Hareton] could want the company of any body else' (II.20, 291). While Nelly repeatedly insists upon Heathcliff's culpability, it is Hindley who must be held responsible for Hareton losing the property. Hareton is not spectral, but nevertheless, he brings Cathy and Heathcliff's childhood into the present moment. Heathcliff complains, 'Five minutes ago, Hareton seemed a personification of my youth, not a human being – I felt to him in such a variety of ways, that it would have been impossible to have accosted him rationally' (II.19, 288); 'But, when I look for his father in his face, I find *her* more and more! How the devil is he so like? I can hardly bear to see him' (II.17, 269).

Catherine, Linton and Hareton's story occludes Heathcliff's, and it is not until his confession to Nelly prior to Linton's death that we view

[16] Hareton's hanging of the puppies repeats Heathcliff's treatment of Isabella's dog. Brontë's implication—that this behaviour has been taught—is obvious.

events through his perspective: a double narrative is created, and the silencing of Heathcliff's story is retrospectively indicated. Both Cathy and Heathcliff treat Nelly as an interlocutor, although Nelly has significantly more patience for Heathcliff. In this confession, Heathcliff looks back to the night of Cathy's burial, forcing us to reread Isabella's account of this same night. Heathcliff's first exhumation of Cathy is curtailed by the emergence of her haunting non-presence: 'I knew no living thing in flesh and blood was by – but as certainly as you perceive the approach to some substantial body in the dark, though it cannot be discerned, so certainly I felt that Cathy was there, not under me, but on the earth' (II.15, 256). Passing swiftly over the violence which occurred at the window that night, he explains his yearning for Cathy: 'I felt her by me – I could *almost* see her, and yet I *could not*'; from this point, his 'nerves [were] at such a stretch, that, if they had not resembled catgut, they would, long ago, have relaxed to the feebleness of Linton's' (257). Cathy's spectre is felt everywhere after this first exhumation: 'And when I slept in her chamber – I was beaten out of that – I couldn't lie there; for the moment I closed my eyes, she was either outside the window, or sliding back the panels, or entering the room, or even resting her darling head upon the pillow as she did when a child. And I must open my eyes to see. And so I opened and closed them a hundred time a-night – to be always disappointed' (257). Like Orpheus, Heathcliff cannot look back at his Eurydice without her gliding out of sight. The second exhumation scene ends this problem, leading to Heathcliff's drive towards death, and to Hareton and Catherine's marriage. Seeing Cathy's corpse, embalmed in the peat rich soil, Heathcliff is 'pacified'. The reality of her death is the reality of his own, and he begins to starve himself, just as she did eighteen years before: 'there is a strange change approaching – I'm in its shadow at present' (II.19, 287); 'I have a single wish, and my whole being and faculties are yearning to attain it' (289). Tellingly, in his final days, 'he would not consent, formally, to exclude Hareton and Cathy [...] choosing rather to absent himself' (290). His ability to see Cathy signals his impending demise: 'I perceived he was not looking at the wall, for when I regarded him alone, it seemed, exactly, that he gazed at something within two yards distance. And whatever it was, it communicated, apparently, both pleasure and pain, in exquisite extremes' (II.20, 294–295).

The two exhumation scenes operate within the context of the wider traumatic structure. The first occurs just before the murderous encounter between Hindley and Heathcliff at the window of the Heights, which is witnessed by Isabella. Attempting to shoot Heathcliff, Hindley is badly injured himself: 'The charge exploded, and the knife, in springing back, closed into its owner's wrist' (II.3, 157). Hindley's wound parallels the injury Lockwood inflicts on Cathy in his second dream (while predating it chronologically), and the wound Heathcliff causes himself when his gun explodes (II.18, 277). Two other wounds are also relevant; the hurt to Cathy's hand when she hits the tabletop in her delirium, and the graze Nelly sees on Heathcliff's hand in death. All of these (very similar) wounds appear self-inflicted: the owner's weapon is turned back upon the self. These physical injuries testify to the shared trauma: bodies express something that is inexpressible.[17] Damage to one is damage to all. No one wins: to quote Lockwood's dream, 'Every man's hand was against his neighbour' (I.3, 20). These wounds bring an affective complex to the fore. Phrased in abstract terms, the subject attempts to define itself by violently abjecting the other; however, Brontë shows through her use of echoes and parallelisms that this is unsustainable. The novel refuses to sustain dualisms; there is always a third term, another person (or persons), through which relationships are formed.[18] Brontë's own upbringing in a close-knit sibling group would undoubtedly have facilitated this insight: parent-child relationships must be read in relation to the entire sibling group. Heathcliff, Hindley and Cathy are all wounded children.

Heathcliff's death is both suicide and murder. Apparently fulfilling the promise she made before she died, Cathy's ghost comes back for him: 'By God! she's relentless. Oh, damn it! It's unutterably too much for flesh and blood to bear, even mine' (II.20, 297). The image of Heathcliff's corpse is the logical conclusion to the drama that 'began' in Mr. and Mrs. Earnshaw's conflict over the body of the little boy:

[17] Brontë's motif anticipates Cathy Caruth's (1996b) concept of trauma as a voice crying out from a wound. This may not be a coincidence. Drawing on Freud's brief reference to the tale in *Beyond the Pleasure Principle*, Caruth uses Tasso's story of Tancred and Clorinda, originally from *La Gerusalemme Liberata* (1580), to formulate this. Edward Fairfax's translation of Tasso's work *Jerusalem Delivered* (1600) was widely read in the nineteenth century. Charlotte Brontë's poem, 'The Violet', written at the age of fourteen, references Tasso in a footnote, which seems reasonable proof that the siblings had access to Fairfax's translation. Mr. Rochester's full name—Edward Fairfax Rochester—seems to nod towards the author.

[18] This can be related back to Hogg's *Private Memoirs and Confessions of a Justified Sinner*, in which Robert is haunted by George and Gil-Martin; this is caused by both abjection and elevation: Robert's rejection by one father, and the religious indoctrination by the other.

> I could not think him dead – but his face and throat were washed with rain; the bed-clothes dripped, and he was perfectly still. The lattice, flapping to and fro, had grazed one hand that rested on the sill – no blood trickled from the broken skin, and when I put my fingers to it, I could doubt no more – he was dead and stark! (298)

The detail of Heathcliff's grazed hand is vital. This wound speaks eloquently to the shared trauma, and it implies its cessation. No blood flows. The wound is stopped in death. The lack of blood contrasts powerfully with the details of Lockwood's second dream: 'I pulled its wrist on to the broken pane, and rubbed it to and fro till the blood ran down and soaked the bed-clothes' (I.3, 21). The window, flapping gently, is open: the breach between Cathy and Heathcliff is closed. Joseph interprets Heathcliff's death as the conclusion to the drama: 'return[ing] thanks that the lawful master and the ancient stock were restored to their rights' (II.20, 298). Nelly, however, is 'stunned by the awful event; and [her] memory unavoidably recurred to former times with a sort of oppressive sadness' (298). Brontë leaves the end of the novel open. Lockwood's investment in the trauma is worked through: watching Hareton and Catherine enter the house he is 'irresistibly impelled to escape them again' (300). Becoming characteristically withdrawn once more, he prepares to leave. While Hareton and Catherine's relationship undoubtedly heals the family's wounds, Cathy and Heathcliff's fate is more ambiguous. Rumours of haunting abound in the neighbourhood: Nelly uneasily reflects that a little boy, 'probably raised the phantoms from thinking, as he traversed the moors alone, on the nonsense he had heard his parents and companions repeat' (299). Brontë carefully underlines the cross-generational schema: phantoms are summoned up and transmitted in the family circle. This moment also implies a wider narrative process: Cathy and Heathcliff's story haunts spaces beyond the text.

Lockwood's perspective differs from that of the 'country folks' (299): looking at the three graves, he 'wondered how any one could ever imagine unquiet slumbers for the sleepers in that quiet earth' (300). This doubled ending is significant: like *The Turn of the Screw*, *Wuthering Heights* refuses to prescribe meaning. The trauma stops, but it is not necessarily worked through, and the novel's enigmas are transmitted to the reader. Within the novel, forgiveness is bound up with silence. Hareton refuses to listen to Catherine: 'I heard Hareton sternly check his cousin, on her offering a revelation of her father-in-law's conduct to his father. He said he wouldn't suffer a word to be uttered to him, in his disparagement; if he were the devil, it didn't signify; he would stand by him' (II.19, 285). This refusal echoes Mr. Earnshaw's prohibition of his family's speech in the childhood section of the novel. However, at the same time, speech can no longer be wounding and violating. Hareton's unconditional love for Heathcliff both prohibits and enables a process of mourning. Secrets remain secret, and it is physically—through the cousins' love, marriage and joining of property—that reparation for the past is made. The novel's enigmas remain enigmatic, as Nelly reflects prior to Heathcliff's death:

> 'But where did he come from, the little dark thing, harboured by a good man to his bane?' muttered superstition, as I dozed into unconsciousness. And I began, half dreaming, to weary myself with imaging[19] some fit parentage for him; and repeating my waking meditations, I tracked his existence over again' (II.20, 293)

Heathcliff's origins, and the violence of the Earnshaws, remain open to speculation and critical interpretation. Like Nelly, we trace and retrace the novel in the hope of revealing a primary truth. Brontë sets a trap for the reader and critic, in which we—like Heathcliff—are forced to exhume the dead.[20]

Family Longing and the Maternal Blessing: *Shirley*

Shirley, like *Jane Eyre* and *Wuthering Heights*, is founded on primal parental failure: Robert Moore's family debt; Caroline's debauched father and absent mother. Shirley's seemingly protected orphanhood is juxtaposed against this. The novel asks how the present can make reparation for the past. This is a double movement: a ghost of the future haunts the historical world of the novel as deaths are foretold and elegies anticipated.

Shirley is a hybrid novel, with an array of narrators and focalisers. This is probably a result of Brontë's fragmented composition, although it is

[19] The OUP edition of the novel follows the first edition by having 'imaging' here. Later editions replace it with the less powerful 'imagining'. Brontë died before the publication of the second edition in 1850.

[20] Hillis Miller (1982) also notes the necrophiliac mode of reading in *Wuthering Heights*, although from a different interpretative perspective (70).

also possible that she was inspired by her sisters' narrative techniques in *Wuthering Heights* and *The Tenant of Wildfell Hall*. In reading *Shirley*, it is difficult to separate the novel from the tragic context of its composition, and it is not wholly necessary that we do so. Branwell, Emily and Anne all died before Charlotte Brontë began writing the third volume (Barker 2010, 709). Their loss is invoked in the opening of Volume III, 'The Valley of the Shadow of Death':

> The future sometimes seems to sob a low warning of the events it is bringing us, like some gathering though yet remote storm, which, in tones of the wind, in flushings of the firmament, in clouds strangely torn, announces a blast strong to strew the sea with wrecks; or commissioned to bring in fog the yellow taint of pestilence, covering white Western isles with the poisoned exhalations of the East, dimming the lattices of English homes with the breath of Indian plague. At other times, this Future bursts suddenly, as if a rock had rent, and in it a grave opened, whence issues the body of one that slept. Ere you are aware, you stand face to face with a shrouded and unthought-of Calamity – a new Lazarus. (III.1, 351)

This imagery bridges that of *Wuthering Heights* and *Villette*. The sobbing wind is heard in all the key scenes in *Wuthering Heights*: it presages the future, testament to the repeating family trauma. The wind cries out a loss that cannot be acknowledged directly. This moment pre-empts the silencing of Lucy Snowe's symbolic shipwreck in *Villette* (1853), which takes place between her childhood and adulthood, and Monsieur Paul's ambiguous fate at the novel's ending. If it is not pushing biography too far, it is possible that Charlotte Brontë creates these intertextual echoes of *Wuthering Heights* in order to find a language in which to mourn, or highlight the impossibility of mourning, her sister Emily. The reference to Lazarus does not reassure with a sense of blessedness: Brontë implies that what returns never returns as itself (and lacks the 'benedictions' identified by William Wordsworth in 'Ode: Intimations of Immortality from Recollections of Early Childhood', discussed in Chapter 1).

Resurrection is reconfigured as exhumation; there is a sense of the vampiric: the return of the undead. The misery of this is palpable; the crisis of faith is clear. The future may well involve a traumatic return of the past, but in a new and terrifying guise. Woundedness is everywhere—the clouds are 'torn', the rock is 'rent', and the 'grave opened'. There is a physical breach presented in each image. Like Emily, Charlotte Brontë asks what new influences will be permitted to enter through the window, and what will ensue. Emily portrays Heathcliff as a catalyst, rather than the cause, of conflict within the Earnshaw family; the more conservative Charlotte posits a noxious foreign invasion. The 'lattices of English homes' remind us of Cathy's lattice window. In a racial metaphor, the whiteness of the Western isles is set against a murky, yellow, threat from outside. Brontë presents a kind of reverse colonisation, death being brought from outside the community.[21] Caroline's recovery is held back by the 'breath of Asiatic deserts' which 'parched' her lips 'and fevered her veins' (III.2, 370). She cannot recover until the *west* wind blows (ibid.). Brontë's personal grief does not disrupt the novel's scheme: she represents illness as the condition of England during times of war, and this agonising moment sits coherently in Caroline's story.[22] In *Beyond the Pleasure Principle*, Freud moves abruptly from his discussion of war neuroses to consider Ernst's play (14): this manoeuvre implies, without theorising, the penetration of global cataclysm into the familial *mise-en-scène*. Brontë's historical novel performs a comparable gesture.

Brontë represents historical process as a form of familial restitution, but this restitution is also wounding. Her language in the opening of Volume III, which opened this analysis, points towards a fear of the future—the contaminating force of modernity. Rather than opening the 'lattices' to allow fresh air to flow, Brontë implies that the windows should be shut: the parameters between home and outside, self and other, precisely redrawn. The references to emigration throughout *Shirley* reinvest the value of home. By presenting emigration as a potential solution to her male protagonists' plight, Brontë taps into a contemporary—mid-Victorian—topic. With that said, although there was an explosion in the numbers emigrating from Britain and Ireland to America and Canada in the 1840s, this process began *en masse* after the Napoleonic wars ended in 1815. *Shirley* therefore anticipates its own immediate future. While the world of the novel opens up sufficiently to allow the half-Belgian Robert and Louis Moore to return to their father's home county and marry their two Yorkshire girls, the family group is sewn up in a circular fashion.

[21] *Shirley* enters into a dialogue with *Wuthering Heights*; not only does the narrator self-consciously correct southern perceptions of Yorkshire barbarism, she also appears to challenge Emily Brontë's representation of Yorkshire. It would be impossible to imagine a character of Joseph's vitality in the working-class groups of *Shirley*.

[22] The physicality of this language can be compared with Thomas Carlyle's in *Past and Present*.

Shirley's historical trajectory implies that modernity comes at a cost: industrialisation injures nature, and with this comes the loss of the feminine independence and myth-making bound up in the landscape. Caroline and Shirley's marriages lead to the irrevocable loss of the ancient countryside. Robert prophesies: 'The copse shall be firewood ere five years elapse: the beautiful wild ravine shall be a smooth descent' (III.14, 540). Brontë uses the Luddite rebellions as a framework to examine the pace and ethics of change, representing history through female witnessing. She questions men's control over history; after the riot, Shirley rebukes Robert Moore's highhandedness: 'Acute and astute, why are you not also omniscient? How is it that events transpire, under your very noses, of which you have no suspicion? It should be so, otherwise the exquisite gratification of out-manoeuvring you would be unknown. Ah! friend, you may search my countenance, but you cannot read it' (II.9, 304–305). This blindness is contrasted with the watchfulness of Shirley, Caroline and Mrs. Pryor. During the riot, it is Shirley and Caroline's perspective that is prioritised; and it is Mrs. Pryor's attention which ensures Caroline's survival in Volume III. However, this is complicated by the introduction of Louis Moore, who increasingly directs the narration following Caroline's recovery. His comment to Shirley, 'my character is not, perhaps, quite as legible to you as a page of the last new novel might be' (III.4, 402), directly echoes her own earlier words. The novel self-consciously eddies between 'Elf-land' and the 'shores of Reality' (I.7, 83). Shirley and Louis's courtship is mythic: they associate their love with Eden and therefore insist upon its originary status. Cross-generational trauma—the pain of male History—is *seemingly* effaced.

Heart Sickness

Shirley, like *Wuthering Heights*, is concerned with illnesses that bridge the physical and psychological. Psychosomatic illness is shown to be real and potentially deadly. Both novels complicate mid-Victorian medical discourse; in *Wuthering Heights,* the congenital weakness of the Lintons strikes down male and female members of the family: both Cathy and Heathcliff push themselves into death. By feminising 'depression' through Caroline Helstone, Charlotte Brontë comes closer to a mid-Victorian norm, but in so doing, she investigates the gendering of illness in relation to the female condition. The two novels' treatment of 'trauma' differs, but a comparative reading is enlightening. Heathcliff and Cathy starve themselves, will themselves, into death: the trauma that defines their childhood and their love compulsively repeats. In *Shirley*, this is handled more quietly through Caroline. Nevertheless, the locked room of her childhood haunts following Robert's rejection of her. The novel is couched within a cross-generational map of inheritance and loss. Through Caroline's story, Brontë represents the gradual wasting away of depression or melancholia. Caroline's drunken and debauched father brings her up until she is six; and her mother chooses not to come back to her after James Helstone's death. Robert is made heartless and avaricious owing to the inheritance of his grandfather and father's debts and must learn to revalue home (his literal home and the concept). These losses create a cycle of social and psychological damage; however, in a totally different fashion to *Wuthering Heights*, the cure comes from the power of the maternal blessing.

Brontë carefully places Robert within a maternal context. When the (rather pompous) third-person narrator first 'sketches' Caroline, she simply tells us: 'Caroline had never known her mother, as she was taken from her in infancy, and had not since seen her; her father died comparatively young, and her uncle, the Rector, had for some years been her sole guardian' (I.6, 65). This bald account allows the domestic scene at the Moores' cottage to unfold without readerly prejudice, and we, like Caroline, are carried away by the intimacy between the two cousins. Caroline presents *Coriolanus* to Robert so that his mind can be played like Samuel Taylor Coleridge's Eolian Harp: 'It is to stir you; to give you new sensations' (77). However, she herself is also played: 'all scenes made of condensed truth and strength, came on in succession, and carried with them in their deep, fast flow, the heart and mind of reader and listener' (79). *Coriolanus* functions as a play within the play: it opens with the grain riots and concludes with the female intervention which prevents Coriolanus's assault on Rome. Coriolanus denies parental authority: 'I'll never/Be such a gosling to obey instinct, but stand,/As if a man were author of himself/And knew no other kin' (5.3, 35–37). His mother, Volumnia, is the dominant figure in the dialogue that follows, presenting a rhetorical and emotive argument calling off the assault, to which Coriolanus capitulates. Brontë's inclusion of the play cuts in two directions: on one hand, it is a narrative prolepsis; by the end of *Shirley*, Robert, like Coriolanus, surrenders to female influence. Through the repeated scenes of nursing, and Caroline's own dependence on Mrs. Pryor, this is placed in a maternal context. On the other hand, this scene of reading allows

Brontë to develop Caroline's character. Even at this early point, Caroline recognises Robert's primary fault: his potential to cut off emotional connections, and defy the sanctifying function of home. Robert's recognition of Caroline's value in this scene is repressed and negated within twelve hours.

Robert's desertion of Caroline is simultaneous with the first substantial elaboration of her history. Buoyant with love and hope the morning after their reading of *Coriolanus,* Caroline talks of marriage with her uncle. Mr. Helstone's cynicism invokes the memory of his brother:

> Many a time had she reviewed them [his sentiments on marriage] before, and sounded the gulf between her own mind and his; and then, on the other side of the wide and deep chasm, she had seen, and she now saw, another figure standing beside her uncle's – a strange shape; dim, sinister, scarcely earthly: the half-remembered image of her own father, James Helstone, Matthewson Helstone's brother. (I.7, 87)

Her father appears as a revenant: summoned up from the past, he haunts Caroline's life with Mr. Helstone. This unnerving spectre elicits a rush of memory:

> She recollected – a dark recollection it was – some weeks that she had spent with him in a great town somewhere, she had had no maid to dress her or take care of her; when she had been shut up, day and night, in a high garret-room, without a carpet, with a bare uncurtained bed, and scarcely any other furniture; when he went out early every morning, and often forgot to return and give her her dinner during the day, and at night, when he came back, was like a madman, furious, terrible; or – still more painful – like an idiot, imbecile, senseless. She knew she had fallen ill in this place, and that one night when she was very sick, he had come raving into the room, and said he would kill her, for she was a burden to him; her screams had brought aid, and from the moment she was then rescued from him she had never seen him, except as a dead man in his coffin. (87–88)

This is nightmarish, but entirely believable: Brontë refuses to make Caroline's childhood the stuff of melodrama. Before the 1839 Infant Custody Act, women had no rights to their children (of whatever age); even after 1839, mothers could only claim custody rights to children aged seven and under. This dark scene of enclosure and madness is invoked when Caroline falls ill in Volume III. Robert's abandonment of Caroline makes her seriously ill for the second time in her life; this is the first. Mrs. Pryor's reappearance repairs the damage caused by masculine violence and neglect, whether literal in the case of James Helstone, or emotional, as in Robert's case.

The mother is held in a liminal suspension: 'Mr. Helstone never spoke' of her. Caroline reflects: 'This mother was then the drunkard's wife: what had *their* marriage been?' The use of free indirect discourse brings the urgency of the question to the reader, and the narrator takes shared ownership of the problem. Caroline addresses Mr. Helstone once more: 'You term marriage miserable, I suppose, from what you saw of my father's and mother's. If my mother suffered what I suffered when I was with papa, she must have had a dreadful life'. Mr. Helstone's brutal reply, rhetorically constructed, is left hanging in the air: 'she thinks nothing of you; she never enquires about you; I have reason to believe she does not wish to see you' (88). The pain that this should cause is projected into the following scene with Robert in which he rejects Caroline: he tries to move past her like a 'phantom', and offers her a 'cool welcome' (89). The narrator addresses Caroline (and the reader) in a key passage:

> You expected bread, and you have got a stone; break your teeth on it, and don't shriek because the nerves are martyrized: do not doubt that your mental stomach – if you have such a thing – is strong as an ostrich's – the stone will digest. You held out your hand for an egg, and fate put into it a scorpion. Show no consternation: close your fingers firmly on the gift; let it sting through your palm. Never mind: in time, after your hand and arm have swelled and quivered long with torture, the squeezed scorpion will die, and you will have learned the great lesson how to endure without a sob. For the whole remnant of your life, if you survive the test – some, it is said, die under it – you will be stronger, wiser, less sensitive. (I.7, 89–90)

The language here is of penetration, wounding, scarring. The suppression of pain is seen as a moral imperative: it is the means of preserving self-respect. However, this silencing of grief is shown to be highly debilitating to Caroline, who is plunged into a melancholic decline. She cannot mourn Robert because to do so would be to accept her love for him; instead she must accept the 'bitter' 'tonic' of 'stoicism' (90). She has 'pent all her universe' in him (95)—but in so doing, his loss resounds with the devastating resonance of her entire family history.

In the wake of Robert's rejection, Caroline's longing for her mother becomes palpable, but she cannot mourn, because of her mother's abandonment of her: 'She longed for something else: the deep, secret, anxious yearning to discover and know her mother strengthened daily; but with the desire was coupled a doubt, a dread – if she knew her, could she love her?' (159). Mrs. Pryor's first appearance occurs only a few pages on from this, although it is not until she reveals her identity that Caroline is cured of her illness and despair. Deploying the language of melancholia, Brontë anticipates the twentieth-century clinical category of depression (the first written use was in 1904 [*OED*]). As Rose Yorke recognises, Caroline is 'shut up' in a 'black trance': 'tediously dying'. Rose describes the parsonage as a 'windowed grave' (II.12, 335).

Rose is a self-styled 'oracle', speaking truth in a world that protects its secrets (337).[23] The acerbic Mrs. Yorke immediately undermines her daughter's validation of Caroline, an attack which the latter feels 'in her very heart' (339). Before confessing her identity, Mrs. Pryor reinforces Rose's diagnosis: 'your mind is crushed; your heart is almost broken: you have been so neglected, so repulsed, left so desolate' (III.1, 361). Caroline replies: 'I believe grief is, and has always been, my worst ailment. I sometimes think, if an abundant gush of happiness came on me, I could revive yet' (361). Female recognition precedes the curative function of female love: Brontë implies that pain must be recognised—it must be spoken—before it can be healed. This operates in counterpoint to the narrator's fervent call for silence and self-control, but this is not a contradiction. The novel presents the movement towards safe spaces of articulation. Female dialogue is prioritised: after their first full conversation, Shirley tells Caroline, 'I have never in my whole life been able to talk to a young lady as I have talked to you this morning' (II.1, 184).

In her effort to work through her grief, Caroline becomes more active and engaged in her community; she does not exclude herself from Shirley, but nevertheless, she wastes away. Caroline is silenced, unrecognisable as the buoyant and daring young woman we first see in Robert and Hortense's parlour. When Robert walks her home from Briarfield, their intimacy is briefly reawakened as a ghost of its former self. Robert says that Caroline will 'haunt' him, and he will 'permit' himself to 'imagine'

[23]This scene leads Caroline to assert, with some irony at this point, the primacy of maternal love: 'Mothers love their children dearly—almost better than they love themselves' (338).

Caroline looking over his shoulder in the counting house (II.2, 214). He claims that he has seen her shade at the mill: 'I walked up to this group; what I sought had glided away' (215); responding to a similar tale, Caroline says, 'It was not my wraith, then? I almost thought it was' (ibid.). These supernatural details—like the telepathic episode in *Jane Eyre*—affirm the couple's identification with, and therefore their desire for, one another. However, this phantomatic language is also inseparable from the imagery surrounding James Helstone and is therefore symptomatic of the trauma. In *Shirley*, hauntedness points towards radical alienation and exclusion from self and loved other. Caroline becomes progressively wraithlike. To appropriate the language she uses concerning her father, she becomes 'scarcely earthly' (87) to herself and others: 'she was, compared with the heiress, as a graceful pencil-sketch compared with a vivid painting' (II.2, 210). This image is potent: Caroline fades out of the novel in favour of Shirley. This pictorial comparison between the two women raises a question concerning the kind of novel Brontë is trying to write as she moves between a variety of tones and forms of narrative discourse. Paradoxically, perhaps, the faded pencil-sketch of Caroline tends towards 'Reality', whereas the 'vivid painting' of Shirley is never fully detached from 'Elf-Land': the mythic and 'heroic' (I.7, 83).

Brontë's representation of Caroline's decline can be compared to Freud's 'Mourning and Melancholia' and Julia Kristeva's *Black Sun*. After Robert's rejection,

> she wasted, grew more joyless and more wan; with them all, her memory kept harping on the name of Robert Moore: an elegy over the past still rung constantly in her ear; a funereal inward cry haunted and harassed her: the heaviness of a broken spirit, and of pining and palsying faculties, settled slowly on her buoyant youth. Winter seemed conquering her spring: the mind's soil and its treasures were freezing gradually to barren stagnation. (I.10, 158)

This language reminds us that the novel is set in a time of war and want. Caroline's wasting mirrors the wasting of the working-class community; the word 'conquer' hints at the continuing conflict at home and abroad. The aural references imply Caroline's identification with Robert: her internal monologue obsessively voices his name; she hears her own agony resounding and is forced to listen to it, without speaking aloud. Elegy is not simply the yearning recognition of loss, it is also repetition:

a record endlessly looping. Caroline does not suffer dissociation until her final breakdown; her memory is not yet compromised. However, Brontë anticipates this final breakdown. Caroline's attentiveness is propelled by wishful fantasy: 'Life wastes fast in such vigils as Caroline had of late but too often kept; vigils during which the mind, – having no pleasant food to nourish it – no manna of hope – no hived-honey of joyous memories – tries to live on the meagre diet of wishes, and failing to derive thence either delight or support' (II.9, 295). Freud differentiates mourning and melancholia through one distinguishing feature: in melancholia, the loss of the other becomes loss of self. The grieving subject identifies with the lost object and berates her—altered—self for her failures. We see a similar mechanism in Caroline: recollecting the moment when she begged a curl of hair from Robert, she tells Shirley, 'It was my doing, and one of those silly deeds it distresses the heart and sets the face on fire to think of: one of those small but sharp recollections that return, lacerating your self-respect like tiny penknives, and forcing from your lips, as you sit alone, sudden, insane-sounding interjections' (194). Caroline retrospectively constructs and internalises Robert's critical gaze, and this gaze lacerates her. She sees herself in the third person: her conscience (not easily separated from the internal version of Robert) punishes her violently for this innocent loving act. Considering the likelihood of Robert marrying Shirley, Caroline thinks 'Truly, I ought not to have been born: they should have smothered me at the first cry' (I.2, 197). The loss of Robert points back to the primary problem: Caroline's early separation from her mother. The use of the word 'they' is evasive: Caroline seems to imagine a murderous parental force—referring to both father and mother.

Caroline can only identify with her mother by thinking of her neglectful and cruel father; or alternatively, through her emotionally detached uncle and the servants who disliked her. This means that her grief becomes stultified and frozen: 'These expressions were ice to the daughter's heart; they suggested the conclusion that it was perhaps better never to know her parent, than to know her and not like her' (159). Kristeva (1989) argues that clinical depression (or melancholy) results from the failure to mourn the loss of the Maternal Thing and inability to 'recover' the mother in language. The connection between maternal loss and the crisis in language is of relevance here: 'they should have smothered me at the first cry' (*Shirley*, I.2, 197). Caroline is able to articulate a place for her mother in her thoughts prior to losing Robert, albeit in a very liminal and suspended fashion. Caroline's subsequent silencing drives her desire for her mother's presence, but likewise makes such a desire painful and prohibited: it is a 'dread'. Her maternal longing is entombed: walled up in the 'windowed grave' (II.12, 335) of the parsonage, which—despite its material comforts—reminds us of the bare attic room in which James Helstone locked and abandoned her as a child. Grim spaces encompass Caroline's longing for her mother. The 'leprous memory' (III.3, 377) of her childhood stands between them.

Paternal Debts

The debts, which Robert inherits from his father and grandfather, lead to his unfeeling response to his rebellious workers. The narrator carefully (if awkwardly) delineates Robert's mercantile ancestry and the disaster he inherits after the 'shock of the French Revolution' (I.2, 25). Through Robert, Brontë explores the interrelation of the personal and the historical. As a child, he is exposed to the Revolution's tremors: 'if a childhood passed at the side of a saturnine mother, under foreboding of coming evil, and a manhood drenched and blighted by the pitiless descent of the storm, could painfully impress the mind, *his* probably was impressed in no golden characters' (25). While Robert remains relatively aloof from the reader throughout the novel, this passage indicates that we should read Robert, like Caroline, as a wounded child. His mother's depression writes on his mind, the word saturnine signifying poisoning as well as more general gloom (*OED*). Growing up in this atmosphere, he attempts to compensate for paternal dishonour, but in so doing, he replicates it by rejecting Caroline and offending Shirley. By overvaluing the financial debt, itself an emotional inheritance from his mother, he becomes responsible for a far worse wound.

It is logical, then, that the 'cure' for Robert comes from within the familial structure, and—indirectly—from the influence of another mother. Family does not stand outside of business, but, as the ending of the novel reminds us, underpins it. Just as in *Coriolanus*, women intervene. Brontë implies that although History (with a capital 'H') traditionally works to silence female endeavour and social participation, so-called leisured middle-class women are actively involved in their communities. Further, this involvement does not wholly exclude the movement of capital, despite the negation of separate female property in the nineteenth century. This point may not be radical in class terms, but (remembering Leonore Davidoff and Catherine Hall's [2002] argument) in *gendered* class terms, Brontë's intervention is important. However, the contrast between Shirley's and Caroline's stories shows that without some degree of financial independence, single middle-class women engage with their communities through self-abnegation: unlike working-class women, they cannot accrue personal property through their labour. (It is significant that William Farren's wife sets up a successful business thanks to the small loan received from Mr. Hall.) This problem is demonstrated through the 'Jew-basket'. The ladies of the neighbourhood each contribute goods for the basket 'sold perforce to the heathenish gentlemen thereof, at prices unblushingly exorbitant' (I.7, 96). The 'feebler souls' in the neighbourhood 'would rather see the prince of darkness himself [...] than that phantom basket' (ibid.). The basket is phantom-like, not only because it haunts the unwilling women of the neighbourhood, but also because its value is fantasised.[24] Shirley earns her freedom from the phantom Jew-basket because of her self-consciously masculine position in the world.

Shirley reveals the limitations placed on female collective action, while showing the critical role women play in the community. When Shirley sets out to distribute her money amongst the poor, the parsons must ratify Miss Ainley's scheme. For Caroline, positioned as she is, autonomy is correlated with paid employment, which means becoming a governess or teacher. Significantly, the governess trade is directly associated with a *paternal* problem. Attempting to dissuade Caroline from becoming a governess, Mrs. Pryor repeats the words of her first employer's daughter, Miss Hardman: 'WE need the imprudencies, extravagances, mistakes and crimes of a certain number of fathers to sow the seed from which WE reap the harvest of governesses' (II.2, 317). This statement sits uneasily in *Shirley:* despite Miss Hardman's coldness and snobbery, the novel partially legitimises this view. James Helstone's drunken debauchery, coupled with the fact Mr. Helstone has spent his £5000 fortune on building a church (apparently as a vanity project), means that Caroline will inherit nothing.

[24] Karl Marx writes, 'There [in religion] the products of the human brain appear as autonomous figures endowed with a life of their own, which enter into relations both with each other and with the human race. So it is in the world of commodities with the products of men's hands. I call this the fetishism [...]' (1990, 165).

She has little to look forward to beyond dependency and liminality—whether she becomes a governess or stays at home.[25,26]

Brontë, through Caroline, questions the position of women: the historical novel form provokes an interrogation of mid-Victorian conditions. Importantly, the limitations placed on middle-class female labour are correlated with paternal failure and debt. This is an ambivalent gesture: on the one hand, Brontë recognises the devastating restrictions placed on women, but on the other, Caroline directs a plea towards fathers to resolve the situation by appealing to their self-interest:

> Fathers! cannot you alter these things? [...] Keep your girls' minds narrow and fettered – they will still be a plague and a care, sometimes a disgrace to you: cultivate them – give them scope and work – they will be your gayest companions in health; your tenderest nurses in sickness; your most faithful prop in age. (II.11, 330)

As a devoted reader of Shakespeare, it is appropriate that Caroline's reflections take the form of soliloquy and political rhetoric. The idea of restraint—the 'narrow and fettered' minds—raises the shadow of the attic room in which James Helstone locked Caroline. Caroline's plea to fathers consolidates a Victorian norm: women are the adjunct to men, their 'gayest companions' and 'nurses'. Caroline proposes a solution through which every woman can become King Lear's ideal daughter. But Shakespeare is more radical than this. Lear's desire to set his rest in Cordelia's 'kind nursery' (I.1, 125) is shown to be narcissistic and wounding; her silence, or 'Nothing', is not self-abnegation, but rebellion and truth. *Shirley* does not present a unified vision; therefore despite the controlling narrative voice, and the novel's suppression of working-class voices, there is *latent* polyphony, albeit of a very specific and limited form. Caroline's plea for paternal intervention is not answered: it is a woman and a mother who heals the damage caused by fathers, while also making reparation for her own faults. We *are* taken back to a 'kind nursery', but one in

[25] Miss Hardman's statement ignores the possibility of social mobility. Patrick Brontë came from a poor farming family in Ireland before attending Cambridge University. He was an entirely self-made man: because of this, his middle-class daughters had to work.

[26] Lucy R. (one of the Freud's case histories in *Studies on Hysteria*, discussed in Chapter 2) was also a young dependent woman: her hysterical symptoms appeared to result from the psychological conflict engendered by her liminal position in the household, and the messages she received from her own, and her employer's, family.

which mother and daughter are reunited. Carolyn Dever (1998) argues that the Victorian idealisation of the mother emerges in relation to her absence and effacement; this model, certainly prevalent in the period, does not apply to *Shirley* in any straightforward fashion, unless we read Maria Brontë's absence as the provocative force for the novel. It is James and Caroline who are presented as spectral. The reunion between mother and daughter is romanticised, but their separate identities are recognised. Mrs. Pryor is shown to be a faulty individual in her own right. Brontë uses nursing as a trope to show the return to child-like state of dependency, in which the traumatic wounds of the past must be worked through.

Maternal Blessings

In 'The Valley of the Shadow of Death', Brontë presents Caroline's illness and redemption: the narrator opens with the apocalyptic vision of the sobbing wind, circles around the other characters' responses to Caroline's illness and then settles her gaze on the intimate space of the sickroom. Brontë focalises the narrative through Mrs. Pryor's careful watching: Caroline's 'consummated debility puzzled all who witnessed it, except one' (III.1, 354); 'These things were not unnoted by Mrs. Pryor' (354); 'Mrs. Pryor had long sight; she knew Mr. Moore' (355). These instances culminate when Mrs. Pryor overhears Caroline's anguished 'soliloquy' (357):

> Is it for nothing the wind sounds almost articulately sometimes – sings as I have lately heard it sing at night – or passes the casement sobbing, as if for sorrow to come? Does nothing, then, haunt it – nothing inspire it? [...] What are all those influences that are about us in the atmosphere, that keep playing over our nerves like fingers on stringed instruments, and call forth now a sweet note, and now a wail – now an exultant swell, and, anon, the saddest cadence?
>
> *Where* is the other world? In *what* will another life consist?

The presence of Coleridge is felt: the aching strains of 'Dejection: An Ode' reverberate (just as earlier in Robert's parlour we heard happy echoes of 'The Eolian Harp'). Caroline, like Coleridge's poetic speaker in 'The Eolian Harp' and the first stanza of 'Dejection: an Ode', sees herself as a harp to be played—her nerves are tightened and taut.[27] This language is in tune with the burgeoning of physiological discourse at the mid century. William Carpenter's *Principles of Human Physiology* was in its third edition in the year *Shirley* was published.[28] There is no contradiction in this combination of influences. The first version of 'The Eolian Harp' (1798) owed much to David Hartley's theory of associationism presented in *Observations on Man* (1749).[29] Hartley proposed that sensations result from the vibration of the nerves; these sensations coalesce into ideas through association.

Caroline's predicament, delicately as it is rendered, echoes Cathy's in *Wuthering Heights*. Like Cathy, she wanders in delirium fixating on her lost love. Mrs. Pryor uncovers the locket in which Caroline keeps a lock of Robert's hair; her fingers 'clasped as usual her jealously-guarded treasure' (355). On waking, she cries out 'Don't take it from me, Robert! Don't! It is my last comfort – let me keep it. I never tell any one whose hair it is – I never show it' (355). Caroline's love, like Cathy's, is articulated in a dissociated state of consciousness. Like Cathy, Caroline sees herself as a ghost. The hallucinated image of Caroline in the counting house window reminds us that earlier Robert said that he would imagine her standing there. Her hallucination is therefore a wishful fantasy, which directly responds to his words:

> 'I smelt the honeysuckles in the glen this summer-morning,' she said, 'as I stood at the counting-house window [...] I went in to call Robert to breakfast: I have been with him in the garden: he asked me to go: a heavy dew has refreshed the flowers: the peaches are ripening'. (357)

Cathy imagines herself back at Wuthering Heights, sobbing alone in bed. Caroline imagines herself *with* Robert, but even so her separation from him is felt: 'I have been with him in the garden: he asked me to go'. This passage brings their traumatic moment of separation back into the present moment. Her hallucination veils and encodes this memory. Becoming calm and lucid once more, Caroline speaks of her father's grave: 'When

[27] Importantly, of course, 'Dejection: an Ode' questions the model established in the earlier poem. Nature *fails* to play the poetic speaker.

[28] The British publication dates of the first five editions were 1842, 1844, 1846, 1853, 1855.

[29] 'Dejection: an Ode' reveals the shift in Coleridge's thought.

I close my eyes, I seem to see poor papa's epitaph in black letters on the white marble. There is plenty of room for other inscriptions underneath' (359). Caroline anticipates her own epitaph, placed subserviently beneath her father's; she is defined by his destructive legacy. This epitaph is written across her consciousness.

Charlotte Brontë establishes the parallel with Emily Brontë's *mise-en-scène* in order to repair it. Cathy is watched (and doomed) by the shockingly uncompassionate Nelly Dean, while Caroline is saved by the intervention of her mother. Listening to her daughter drifting, Mrs. Pryor is penetrated: 'Strange words like these from pallid lips pierce a loving listener's heart more poignantly than steel. They sound romantic, perhaps, in books: in real life, they are harrowing' (357). The trauma is transmitted from daughter to mother. The scene increases in physical intensity: 'Some minutes passed in silence. The patient lay mute and passive in the trembling arms – on the throbbing bosom of the nurse' (358). Mrs. Pryor trembles under the close influence of her daughter's presence. Brontë sustains this language when describing Mrs. Pryor's song, which 'trembled' with the 'tender vibration from a feeling heart' (359). In deploying this language of vibrations, Brontë creates a linguistic bridge between the happy scene in Robert's cottage and this moment. Mrs. Pryor's loving but mournful influence, heard resonating in her voice, supersedes the terrifying sobbing of the wind, which presaged Caroline's impending death, and the traumatic return of the past:

> No wonder Caroline liked to hear her sing: her voice, even in speaking, was sweet and silver-clear; in song, it was almost divine: neither flute not dulcimer has tones so pure. But the tone was secondary compared to the expression which trembled through: a tender vibration from a feeling heart. (359)

Even the cold-hearted Mr. Helstone is affected by this song: 'Why it reminded him of his forgotten dead wife, he could not tell; nor why it made him more concerned than he had hitherto been for Caroline's fading girlhood' (359). Mrs. Pryor's song is elegiac: it enables mourning of the past. Brontë once more uses aural detail to great effect. Caroline's internal monologue becomes repetitive, fixated, continually voicing Robert's name: 'a funereal inward cry haunted and harassed her' (I.10, 158). Her grief is perpetually *heard*, but silenced: Mrs. Pryor's song heals.

Women take a central role in mourning in *Shirley*, *North and South*, and *The Mill on the Floss*, but nevertheless, the dynamic of mourning presented in *Shirley* differs from what we see in Elizabeth Gaskell's and George Eliot's novels. For both of these authors, mourning the past effectively means moving outwards. In *Shirley*, the movement is reversed: mourning is private and enclosed. Before confessing her identity, Mrs. Pryor, 'glided to the door, softly turned the key in the lock' (361). She asserts the intimate physical connection between herself and Caroline: 'it will be neither shock nor pain for you to know that *that* heart is the source whence yours was filled; that from *my* veins issued the tide which flows in *yours*; that you are *mine* – my daughter – my own child'. This bodily affinity drives Caroline's recovery: 'I bore you – nursed you' (361). Mrs. Pryor's positive affirmation of motherhood as a bodily experience, the source of redemptive love, feels quite different from anything we see in Dickens's or Collins's novels, although Gaskell's *North and South* contains comparable moments. The mother is not spectral, she is flesh: she is not an abstract ideal; she is a person. The sheltered space of the sickroom rewrites the enclosure that has defined Caroline thus far. Rather than her being locked into a bare space by herself, as she was in childhood by her father, she is 'softly' locked in with her mother. The 'moonlight' shines into the room, creating a feeling of purity and even grace. As previously argued, *Shirley* is concerned with finding safe spaces of feminine articulation, and this scene is the culmination of that search. However, Brontë's use of the name Agnes Grey for Mrs. Pryor's maiden name undoubtedly creates a textual hauntology. She reveals the name at two different moments, separated by fifty pages (II.10, 317; III.1, 367). It is a suspended revelation and does not impact upon the novel's world. For the reader, though, Brontë carefully encodes the loss of her sister Anne and validates her sister's writing. The revelation that Mrs. Pryor's Christian name is Agnes is not made until the third volume, by which time Anne Brontë was dead. The redemptive quality of this sickroom scene is counterpoised by Charlotte Brontë's use of *Wuthering Heights* and *Agnes Grey*: Caroline recovers; Emily and Anne haunt.

In a decisive passage, Mrs. Pryor accepts her daughter verbally for the first time:

> James Helstone was *my* husband. I say you are *mine*. I have proved it. I thought perhaps you were all his, which would have been a cruel dispensation for me: I find it is *not* so. God permitted me to be the parent of my

> child's mind: it belongs to me: it is my property – my *right*. These features are James's own. He had a fine face when he was young, and not altered by error. Papa, my darling, gave you your blue eyes and soft brown hair: he gave you the oval of your face and the regularity of your lineaments: the outside *he* conferred; but the heart and the brain are *mine*: the germs are from *me*, and they are improved, they are developed to excellence. I esteem and approve my child as highly as I do most fondly love her. (362)

Mrs. Pryor's reaffirms the possibility of maternal property: she lays claim to her daughter's subjectivity. Bearing in mind the novel's (fragmentary) proto-feminist discourse, this feels heavily laden: she asserts her rights of property and her own separate identity through her daughter. However, her claim ignores the haunting presence of James Helstone in Caroline's consciousness: the epitaph written across her eyes. Mrs. Pryor's knowledge of James Helstone necessarily exceeds Caroline's: 'it was my lot to witness a transfiguration on the domestic hearth: to see the white mask lifted, the bright disguise put away, and opposite me sat down – oh God! I *have* suffered!' (363). *Shirley* gestures towards Shakespeare's *The Winter's Tale*; the novel relies on the mother's resurrection, and this is inseparable from the father's crimes. However, Brontë plays with the source: Caroline has become frozen and statue-like, and it is the living, 'trembling', mother who revivifies her:

> You *must* recover. You drew life and strength from my breast when you were a tiny, fair infant, over whose blue eyes I used to weep, fearing I beheld in your very beauty the sign of qualities that had entered my heart like iron, and pierced through my soul like a sword. Daughter! we have been long parted: I return now to cherish you again. (III.1, 362)

In this potentially shocking confession, we learn that the daughter's resemblance to the father traumatised, 'pierced', the mother and led to her later rejection of her; the marital abuse Mrs. Pryor experiences impacts on the bond with her baby. She relates how Mr. Helstone, 'and all the world thought hardly of me for my strange, unmotherly resolve, and I deserved to be misjudged' (365).[30] Mrs. Pryor's paranoiac response is propelled by her experiences as a governess. She insists upon the validity of her own pain: 'I *have* suffered! None saw, – none knew: there was

[30] George Lewes complained that no mother would be capable of such feelings; Brontë found his review 'very brutal and savage' (Barker 2010, 725).

no sympathy – no redemption – no redress!' (363). This reminds us that Caroline, in reality, is not so disadvantaged. Both Mrs. Pryor and Shirley watch over her. The reunion complicates our understanding of what cross-generational traumatisation might involve. The dynamism of the trauma is doubled—passed and then passed back from the elder to the younger.

Caroline is opened to her mother's influence. Brontë presents this in positive and idealised terms; returning to infant-hood physically heals Caroline:

> The off-spring nestled to the parent: that parent, feeling the endearment and hearing the appeal, gathered her closer still. She covered her with noiseless kisses: she murmured love over her, like a cushat fostering its young.
>
> There was silence in the room for a long while. (362)

This is the source for a wider process of healing. Mrs. Pryor redeems the paternal 'debt':

> James, slumber peacefully! See! your terrible debt is cancelled! Look! I wipe out the long, black account with my own hand! James, your child atones: this living likeness of you – this thing with your perfect features – this one good gift you gave me has nestled affectionately to my heart, and tenderly called me 'mother'. Husband! rest forgiven! (364)

The mother's blessing of the father heals the daughter, and the daughter makes the mother reparation. Soothing Mrs. Pryor's grief: 'the child lulled the parent, as the parent had erst lulled the child' (364). Cross-gendered parental conflict drives the child's traumatisation throughout the mid-Victorian novel. This moment of forgiveness is therefore, in many ways, the emotional climax of *Shirley*, and it is not surprising that Brontë moves away from Caroline after this point: her story is worked through. Mrs. Pryor's forgiveness of James Helstone means that Caroline is also permitted to forgive him: as Shirley pertinently observes, Caroline's 'natural tears' (377), now flowing and no longer 'ice' (I.11, 159), 'cleanse' a leprous memory' (III.3, 377). Even Mr. Helstone is briefly humanised after the reunion: 'he stooped over her pillow, kissed her, and said with a broke, rugged accent, – "Good-night, bairnie! God bless thee!"' (III.1, 368).

Nursing is a larger trope in *Shirley*. Robert's incompetent nursing in the Yorke household is contrasted to Caroline's delicate nursing at the hands of her mother. Robert is punished by being brought back to a state of infant dependency and being brutally handled by an uncaring woman. Caroline and Robert's stories work contrapuntally. Caroline is saved by the reappearance of her mother; her nullification is repaired through her validating gaze and presence. This means Caroline, in turn, is able to heal Robert. Her visit to his sick chamber, aided and abetted by the charming teenage schemer, Martin Yorke, is the turning point in Robert's recovery. Robert is put on trial; in another locked room, he relives Caroline's own enclosure and restraint in order to become worthy of her: 'I despaired of ever seeing you again. Weakness has wrought terrible depression in me – terrible depression' (III.10, 488). The wind, 'wuthering' 'wildly', is not heard by the couple: 'each seemed conscious but of one thing – the presence of the other' (487). Their stories echo, and Robert repents:

> Moore sighed – a sigh so deep, it was nearly a groan: he covered his eyes with his hand.
> 'May I be spared to make some atonement!'
> Such was his prayer. (489)

Kissing his hand, Caroline releases Robert's grief: a 'large tear or two coursed down his hollow cheek' (489). This is a moment of catharsis: his 'large tear' is similar to the redemptive 'natural tears' Caroline sheds for her father. The past is acknowledged and mourned; male debts are redeemed. The reader is left in little doubt that the couple will be granted a happy ending, but this ending remains inseparable from the mother-daughter reunion. In the proposal scene, Brontë physically manoeuvres Caroline from daughter to lover: looking up at the night sky, Caroline mistakes Robert's touch for that of Mrs. Pryor:

> 'I am looking at Venus, mama: see, she is beautiful. How white her lustre is, compared with the deep red of the bonfires!'
> The answer was a closer caress; and Caroline turned, and looked, not into Mrs. Pryor's matron face, but up at a dark manly visage. (III.14, 535)

Caroline does not invest 'all her universe' (I.7, 95) in Robert again. When she marries, Mrs. Pryor comes with her. Robert, in his turn, discusses his marital plans with Mrs. Pryor before formally proposing to Caroline. The maternal blessing enables the mourning of loss, the restitution of the wider family and forwards the romance plot. This contrasts with the ending to *Jane Eyre*: the insularity of Jane and Rochester's life at Ferndean uneasily perpetuates the idea that romantic love and kinship are equivalent. *Shirley* complicates this concept through Robert, Caroline and Mrs. Pryor, only to reinscribe it through Louis and Shirley.

Eva

Despite giving the novel its name, Shirley's history is repeatedly effaced: like her supposed real-life counterpart Emily Brontë we know very little about her. Shirley's privacy is jealously guarded, not only by the character herself, but also by the third-person narrator. There are two stories in *Shirley*: the one, idealised, mythic and erotic (associated with Shirley); and the other, pragmatic and pained (associated with Caroline). However, these two modes of representation share the same space and are blurred through the young women's friendship. Shirley and Caroline's adopted sisterhood is presented as a source of emotional and aesthetic value: 'The minds of the two girls being toned in harmony, often chimed very sweetly together' (II.1, 189). Their love for one another is based in a shared sensibility; a shared openness to the influence of nature and literature:

> Shirley sat at the window, watching the rack in heaven, the mist on earth, listening to certain notes of the gale that plained like restless spirits – notes which, had she not been so young, gay, and healthy, would have swept her trembling nerves like some omen, some anticipatory dirge: in this her prime of her existence and bloom of beauty, they but subdued vivacity to pensiveness. Snatches of sweet ballads haunted her ear; now and then she sang a stanza: her accents obeyed the fitful impulse of the wind; (189)

The intertextual echo of *Wuthering Heights* is heard here; Shirley's difference from Cathy and Heathcliff is established through her ability to heal the 'fitful impulse of the wind' through her attentive listening. This anticipates the later representation of Mrs. Pryor in 'The Valley of the Shadow of Death', in which Caroline is at the mercy of the wind's wuthering. Here, Shirley responds to the gale by joining her voice with its own in song. Caroline, herself inspired, recites William Cowper's poem, 'The Castaway': she 'vividly' 'realized the heart of the poet' (190). Both women are creative: Caroline is presented as an attentive, sensitive, even philosophical reader. Responding to Shirley's question as to who taught her to analyse Cowper and Rousseau, she replies: 'Why should anybody have told me? Have I not an instinct? Can I not define by analogy? Moore never talked to me either about Cowper, or Rousseau, or love. The voice we hear in solitude told me all I know on these subjects' (191). The narrator presents Shirley as an artist, but an unfulfilled one: 'If Shirley were not an indolent, a reckless, ignorant being, she would take a pen at such moments [...] she would take a good-sized sheet of paper and write plainly out, in her own queer but legible hand, the story that has been narrated, the song that has been sung to her, and thus possess what she was able to create'. She will 'die without knowing, the full value of that spring' within her (II.11, 326). The female novelist—Brontë—must recuperate and mourn the incompletion of female history.

Shirley presents a double vision. Caroline's story is founded on a primal trauma, operating like a screen memory: the scene in the attic compacts Caroline's childhood conflicts and fears into one paradigmatic moment. When Robert rejects her, this enclosure is reactivated, and she is immured once more. For much of the novel, Shirley provides the foil to Caroline's unhappiness: 'Fate had been benign to the blissful dreamer, and promised to favour her yet again' (II.1, 195). However, the narrative shifts following Caroline's recovery; Brontë reframes female identity through Shirley's mythic account: her French *devoir*. Femininity is conceived in relation to male generative power. Speaking to Caroline, Shirley says: 'the minutest spark of His spirit lifts them almost above mortality. Indisputably, a great, good, handsome man is the first of created things' (183). This fantasy is realised in Shirley's relationship with Louis. Shirley's childhood cannot be analysed in the same way as Caroline's. We know little concerning the death of her parents, and her early life with her aunt and uncle, and what we do learn comes from Henry. However, this does not mean that her early life is simply irrelevant: it is the motive force of her love for Louis. It is only when we read her mythic story that we realise that she may have been vulnerable and unhappy. Louis is more than lover, and more than teacher: he is Promethean. This complicates the novel's treatment of gender. Caroline's story serves to undermine the primacy of the male and paternal; Shirley insists upon primeval maternal power *and* recuperates masculine agency. The authenticity of feminine erotic fantasy is reasserted, while this fantasy, through a sleight of hand, allows Shirley to affirm the validity of female creativity.

Shirley's affirmation of primal maternal power is simultaneous with Caroline's longing for her absent mother. Shirley represents Nature as the first woman: 'she is like what Eve was when she and Adam stood alone on earth' (II.7, 269). Shirley, deploying (in Caroline's words) a 'hash of Scripture and mythology', criticises John Milton's representation of Eve: 'I would beg to remind him that the first men of the earth were Titans, and that Eve was their mother: from her sprang Saturn, Hyperion, Oceanus; she bore Prometheus'; 'The first woman was heaven-born: vast was the heart whence gushed the well-spring of the blood of nations' (270). Shirley's grandiose vision contrasts with Caroline's:

> Shirley had mentioned the word 'mother:' that word suggested to Caroline's imagination not the mighty and mystical parent of Shirley's visions, but a gentle human form – the form she ascribed to her own mother: unknown, unloved, but not unlonged for. (271)

Bearing in mind women's lack of legal rights in the mid-nineteenth century, Shirley's representation of primaeval maternal power could appear painfully ironic. *Shirley* self-consciously moves between 'Elf-Land'—the joyous realm of fantasy—and the 'shores of Reality' (I.7, 83), a motion driven through Caroline and Shirley, and their maternal visions. In this scene, Brontë provides a clue as to how we should read this: Shirley's mythic narrative provides a safe *imaginative* space in which Caroline can articulate—internally—her longing for her mother for the first time: listening to Shirley's vision, the 'desire' for her mother is 'relit'; it 'glowed warm in her heart' (II.7, 271). Elf-land serves a curative function.

However, these ideas are complicated by the *devoir.* Shirley represents a lost child in a primaeval English landscape: 'There is one in this tribe too often miserable, – a child bereaved of both parents. None cares for this child: she is fed sometimes, but oftener forgotten: a hut rarely receives her; the hollow tree and chill cavern are her home' (III.4, 406).[31] This girl is a 'desolate young savage […] On the evening of one summer day, before the Flood' (406). She feels herself 'the centre' of everything: '– a small forgotten atom of life, a spark of soul, emitted inadvertent from the great creative source, and now burning unmarked to waste in the heart

[31] The tone of Shirley's vision is comparable to Felicia Hemans's poem 'The Indian Woman's Death Song' in which the speaker calls to the 'father of waves' (l.27) to 'roll on' (l.20) and take her and her baby to death. In 1842, Brontë gave an inscribed copy of Hemans's *Songs of the Affections and other Poems* to her friend Ellen Nussey, now in The Brontë Society's collection at Haworth.

of a black hollow' (407). A spark of divine creativity—lost in the wilderness: 'her living light doing no good, never seen, never needed' (ibid.). She cries for help: 'At last, one over-stretched chord of her agony slacked: she thought Something above relented: she felt as if Something far round drew nigher: she heard as if Silence spoke. There was no language, no word, only a tone' (ibid.). This 'deep, soft, sound, like a storm whispering' (ibid.) speaks a name: 'Eva!' (408). The male divinity interpellates the girl, and she responds: 'The dark hint, the obscure whisper, which have haunted me from childhood, are interpreted. Thou art He I sought. God-born, take me, thy bride!' (408).

In highly stylised terms, the girl is formed by the other's message: in this case, the whisperings of male Genius. When Caroline pleads for paternal intervention, for a benevolent male to protest against female enclosure and restraint, her pleas go unanswered. Instead, Mrs. Pryor saves her and legitimises her marriage to Robert. In the *devoir*, we see the female cry answered by deep masculine tones: 'I come: a Comforter' (408). In the gospel of St. John, 'Comforter' refers to the Holy Spirit (14:16–17). This masculine power is divine (although it is not God the 'Maker' [409]): the girl's 'spark of soul' has been 'emitted' 'from the great creative source'. Shirley's rewriting of Genesis is conservative and radical: Eva is a fragment of a larger divinity, and this divinity is presented as masculine. However, the *devoir* also presents the first woman as a creative being. Her genesis—'emitted inadvertent from the great creative source'—is reminiscent of Athene's birth from the brain of Zeus. The title of the chapter in which the *devoir* is presented, 'The First Blue-Stocking', wryly (perhaps ironically) points us towards a specifically female and proto-feminist history.

Shirley's treatment of myth is complex: in the *devoir*, feminised Humanity is presented as a fragment of masculine divine Genius (a Promethean image); however, by referring to Pygmalion, Shirley presents women as a function of male creativity. As the novel moves to its conclusion, the Pygmalion paradigm becomes more dominant.[32] Arguing with Louis after reading out her *devoir*, defending her aloofness, Shirley says: 'One man in times of old, it is said, imparted vitality to the statue he had chiselled. Others may have the contrary gift of turning life to stone' (412). Louis's voice—expressed through his diary—takes control of events. Like

[32] It is worth remembering that Shirley insists earlier that Eve bore Prometheus: Shirley is defined by masculine power, but does not simply accept its generative primacy.

Mrs. Pryor, he is a careful watcher: he guarantees Shirley's identity. In the *devoir*, the male Genius's voice 'vibrated through her heart like music' (409): this moment echoes the language used to describe Mrs. Pryor's song. Considering Caroline in his diary, Louis writes: 'There she is, a lily of the valley, untinted, needing no tint. What change could improve her? What pencil dare to paint?' His desire for Shirley is artistic and controlling. He wishes to 'touch up' areas that are lacking: 'she must be curbed' (III.6, 439). As we also see in *Jane Eyre*, there is a (not particularly) latent sado-masochism in Brontë's erotic vision. Through Louis and Shirley's courtship, the novel situates pedagogical erotics in the place of *parental* power.[33] This gendered power play complicates Shirley's earlier evocation of Eve as the primaeval force of nature. However, Louis's description of himself as 'Adam's son' (III.3, 383) reveals the couple's shared fantasy. Their courtship is placed in Eden; it is granted all the force of originality—of being first. Robert and Caroline express their love through shared fantasies of haunting, relating back to their compromised parental inheritances. Louis and Shirley's Edenic visions seem like a denial of history—a denial of cross-generational *determination*. We cannot quite synthesise the novel's doubled vision. And neither—I argue—are we meant to. Elf-Land and Reality are permitted to coexist.

Works Cited

Literary Texts

Aeschylus. 1984. *The Oresteia: Agamemnon; The Libation Bearers; The Eumenides*. Translated by Robert Fagles. Edited by W. B. Stanford. London: Penguin.

Brontë, Anne. 2008. *Agnes Grey*. Edited by Robert Inglesfield and Hilda Marsden. Oxford: Oxford University Press.

———. 1996. *The Tenant of Wildfell Hall*. Edited by Stevie Davies. London: Penguin.

Brontë, Charlotte. 2008. *Jane Eyre*. Edited by Margaret Smith. Oxford: Oxford University Press.

———. 2008. *Shirley*. Edited by Herbert Rosengarten and Margaret Smith. Oxford: Oxford University Press.

[33] This manoeuvre refers back to Brontë's unrequited love for Monsieur Constantin Héger, her married teacher in Brussels.

———. 2008. *Villette*. Edited by Margaret Smith. Oxford: Oxford University Press.
———. 1916. 'The Violet'. London: Privately printed by Clement Shorter. http://contentdm.baylor.edu/cdm/ref/collection/ab-wpc/id/96789.
Brontë, Emily. 2008. *Wuthering Heights*. Edited by Ian Jack. Oxford: Oxford University Press.
———. 1992. *The Complete Poems*. Edited by Janet Gezari. London: Penguin.
Carlyle, Thomas. 1971. *Past and Present*. In *Selected Writings*, edited by Alan Shelston, 257–312. Harmondsworth: Penguin.
Chaucer, Geoffrey. 1872. 'The Parlement of Briddes, or the Assembly of Foules'. In *The Poetical Works of Geoffrey Chaucer*, edited by Richard Morris. Vol. 4, 51–74. London: Bell and Daldy.
Coleridge, Samuel Taylor. 2002. *Coleridge's Poetry and Prose*. Edited by Nicholas Halmi, Paul Magnuson and Raimonda Mondiano. New York: W. W. Norton.
Eliot, George. 1981. *The Mill on the Floss*. Edited by George Haight. Oxford: Oxford University Press.
Gaskell, Elizabeth. 1971. *The Life of Charlotte Brontë*. London: Everyman.
———. 2008. *North and South*. Edited by Angus Easson. Oxford: Oxford University Press.
Hemans, Felicia. 1875. *The Poems of Felicia Hemans*. London and Edinburgh: William P. Nimmo.
Hogg, James. 2001. *Private Memoirs and Confessions of a Justified Sinner*. Edited by Adrian Hunter. Ontario: Broadview Literary Texts.
James, Henry. 1992. *The Turn of the Screw and Other Stories*. Edited by T. J. Lustig. Oxford: Oxford University Press.
Ovid. 1826. *Ovid's Metamorphoses: Translated by Various Authors*. Translated by John Dryden et al. London.
Shakespeare, William. 2008. *The Norton Shakespeare*. Edited by Stephen Greenblatt. London and New York: W. W. Norton.
Sophocles. 1984. *The Three Theban Plays*. Translated by Robert Fagles. Rev. ed. London: Penguin.
Wordsworth, William. 1984. *The Major Works*, edited by Stephen Gill. Oxford: Oxford University Press.

Primary Psychoanalytic Texts

Abbreviations

SE: *The Standard Edition of the Complete Psychological Works of Sigmund Freud*. 2001. Translated from the German under the general editorship of James Strachey, in collaboration with Anna Freud and assisted by Alix Strachey and Allan Tyson. London: Vintage.

Abraham, Nicolas and Maria Torok. 1994. 'The Topography of Reality: Sketching a Metapsychology of Secrets'. In Nicholas Abraham and Maria Torok, *The Shell and the Kernel: Renewals of Psychoanalysis*. Edited and translated by Nicholas Rand, 157–161. Chicago: University of Chicago Press.

Breuer, Josef and Sigmund Freud. 2001. *Studies on Hysteria*. *SE* 2.

Freud, Sigmund. *Beyond the Pleasure Principle*. *SE* 18:3–64.

———. 'Mourning and Melancholia'. *SE* 14:237–260.

———. 'A Project for a Scientific Psychology'. *SE* 1:283–397.

———. 'Screen Memories'. *SE* 3:301–322.

———. 'The Unconscious'. *SE* 14:161–215.

Kristeva, Julia. 1989. *Black Sun: Depression and Melancholia*. Translated by Leon S. Roudiez. New York: Columbia University Press.

Laplanche, Jean. 1999. 'Reference to the Unconscious'. In *The Unconscious and the Id*, translated by Luke Thurston and Lindsay Watson, 1–121. London: Rebus Press.

Secondary Texts

Auerhahn, Nanette and Dori Laub. 1998. 'The Primal Scene of Atrocity: The Dynamic Interplay between Knowledge and Fantasy of the Holocaust in the Children of Survivors'. *Psychoanalytic Psychology* 15, no. 3: 360–77.

Barker, Juliet. 2010 [1994] *The Brontës*. London: Abacus.

Carpenter, William. 1855. *Principles of Human Physiology: With their Chief Applications to Psychology, Pathology, Therapeutics, Hygiene and Forensic Medicine*. 5th ed. London: John Churchill.

Caruth, Cathy. 1996b. *Unclaimed Experience: Trauma, Narrative, History*. Baltimore: Johns Hopkins University Press.

Davidoff, Leonore and Catherine Hall. 2002. *Family Fortunes: Men and Women of the English Middle Class 1780–1850*. Rev. ed. London: Routledge.

Derrida, Jacques. 1976. Foreword: *Fors*: The Anglish Words of Nicholas Abraham and Maria Torok. In *The Wolf Man's Magic Word: A Cryptonymy*, translated by Nicholas Rand, xi–xlviii. Minneapolis: Minneapolis University Press.

Dever, Carolyn. 1998. *Death and the Mother from Dickens to Freud: Victorian Fictions and the Anxiety of Origins*. Cambridge: Cambridge University Press.

Hartley, David. 1834. *Observations on Man: His Frame, His Duty and His Expectations*. 6th ed. London: Thomas Tegg and Son.

Hillis Miller, J. 1982. *Fiction and Repetition: Seven English Novels*. Cambridge, MA: Harvard University Press.

Lukits, Steve. 2008. 'The Devastated Nest: Crises of Identity in *Wuthering Heights* and *Antigone*'. *Mosaic: A Journal for the Interdisciplinary Study of Literature* 41, no. 3 (September): 103–116.

Marx, Karl. 1990. *Capital.* Vol. 1, translated by Ben Fowks. London: Penguin.
Miller, Lucasta. 2001. *The Brontë Myth.* London: Vintage.
Nares, Robert. 1825. *A Glossary or, Collection of Words, Phrase, Names, Allusions to Customs, Proverbs, etc. in the Works of English Authors, Particularly of Shakespeare and his Contemporaries.* Stralsund: Charles Loeffler.
Thormählen, Marianne. 2014. *The Brontës in Context.* Cambridge: Cambridge University Press.
Vine, Steve, 1999. 'Crypts of Identity: The Refusal of Mourning in *Wuthering Heights*'. *English* 48, no. 192 (Autumn): 169–186.

CHAPTER 4

Charles Dickens—Lost Children and 'Primal Scenes': The 'Autobiographical Fragment', *Dombey and Son* and *Great Expectations*

Charles Dickens was well placed to understand the power of childhood trauma as numerous critics and biographers (beginning with John Forster, Dickens's friend and first biographer) have observed, and in his novels, he privileges childhood as the locale for the most profound traumatic events. Childhood was a focus in itself throughout his early and middle stage career: Dickens was passionately concerned about what it meant to be a child. From *Dombey and Son* (1848) onwards, he also represented childhood as a haunting presence within the adult subject, psychologising parent-child relationships in a new way. Both orphanhood and 'parental' failure (including the failure of surrogate or foster parents) are central to the plots of *Oliver Twist* (1838), *The Old Curiosity Shop* (1841), *Nicholas Nickleby* (1839) and *Martin Chuzzlewit* (1844); however, in *Dombey and Son* Dickens represents parent-child relationships in a state of psychological damage. This sense of damage is not limited to the Dombey family, but appears endemic to the structure as a whole.[1] Crucial to this change was Dickens's move towards greater narrative organisation and cohesion. Improvisation—such as the famous decision to move Martin Chuzzlewit to America to garner more readers—was replaced by greater discipline

[1] We do not have to see this as an abrupt change of direction, but as a continuation of a theme: in *Martin Chuzzlewit* the Chuzzlewits are characterised by their betrayals, hypocrisies and failures—this does not, however, become internalised in quite the same way as we see in *Dombey* through Paul and Florence.

M. Wood, *Parents and Children in the Mid-Victorian Novel*,
https://doi.org/10.1007/978-3-030-45469-2_4

in the composition of *Dombey and Son*. As the number plans to *Dombey* reveal, a specific temporal model was shaped in order to achieve this: a model in which traumatic repetition was central. This model was elaborated in his own 'autobiographical fragment', in which we see Dickens's self-conscious construction of a temporal model of selfhood. 'Traumatic' return (present in all but name) is created as both a narrative mode and as the core of subjectivity.

Like Jane Eyre, Cathy, Heathcliff and Hindley,[2] Dickens's protagonists (including, in his own account, himself) come into being through a state of delayed and repetitive wounding. Throughout the 1850s, Dickens explored comparable themes; each of his major novels returns in differential form to the parent-child relationship. Even *Hard Times* (1854) and *A Tale of Two Cities* (1859)—which stand out due to their shorter lengths, and more concise focuses—engage with this theme. *Hard Times* represents the persecutory parent-child relationship through the Gradgrind family: here, Dickens returns to the idea of parental 'forcing' so critical to *Dombey*. In *A Tale of Two Cities*, Dickens uses the idea of the maternal daughter (already of importance to *The Old Curiosity Shop* and *Dombey*, as well as lying at the heart of *Little Dorrit*) through Monsieur Manette and his daughter Lucie. However, the historical form undoubtedly alters the timbre of the latter as the primary trauma at stake is the revolution itself. His three longer novels of the 1850s, *David Copperfield*, *Bleak House* and *Little Dorrit*, extend and manipulate the idea of 'trauma' as a narrative mode, while remaining true to the idea that subjectivity is engendered or indeed prohibited by 'parental' acts (whether death, desertion, inheritance or ethical failure). Arthur Clennam is a striking example: his stepmother's intrusive religious ideology, in combination with the unknown loss of his real mother, engenders him as 'nobody': son of a 'hard father and mother', he tells Mr. Meagles that he has been 'Trained by main force; broken not bent, heavily ironed with an object on which I was never consulted and which was never mine' (Ch. 2, 20). In *Great Expectations*, Dickens foregrounds the problematisation of identity: he explores how 'children' (in infancy, youth and adulthood) are created, written-on, broken and nurtured by the elder generation, and in both *Dombey and Son* and *Great Expectations*, parental demands are represented as formative.

[2] The writing of *Wuthering Heights* in the winter and spring of 1846 preceded the publication of the first number of *Dombey and Son* in October; *Jane Eyre* was begun in the autumn of 1846 (see Barker 2010 [1994], 590–600).

Dickens and the 'Autobiographical Fragment': Memory and Writing

Dickens's time in Warren's Blacking factory has taken on an almost mythic status for biographers; as Rosemarie Bodenheimer (2001) has noted it holds the 'place of honor in the early portions of biographical accounts' (216); it is interpreted as, and has become, a kind of primal scene. Robert Douglas-Fairhurst attempts to correct Dickens's memory of the event, but his confident assertion that despite the 'false trails and dead ends it is possible to reconstruct the true sequence of events with some accuracy' (29), appears to miss the point of why we might wish to do so. It is Dickens's emotional and authorial investment in his own history—how the events were shaped, filtered, appropriated, repressed or understood—that is of significance. In the fragment, Dickens not only presents the compulsive operation of trauma (as indeed Edmund Wilson first highlighted in *The Wound and the Bow* [1941]), but also a scenography of trauma, in which the compromising parental 'demand' is decisive. Peter Ackroyd (1994, 56), Fred Kaplan (1988, 44) and Michael Slater (2009, 24) highlight the disagreement between John and Elizabeth Dickens, in which the child was implicated.

Steven Marcus (1985) charts the scenes of spectatorship throughout *Oliver Twist*, arguing that Bob Fagin represents a threatening and castrating father; he relates this point back to Dickens's unconscious ambivalence towards John Dickens, deploying Freud's idea of the primal phantasy in order to speculate that the young Charles had witnessed and then repressed the memory of his parents having sex (373–374). He argues that the moment at which John Dickens watches his son working at the window of the factory is a screen memory for this repressed 'primal scene'. This—purely speculative—point results in Marcus drawing an unconvincing, not to say unnecessary, symbolic connection between the murderous Bill Sikes and the feckless John Dickens, reliant on the problematic notion that in infancy we *all* imagine our father as 'terrible' (374). Looking is indisputably critical to the fragment and to Dickens's fiction as a whole; however, as Bodenheimer notes in both her readings of the 'autobiographical fragment', the gaze must be understood in terms of social scrutiny, narrative focalisation and the rhetoric of memory.

Marcus correctly highlights the overdetermination at work in the fragment, but he does not push this point to consider the wider family structure, Elizabeth Dickens, nor indeed the plurality of the scenic narrative. As Slater's biography clearly shows, Dickens's history was acted on by an extended family structure, taking in his sister Fanny, James Lamert and John Dickens's mother (whose timely death and legacy saved the family) (Slater 2009, 23), to name only three people. We should not, therefore, limit our understanding to an Oedipal triad. While Dickens's novels are grounded in cross-generational conflicts, these conflicts are not restricted to an Oedipal schema and exist in a constant state of disruption or extension. James Lamert is an interesting figure in his own right; a cousin by marriage, he used to take his young relative to the theatre, but was later responsible for Charles's job in the factory (Newsom 1983, 21). Feelings of betrayal were therefore very likely at work in relation to him as well. Further, in the 'autobiographical fragment' the tears Dickens sheds at his sister Fanny's prize-giving do not relate to castration anxiety, nor indeed to a threatening sense of paternal authority. It is, however, a formative scene, which speaks to a sense of unfairness, familial exclusion, and sadness, which becomes wounding: 'I felt as if my heart were rent' (Forster 1874, 1:47). As we saw clearly in the Wolf Man's case, the search for a definitive and *singular* origin is inherently problematic. The fragment is not grounded in a single scene; it presents a veritable scenography of trauma in which every scene becomes formative. Exclusion becomes a repetitive feature, as does the image of a broken heart.

It is the affective structure created through Dickens's retrospective account of the past with which I am concerned. What is at stake is the ongoing effect of Dickens's childhood experience: namely, his consistent presentation of the parent-child relationship as grounded in trauma, disruption or loss. Dickens self-consciously creates a specific temporal model in the fragment. It seems clear that Dickens's experience provoked his understanding of 'trauma' as a category of being. Childhood experience is formative, inescapable, haunting and possessing: parents appear as 'downright culpable' (Slater 2009, 22). Dickens's depiction of traumatisation intersects with the mid-nineteenth-century category of shock without being contained by it. Reading across Dickens's works, we can suggest that the mere state of being human within a family engenders shocking 'events' (in the medical *and* in the common sense). Importantly, dissociation is not simply a pathological state in Dickens's writings; it is implicated in the experience, and manifested in the memory, of childhood. Dissociation is represented as physical and psychological: remembering his feelings of alienation, Dickens writes, 'If I ever find myself in a very different kind of coffee-room now, but where there is such an inscription on glass, and read it backward on the wrong side MOOR-EEFFOC (as I often used to do then, in a dismal reverie), a shock goes through my blood' (Forster 1874, 1:37). This moment refers to a temporal experience that Freud was to call *Nachträglichkeit*. The 'traumatic symptom' (the 'shock' in the blood) is created through the symbolic correlative between two moments: the first, the little boy's lonely gazing, and the adult's later differential experience. Dickens knew what he was doing; he brings together past, present and symptom in precise fashion.

For Dickens, the wounds are of self and soul: the crushing effect of social exclusion; the psychologically haunting state of loss; the remembrance and allocation of guilt. To be a child, to become an adult, is to be wounded. Dickens's use of his own history was far from consistent or repetitive; even in *David Copperfield* he thoroughly reworks his parental source material. Like Douglas-Fairhurst, Bodenheimer and Newsom, I read the 'autobiographical fragment' as *writing*; like Bodenheimer (2001), I read it as possessing 'hermeneutical power' (217). However, this does not lessen its significance as a self-conscious act of memorisation. In her second analysis of the fragment (2007), Bodenheimer modifies her earlier analysis through the idea of trauma. She argues rightly that the fragment hints at the 'unknowable' aspects of traumatic experience through the varying narrative tonalities Dickens employs (70). I work on a similar premise, but read these tones differently. While Bodenheimer reads the piece in terms of 'memory writing' and 'trauma writing' (71),[3] I complicate this division through the notion of phantasmatic investment, and the primacy of the parental demand upon the child. In fact, as Bodenheimer seems to imply at certain points in her reading (although she does not clarify the subtext of her own analysis), 'memory writing' is inseparable from traumatic writing, especially if we are willing to accept Dickens's own proposition presented in the fragment: namely, that trauma and traumatic return underpin the production of identity.

Using Cathy Caruth's theory of trauma, Bodenheimer reads Dickens's angry present-tense interjections into the fragment as 'traumatic', suggesting they bear witness, through their very hyperbole, to the

[3] Bodenheimer creates this distinction by appropriating and modifying Bessel van der Kolk's categorisation of 'traumatic memory' and 'narrative memory' (set out in *Psychological Trauma*, 1987). This latter distinction is equally problematic since van der Kolk does not address the complexity of narration as act or phenomenon.

'unknowability' of traumatic experience (72). However, this does not acknowledge the manner in which Dickens formulates traumatic return knowingly in the 'autobiographical fragment'. Dickens may—like all of us—have been a psychological 'case'; however, he was also an important contributor to the development of trauma as a medical and psychological concept. The fragment demonstrates Dickens's sophisticated conceptualisation of memory; more specifically, he grounds the process of memory *within* a traumatic model. By Forster's account, Dickens's experience continued to reverberate; he writes that Dickens 'felt the weight upon his memory as a painful burden until he could lighten it by sharing it with a friend' (Forster 1874, 1:20). However, as we have already seen through the coffee-room detail, Dickens himself implies that the affect associated with the events is activated—felt—through afterwardsness. (As outlined in Chapter 2, this term comes from Jean Laplanche's translation of Freud's *Nachträglichkeit*; James Strachey translates this as 'deferred effect' in *The Standard Edition*.)

This idea resonates strongly with what we see in the fragment (and indeed Dickens's mid-period novels as a whole). Dickens's protagonists—as children and adults—attempt to translate parental communication, or indeed the absence of communication. In the 'autobiographical fragment', Dickens searches for understanding of his parents' motives, actions and thoughts. His father's descent into debt was, according to Forster, misunderstood with an almost supernatural intensity: 'He knew it [the 'deed'] in later days to have been a composition with creditors; though at this earlier date he was conscious of having confounded it with parchments of a much more demoniacal description' (Forster 1874, 1:16). There is a fluctuating process of comprehension: Dickens clearly maintained belief in his childhood powers of perception, but nevertheless, his parents remain enigmatic; relating the now infamous moment when John Dickens saw his son working at the factory window, Dickens writes 'I wondered how he could bear it' (1:48). The retrospective narrator cannot or does not rationalise the father's feelings, and instead perpetually speculates about John Dickens's attitude towards his son's work. Dickens's childhood bewilderment is clearly carried through into the present day when he writes, 'It *is* wonderful to me that, even after my descent into the poor little drudge I had been since we came to London, no one had compassion enough on me – a child of singular abilities, quick, eager, delicate, and soon hurt, bodily or mentally' (1:31 [my emphasis]). This tone does not seem to me to be indicative of a 'loudly "remonstrating" biographer' (Bodenheimer 2001, 222), but of a pained human being: the point being, of course, that there may not be much difference between these two tonalities. What is noticeable is the horror with which the adult watches his child self's situation. Knowledge appears, then, not so much as empirical reality, but as affective truth.

However, at points in the fragment, Dickens self-consciously distinguishes the child's perspective from the remembering adult's. In one of his narrative interjections, he creates an epistemological rhetoric through the anaphoric repetition of 'I know', beginning with the powerful statement: 'I know I do not exaggerate, unconsciously and unintentionally, the scantiness of my resources and the difficulties of my life' (Forster 1874, 1:37). But there is of course an epistemological impossibility: the knowingness and unconsciousness cannot be resolved, Bodenheimer (2007) arguing that this semantic problem demonstrates Dickens's 'effort to claim mastery over unknown parts of the mind' (72). Modifying this point, in Laplanche's terms, we could interpret Dickens's rhetoric as responding to the 'compromised parental message': his present-day interjection operates as a translation, which must—by definition—remain partial. In her earlier analysis, Bodenheimer (2001) emphasises Dickens's control of the material (222); in her second reading (2007), she affirms a similar point in a slightly different way, by claiming that Dickens's forms of 'memory writing are concrete and persuasive' (71). However, despite the anecdotal virtuosity Dickens displays, there are significant moments of hesitation where knowledge is superseded by uncertainty. He admits repeatedly that he could not remember how events progressed in sequence: the qualifying phrase, 'I think' recurs numerous times (see Forster 1874, 1:30, 32, 35, 36); 'I suppose my lodging was paid for, by my father' (35); and 'I am not sure that it was before this time, or after it' (47). Despite the boy's observational prowess, he cannot have seen, or more importantly, understood, the family's situation in its totality, and—crucially—the retrospective narrator does not claim to have done. In *The Uncommercial Traveller*, Dickens returned to similar ideas of perception and comprehension, writing, 'It would be difficult to overstate the intensity and accuracy of an intelligent child's observation. At that impressible time of life, it must somehow produce a fixed impression. If the fixed impression be an object terrible to the child, it will be (for want of reasoning upon) inseparable from great fear' ('Travelling Abroad', Ch. 7, 98). This passage does not of course negate the child's perception, but it does reinforce the gap between perception and understanding, suggesting that this gap provokes the retention of memory.

Dickens has often been criticised for exaggerating or manipulating the truth in the 'autobiographical fragment'. However, whether or not Dickens consciously exaggerated the events in his writing (or indeed in his own mind) does not undermine the value of the 'fragment', since what is at stake here is not the child's immediate experience, but his presentation of the affect provoked by the experience. By analysing their relationship to structures of fantasy, memory and writing can be brought together theoretically, without looking back hopelessly for some unattainable truth which history could reveal to us. The point is surely not whether Dickens 'lied'—for how could we ever know that he *knew*?—but the fact that memory is unavoidably, irredeemably tendentious, within any narrating subject. Dickens's phantasmatic investment in the event relies on a certain notion of himself and his own superiority: an investment that draws together these early experiences with his later authorial persona. The fragment knowingly represents a trauma of identity.

Laplanche argues that the location of fantasy can change through repression, without the content undergoing significant modification. In fantasy, as in Freud's idea of childhood memory and screen memory, we can enter a scene as a point of view, as a spectator, rather than an active participant: as Dickens does. For much of the fragment, Dickens perceives himself as a child in the third person—as a character in his own history—rather than looking through his child-self's eyes. Dickens's use of the third-person—'a child of singular abilities'—is related to his authoring of his history within the fragment, but also speaks to the nature of memory. As I discussed in Chapter 2, Freud posits that childhood screen memories condense formative affective conflicts in operation from childhood, *and/or* adult concerns pushed back onto the childhood scene ('Childhood Memories', 44). This temporal dualism likewise underpins the structure of the *Bildungsroman* form where retrospection is the central narrative mode. As a genre, the autobiography is not only a recitation of childhood events, but also the exposition of the protagonist's retention of childhood, and the relation between traumatic and nostalgic constructions of the past.

Unlike *Dombey and Son* and *Great Expectations*, the fragment does not present us with a neat primal scene. However, Dickens unquestionably constructs his own childhood history through a complex scenography. As Bodenheimer (2001) observes, Dickens repeatedly places his child self in the context of social scrutiny, underscoring his sense of shame and alienation (219). This alienation, and concomitant visibility, is of 'primal' importance; Slater writes that the 'public gaze must have had a searing impression' on the young Dickens (24). Significantly, there are several moments where Dickens describes past and present collapsing into one another. Importantly, these are not identical with the narrator's present-tense interjections, although they do cross over at certain points. These moments create a temporal and scenographic model, in which traumatic repetition is represented. The first instance is Dickens's visit to the Marshalsea following the arrest of his father. Interestingly, this scene is not placed with Forster's ostentatious presentation of the Blacking factory material in Chapter 2 of the biography, which Forster prefaces with the words, 'I give now the fragment of the autobiography of Dickens' (1:30). This is especially curious if we bear in mind that this earlier moment is apparently reliant on the fragment as well: Forster marks the margin with '*C.D. loq*', which Philip Collins (1984) argues refers to material taken from the fragment, rather than from letters or other sources (91). Here in the Marshalsea, we see through the child's eyes:

> [...] we went up to his room [...] and cried very much. And he told me, I remember, to take warning by the Marshalsea, and to observe that if a man had twenty pounds a-year and spent nineteen pounds nineteen shillings and sixpence, he would be happy; but that a shilling spent the other way would make him wretched. I see the fire we sat before, now; (Forster 1874, 1:24)

Going on to describe the dinner with Captain Porter, Dickens immerses himself within this scene; it is both pathetic and affirming. His simple language, we 'cried very much' evokes the sense of a child's voice. This little scene between father and son underscores rather than negates the misery expressed in the remainder of the fragment; it is precisely because Dickens loved his family that their subsequent absence is so bitterly resented. Looking at the fragment in scenographic terms, this moment in the prison could not be conceived of as 'traumatic' in isolation. The narrator willingly places himself within the scene. It is only when he repeats the same phrasing in a different context that it signifies in a new way. When recounting his lonely meal at the beef-house, Dickens writes of the waiter, 'I can see him now, staring at me as I ate my dinner, and bringing up the other waiter to look' (34). Here, the persistence of the child's perspective within the adult testifies to the ever-present sense of shame, engendered *first* by the father's existence in the Marshalsea. The feeling created operates through afterwardsness. The repetition of the phrase, 'I see now', in the beef-house scene, creates an echo, which implicates our understanding of the Marshalsea scene. However, unlike the first usage, this later scene creates a sense of the past's continuing action through the use of the present participles, 'staring', and 'bringing'; the child's action is, of course, rendered in the past tense: 'I ate'. The present participles create an uncanny sense of repetition compulsion, quite unlike the nostalgic tone of the scene in the Marshalsea, while also refracting back upon it.

The scenography of the 'autobiographical fragment' operates by creating constellations of feeling, which are heavily overdetermined. So as readers, it is only when we follow Dickens to the factory that we realise what was at stake in the Marshalsea: somehow home has been mislaid. The factory is introduced in Chapter 2 of Forster's biography through an intense and evocative sketch:

> Its wainscoted rooms, and its rotten floors and staircase, and the old gray rats swarming down in the cellars, and the sound of their squeaking and scuffling coming up the stairs at all times, and the dirt and decay of the place, rise up vividly before me, as if I were there again. (1:31)

The crumbling building is in stark contrast to the makeshift 'home' which Dickens and his father created in the Marshalsea scene. The image of the rats produces a physical sense of contamination and intrusion. This moment becomes indicative of the shock and terror of Dickens's childhood experiences, compacted into one brightly lit moment. There are key differences between the temporal structures created. In the Marshalsea, Dickens represented the action in the past tense, although his perception was rendered in the present: 'I see the fire we sat before now' (24). Something more uncanny—or traumatic—is happening in the factory; as in beef-house scene, the action itself is continuous. In this passage, however, it is not demarcated by the past tense at all: instead, Dickens uses a series of present participles, indicating continuing movement: the rats' 'swarming' squeaking' 'rustling' 'rise up before' him. Dickens, then, does not simply bear witness to—he essentially conceptualises, on a grammatical level—the repetition compulsion of 'trauma'. This is sustained at other moments: his account of the alehouse once more breaks down the barriers between past and present. Speaking of his child self and the landlord and landlady, he writes, 'Here we stand, all three, before me now, in my study in Devonshire terrace' (Forster 1874, 1:44). While Bodenheimer (2007) analyses the 'split' created here in terms of the narrator's 'stable perspective' (71), something more uncanny is happening: the narrator describes himself as continually divided: 'I' stands in front of 'me'. We can just as easily interpret this as an intrusion into Dickens's study, rather than the narrator's inhabiting of a 'stable perspective'. Here, it is not only the perception that is rendered in the present, but also the action itself: 'Here we stand' (Forster 1874, 1:44). Once more Dickens is confronted with an interrogatory adult gaze, but the gaze splits his self in two.

Dickens's "traumatic" model is made wholly explicit in one of his narrative interruptions:

> The deep remembrance of the sense I had of being utterly neglected and hopeless; of the shame I felt in my position; of the misery it was to my young heart to believe that, day after day, what I had learned, and thought, and delighted in, and raised my fancy and my emulation by, was passing away from me, never to be brought back any more; cannot be written. My whole nature was penetrated with grief and humiliation of such considerations, that even now, famous and caressed and happy, I often forget in my dreams that I have a dear wife and children; and even that I am a man; and wander desolately back to that time of my life. (33)

In this passage, Dickens's dreams return him to the source of his pain: his 'penetration' with 'grief and humiliation'. The fact that Dickens phrases this in the language of physical trauma is telling: he is 'penetrated' by his parents' failure. In his novels, Dickens eloquently represents trauma—or psychological wounding—in terms of the familial and the personal: the emergence of subjectivity, and the creation of identity. In so doing, he pushed far beyond contemporary medical discourse. For Dickens, it is not just that 'bad stuff' happens—it recurs, it haunts—and this implicates who you are and who you can be. The mimetic quality of trauma is crucial here; Dickens's childhood trauma is not the story of his deprivation per se, but his parents' culpability for this deprivation: his shame in his parents and in himself.[4] The parents' failure is represented as primal, and by his own account, he identifies with it. It is this which 'penetrates him'.

[4]As Newsom also points out (9).

It is important to note that following his dismissal from the factory, Dickens's resentment became increasingly bound up with his mother, rather than his father:

> My mother set herself to accommodate the quarrel, and did so next day. She brought home a request for me to return next morning, and a high character of me, which I am very sure I deserved. My father said I should go back no more, and should go to school. I do not write resentfully or angrily; for I know how all these things have worked together to make me what I am; but I never afterwards forgot, I never shall forget, I never can forget, that my mother was warm for my being sent back. (49)

This rhetoric of memory negates Dickens's supposed lack of anger: reading across the final sentence, the threefold repetition of 'never', 'never', 'never' echoes Lear's despairing cry following the death of Cordelia. Dickens's words towards the end of the fragment are telling: 'From that hour until this my father and mother have been stricken dumb upon it' (49). This total silence on the topic (whether real or exaggerated) is provocative. Dickens's language implies a punitive *deus ex machina*: they were 'stricken dumb'. The phrase implies an inability rather than an unwillingness to speak: a kind of enforced secrecy in which the child is implicated. The parents' vocal agency is ambiguous. The unreadable, or to use Laplanche's terminology, the untranslatable parental demand on the child is critical throughout Dickens's novels: demands are made in silence and in speech. The compromised and compromising parental message underlies the fragment, and so John and Elizabeth's ultimate silence becomes heavily weighted. In the portion of the narrative that deals with the factory, Dickens refers to his home life as a 'blank' (38); this term is directly picked up by Forster to describe the lack of narrative cohesion in the fragment itself: 'There is here another blank, which it is however not difficult to supply from letters and recollections of my own' (39). The blanking out of home becomes a negative space that actively signifies something to the child and indeed to Forster as biographer. Negativity is projected back onto the parents through the language that Dickens employs in his final remarks: 'never', 'never', 'never'.

The combination of paternal failure and (perceived) maternal cruelty expressed above was reworked compulsively in various forms throughout Dickens's novels. For Dickens, both as a subject and an author, the child's primal scene of fantasy or trauma was unavoidably bound up with forms of parental failure. The irresolvable tension between the father's failure and the mother's apparent cruelty is played with consistently (although the parental roles are far from static). The childhood traumas are, over and over again, correlated with a primal conflict between the maternal and paternal; Dombey opposes Edith; the feckless William Dorrit is set against the steely Mrs. Clennam; Magwitch symbolically opposes Miss Havisham; Mrs. Joe and Joe are set in comic but violent conflict.

Paul Dombey's Life, Death and Afterlife: Traumatic Echoes in *Dombey and Son*

Dombey and Son traces and retraces the influence of parent upon child with an almost obsessive compulsion; despite the sustained relationship Dickens creates between the colonial mercantile context and the Dombey family itself, ultimately the story of the firm's fall is brought back within the confines of the familial narrative, as becomes apparent when the firm's ship, the *Son and Heir*, disappears without a trace shortly after Paul Dombey's death. There is a sense of Gothic excess, far greater than anything Dickens created prior to this date: family is represented with an almost supernatural intensity. While Dickens's didactic narrator does not explicitly condemn Dombey's mercantile enterprise in moral terms, it is (productively) destabilised through these symbolic connections. Fanny Dombey's death in the first chapter of the novel inscribes parental loss as a primal moment that is subsequently constituted through a series of differential repetitions, with Paul's own death reinscribing the trauma.

Paul himself has tended to get lost in previous interpretations of the novel; however, on a psycho-symbolic level he is at his father's mercy in a far more sinister way than Florence: death shadows him from birth. His selfhood is crushed before it is begun: as we see in the opening scene, he is only ever 'Son'. The critical neglect of Paul's story occludes the traumatic structuring of the novel; Paul himself, denied an identity of his own, becomes a talismanic narrative presence: a force through which other characters orientate themselves, both before and after his death. The novel's traumatic structure underlines the thematic centrality of the parent to child relation: the affect passed from parent to child emerges as a pervasive and encroaching power that transcends death itself; Dombey's fantasies are an intrusive force, which, when coupled with the uncanny re-emergence of the dead mother, propel Paul to a certain death. Dickens reveals a deep awareness of psychical reality in *Dombey*;

dream-like sequences merge with the primary narrative, and Paul's life is characterised by a strange hallucinatory feel in the wake of his mother's death and the loss of his nurse. Dickens uses maternal death as the traumatic event that subsequently allows a thorough exposition of the problematised relationship between parent and child; however, further, as Fanny's death reveals, mothers and fathers operate in an unavoidably dialectical fashion: their children, whether in childhood or adulthood, form the point of intersection for a specifically gendered conflict. This conflict is perpetuated, rather than resolved, by the death of the mother. The centrality of parental death or absence not only testifies to the psychological problems engendered by mourning, but also implies a fault line in parenthood itself.

Mimetic identification—key to the Wolf Man case—is crucial for an understanding of *Dombey*: the trauma of the mother's death cannot be separated from Paul's and Florence's subjectivities.[5] Fanny's death is not simply an event that happens *to* them since it forms the crux of their selves. Paul identifies with the moment of loss itself: the repetitive refrain that he is 'old fashioned' is finally translated on his sickbed, where the 'old-fashion' is neither more nor less than death itself. Florence, on the other hand, is closely identified with the dead mother; at times, this association is so pronounced that Florence seems little more than a shadow or a ghost. The Dombey family as a whole can be analysed in terms of its shifting identifications. Following Dombey's second marriage, Florence disastrously identifies with both her father and her stepmother Edith, and the ensuing conflict between the two identifications engenders the violence between father and daughter. Dickens creates repetitive echoes that collectively point towards the fundamental familial conflicts. Cathy Caruth's (1996b) idea of attentiveness involves an ethical imperative, and we see a similar imperative enacted in the novel; after Paul's death, the story of Dombey and Florence is figured in comparable terms: Florence's voice, calling out from the wound of Paul's death, is not attended to by Dombey, and chaos ensues. Judith Greenberg's idea that the mythic figure of Echo can helpfully represent the disrupted and belated act of 'telling' in a traumatic stress disorder also resonates with Dickens's technique: through the echoing motif of the mother's song, sung by the grieving Florence both before and after Paul's death, Dickens beautifully

[5] In Chapter 2, I discussed the mimetic theory of trauma, which 'posits a moment of terrorized identification with the aggressor' (Leys 2007, 9).

implies Florence's inability to tell her *own* story, compounded, of course, by Dombey's narcissistic inability to listen to it.[6] Significantly, Florence's voice is not itself enough to enable a process of working-through; it is only when the 'sun/son' shines upon her that her voice achieves potency.

As P. Ikonen and E. Rechardt (1984) argue in relation to primal phantasies, in order to come into being the subject must be both included and excluded from certain structures (65). Paul Dombey's problem is that he is not excluded *enough*: Dombey's mercantile ideal embraces Paul, while rejecting his wife, Fanny, and daughter Florence: Paul's subjectivity is essentially prohibited as a consequence. He is, in Ikonen and Rechardt's terms, 'somebody else': he is 'Dombey and Son'. As I go on to show, the scene by Fanny's deathbed reveals the extent of Dombey's paternal obsession, rather than suggesting a shared parental love or desire, and everything that happens in the novel speaks back to this primary problem. The opening scene retrospectively reveals the fundamental problematic explored by Dickens: the irresolvable conflict between mother and father in which the child is implicated. Paul Dombey is the direct point of intersection for these issues, Florence becoming the Echo who lives, potentially to tell and work through the trauma. The primal scene by Fanny's deathbed introduces a series of compromised parental messages which Paul and Florence attempt to translate; Paul's ultimate failure to survive this process is indicative of the affective violence created by Dickens in this opening scene, a violence replayed and repeated throughout the novel.

Bad Blood

Dombey and Son falls naturally into well-defined narrative sections, the first dealing almost exclusively with the birth, education, and death of Paul Dombey. The question of parental influence predominates throughout this section, with a dialogue created between the maternal and paternal. Maternal influence appears in this first part of the novel as a flux, represented in fluid form, and bearing the possibility of moral,

[6] In Ovid's *Metamorphoses*, Echo is a nymph, cursed to repeat others' speech, who falls in love with Narcissus. Narcissus spurns her love, and she retreats into the wilderness, until nothing remains except her fragmented voice. Greenberg uses the story of Echo to represent the disrupted act of telling within trauma, 'the inaccessibility of the original event and the impossibility to narrate it' (1998, 332).

social and physical pollution. The search for an appropriate wet nurse for Paul is, after all, a search for a worthy source of milk. Milk is not the only fluid correlated with maternal influence since it stands for that more primal presence: blood. Laura Berry (1999) explores the contemporary discourses that surrounded breast-feeding: milk was deemed to be far more than food, since it also provided moral sustenance via the bond created between mother and child (66). Childhood was a time of danger, both physical and moral. As Melisa Klimazewski (2006) argues further, milk was a commodity, capable of exposing the economic foundation of the family institution (139). The loss of Fanny reveals the compromised ideological underpinning of the bourgeois family.

Fanny Dombey's failure to provide her husband with a boy for the first ten years of their marriage is perceived by Dombey and his sister, Mrs. Chick, as a sign of failure, even neglect of duty: in Mrs. Chick's eyes, Fanny hasn't made enough 'effort', and her death is likewise seen as a personal failing. But Fanny's death is undoubtedly presented as the novel's primal traumatic moment: the first chapter ends with her death, described by Dickens with portentous words, establishing for the first time the shadowy symbolic presence of the sea found persistently throughout *Dombey and Son*: 'the mother drifted out upon the dark and unknown sea that rolls round all the world' (Ch. 1, 11). Death is a drowning: Fanny clinging to Florence as her 'slight spar' (10). These first references ensure that the idea of maternal loss is inseparable from the recurring image of the sea. Despite the brief sense of grand tragedy, Fanny herself is largely obscured throughout the chapter; far more description is expended on Miss Tox and Doctor Peps. Dickens effectively holds back the pathos, creating it subtly through Fanny and Florence's final desperate embrace. Through the use of the free indirect style, the chapter's dominant tone is Dombey's own, as the narrator looks over his shoulder to build the scene and the character's psychological condition: 'But what was a girl to Dombey and Son! In the capital of the House's name and dignity, such a child was merely a piece of base coin that couldn't be invested – a bad Boy – nothing more' (3). The humorous second paragraph, in which Dickens compares the appearances of Dombey and 'Son', establishes the pattern whereby Paul is subsumed into his father's identity:

> Dombey was about eight-and-forty years of age. Son about eight-and-forty minutes. Dombey was rather bald, rather red, and though a handsome well-made man, too stern and pompous in appearance, to be prepossessing.

> Son was very bald, and very red, and though (of course) an undeniably fine infant, somewhat crushed and spotty in his general effect, as yet. (1)

The repetition of the family name emphasises its various resonances, with its hints of 'dominating,' 'dominial' (the latter meaning 'of or pertaining to ownership' in the *OED*), and even 'domesticate.' By naming the family 'Dom-*be*,' Dickens hints at the overriding passion for control which is Dombey's *raison d'être*, and which becomes increasingly apparent as the story progresses. If we interpret Fanny's death as a primal loss, as indeed Dickens encourages us to do in the chapter's final words, it is significant that the source of loss is simultaneously obscured: the mother's suppression in this scene provokes her uncanny return. Maternity in *Dombey and Son* is both too absent, and all-too present; maternal loss is placed at the heart of the narrative, but can only be conceived of via the paternal fantasy that dominates the first chapter. Maternal ideals are, in fact, curiously lacking from *Dombey and Son*. Fanny Dombey's death paves the way for a plethora of figures to perform the maternal function for little Paul: Polly, Mrs. Chick, Miss Tox, Mrs. Pipchin, Susan Nipper and ultimately Florence herself; but at no point in the novel does Dickens present such a eulogy on motherhood as he does later in his career through the 'little mother', Amy Dorrit. The death of the primal mother leads not to a clear narrative ideal, but to a split and fragmented representation of motherhood.

The patent lack of love between Dombey and Fanny operates as an enigmatic signifier or compromised message in the psychical development of their children (and in the novel's own symbolic processes). The scene reveals Dickens's brilliance at rendering minutiae: every gesture and act is encoded and points towards the fundamental problem. Each of the parents claims ownership of a different child; Florence is aligned with their mother, Paul with their father. The opening sentence finds Dombey sitting at the hearthside, toasting his son like a muffin (1); calling his wife 'my – my dear,' as her face flushes with embarrassment and surprise (1). Her eyes close at the mention of her son's proposed name (2), and open only as a response to her daughter's gaze (3). She clasps her daughter to her, but cannot rouse herself to look at her son (9). At the sound of her daughter's voice, a final 'shadow' of a smile appears on her face (10). Fanny's motherhood is idealised through her relationship with Florence, rather than through Paul, and Mrs. Chick chastises the dying woman for having spent little time with her son. It is the lurking pathos of the love between mother and daughter which provides any kind of sentimental ideal, but even so, this is presented quite distantly by Dickens: the small six-year-old girl is described (perhaps ironically, but no less coldly) as clinging to her mother 'with a desperate affection very much at variance with her years' (3). Fanny's death appears to be hurried along by the inexorable march of her husband's watch, which seems to assume a faster and faster pace as she fades away:

> 'Fanny! Fanny!'
> There was no sound in answer but the loud ticking of Mr. Dombey's watch and Doctor Parker Peps's watch, which seemed in the silence to be running a race. (10)

The watch takes the place of her heartbeat. Through this eloquent displacement, we can imagine a quickening of her pulse followed by nothing: 'The race in the ensuing pause was fierce and furious. The watches seemed to jostle, and to trip each other up' (10). The disjunctive correlation implied between heart and watch establishes the fundamental schism found in the novel between feminised and masculinised forms of time and value—cyclical physical time, opposed to regimented watch-time: love opposed to materialism. The feminine image is submerged under the male: there is a sense of symbolic oppression suggested by Dickens's narrative technique. We cannot hear Fanny's heartbeat directly.

Rather than the children intruding upon the parents' intimate good-byes, it is Fanny and Florence who are the unwelcome intruders in Dombey's eyes. Dickens's narrative technique means that there is a disjunction created between the tragic event and its mode of narration. The question of exclusion is inverted when later Dombey cannot forget that he was excluded from this scene; he remembers the 'two figures clasped in each other's arms, while he stood on the bank above them, looking down a mere spectator – not a sharer with them – quite shut out' (Ch. 3, 31). Fanny's death is a shared traumatic event, but the event is crossed over by conflicting desires. Even in Freud's theory of the primal phantasy as the scene of parental sex, the notion of exclusion is key: children are forced to situate themselves in relation to a parental desire to which they are refused access, as Florence does later when Dombey marries Edith. Dickens consistently implies that trauma is bound up with familial exclusion; this is not only relevant to Florence, but also (in mutated form) to Dombey himself.

Dombey feels the loss of his first wife solely as the loss of Paul's natural nurse, and the consequent socio-sexual anxiety that follows upon this. He pities himself through the child (Ch. 2, 20). Following Fanny's death, Dickens reveals the potent social and psychological implications of Paul's having a wet nurse rather than being nursed by his mother, a woman of his own class, in 'In which Timely Provision is Made for an Emergency that will Sometimes Arise in the Best Regulated Families' (11). The obsessive concern shown regarding the Toodles family's respectability blurs naturally into comedy. Mrs. Chick checks Polly's 'marriage certificate, testimonials and so forth', and Miss Tox ascertains that the blister on the nose of little Biler is 'accidental', rather than 'constitutional' (Ch. 2, 16). As Margaret Wiley (1996) reminds us, this remark about a 'constitutional' blister probably refers to a secondary syphilitic lesion (220). While Dickens undoubtedly intends the Toodles family to represent a positive familial ideal, its members are also caricatured and undifferentiated: each is 'apple-faced' and identical to the next. Polly Toodles is (to appropriate Shakespeare's term) the thing itself: a soft, round, cushioned representation of motherhood. This operates through synecdoche; as an abstract vision of 'wholesome' motherhood, Polly actually seems more like a personified, disembodied, breast. Dombey represents the transaction between the two families as a whoring of motherhood, in which, tellingly, no memory traces will be left of the bond between nurse and child: 'The child will cease to remember you; and you will cease, if you please, to remember the child' (Ch. 2, 18).[7] It is interesting that in his ponderings Dombey perceives a symbolic sexual relation between himself and the wet nurse: she will be neither more nor less than a stand-in for Fanny Dombey. Dombey's enjoyment in rejecting the maternal candidates displaces the punishment he feels his dead wife deserves for deserting their son; through her very absence, Fanny Dombey is a potentially dangerous force. Dombey attempts to abnegate his own anxiety by removing Polly's womanhood at one fell, and unknowingly comic, stroke by renaming her 'Richards'. This strong decisive name, with its connotations of male leadership, could not be further away from the round and comfortable sound of 'Polly Toodles,' and Dombey undoubtedly intends to emphasise his own centripetal power with the name. However, this renaming, while

[7] In his analysis of *Bleak House*, John O. Jordan (2011) insists upon the importance of infantile memory traces to the novel, reinforcing this by referencing Dickens's interest in the issue (89).

removing Polly's femininity, potentially posits *her* as a source of power in Paul's life, a supposition that is supported by the fact that the little boy calls for her upon his deathbed, much to Dombey's chagrin.

Despite the life-giving nourishment provided by Polly, Paul's infancy takes on an overtly funereal character. Although the traumatic affect bound up in the mother's death has not yet been reinforced by the loss of Polly, the Dombey house is transformed into a dead space. The affect is displaced from the subjective to the material: the whole house seems consumed with melancholy, as the 'shadow of the lost object' falls upon it (Freud 'Mourning', 249). Fanny's death is not openly mourned. Her portrait is shrouded in bandages, as if she is an Egyptian mummy, waiting for her chance to return and wreak violence upon the family: 'Odours, as from vaults and damp places, came out of the chimneys. The dead and buried lady was awful in a picture-frame of ghastly bandages' (Ch. 3, 24). This description prefigures the vision of Miss Havisham in *Great Expectations*. As this passage suggests, no fresh influence can enter, not even from the sky above the house: it is as if the chimneys reach down into the ground, rather than rise up to the sky. Dickens relentlessly emphasises the air of melancholia through the house's physical presence:

> Every gust of wind that rose, brought eddying round the corner from the neighbouring mews, some fragments of the straw that had been strewn before the house when she was ill, mildewed remains of which were still cleaving to the neighbourhood: and these, being always drawn by some invisible attraction to the threshold of the dirty house to let immediately opposite, addressed a dismal eloquence to Mr. Dombey's windows. (24)

This image of the straw returning magnetically to the street echoes the sea imagery used by Dickens throughout the novel: a gentle flow, a passing and return, which becomes suggestive of the lost mother. The returning fragments 'address' a rebuke towards the Dombey house. The fact that this dirty straw stands in for the mother's absence is suggestive; these mouldering remnants returning on the wind are indicative of the fragmentary (and compromised) nature of maternity in the novel. Edith's mother, Mrs. Skewton, clinging onto her grotesque illusion of youth, emerges as the embodied reality of this idea when Dombey travels to Leamington Spa with Major Bagstock. Dickens's narrative treatment of Mrs. Skewton's death is one of the most effective elements in *Dombey and Son*, but the ghastly disintegration of the mother is foreshadowed from the beginning of the novel.

Paul's second maternal trauma occurs when Polly is dismissed and he is hastily weaned, an event described as 'Paul's second deprivation' in Dickens's plan for the novel (Dickens, 'Number Plans', 836). Dickens clearly underlines this as a key moment; Chapter 6 concludes with Paul's 'crying lustily': 'for he had lost his second mother – his first, so far as he knew – by a stroke as sudden as that natural affliction which had darkened the beginning of his life' (Ch. 6, 84). This is a crucial moment in the development of Dickens's traumatic model. Tellingly, like Freud's, it is characterised by belatedness, by a relationship between two temporal moments: Fanny's death, and Polly's loss. Dombey wonders uneasily what consequences this loss had for his young son, the narrator referring much later to the fact that Paul had not been 'weaned by degrees' (Ch. 11, 141). Crucially, as in Emma's case history (in 'A Project for a Scientific Psychology'), there is a series of symbolic correlatives between the two moments. The question of maternal blame is again placed at the forefront of the narrative: Polly's dismissal follows upon her visit to the Toodles family in Staggs's Gardens, a visit that, in Dombey's eyes, could potentially contaminate Paul. He is much more concerned with this possibility than the very real fact that Florence has been kidnapped by Good Mother Brown (the maternal pimp). In the wake of his mother's death, and the loss of Polly, Paul grows up into a fragile, thoughtful, little boy. The narrator places the responsibility for Paul's ill health onto the second maternal loss: 'Naturally delicate, perhaps, he pined and wasted after the dismissal of his nurse' (Ch. 8, 91). The problem is not now one of maternal pollution (as with the Good Mother Brown episode), but of glaring maternal absence. Mrs. Chick notes with anxiety that 'His soul is a great deal too large for his frame' (Ch. 8, 96): it is as if his father's soul has been forced upon him, and Paul is physically crushed by the weight of being the 'Son'.

This second traumatic loss reinscribes (even to a great extent *creates* in subjective terms) the emotional potency of the first, while subtly re-presenting the notion of maternal culpability, which was ironically commented upon by Mrs. Chick in the first scene when blaming Fanny Dombey for her lack of 'effort'. Significantly, the repetition dispenses with the irony; Dickens augments the question of maternal responsibility through Florence's childhood episode. Although Dombey's insistence that Polly must abstain from contact with her own family is undoubtedly brutal, her decision to ignore his prohibition leads directly to Florence's falling into the hands of Good Mother Brown. The narrative colludes with Dombey's prohibition through this course of events. Motherhood is not only disrupted but dangerously fragmented by not having a domestic centre. As Alice Marwood remarks about Good Mother Brown later in the novel, 'She's as much a mother as her dwelling is a home' (Ch. 33, 464). Florence's encounter heightens the sense of maternal threat; London becomes associated with sexual danger. Importantly, Florence's encounter with Good Mother Brown leads to the latter spying on the Dombey family, 'In memory of [her] poor gal' (Ch. 34, 470), a peripheral plot line which Dickens integrates. The novel, then, consistently works against its unifying tendencies; despite the centrality of the Dombey family, the traumatic structure proliferates, and echoes across different classes. On the level of character, parental failure is not the sole province of the bourgeoisie or the working class, but appears endemic within 'family'. However, this is complicated if we remember the centrality of economics—the firm—to the novel's overall structure: Dombey's mercantile overreaching runs parallel to the maternal pimping perpetrated by Good Mother Brown and Mrs. Skewton; significantly, Walter Gay's father has also failed to provide for him. The difficulty of maintaining parental ethics in the context of economic enterprise is repeatedly underscored, and this problem can be related back to Dickens's 'autobiographical fragment'. The family as a bourgeois institution is the object of a profound double bind. On the one hand, it *is* an economic structure that must maintain itself as such: on the other hand, in order to function as a loving family, money must be in some sense occluded from view. The mid-Victorian fantasy of family relies on the premise that it is a sentimental grouping that we *choose*, rather than an economic institution that we are placed within. In this context, it is significant that the Dombey family only finds healing in the Midshipman—the shop that does not sell anything.[8] Dickens does not solve the familial problem, but in *Dombey* he represents it more powerfully—with greater unease—than anywhere else in his fiction.

[8] My interpretation of this differs from Holly Furneaux's (2009, 52). While *Dombey and Son* seemingly recuperates the family through the 'queered' non-biological unit in The Midshipman, the novel continues to coalesce around Paul Dombey and his haunting presence as 'Son'/Sun. Moreover, the fact that the shop does not sell anything shows the tension between the actual economic basis of the Victorian family and the *fantasised* occlusion of economics.

Arrested Development

The traumatic structuring of *Dombey* is by no means linear or straightforward; as in Freud's own case histories, the identification of a stable 'origin' is inherently problematic. In Freud's history of Lucy R. (discussed in Chapter 2), the key traumatic scenes constantly referred back to an earlier moment. While in *Dombey*'s traumatic structure the two maternal losses are undoubtedly central, Paul's christening is also a key moment, referring back to his birth, as well as looking forward with a gloomy premonition to his sentimental demise and subsequent interment: two very private moments, flanked neatly by their social performances. Although we are told that Paul 'pined and wasted after the dismissal of his nurse', the atmosphere of the christening is also retrospectively interpreted as a negative influence, the narrator speculating that 'The chill of Paul's christening had struck home, perhaps, to some sensitive part of his nature' (Ch. 8, 91). Dickens juxtaposes the private (maternal) losses, with the public (paternal) ceremonies, reinforcing the tension between maternal and paternal culpability in Paul's demise. In this christening scene, Dickens reminds us that the crisis set in motion by the opening scene was not only one of maternal loss, but also of intrusive paternal fantasy. Paul is born into death: his mother's and his own. The christening is a freezing affair: the narrator notes, the 'chief difference between the christening party and a party in a mourning coach, consisted in the colours of the carriage and horses' (Ch. 5, 58): 'It happened to be an iron-grey autumnal day, with a shrewd east wind blowing – a day in keeping with the proceedings' (54). Paul is welcomed into a deathly world: 'dusty urn[s]' adorning the drawing room, as if 'dug up from an ancient tomb'. Melancholy details abound; even the leaves fall 'blighted' as autumn passes into winter. The 'chimney-glass' bears witness to Dombey and his portrait and 'seemed fraught with melancholy meditations'. With this image, Dickens subtly implies the function that Paul (as well as the christening) serves in Dombey's narcissistic conception of self. Dickens constructs the scene with a moralising and sustained symbolism. In the church, Mr. Chick accidentally reads out 'the reference to Mrs. Dombey's tomb in full, before he could stop himself' (Ch. 5, 59). Maternal loss, melancholia and premature death: all are invoked. Dombey's emotional frigidity is extended to his surroundings, and, with a typical Dickensian flourish, affect permeates even the food:

> 'This,' returned Mr. Dombey, 'is some cold preparation of calf's head, I think. I see cold fowls – hams – patties – salad – lobster. Miss Tox will do me the honour of taking some wine? Champagne to Miss Tox.'
>
> There was toothache in everything. (Ch. 5, 60–61)

Dombey's paternal influence is overwhelming and his 'cold and distant nature' refuses to share ownership of his son (Ch. 5, 49); while he is happy to concede the role of godmother to Miss Tox 'in virtue of her insignificance', he does not recognise the need for the traditional role of godfather. This narrowing of male influence is clearly intended to alert the reader to the danger that Paul will be crushed by the concentration of his father's love. The dialectical relation between maternal and paternal influence is firmly reinforced; Dombey symbolically forces an icy particle into his son's heart. While, as we saw in the previous section, maternal influence was a dubious flux, a stream that bore the risk of contamination and fragmentation, Dombey's influence is hard and inflexible: the rigid application of a pre-existing set of values. In an eloquent passage, the narrator describes how Dombey incorporates the birth of his son into his worldview:

> And now when that nature concentrated its whole force so strongly on a partial scheme of parental interest and ambition, it seemed as if its icy current, instead of being released by this influence, and running clear and free, had thawed for but an instant to admit its burden, and then frozen with it into one unyielding block. (Ch. 5, 49)

Dickens does not allow us to soften towards Dombey's obsession. The word 'partial' in the passage is telling; Dombey's fatherhood not only excludes Florence, but also excludes Paul's own childhood. Dombey's manner is impatient and irritable. Paul's infancy is a matter of acute indifference to him: 'So that Paul's infancy and childhood pass away well, and I see him become qualified without waste of time for the career on which he is destined to enter, I am satisfied' (Ch. 5, 48–49). The irony is, of course, that Paul's childhood 'passes away' far more literally than Dombey could possibly foresee. Dickens's use of this phrase subtly creates a link between Dombey's fantasy and Paul's premature death: without realising it, Dombey wishes away his son's childhood and consequently, his life. He destroys both the symbolic and physical vitality of childhood, a criminal act in the eyes of the author who showed a passionate concern for educational standards and reform throughout his writing career. Like the Medusa's head, Dombey has the magical ability to turn those around him into stone; he is 'not only a constraint upon [Florence's] mind, but even upon the natural grace and freedom of her actions' (Ch. 3, 32–33). When she first meets him again after her mother's death, 'The tears that stood in her eyes as she raised them quickly to his face, were frozen by the expression it wore' (32). He petrifies his children.

Paul becomes increasingly otherworldly as the novel progresses. The death into which he is born surrounds him. The narrator presents us with the pathetic figuration of a dying child, struggling to come to terms with the world around him; but Paul is also ageless, deathless, evading time itself. In Brighton, he avoids the company of other children aside from Florence, picking out 'a weazen, old, crab-faced man, in a suit of battered oilskin' to pull his carriage (Ch. 8, 110). Paul instinctively feels that he has more in common with those close to death, with those who can hear the seductive call of the sea. He reminds us of those changelings in fairy tales who cannot grow older, but who have an aged quality nevertheless; Dickens self-consciously uses fairy-tale imagery to codify a dark reality. Paul's decline and death are presented as an answer to a seductive call encoded in the sea's murmurs. He senses that only those closer to death can hear the call: 'And though old Glubb don't know why the sea should make me think of my Mama that's dead, or what it is that it is always saying—always saying! – he knows a great deal about it' (Ch. 12, 151). Paul struggles to make sense of the loss of his mother, even while the sea itself becomes the location for her uncanny reappearance. As we saw in the opening scene, the sea is feminised through its symbolic relation to Fanny Dombey and its later association with Florence's feminine influence.

In the wake of Polly's departure, Paul is plunged into a liminal state where maternal love is correlated with a kind of erotic seduction. The sea's call is not simply the maternal voice crying to the young boy—it is also a call to death. The sea is a symbol of eternal maternal love, a love that returns as inevitably as the waves breaking on the beach. In this context, Lynn Cain (2008) interprets the sea as not only maternal, but 'amniotic', drawing upon Julia Kristeva's idea of the maternal 'chora'. In this schema, Paul's return to the sea is a regressive return to the womb (Cain, 70). While the symbolic connection between the mother and the sea is irrefutable, Cain's interpretation of the sea as choric (and therefore relating to primal bodily drives), rather than symbolic, means that the mother necessarily emerges as an 'archaic' archetype (78) rather than the seductive presence I interpret her to be.[9] Maternity in *Dombey* is not represented by one cohesive image, but is represented through a proliferation of bodies: the novel is wary of mothers, but it is erroneous to perceive this wariness as solely emerging from the idea of a 'regression' to the womb. In fact, this wariness indicates Dickens's deep awareness of maternity's relentless symbolic permutations, its differential quality: its undying ability to reproduce itself. Even the sterile Edith has a dangerous double, her cousin Alice. The traumatic loss of the mother(s) provokes the re-emergence of an enigmatic maternal presence that possesses Florence, while haunting Paul. Through the narrative's convoluted symbolic processes (which crucially also take in Edith, Mrs. Skewton, Good Mother Brown and Alice), Dickens poses an underlying and unanswerable question: *What is it that mothers want from their children?* (We could pause at this point on Dickens's professed resentment towards his own mother expressed in the 'autobiographical fragment'.) The sexualisation of the maternal demand is apparent in Mrs. Skewton and Good Mother Brown. These maternal pimps simply wish to sell their daughters to the highest bidder; both old women, however, also desire their daughters' love and absolute loyalty. This impossible dichotomy underpins the representation of maternity in *Dombey and Son*, and Fanny Dombey's haunting presence seems to stand in for this paradox: this parental fault line.

Fanny beckons Paul, and it is only Florence, the living maternal substitute, who can keep him alive in the build-up to the annual school dance at Blimber's. Paul is plunged into a perpetual dreamlike state: he cannot fully access the source of his trauma, and therefore, his mourning is circular and impotent. As Dominick LaCapra (2001) argues, 'when absence, approximated to loss, becomes the object of mourning, the mourning may (perhaps must) become impossible and turn continually back into endless melancholy' (68). Florence's subjectivity, as in Freud's model of the melancholic ego, is obscured by the shadow of what she has lost. In a key passage, Paul describes the night-time sea by the 'lonely shore':

> 'Not blowing at least', said Paul, 'but sounding in the air like the sea sounds in the shells. It was a beautiful night. When I had listened to the

[9] In this context, it is appropriate to note that the sea is the site of mercantile activity and the source of capitalist profit in *Dombey*: by implication both profit and death are feminised concerns.

> water for a long time, I got up and looked out. There was a boat over there, in the full light of the moon: a boat with a sail [...] in the full light of the moon. The sail like an arm, all silver. It went away into the distance, and what do you think it seemed to do as it moved with the waves? [...] It seemed to beckon,' said the child, 'to beckon me to come! – There she is! – There she is!'
>
> Toots was almost beside himself with dismay at this sudden exclamation, after what had gone before, and cried 'Who?'
>
> 'My sister Florence!' cried Paul, 'looking up here, and waving her hand. She sees me – she sees me!' (Ch. 12, 169)

A summoning spell is woven about Paul, a magical call that he cannot resist. The traditional symbolic connection between the moon and femininity, found from the Greeks onwards, is invoked here to hint at the potency of the mother's absent-presence: the Greek goddess, Artemis, and her Roman equivalent, Diana, were not only moon goddesses, but goddesses of the hunt, of entrapment. The slippage between Fanny and Florence in Paul's speech—a slippage that terrifies the simple Toots—means that Florence also briefly emerges as an uncanny emanation: a maternal revenant. By sending Paul to school, Dombey had undoubtedly hoped to 'wean' Paul from his sister, but in fact, he opens the way for the more insistent call of the dead mother. However, it is not Florence's actions, but Paul's entry into the school that signals his demise. Florence nurtures and educates her brother in Brighton before he enters Doctor Blimber's establishment. Dickens constructs the prosaic dance at the school at which Florence will appear as a potent fantasy, which (as his Doctor observes) has the capacity to keep Paul alive for a number of days (Ch. 14, 204). Florence is both the nurturing sister *and* a seductive maternal revenant. Dickens does not choose, but neither does one aspect negate the other. As Freud demonstrates in relation to Frau Emmy Von N., Lucy R., 'A Case of Paranoia', and the Wolf Man, the individual subject assumes multiple familial positions, actual and symbolic, which become determinant for the formation of fantasy. At the end-of-term dance, Florence's presence is connected over and over again to the dead mother's call, emanating from the sea: 'The same mysterious murmur he had wondered at, when lying on his couch upon the beach, he thought he still heard sounding through his sister's song' (200). The tie between Florence and the dead mother is created persistently throughout these final scenes: the mother is correlated with the call of the sea, which is, in its turn, correlated with Florence's song. Reading across Dickens's use of imagery, we find that the dance at Doctor Blimber's represents Paul's passing from his sister's hands into his mother's: the collapsing in of past and present, described by the narrator, signals the uncanny re-emergence of the mother and Paul's inevitable death.

Paul's deathbed becomes a magical site, translating, as the title of the chapter says, 'What the Waves Were Always Saying'. Before meeting Polly for the first time since infancy he asks, 'Is she dead too? Floy, are we *all* dead except you?' (Ch. 16, 223). Florence is defined in relation to what she has lost, or what she lacks. Lying waiting, the boy calmly watches the golden light playing on his bedroom wall. He experiences death as a journey down a river, passing to the sea, where his mother waits for him, the river 'running very fast, and confusing his mind' (Ch. 16, 223); he boards the boat which he had earlier described to Toots:

> Now the boat was out at sea, but gliding smoothly on. And now there was a shore before him. Who stood on the bank! –
>
> Mama is like you, Floy. I know her by the face! But tell them that the print upon the stairs at school, is not Divine enough. The light about the head is shining on me as I go! (225)

As in the earlier scenes at Doctor Blimber's, Florence and Fanny Dombey merge into one welcoming, or seductive, presence. The repeated mantra that Paul is 'old-fashioned' is finally explained, with heavy emphasis: 'The old, old, fashion! The fashion that came in with our first garments, and will last unchanged until our race has run its course, and the wide firmament is rolled up like a scroll. The old, old fashion – Death!' (225). The call from the mother welcomes Paul to death, and implicitly (but only implicitly) to God. As we have seen, this can also be read as a dangerous maternal seduction, urging Paul away from Dombey and life itself. The maternal call is destabilising: ultimately, Paul must renounce life and remain ever a child in his mother's arms. The maternal embrace, never realised in the first scene (Ch. 1, 9), is finally imminent. But the effectiveness of the call is undoubtedly not only compounded, but also *created* by Dombey's interest, or investment, not in Paul as a child, but speculatively as a future adult companion and business partner. Dickens is doing something quite complicated with the parental dialectics here: motherhood is an a-temporal force, while fatherhood is cold and 'forcing' (the term applied to Doctor Blimber's educational techniques). Crucially, both are equally compromised through the density of Dickens's writing.

While Paul Dombey's death may seemingly stand out within Dickens's fiction because of its sentimental portrayal of a child's innocent bravery in the face of tragedy, it is in fact much more notable for its depiction of a child caught, even crushed, between two parental powers over which he has no control: the father—a 'tall shadow on the wall' (Ch. 14, 204), the mother—a powerful, but whispering voice.

Echoes

Paul's death functions in relation to the maternal loss; as the narrator's repeated mantras reveal, it is the 'destiny' that Dombey unconsciously foresaw for his son in the first chapter (3). Further, however, Paul's death reconfigures the novel's phantasmatic structure: it replaces the mother's death as the key trauma while remaining inseparable from it. Again, Dickens creates a sense of afterwardsness: Paul's death leads to the inevitable crisis in Florence and Dombey's relationship (prefigured in the first scene), a crisis that becomes even more pronounced following Edith's entrance into the household. It is ultimately *only* through Paul's posthumous influence that the father and daughter can begin to be healed, potentially enabling a process of working-through.

For both children, the sibling relationship had filled the void left by the mother's death, and so, with the loss of Paul, Florence is completely bereft for the first time. Absence is figured as a glaring void, free of the parental whispers and shadows that passed through Paul's childhood. This deathly silence is a potent message in its own right, and one that precipitates Florence's obsessive (and uncomfortable) desire to make her father love her. It is at this point in the novel that Florence is reconfigured as Echo, desperately trying to articulate what has passed. Following Paul's death, when confronted with the horrific absence of both mother and brother, Florence appears to reaffirm her relation to her dead mother, which had been such a central aspect of her relationship with her brother:

> It was not very long, before, in the midst of the dismal house so wide and dreary, her low voice in the twilight, slowly and stopping sometimes, touched the old air to which he had so often listened, with his drooping head upon her arm. And after that, and when it was quite dark, a little strain of music trembled in the room: so softly played and sung, that it was more like the mournful recollection of what she had done at his request on that last night, than the reality repeated. But it was repeated, often – very

> often, in the shadowy solitude; and the broken murmurs of the strain still trembled on the keys, when the sweet voice was hushed in tears. (Ch. 18, 242)

A refashioned Echo, Florence's broken voice covers over the dead mother's silence, but she has no words of her own. Fanny Dombey summoned Paul, but Florence has been left behind: she simply represents the resonance of the lost call. In symbolic terms, Dickens portrays Florence as a kind of maternal remainder, a redundant household presence. Denied her role as daughter, unable to be a sister, Florence is meaningless: her singing is a 'broken' fragmented collection of dead utterances. Whether he did so knowingly or not, Dickens undoubtedly translates the metamorphic logic of Echo and Narcissus into the Dombey family. Florence cannot express her desire for her father's love and is condemned to reiterate the whispers of her dead mother; Dombey is, like Narcissus, captivated by his own reflected greatness—previously passed on to Paul. Greenberg (1998) argues that the story of Echo and Narcissus acts as a 'didactic parable', which 'emphasises the need to confront one's own echoes to avoid falling into the pool of one's own reflection, death' (339); Dickens likewise highlights the danger of not attending to echoes: the narrator's repeated portentous call 'Let him remember' (used when referring to Dombey and Florence) underscores this. Directly after Paul's death the daughter is caught obsessively reproducing familial loss, while the father cannot tear himself away from his own representation. The two forms of frustrated love are inextricably connected. Just like Echo, Florence compounds her father's narcissism by feebly echoing the primary enigma: his inability to love her. When Florence enters his study after Paul's death, she cries out 'Speak to me, dear Papa!' (Ch. 18, 252): her speech constitutes a demand for his words, rather than operating as an effective articulation in its own right. Like Narcissus, Dombey already knows that he is an object of desire; the tragedy is that he does not care. Florence's realisation of this leads to her 'prolonged low cry' (252). Following Paul's death, Florence can only exist through others, dead or alive; Dombey will perish from himself. As Jacqueline Rose (1991) explains in relation to Sylvia Plath's 'Daddy', the father demands an identification which he then refuses to accept (230): the double bind of daughterhood is revealed. Florence's obsessive desire to love Dombey in the wake of Paul's death is a proportionate mirroring of Dombey's own self-love, which is likewise dealt an irretrievable blow by this same event.

While the figure of the daughter is undoubtedly problematised throughout the novel, this becomes increasingly anxiety-ridden following Dombey's second marriage. The entry of Edith into the family provides Florence with the 'Mama' she has always craved, and, as a result of the crisis that follows, the primal conflict between the 'mother' and 'father' that was established symbolically by Fanny Dombey's death is fully realised in the plot. Dombey's second marriage testifies to a crisis in the family's conflicting desires: Florence's association with her own neglected mother and the despised Edith engenders her as a dangerous sexual object in the household: this culminates in Dombey striking Florence across her breast after Edith has fled with Carker. The negative relation between Dombey and Florence is revealed in all of its interpretative violence here: owing to the identification between Florence and Edith (itself a differential repetition of Florence's identification with Fanny in the primal scene), Florence is also rendered guilty in her father's eyes; the irony being that the identification Florence felt for Edith (described as the 'old association' by the narrator [Ch. 47, 621]) was based upon her voyeuristic desire to gain her father's love. The blow destroys the identification Florence has tentatively felt for Dombey himself, the desire she had cherished that he would love her:

> But she looked at him, and a cry of desolation issued from her heart. For as she looked, she saw him murdering that fond idea to which she had held in spite of him. She saw his cruelty, neglect, and hatred, dominant above it, and stamping it down. She saw she had no father upon earth, and ran out, orphaned, from his house. (Ch. 47, 637)

The dangerous circling of identification and desire is presented at its most extreme here: nowhere else in Dickens's fiction do we see quite so painfully the way in which self and other become locked into ambivalent processes of self-constitution and destruction. In an extraordinary passage, standing in front of the mirror at the Midshipman, Florence remembers her feeling that she had witnessed a murder:

> She had seen the murder done. In the last lingering natural aspect in which she had cherished him through so much, he had been torn out of her heart, defaced and slain [...] If her fond heart could have held his image after that, it must have broken; but it could not; and the void was filled with a wild dread that fled from all confronting with shattered fragments – with

> such a dread as could have risen out of nothing but the depths of such a love, so wronged.
>
> She dared not look into the glass; for the sight of the darkening mark upon her bosom made her afraid of herself, as if she bore about her something wicked. (Ch. 49, 655–656)

There is a slippage here; no one has destroyed the image of Dombey but Dombey himself, but the gaping void left behind testifies to Florence's inability and her unwillingness to recreate his image in the wake of the blow. Much like the speaker of 'Daddy', Florence therefore sees herself as implicated in the murder. It is significant that Dickens uses the metaphor of glass-like 'shattered fragments' to describe Florence's picture of her father: it is as if the 'mirror' itself (as the abstract guarantor of identity) is shattered, the mirrored image of ourselves that we find in the other, and which assures our identity. The key point to note here is not that Florence bears the murderous mark of Cain (2008, 72), but that identification *necessitates* desire—a desire brutally repudiated by Dombey himself. The violence is engendered by Dombey alone: as we have seen, the obsessiveness of Florence's desire for his love is a mirror image of his desire for himself, as well as being the foundation for her sense of self after Paul's death.

The supposed irony of *Dombey and Son*, hinted at by Dickens himself in his notes to John Forster, is that rightly it should be named *Dombey and Daughter* (*Dombey*, introduction, xv). Considering that Paul dies only a quarter of the way through the novel (at the end of the fifth number), this can be seen as a literal truth, without being an accurate textual analysis. As we may expect from the opening birth scene, the 'Son' is an overarching schema. The material presence of the 'Son' is replaced with Paul's magical, talismanic non-presence, without which the father and daughter would remain locked in their torturous processes of identification and repudiation: the 'Son' allows the trauma to be partly worked through. Without Paul's blessing, the union between Walter and Florence would be meaningless. Florence describes the relationship between herself and Walter to Edith after her father's marriage:

> He was my brother, Mama. After dear Paul died, we said we would be brother and sister. I had known him for a long time – from a little child. He knew Paul, who liked him very much; Paul said, almost at the last, 'Take care of Walter, dear Papa! I was fond of him!' (Ch. 35, 485)

Walter's character is almost irrelevant; structurally he is destined to rescue Florence because he takes the place of Paul—her only stable (if curtailed) family bond. His survival from the sinking of the ship, 'The Son and Heir', reinforces the sense that, Lazarus-like, he has the power to take Paul's privileged place. Dickens was clearly aware of the difficulty of manoeuvring Walter from the position of surrogate brother to lover. In Chapter 50, in a protracted dialogue between the two young people, Walter explains to Florence that he must renounce the brotherly closeness he had with her, saying 'I left a child, I find a woman' (Ch. 50, 678). The right to 'protect' the woman is seen as either a (biologically) fraternal or a husbandly concern. This scene constitutes a moment of sexual recognition for Florence, as 'The colour overspread her face' (678). With her 'bosom swelling with its sobs' (679), she proposes Walter's transition from brother to husband herself: 'If you will take me for your wife, Walter, I will love you dearly. If you will let me go with you, Walter, I will go to the world's end without fear' (679). Florence's recognition is key to creating the union as a reciprocal exchange between two adults, although Dickens could not resist a final flourish at the end of the scene, with Florence falling asleep 'like a hushed child' on Walter's bosom (679).

The role of the 'son' as a centre of gravitation is clear, and it is probable that Dickens had the son/sun pun in mind throughout his writing of the novel.[10] Paul's posthumous influence does not end with his blessing of Walter Gay. His symbolic reincarnation in Florence's own son provokes the former's return to her father as a married woman in Chapter 50: having been neglected, and then physically abused by her father, Florence returns to him in continuing self-abasement to beg for his forgiveness for abandoning him. This disturbing scene can only make sense if we take into account the way in which Paul's influence reverberates through the book after his death. Paul's talismanic role in the text is clear, even before Florence enters the scene. Dombey, pondering his family life, realises that he should have conceived of his children as one being: 'Oh, how much better than this that he had loved her as had his boy, and lost her as he had his boy, and laid them in their early grave together!' (Ch. 59, 796). Dombey reformulates the question of familial exclusion (so key to the primal scene) by situating Florence in relation to Paul, rather than to the

[10] Shakespeare also uses this pun in *Hamlet*; in Act I, Scene 2, Hamlet mockingly remarks to Claudius, 'I am too much in the sun' (1.2.67). *Hamlet* is a key source for *Great Expectations*, and echoes throughout *Dombey*.

dead mother, or indeed to Edith. Dickens demonstrates the potency of psychical reality here. It is only through Paul's mediating (non-)presence that Dombey is able to conceive of Florence as his daughter and a potential recipient of his love. As a consequence, he continues to wish her dead, as he has done since Paul's demise: Florence is a ghostly presence who has 'never changed' (Ch. 59, 796). Dombey thinks of his children in terms of a 'double childhood' and a 'double loss' (797). Florence is meaningless without Paul: 'It was one child no more. He re-united them in his thoughts, and they were never asunder' (798). Dombey's mirror image is again seen, just as it was at the christening party, but now it appears as a 'picture': a 'spectral' 'it', which imagines the blood of a 'wounded man' wending a path into the hallway (801). Dombey's suicidal alienation is beautifully rendered here; it is the mirror image who thinks, the mirror image whose hand looks 'wicked and murderous' (801). As Cain argues, the absolute collapse of Dombey's narcissistic conception of self is at hand prior to Florence's return, 'which re-establishes Dombey as subject' (66). As Florence enters, Dombey looks to the glass and 'only saw his own reflection […] and at his knees, his daughter!' (802). However, something must be added to this analysis. Just as Florence enters, a 'gleam of light' finds its way into the darkened room, 'a ray of sun' (801). The slippage between sun/son is used to indicate Paul's necessary presence in this encounter between father and daughter: the text's symbolism colludes with Dombey's earlier idea of the children as one being. Further, Florence's identification with her son, Paul Gay, 'teaches her' to return to her father: 'We will teach our little child to love and honour you; and we will tell him, when he can understand, that you had a son of that name once, and that he died, and you were very sorry' (802). This child is a new talisman, a living point of emotional orientation, correlated with 'glorious sun [son] shine' (802). The rebirth of 'Paul' means that Florence's internal image of her father coalesces, and she feels retrospectively guilty that she was not able or willing to achieve this previously. The continuing tragedy for the reader is that Florence can only situate herself in the 'expectation' of her father's desire if she is the keeper of a boy: little Paul Gay becomes the conduit for a heterosexual father-daughter romance. Later, in the Midshipman, while Dombey lies on his sickbed, 'Florence, having her baby in her arms, began in a low voice to sing to the little fellow, and sang the old tune she had so often sung to the dead child' (Ch. 61, 819). Florence reappropriates her old maternal role with this echo of the tune and, through the baby, assumes her daughterly place for the first time. The birth of Paul Gay legitimises Florence's association with maternity, drawing it out of the shadows of the old house into the light, and into life in the Midshipman under the auspices of the appropriately named Uncle *Sol*.

In the deleted passage with which Dickens initially planned to conclude the novel, Dombey is haunted by the whispering waves for the first time:

> They speak to him of Florence and his altered heart; of Florence and their ceaseless murmuring to her of the love, eternal and inimitable, extending still, beyond the sea, beyond the sky, to the invisible country far away.
>
> Never from the mighty sea may voices rise too late, to come between us and the unseen region on the other shore. Better, far better, that they whispered of that region in our childish ears, and the swift river hurried us away! (833*n.*)

He hears a maternal call, a call that urges him to remember: to perform a reparative mourning which simultaneously acknowledges that he too must die. In Greenberg's terms, Dombey allows himself to hear the traumatic echoes, thus enabling the trauma to be worked through. The need to live in death is an ethical one, and in Dickens's final scheme, the maternal voices terrifyingly, but inescapably, negotiate our journeys between life and death.

Despite this ethical exhortation the parental problematic remains unresolved, and symbolically irresolvable. The published ending to the novel again complicates the familial dynamics: 'But no one, except Florence, knows the measure of the white-haired gentleman's affection for girl. That story never goes about. The child herself almost wonders at a certain secrecy he keeps in it. He hoards her in his heart. [...] He is fondest of her and most loving to her, when there is no creature by' (Ch. 62, 833). While Dombey's celebrated love for his grandson is a straightforward reformulation of his love for his dead son, the love for the granddaughter is an entirely new phenomenon. Dickens undoubtedly intended this love to represent a displaced reparation towards Florence herself, and yet it is kept secret. Without being mediated through the male figure, whether the son or the grandson, there is still something potentially dangerous about love for the (grand)daughter. Considering the centrality of the firm 'Dombey and *Son*' in his world view, Dombey's untold desire for another son must logically have been the motive for his second marriage, and yet the novel never refers to this, perhaps because it would make it all too clear that symbolically it is his own daughter who finally gives birth to the longed-for second son. The love that Dombey develops for Florence is primarily displaced onto her daughter, and remains hidden from the world, if not from Florence herself. This is a highly compromised resolution of the maternal and paternal conflicts established in the novel's primary trauma; the father-son narrative is still openly embraced and celebrated, a 'story' to be told to the world (833); the father-daughter story is private, a love happening behind closed doors. Further, while at the beginning of the novel, the daughter was a 'base coin' who could not be traded, by the end of the novel, the (grand)daughter emerges as a coin who will be possessively 'hoarded'. A sense of thwarted possession underlies both images. As we may expect based upon our reading of the novel's primal scene, the circulation of desire between father and daughter is dependent on the emotional potency of the son and the tacit blessing of the mother,[11] but despite all of Dickens's manoeuvres, this working-through remains, provocatively, only a 'partial' scheme.

Parental Substitutions and the Ethics of Guilt: *Great Expectations*

In Dickens's earlier *Bildungsroman*, *David Copperfield*, the ironic, playful, account of David's birth which opens the novel points towards the epistemological problem which underpins the autobiographical genre: how the author can take ownership of their experience in writing:

> Whether I shall turn out to be the hero of my own life, or whether that station will be held by anybody else, these pages must show. To begin my life with the beginning of my life, I record that I was born (as I have been informed and believe) on a Friday, at twelve o'clock at night. It was remarked that the clock began to strike, and I began to cry, simultaneously. (Ch. 1, 1)

Dickens wrote *David Copperfield* directly after the 'autobiographical fragment' and as numerous critics have argued his self-conscious exploration

[11] Edith gives this blessing when Florence visits her in the care of uncle Feenix: 'When he loves his Florence most, he will hate me least. When he is most proud and happy in her and her children, he will be most repentant of his own part in the dark vision of our married life. At that time I will be repentant too—let him know it then' (Ch. 61, 827).

of what it means to write autobiography is of relevance throughout (see Welsh 1987, 110–112). *Great Expectations* reads differently: the problem is not only about how to write one's own story, but also who authors the child's life. *Great Expectations* can be read as a sequence of parental epitaphs; nevertheless, Pip not only writes parental epitaphs, but also his own. When confronting Old Orlick towards the end of the novel he writes, 'far more terrible than death was the dread of being misremembered after death' (III.14, 442). Pip's identity is rendered uncanny in the opening lines of the novel, where as an orphan, he is defined by a series of parental surrogates; Dickens charts the return of the repressed in Gothicised terms. Pip creates a complex fantasy structure around these surrogates, which determines his progress through the novel. The novel's intertextual echoes create a deeper sense of textual haunting. Through the repetitive, and frequently ironic, use of *Hamlet* Dickens investigates the effect of the parental demand, and the spectrality of the familial. Through his more subtle, varied, use of *Frankenstein*, he poses a question concerning creation: who makes the child—and for what purpose? This is a direct extension of his enquiry in *Dombey*.

Unlike *Dombey*, critics have read *Great Expectations* in terms of trauma; the opening scene in the graveyard is an exemplary literary primal scene.[12] The messages passed from parents to children are, again, problematised, and Dickens frames the question in terms of material inheritance and psychological influence. In *Dombey and Son*, the didactic, omniscient, narrator self-consciously shadows the novel: in *Great Expectations*, Dickens plays with the limitations of perspective and explores the possibilities of focalisation through Pip. In *Dombey*, Florence's illogical guilt is a refraction of Dombey's own violating self-importance. By bringing his child protagonist centre stage in *Great Expectations*, guilt is shown to be an all-pervading concern.

Pip or Pig

Pip's terrifying 'vivid' encounter with Magwitch in the graveyard stands in for the horrific loss of his parents and siblings, which is never fully

[12] Peter Brooks (1992) analyses the novel through a systematic exploration of 'official' and 'repressed' plots: he argues that the energy released in the novel's primal scene is unsuccessfully bound within the official plots, surfaces intermittently, and then bursts through upon the return of Magwitch.

acknowledged by the narrator. This primal scene is inscribed in the novel as a precipitating force. It can, however, make little sense without the two further meetings with Magwitch which follow. As we see from the unfolding of events, the encounter continues to resonate—to echo; the meeting with Magwitch determines Pip's subsequent attitude to his 'expectations' and to Miss Havisham and Estella. The structure of *Great Expectations* is far from straightforward; while the Magwitch plot can be charted through an uncanny process of repetition and return as Peter Brooks (1992) shows, this plot is inseparable from the two other familial constellations which define Pip: Mrs. Joe and Joe, and Miss Havisham and Estella. These three groupings create an extended topography formative for Pip in the childhood section of the novel. The narrator constructs his story through juxtaposed chapters, which move between the three family groupings. The novel must be read in two time frames: the first, the level of experience where the child and young man fail to interpret the world correctly; and the second retrospective level where the much older Pip corrects his previous perspective. It is evident, however, that the retrospective narrator cannot simply stand apart from his past self: as in the 'autobiographical fragment', past collapses into the present, while the present redefines the past.

Pip's meeting with Magwitch establishes the first in a series of familial displacements where surrogate parental figures are found, or inflicted upon him. Pip's guilty identification with Magwitch renders him criminal in his own eyes, but also displaces the very real guilt he should (and later does) feel for his snobbish behaviour towards Joe. Dickens inscribes the loss of family in the opening lines:

> My father's family name being Pirrip, and my Christian name Philip, my infant tongue could make of both names nothing longer or more explicit than Pip. So, I called myself Pip, and came to be called Pip. (I.1, 3)

There is boldness and vulnerability in this statement. Pip connects and distances himself from his family in the graveyard, rejecting his father's name, while using it as the basis for his own self-created identity. His family are humorously portrayed in their inadequacy through the description of their gravestones: his mother is 'freckled and sickly' (3). The narrative voice is focalised through the child's perspective, but the adult retains an ironic distance from his child self. The graveyard scene provokes

Pip's first realisation of himself as an individual operating in relation to a larger structure:

> My first most vivid and broad impression of the identity of things, seems to me to have been gained on a memorable raw afternoon towards evening. At such a time I found out for certain, that this bleak place overgrown with nettles was the churchyard; and that Philip Pirrip, late of this parish, and also Georgiana wife of the above, were dead and buried [...] and that the small bundle of shivers growing afraid of it all and beginning to cry, was Pip. (3–4)

Pip is excluded from his family. He is unable to visualise them effectively, and this originary occlusion of sight leads to his compensatory *conceptualisation*: a paradigm decisive for the novel as a whole. The use of the present participles—'growing' and 'beginning'—underscores the continuing importance this scene holds for Pip: his self-awareness begins here. The boundary between retrospective narrator and child protagonist is blurred. When telling Pip the story of his life, Magwitch presents a comparable notion of self-consciousness, saying 'I first become aware of myself, down in Essex, a thieving turnips for a living' (III.4, 344). In the opening passage, the use of the continuous grammatical form means that Pip's first realisation of himself appears inseparable from Magwitch's intrusion, which directly follows it. Looking at this scene in the context of Pip's retrospective narration, it is comparable to a screen memory, 'vivid', 'broad' and almost disproportionally significant in itself: after all, if Pip's acquaintance with Magwitch ended at the end of the first chapter, the novel itself could not exist, and Pip's guilty identification with Magwitch would not be possible. Afterwardsness is therefore important to the construction of the scene. Magwitch functions in psychological and metonymic terms: he is the symbol of the criminality that *already* shadows the orphan Pip.

At the same time, this is the moment at which change becomes possible. The scene is defined by a temporal dualism. Although Chapter 1 defines *Great Expectations*, it also points towards a mythic origin which evades direct representation, and which is intimately connected to the relation between adults and children. The representational impasse is revealed through Pip's naïve identification of his parents with their gravestones, underscoring the parental absence, as well as accurately portraying the littleness of the child protagonist. The mythic origin is unknown and unknowable. In his analysis of *Bleak House*, Jordan (2011) suggests that Esther's primal scene is based on her imagined abandonment at the hands of Lady Dedlock (47). Pip's primal scene is not constructed in quite the same way: prior to the appearance of Magwitch, Pip's imagination centres round his lack of comprehension regarding his parents, dead brothers, and Mrs. Joe. It is not abandonment, then, that structures his fantasy, but negation. However, in both cases, it is the child's exclusion from the family structure which is formative.

There is a forcible parental substitution: Magwitch appears by the grave of Pip's father, bursting in on Pip's reverie as an excessive presence, aggressively filling the absence represented by the gravestones:

> 'Hold your noise!' cried a terrible voice, as a man started up from among the graves at the side of the church porch [...] A fearful man, all in coarse grey, with a great iron on his leg. A man with no hat, and with broken shoes, and with an old rag tied round his head. A man who had been soaked in water, and smothered in mud, and lamed by stones, and cut by flints, and stung by nettles, and torn by briars; who limped, and shivered, and glared and growled; (I.1, 4)

Magwitch's appearance, scarred by his escape across the marsh, lies in sharp contrast to Pip's initial description of the deadened landscape. There is an intense physicality, underlined by the anaphoric 'A man'. The alliteration of 'soaked', 'smothered', 'stones', 'stung' creates a rhythmic impetus and a sense of the violence that has been perpetrated against Magwitch. The final list of verbs, 'limped', 'shivered', 'glared', 'growled', defines Magwitch in terms of action and movement. He causes literal upheaval as he repeatedly throws Pip up in the air, making the church go 'head over heels' (4). From being radically excluded by his dead family's stony incomprehensible silence, Pip is forcibly incorporated into Magwitch's story. Magwitch's association with the dead is hinted at, however, as Pip imagines him 'eluding the hands of the dead people', and then as the hanged pirate 'come to life' (7).

Magwitch represents the spectral power of the paternal: like Hamlet's father, he makes a formative demand on the child. This demand is brought back to the question of identity when Pip receives his expectations and Jaggers tells him that he must be known as 'Mr. Pip': by making this stipulation, Magwitch retrospectively endows Pip's name with quasi-paternal authority. In a beautifully suggestive passage, Pip describes the landscape as he watched the convict retreat: 'The marshes were just a long black horizontal line then, as I stopped to look after him; and the river was just another horizontal line, not nearly so broad nor yet so black; and the sky was just a row of long angry red lines and dense black lines intermixed' (7). The marshes appear like an overwritten page, replacing the blankness that defined Pip's initial description of the view: the 'dark flat wilderness' (4). This 'writing' of the landscape refracts back onto our understanding of the scene as a whole, and what is at stake within it: the authoring of Pip himself, as well as Pip's role as author.

The childhood portion of the novel is saturated with Pip's youthful ideas of criminality, whether ethical, legal, fanciful or symbolic. Two violent actions are repeatedly referred to, either directly or symbolically: hanging and cannibalism. The first represents the criminal's fate; the second is the definitive crime. Both of these images are introduced in the first chapter, and both become associated with family, and more specifically with parental surrogates. The child Pip's fanciful association of the convict and the pirate leads to his thought that Magwitch was 'going back to hook himself up [on the gibbet] again'. This is a grim prolepsis (or expectation) provided by the narrator, as well as an example of the child's imaginative vision, an ironic dual perspective critical to the novel's functioning. As the novel progresses, the idea of hanging recurs, representative of criminality in the abstract, and indicative of Pip's identification with this primary moment. Hanging becomes closely related to Miss Havisham; as a child at Satis House Pip thinks he sees her hanging from the beam of the brewery, 'a figure all in yellow white, with but one shoe to the feet' (I.8, 65); just prior to her final conflagration, the 'childish association' is revived and Pip sees this vision once again (III.10, 398). Miss Havisham is implicitly presented as criminal, suicide and ghost. Through the text's symbolic processes, she is closely associated with Magwitch.

In the opening scene, Magwitch introduces the idea of cannibalism through his reference to the unnamed Compeyson:

> You fail, or you go from my words in any partickler, no matter how small it is, and your heart and your liver shall be tore out, roasted and ate. Now I ain't alone, as you may think I am. (I.1, 6)

This threat introduces the idea that adults feast upon children. The trauma underlying *Great Expectations* is undoubtedly one of identity, but here Dickens renders the parental demand Gothicised, violating, and perverse through its association with cannibalism. The manner in which parents violently possess or alternatively prohibit the child's identity is a recurrent concern. Pip is framed (consciously by Dickens, incidentally by Magwitch) as the Promethean figure, punished for his hubris in Hades by having his heart and liver torn out daily while being chained to a rock. This subtle use of *Frankenstein: or the Modern Prometheus* introduces the ideas of creation, overreaching and binding, which are critical to Pip's story. (Later, Pip compares himself to Frankenstein and Magwitch to the creature [III.1, 337].) Bearing in mind the Promethean myth deployed by Mary Shelley and Dickens, the same questions are posed in each case, who creates, for whom, and for what? Magwitch's Promethean threat creates the first link between the unnamed but horrifying Compeyson, and the repetitive image of broken hearts. This image, critical to the novel as a whole, can be linked back to the fragment. The idea that the heart can be 'rent' with emotional pain (Forster 1874, 1:47) which penetrates it with corrosive force is crucial to the traumatic model elaborated in Dickens's own history, and he uses it as one of the structuring metaphors of *Great Expectations*.

The symbolic significance of eating is reinscribed when Pip returns to the marsh to give Magwitch the stolen food. As Brooks rightly points out, there is a fundamental duality to Pip's feeling; while he is clearly terrified, he feels pity for Magwitch's 'desolation' (I.3, 18): Brooks reads this scene as a 'communion' (Brooks 1992, 117). The child nurtures the starving adult—as Pip's heart and liver could have done, if Magwitch had been in earnest previously—and it is this nurturance that creates the indissoluble bond between them. Throughout Dickens's fiction, the child's nurturance of the parent is presented as ethically meaningful. There is always the danger; however, the parent will thrive at the cost of the child's starvation, as we see in the case of Amy and William Dorrit. Regardless of Pip's increasing horror at his child self's actions (a horror handled equivocally by the narrator), this moment of communion is a moral one as it is governed by fellow feeling rather than shame. The guilty identification with Magwitch is self-consciously returned to throughout Pip's narration, but is also part of the text's wider processes: looking at Magwitch eat, the child notices 'a decided similarity between the dog's way of eating, and the man's' (I.3, 20); this is echoed at Satis House, where Pip is fed by Estella 'as if I were a dog in disgrace' (I.8, 63). In the final childhood encounter with Magwitch, Pip reaches out to him with a sense of fellowship. The whole scene is rendered in legalistic terms as Compeyson calls upon the arresting officers to 'bear witness' (I.5, 37). Compeyson's continuing failure to 'look at' (38) Magwitch is indicative of his social oppression of the latter: the absolute refusal to recognise him or validate his identity. This is set against the child Pip's urgent desire for Magwitch's attention:

> I had been waiting for him to see me, that I might try to assure him of my innocence. It was not at all expressed to me that he even comprehended my intention, for he gave me a look that I did not understand, and it all passed in a moment. But if he had looked at me for an hour or a day, I could not have remembered his face ever afterwards, as having been more attentive. (39)

Pip's identification with Magwitch is underscored by Joe, who remarks, 'we wouldn't have you starved to death, for it, poor miserable fellow-creature – Would us, Pip?' (37). This is an important moment: as Pip finally shows through his own actions, this is the moral response to the situation. When Pip attempts to secure Magwitch's escape out of London, he does not reflect on the possible dangers he might himself suffer, in either the narration or in the past-tense action. It is simply the right thing to do. However, at this early point in the novel, even the narrator seems unsure of the ethics; in a short and wholly reflective chapter, he dwells on his failure to tell Joe what had happened, writing, 'In a word, I was too cowardly to do what I knew to be right, as I had been too cowardly to avoid doing what I knew to be wrong' (I.6, 42). While the novel does not openly condone Pip's theft, his pity for Magwitch must redeem the act in the eyes of the reader, as Joe's comment indicates.

Joe is the ethical heart of the novel, but this can only be actualised through the introduction of Magwitch into the story. The two paternal figures provide working-class narratives of identity, which are formative for Pip's understanding at different points. At first glance, following the opening scene, *Great Expectations* pushes male violence into an extra-familial space through Old Orlick and Compeyson; however, Joe's childhood memories demonstrate the formative importance of paternal violence. Pip reassesses Joe's seeming impotence when he hears his childhood story, in which Joe describes his mother's frequent attempts to escape from the brutality of her husband:

> my father were that good in his hart that he couldn't abear to be without us. So, he'd come with a most tremenjous crowd and make such a row at the doors of the houses where we was, that they used to be obligated to have no more to do with us and to give us up to him. And then he took us home and hammered us. (I.7, 47)

It is a disturbing account, perhaps rendered all the more so because of Joe's pragmatism and forgiveness. Joe explains that his toleration of Mrs. Joe's excesses came of his desire not to be his father: 'I see so much in my poor mother, of a woman drudging and slaving and breaking her honest hart and never getting no peace in her mortal days, that I'm dead afeerd of going wrong in the way of not doing what's right by a woman, and I'd fur rather of the two go wrong the t'other way, and be a little ill-conwenienced myself' (50–51). Importantly, bearing in mind the opening scene in the graveyard, Joe had wanted to write an epitaph for his father, defending him from future judgment: 'Whatsume'er the failings on his part, Remember reader that he were that good in his hart'. Joe goes on to say that 'I made it [...] my own self. I made it in a moment. It was like striking out a horseshoe complete, in a single blow' (48). His rhyming couplet is laden with Dickensian sentiment, but should not be overlooked as a result. Both Joe and Magwitch are strong authorial presences in Pip's own story: the need to translate their stories, as well as his own, provides narrative dynamism. Joe's loyalty towards his father contrasts with Pip's own neglectful behaviour towards Joe, and his initial rejection of Magwitch. This is not, then, simply a moment of ironic pathos. The epitaph's address to the 'reader' is a self-conscious moment, which draws attention to *Great Expectations*' status as text, and reminds us to think of Pip's 'hart'. Pip is also an author, whose narrative can be read as a series of extended parental epitaphs. His role as narrator can be related back to this moment, and to the opening scene in the graveyard. However, as in the 'autobiographical fragment', past affect is both formative and activated in the moment of writing. Describing Joe's confrontation with Jaggers, the narrator interjects:

> O dear good Joe, whom I was so ready to leave and so unthankful to, I see you again, with your muscular blacksmith's arm before your eyes, and your broad chest heaving, and your voice dying away. O dear good faithful tender Joe, I feel the loving tremble of your hand upon my arm, as solemnly this day as if it had been the rustle of an angel's wing! (I.18, 140)

The description of the 'voice dying away' and the 'angel's wing' leaves us in little doubt that the *narrating* Pip mourns the permanent loss of his foster father. Despite this, the past continues to haunt: he can 'see' and 'feel' Joe in the present tense of the narration. Pip employs an elegiac tone when recounting key episodes with both Joe and Magwitch, and this correlation supports the idea that Joe is equally lost to him at the time of writing.

Refusing to identify with his father, Joe fails to protect the little boy whom he loves. His protection of Mrs. Joe's 'hart' leads to the scarring of Pip's: the deep-seated sense of injustice and sensitivity Pip refers to at Satis House (I.8, 64). After nursing Pip back to health towards the end of the novel, Joe repeats the lesson he has learnt from the wiser Biddy: 'Supposing ever you kep any little matter to yourself, when you was a little child, you kep it mostly because you know'd as J. Gargery's power to part you and Tickler in sunders, were not fully equal to his inclinations' (III.18, 464). Joe's failure to protect Pip is formative: another 'compromised message' he must interpret, just as he falteringly deciphered the tombstones in the opening scene. Dickens describes the complex network of conflicting adult messages from the child's perspective: as Pip says, he must 'find out for [him]self' (I.2, 8) what expressions mean. Pip is actively caught between his 'all-powerful sister' and the self-willed impotence of Joe. Mrs. Joe represents guilt and conscience; her cleanliness is 'more uncomfortable and unacceptable than dirt itself' (I.4, 23), and her lessons teach him that childhood curiosity leads directly to crime:

> People are put in the Hulks because they murder, and because they rob, and forge, and do all sorts of bad; and they always begin by asking questions. (I.2, 15)

Mrs. Joe's unloving emphasis on her duty and obligation, shown in the repetitive sayings about her apron and her 'bringing up by hand', means that the performance of duty seems more criminal than neglect itself: even feeding Pip takes on a brutal character, as the bread and butter could be laced with pins and needles (I.2, 10). Mrs. Joe's clichéd language mystifies her maternal role, which is therefore—in itself—deeply compromised ideologically. The Christmas dinner scene is vital in illuminating Pip's position in relation to his adult circle. He metaphorically lies in the same position as the pig, 'the four-footed Squeaker', which sits on the

Christmas table (I.4, 27). He is cut with adult criticisms that operate like a knife. Pumblechook describes Pip's alternative life as a little pig:

> You would have been disposed of for so many shillings according to the market price of the article, and Dunstable the butcher would have come up to you as you lay in your straw, and he would have whipped you under his left arm, and with his right he would have tucked up his frock to get a penknife from out of his waistcoat-pocket, and he would have shed your blood and had your life. No bringing up by hand then. Not a bit of it! (I.4, 28)

Here, we see another detailed exposition of adult cannibalism, an image introduced by Magwitch. The intricate detail of Pumblechook's speech is comic and horrific. It seems that certain death and ruin would have ensued if Mrs. Joe had not adopted Pip. Despite the cruel excess of Pumblechook, Dickens makes a serious point, similar to that made by Thomas Carlyle in *Past and Present*, as discussed in Chapter 1: the elder generation preys upon the younger. This moment underscores the violence that defines the novel: the sense of being wounded and violated. Despite being her only living relative, Pip is completely excluded from his sister's love or esteem. It is unclear why Mrs. Joe despises him, and this uncertainty is important to her function in the novel: in Laplanche's terms, it is the 'noise' inhabiting the message. In *Freud and the Sexual* (2011) Laplanche writes, 'an interference or 'noise' comes to inhabit this communication like a parasite' (21). There is a disjunction between the child's perception of what should be, and what is: his sister hates him, while Magwitch protects him following the capture on the marshes. This disjunction constitutes the unformed question that follows Pip throughout the novel, and which he attempts to translate into his search for gentility, his relation to Miss Havisham and his aspirations for Estella.

Haunted

Pip does not simply accept the messages he receives as a child: although he accepts the guilt Mrs. Joe ascribes to him, he also realises she is 'unjust' (I.8, 64). The attack on Mrs. Joe is a key scene in adding to his accumulation of guilt: Pip immediately connects himself to the crime: 'I was at first disposed to believe that *I* must have had some hand in the attack upon my sister, or at all events that as her near relation, popularly known to be under obligations to her, I was a more legitimate object of suspicion than any one else' (I.16, 119). The plot metes out a horrific, hyperbolic, punishment to Mrs. Joe, and the punitive violence against the feminine is later perpetuated against Miss Havisham and Estella. Pip's initial feeling of guilt is reinforced when he realises that Mrs. Joe was attacked with Magwitch's discarded leg iron, writing, 'It was horrible to think that I had provided the weapon, however undesignedly, but I could hardly think otherwise' (I.16, 121). Dickens reinforces Pip's symbolic connection to the attack when Old Orlick confesses that it was jealousy of Pip that pushed him to commit the crime. The guilt is doubled: the weapon is associated with Pip and so, eventually, is the motive. In some ways, structurally, it is irrelevant that Pip does not commit the crime himself. Old Orlick is Pip's double: he names himself (in the third-person); he slouches and sulks in resentment at his position; and he stalks Biddy in a sinister echo of Pip's 'haunting' of Estella. Reduced to a state of near childhood after the attack, with the 'bearing of a child' towards Old Orlick (I.16, 122), Mrs Joe 'would often put her hands to her head, and would then remain for about a week at a time in some gloomy aberration of mind' (122). In this liminal state, she represents those parts of Pip's childhood history that cannot be fully assimilated. Her final words 'Joe', 'Pardon' and 'Pip' indicate the disturbingly redemptive quality of her punishment (II.16, 282).

Pip's ambivalent attitude towards Magwitch is an essential part of his mental life, and adds to his sense of guilt, and the ever-pervading air of crime actualised in Little Britain and Newgate. As with Paul and Florence Dombey, the trauma is not simply something that happens *to* Pip, it provides the dynamism for his subjectivity. Just as the narrator identifies the primal encounter with Magwitch as the determining moment in his childhood, Pip clearly describes Magwitch's return as the pivotal event in his adult life: 'I pass on, unhindered, to the event that had impended over me longer yet; the event that had begun to be prepared for, before I knew that the world held Estella' (II.19, 311). Between Magwitch's capture and his return, Dickens creates a series of moments that refer back to the childhood encounter, creating a recurring sense of dissociation. When Pip meets the unnamed convict in Chapter 10, he claims to have 'forgotten' the encounters with Magwitch: 'a feature in my low career' (79). However, from this point on, Dickens does not imply that Pip represses the encounters from conscious memory; instead, the *consciousness* of his memory is loaded with a disorientating, destabilising force. When he is given the two 'sweltering 1-pound notes' by the unnamed convict, Pip tells us he felt 'stupefied' (I.10, 79) and 'spellbound' (78). Following this meeting, he is troubled by the memory of the file in his sleep: 'I saw the file coming at me out of a door, without seeing who held it, and I screamed myself awake' (79). This dream implies an invisible authority and control; the hand holding the file is unseen, but could refer to Magwitch, the unknown convict, Pip, or indeed someone else entirely. Pip is not the agent of his own story. After attending Mr. Wopsle's performance in London, another dream underscores this idea:

> I had to give my hand in marriage to Herbert's Clara, or play Hamlet to Miss Havisham's Ghost, before twenty thousand people, without knowing twenty words of it. (II.12, 258)

Parental figures become associated with death, spectrality and haunting. Children are not only pre-determined, they are also possessed. When Mrs. Joe is attacked, Pip writes that 'I suffered unspeakable trouble while I considered and reconsidered whether I should at last dissolve the spell of my childhood, and tell Joe all the story' (I.16, 109). The initial wound becomes silenced: clearly echoing the tone of Dickens's 'autobiographical fragment', Pip writes it is a 'secret' which 'had so grown into me and become a part of myself, that I could not tear it away' (110).[13] Each time the memory intrudes it brings with it an indefinable terror—a traumatic return: in London, listening to the unnamed convict recounting the story of Magwitch and the two one-pound notes, Pip's dissociation recurs again:

> As I walked on to the hotel, I felt that a dread, much exceeding the mere apprehension of a painful or disagreeable recognition, made me tremble.

[13]The primacy of the secret in Dickens's psychological vision can be compared to Nicolas Abraham and Maria Torok's theory of the crypt: the crypt contains a 'memory they buried without legal burial place: The memory is of an idyll, experienced with a valued object and yet for some reason unspeakable' ('The Lost Object', 141). Pip's story can be read in comparable terms; his moment of communion with Magwitch is both valued *and* unspeakable. There are further avenues of thought that could be developed here in terms of the way in which the child Pip is—in twenty-first-century terminology—"groomed" into secrecy. Ultimately of course, Dickens recuperates this in ethical terms.

> I am confident that it took no distinctness of shape, and that it was the revival for a few minutes of the terror of childhood. (II.10, 230)

The disjunction here between the experiencing self and the narrating self is used to emphasise the young man's inability to take ownership of his own childhood story. The older Pip intervenes in the present tense: 'I *am* confident.' This resonates with the tone taken by Dickens in his own 'autobiographical fragment'. The fragment is again directly echoed when Pip reflects on the impossibility of making reparation to Joe and Biddy, writing 'I could never, never, never, undo what I had done' (II.20, 321).[14] While in the fragment Dickens echoes Lear's words to underline the impossibility of forgetting his mother's actions, Pip reflects on the impossibility of his own actions being forgotten. Memory is a trap, a binding structure, as well as the source of destabilising affect. When Magwitch appears in Pip's London lodgings, Pip's recognition takes him back to the churchyard:

> Even yet, I could not recal a single feature but I knew him! If the wind and the rain had driven away the intervening years, had scattered all the intervening objects, had swept us to the churchyard where we first stood face to face on such different levels, I could not have known my convict more distinctly than I knew him now, as he sat in the chair before the fire. (II.20, 313)

This recognition is still a misrecognition; when Pip realises shortly afterwards that Magwitch is his benefactor, he is physically broken down by it: 'With my heart beating like a heavy hammer of disordered action [...] All the truth of my position came flashing on me; and its disappointments, dangers, disgraces, consequences of all kinds, rushed in in such a multitude that I was borne down by them and had to struggle for every breath I drew' (II.20, 315). In the opening chapter, Magwitch turned Pip upside down; here, the psychological effect is the same. Pip's brain fever is critical in this scheme; through illness, Pip is returned to a state of childhood, writing 'I fancied I was little Pip' (III.18, 462). This return to 'little Pip' enables a partial working-through of the childhood traumas.

[14]The refrain is also echoed in the following exchange between Magwitch and Pip: '"But didn't you *never* think it might be me?" "O, no, no, no," I returned. "*Never, never*!"' (II.20 318 [my emphasis]).

Pip is able to attend to Joe's speech for the first time since receiving his expectations. The (partially) curative function of his brain fever parallels Dombey's infantilisation at the hands of his daughter in the final chapters of *Dombey and Son*. Dickens posits, what sociologist Jeffrey Weeks calls, the 'equality of vulnerability' as an ethical force, 'our equal fallibility in negotiating the conditions of our intimate life' (Weeks 2008, 654).

Pip is propelled through the plot by the movement between different parental figures, and the underlying question: with whom should he identify? The attentions Pip receives from Miss Havisham appear, falsely, to close the gap of interpretation: he expects great things that will justify the weakness of his family and his own failings. Pip claims as an adult that Miss Havisham 'had adopted Estella, she had as good as adopted me' (II.10, 232). His visit to Satis House forces him to place himself within a wider social context, as a 'common labouring boy' (I.8, 61). This reframes the primary sense of exclusion Pip felt in relation to his own family. Through Estella, Pip's aspirational class identification becomes correlated with his desire[15]: as a child, her 'contempt [...] was so strong, that it became infectious and [he] caught it' (61). There is a temporal paradox: Satis house is unmoving, but for Pip, it represents the progression of time within his own history. After his first visit there he writes,

> That was a memorable day for me, for it made great changes in me. But, it is the same with any life. Imagine one selected day struck out of it, and think how different its course would have been. Pause you who read this, and think for a moment of the long chain of iron or gold, of thorn or flowers, that would never have bound you, but for the formation of the first link on one memorable day. (I.9, 73)

This passage describes the binding nature of childhood experience and of time itself. In contrast to the encounters with Magwitch, Pip does not attempt to suppress his experiences at Satis House; instead, they forcibly usurp his prior experience. However, this usurpation not only inscribes Satis House in his memory, it also creates a new source of dissociation. The narrator repeatedly refers to the cloudiness, confusion and dreamlike influence of Satis House: 'Is it to be wondered that my thoughts were

[15]The connection between love and class-identification is reinforced in inverse fashion through Magwitch, who plays out his love by elevating Pip's class. His love for Pip becomes the identification of a father, but it is also indicative of an aspirational class feeling, which he cannot enact himself.

dazed, as my eyes were, when I came out into the natural light from the misty yellow rooms?' (I.12, 96). Dickens constructs an extended allegory for traumatisation through Satis House, and like Wemmick, Miss Havisham is herself a literalised metaphor. Miss Havisham fixates on her moment of pain. In her case, trauma is directly correlated with the actual event, rather than the echoing repetition of it; however, despite this, the event pales in comparison with her response to it. Her self-willed incarceration freezes her at the moment of traumatisation. That is not to say that repetition is unimportant; despite the seeming stasis of Satis House, the uncanny repetition of trauma is played out in the next generation through Estella and Pip. The trauma at Satis House is inherited. Although female spectres and maternal zombies are found in *Dombey and Son* and *Little Dorrit*, Miss Havisham is the most extreme representation of the melancholic subject found in any of Dickens's novels. Miss Havisham identifies with the act of cruelty which was committed against her, and she ponders upon herself as if she were already a corpse: 'When the ruin is complete [...] and when they lay me dead, in my bride's dress on the bride's table – which shall be done, and which will be the finished curse upon him' (I.11, 89). She retains the love relation as a traumatising self-punishment. Miss Havisham's refusal to acknowledge change transforms her love and hatred into putrefying objects and even the bridal decorations take on a swarming life of their own. It is significant that she, alone of the parental characters, refers to herself as the victim of cannibalism: looking at her wedding cake she says, 'It and I have worn away together. The mice have gnawed at it, and sharper teeth than teeth of mice have gnawed at me' (89). The emotional violence Compeyson has perpetrated against her, the eating away of her heart, is replayed in her own behaviour towards Estella. Her sexual obsession is displaced in her 'burning' love (II.19, 302). Miss Havisham is forever caught between bride and wife; both wicked witch and sleeping beauty.

In *Dombey and Son*, the seductive maternal presence is subtly presented through Fanny Dombey, but there is nothing subtle about Dickens's representation of Miss Havisham. She is persecutory, threatening and fixated on a sexual moment. She damages both Pip and Estella; when he is apprenticed to Joe, Pip writes that 'some confounding remembrance of the Havisham days would fall upon me as a destructive missile, and scatter my wits again' (I.17, 131). His primary encounter with Magwitch becomes subsumed under his desire for Estella. He is bound within Miss Havisham's vicarious sexual revenge and is therefore a stand-in for

Compeyson. Children become the point of intersection for adult conflicts. The *explicitly* sexual nature of this conflict is foregrounded in *Great Expectations*. Estella herself is curiously static, and Miss Havisham's attempt to pursue a work of sexual mourning through her ultimately fails. Miss Havisham discovers that she has taught Estella too well when the latter decides to marry Drummle. Estella is incapable of love, rebuking her foster mother, 'I am what you have made me' (III.5, 358). Pip is likewise bound by Miss Havisham and endlessly replays *her* obsession with Estella. Miss Havisham's later claim that Pip had 'made [his] own snares' (III.5, 358) is true but also a sophistical lie. Pip's response to Miss Havisham ensnares him, but nevertheless, she encourages him, provokes him and traps him in his response. The constraint explicit in Pip's relationship with Miss Havisham and Estella is perpetuated in the novel's dialogue with money. Through the symbolic use of 'apprenticeship' as a concept, the relation between parents and children is portrayed as binding and repressing.

Class Spectres

Dickens mobilises social concerns through the family; Pip's expectations are inextricable from the parental addresses that alternately negate him, adopt him and name him. However, this has ramifications, not only for the representation of family and subjectivity, but also for our understanding of *social* identity. Dickens draws together the formation of personal and social identity conceptually through the primary importance the novel grants to the 'address'. As in Louis Althusser's model of 'interpellation', becoming a social subject in *Great Expectations* means being 'subjected to' a class-based ideology (Althusser 1971, 128). However, the parental address cannot be seen as separate from the 'social' address: as Althusser argues, the family can be interpreted as part of the 'state apparatus' which interpellates the individual (138).

Class is represented not as a naturalised social state, or even in monetary terms, but as social performance. In London, Pip refers to himself as living in 'bondage and slavery' to the 'Avenger', the monstrous manservant he has 'made', who 'haunted [his] existence' (II.8, 218). The 'Avenger' is a comic refraction of Pip, who is himself the 'creation' of Magwitch: Pip writes, 'The imaginary student pursued by the misshapen creature he had impiously made, was not more wretched than I, pursued by the creature who had made me' (III.1, 337). Dickens's use of *Frankenstein* positions Pip as both creature and creator. Class emerges as a haunting spectre, rather than as a designator of social positionality. It is not a given, but part of a process of (familial) creation, which can create 'monsters' such as the Avenger and Pip, who are defined by their idleness and posturing. Bourgeois and criminal identities become curiously interrelated throughout the novel. Magwitch occupies an uneasy space in these figurations: he has, according to Pip, 'Convict in the very grain' (III.1, 336); his identity cannot be concealed with clothes, or hair powder. However, Dickens complicates this when we hear Magwitch's history: he is a pauper and career criminal, who has come into self-consciousness *through* his criminal activities. Magwitch tells Pip how he was addressed and named as a criminal at his trial, unlike his partner, the middle class and educated, Compeyson:

> My lord and gentlemen, here you has afore you, side by side, two persons as your eyes can separate wide; one, the younger, well brought up, who will be spoke to as such; one, the elder, ill brought up, who will be spoke to as such; (III.3, 349)

This parallels what we see happening between parents and children throughout the novel. The idea that society has a responsibility to name and form identity ethically mirrors what we see happening in the family; moreover, these two aspects are conceptually inextricable for Dickens.

To move outwards from Magwitch's history briefly, it is important that in all of the disciplinary institutions presented by Dickens—prison, workhouse, factory, school, Chancery—power is deployed in order to hamper rather than enact positive social change. This is a micro- and macrocosmic concern for Dickens: as we see throughout *Great Expectations*, both society and family repeatedly fail to produce community. This failure of community has manifest implications for the individual subject; Dickens indicates how moral responsibility is deferred through the enactment of authority. In *Bleak House*, this is succinctly expressed by the imperative command of the police: 'Move on'. This command becomes symptomatic of the orphan Jo's state of being; he has no home, no family, no history, and no writing, other than the notice he dictates to Mr. Snagsby on his deathbed. His story, defined by the police's command, is both a realistic working-class tragedy and a parody of bourgeois social mobility. His identity is created in relation to negation: speaking of Jo and his fear of Detective Bucket, Allan Woodcourt remarks, 'he is possessed by an extraordinary terror of this person who ordered him to keep out of the way; in his ignorance, he believes this person to be everywhere, and cognisant of everything' (Ch. 47, 667). As his fear indicates, Jo is the inverse mirror image of Detective Bucket; he is the social subject called into being through the punitive 'hail' of the police. The police take the place of his absent parents in forming his (non-) identity. A similar model is reflected in Magwitch's history: 'in jail and out of jail [...] I've been carted here and carted there, and put out of this town and put out of that town, and stuck in the stocks, and whipped and worried and drove' (III.5, 344).

The act of interpellation addressing Magwitch as criminal does not prevent him from loving Pip. Neither, however, does it prevent his wishing to create and own his own gentleman, in vicarious revenge against Compeyson; the latter sentiment defined by Magwitch as 'lowness'. There is nothing reassuring about Dickens's representation of class; the coded gestures that make up class-based identity are repeatedly represented, as we see through the 'Avenger'. This empty posturing is set in opposition to the idea of 'hard work', which remains the goal of bourgeois man and working man alike. On the one hand, *social* position is up for grabs; on the other hand, true gentlemanly behaviour is correlated with an honourable heart, and represented through Herbert, Matthew Pocket and Joe. Joe's good-heartedness cannot simply be explained by nature. It is a self-conscious strategy, and a response to his childhood traumatisation, designed to protect women from masculine violence. The representation of class in the novel is far from simple: old-fashioned—pre-Victorian—working-class identity is only *seemingly* elevated through the true 'gentle Christian man', Joe (III.18, 459). Joe's account of his father's brutality adds psychological depth to his characterisation. As we see through Pip, Estella, Miss Havisham and Magwitch, hearts can be contaminated and wounded. The repetitive image of broken hearts undermines the idea that people can be unconditionally good in their 'hart'. Estella declares in response to Pip's rebuke, that her cold-heartedness 'is in *my* nature [...] It is in the nature formed within me' (III.5, 361).

The representation of women further complicates Dickens's representation of class, and once more, this is a familial concern. In his powerful speech to Pip following the return of Magwitch, Jaggers describes what would have happened to Estella if he had not taken her up and given her to Miss Havisham: 'qualified in all ways for the hangman, and growing up to be hanged' (III.12, 410). As the daughter of a murderess and career criminal, Estella is unquestionably *made* a 'lady' (III.17, 456), and the haunting condition of bourgeois identity is hinted at repeatedly. Molly appears, to the well-attuned reader of Dickens, like Jacob Marley, her face in flux as if seen through wavering fires (II.7, 212). In a strangely digressive detail, Pip writes that 'Years afterwards, I made a dreadful likeness of that woman, by causing a face that had no other natural resemblance to it than it derived from flowing hair, to pass behind a bowl of flaming spirits in a dark room' (212). This temporal shift indicates the continuing influence of Pip's vision. Pip is haunted by Estella's resemblance to her mother in past and present time frames: when Pip is in company with Estella following his first meeting with Molly, the middle-aged *narrator* Pip employs free indirect discourse to relate and enact his past feeling of disorientation:

> What *was* it that was borne in upon my mind when she stood still and looked attentively at me? Anything that I had seen in Miss Havisham? No. In some of her looks and gestures there was that tinge of resemblance to Miss Havisham which may often be noticed to have been acquired by children, from grown person with whom they have been much associated and secluded, and which, when childhood is passed, will produce a remarkable occasional likeness of expression between faces that are otherwise quite different. And yet I could not trace this to Miss Havisham. I looked again, and though she was still looking at me, the suggestion was gone.
>
> What *was* it? (II.10, 238)

The use of the free indirect style partially closes the gap between protagonist and narrator, emphasising the continuing question posed by Estella in the present day of the narration. John O. Jordan (1983) argues that the narrative is predicated on Pip's continuing and unfulfilled desire for Estella, and the fact she 'remains an enigma' (80). This is supported by Pip's account of his sad courtship; he writes, 'If that staid old house near the Green at Richmond should ever come to be haunted when I am dead, it *will be* haunted, surely, by my ghost' (II.19, 298 [my emphasis]). The future tense employed here effectively prohibits the possibility of reading Dickens's revised ending as a happy one: the middle-aged or elderly Pip continues to be haunted by his past experience. Further, he himself has been rendered ghostly and unreal as a consequence of his desire, which is always—where Estella is concerned—social, familial and erotic.

Anticipating Fyodor Dostoyevsky's focus in *Crime and Punishment* (1866), Dickens explores the construction of identity in relation to authority and transgression: the law and criminality. Dickens consistently focalises this question through the family and trauma. The vulnerability of the subaltern classes is represented as social and familial. Jaggers's speech to Pip, defending his actions towards Estella, ventriloquises Dickens's own concerns:

> Put the case that he lived in an atmosphere of evil, and that all he saw of children, was, their being generated in great numbers for certain destruction. Put the case that he often saw children solemnly tried at a criminal bar, where they were held up to be seen; put the case that he habitually knew of their being imprisoned, whipped, transported, neglected, cast out, qualified in all ways for the hangman, and growing up to be hanged. Put the case that pretty nigh all the children he saw in his daily business life, he had reason to look upon as so much spawn, to develop into the fish that were to come to his net – to be prosecuted, defended, forsworn, made orphans, bedevilled somehow. (III.12, 410)

Orphanhood appears as more than a familial state here. Society, as parent, fails to nurture its children, and orphanhood is seen as a continuing, degenerative process. Jaggers feeds off the vulnerability of the criminal classes and their children, but his compulsive hand washing—reminiscent of Lady Macbeth and Pontius Pilate—implies his unease. While the action of the novel is ostensibly set in the early nineteenth century, it speaks to specifically mid-Victorian themes. The depiction of the lawyer as an individual who can move between social classes, actively intervening in both criminal and familial concerns, is a modern possibility, linked to the development of legislation surrounding property, inheritance, marriage, child custody and welfare from 1834 onwards. The evolving status of the lawyer in relation to the family is borne out by Jaggers's plotting power, and his 'taming' of Estella's murderous mother.

Jaggers is an ambivalent presence: an authorial figure, he is the point of intersection for the novel's complex plotting; however, he is also a quasi-parental figure, who perceives his own role as persecutory and entrapping. The novel implies society's increasing intervention in the family institution; however, at the same time, Dickens's focalisation of social issues through the family means he foregrounds the manner in which society interpellates the individual. As Lyn Pykett argues, the self-division of Dickensian heroes mirrors, even enacts, the processes of capitalist society through which the self becomes a cultural commodity, necessitating the creation of public and private identities (168–170). The uncanniness of bourgeois identity is underscored in comic fashion through Wemmick's schizoid functioning: the kindly son in Walworth, he is then the 'gardener' amongst his human plants in Newgate (*Great Expectations*, II.13, 260). Wemmick's ability to be a loving son is geographically specific: his important role in Little Britain and Newgate renders him thing-like until he goes home. Bedecked in 'portable property', he is a parody of the mournful Victorian middle-class gentleman, displaying his personal—quasi-familial—grief through social performance. Wemmick's mourning paraphernalia implies the power of mid-nineteenth-century commodity fetishism: human relationships are constantly mediated through things. Things are haunted, possessed, endowed with life; humans are, in their turn, deadened, or made 'dry' and 'hard' in the case of Wemmick (II.6, 209). The fact that Wemmick's 'portable property' is inextricable from the motif of mourning implies the economic bases of family, law and crime alike. It is a hideous parody of family feeling, which refracts back onto our understanding of the family, as well as the ethical failings of the Law. Dickens shows a deep awareness of the mythical construction of home: its status as an ideological fantasy. Wemmick's 'castle' is a preposterous fiction, but also gives a charming indication of his boyish imagination. Importantly, Wemmick's moral character is already redeemed through his father, the (rather twee) Aged P before he offers help to Pip. This evocation of father-son sentiment is indicative of Dickens's wider concern in the novel: the idea that loving filial sympathy can heal the wounds of identity formation, even though the novel likewise shows that identity is formed through parent-child relationships. This dynamic is critical to Pip and Magwitch (and in displaced form through Joe and his father). Despite this, the idea that bourgeois identity is somehow based on fraud, forgery, unnatural creation or even an act of cannibalism pervades the novel without being resolved.

Dickens modifies ideas of monstrosity throughout *Great Expectations*; unlike the unrepentant Victor Frankenstein, Pip eventually learns that appearances cannot be relied upon, that a rough exterior can house—in the novel's own terminology—a good heart. The ethical status of capital, or of 'portable property', remains uncertain in this scheme. Pip renounces Magwitch's money on the basis that it would create an identification with him, which he repudiates. However, the worthy Herbert can only flourish through Magwitch and Miss Havisham: his 'looking around' achieves nothing without capital investment. Pip's story speaks to the fundamental difficulty of how to move from family to society and back again. When leaving Pip after his first devastating visit to London, Joe describes life as 'made of ever so many partings welded together' (II.8, 224), and it is difficult to overstate the importance of this eloquent thought. The repetitive image of the mist rising from the marshes stresses the formative power of departure, and the impossibility of a true return. Pip identifies with his childhood experiences: the primary trauma determines both his narrative and his subjectivity. Unlike Florence Dombey, he is able to bear witness to his own and others' wounds, but as we see from the liminal close to the novel this does not mean that his plot can be concluded. Trauma is again far more than a structural device: it is represented as the core of parent-child relationships. This is not only a psychological concern, but also an ethical one. Moving beyond traumatic experience involves an ethical realisation: other people are also traumatised. In *Great Expectations*, Dickens is able to prioritise this issue of translation by constructing Pip as both protagonist and narrator.

Like *Dombey and Son*, *Great Expectations* creates a formative conflict between maternal and paternal authorities. *Great Expectations* is relentlessly violent in both literal and symbolic terms, and this violence becomes associated with the maternal threat posed by Mrs. Joe, Miss Havisham, and Molly (who tells Magwitch she has killed their child). This paradigm engenders the physical brutality perpetuated against female figures throughout the novel. This punitive violence towards the feminine is echoed in the final scene: Estella must also be 'bent and broken' before she can understand 'what [Pip's] heart used to be' (III.20, 480). She does not admit love, but recognises his pain: she must be wounded again, in order to work through her initial trauma. This problematic affective complex is set against the paternal idealism that dominates the latter half of the novel: father-son relationships are endowed with eloquent feeling and pathos. The attentiveness to paternal wounds is critical to Pip's familial redemption. By finally accepting Magwitch, and listening to his story, Pip learns to attend to others' experiences, to their wounds or losses: only then is he is able to take ownership of his guilt. Miss Havisham must also attend to Pip's pain in order to move beyond her own: he is the 'looking-glass' (III.10, 396) in which she must confront herself. Problematically, however, this attentiveness only forms part of Miss Havisham's redemption: in a brutal purgative gesture, she is consumed by fire directly afterwards. She is kept in a deathly liminal state—much like Mrs. Joe—until she dies, shortly after Compeyson is drowned. Women are condemned to leave abbreviated narratives. Mrs. Joe only manages to articulate, 'Joe', 'Pardon', 'Pip' (II.16, 282), while Miss Havisham repeats her final message endlessly: 'Take the pencil and write under my name, "I forgive her"' (III.10, 401).

Works Cited

Literary Texts

Brontë, Charlotte. 2008. *Jane Eyre*. Edited by Margaret Smith. Oxford: Oxford University Press.

Brontë, Emily. 2008. *Wuthering Heights*. Edited by Ian Jack. Oxford: Oxford University Press.

Dickens, Charles. 1861. *The Uncommercial Traveller*. London: Chapman and Hall.

———. 1974a. *Dombey and Son*. Edited by Alan Horsman. Oxford: Clarendon Press.

———. 1974b. 'The Number Plans'. Appendix to Dickens, *Dombey and Son*, 835–855. Oxford: Clarendon Press.

———. 1979. *Little Dorrit*. Edited by Harvey Peter Sucksmith. Oxford: Clarendon Press.

———. 1981. *David Copperfield*. Edited by Nina Burgis. Oxford: Clarendon Press.

———. 1982. *Martin Chuzzlewit*. Edited by Margaret Cardwell. Oxford: Clarendon Press.

———. 1993. *Great Expectations*. Edited by Margaret Cardwell. Oxford: Clarendon Press.

———. 1998a. *Hard Times*. Edited by Paul Schlicke. Oxford: Oxford University Press.

———. 1998b. *The Old Curiosity Shop*. Edited by Elizabeth M. Brennan. Oxford: Oxford University Press.

———. 1966. *Oliver Twist: Or the Parish Boy's Progress*. Edited by Kathleen Tillotson. Oxford: Clarendon Press.

———. 2008a. *Nicholas Nickleby*. Edited by Paul Schlicke. Oxford: Oxford University Press.

———. 2008b. *Our Mutual Friend*. Edited by Michael Cotsell. Oxford: Oxford University Press.

———. 2008c. *A Tale of Two Cities*. Edited by Andrew Sanders. Oxford: Oxford University Press.

———. 2008d. *Bleak House*. Edited by Stephen Gill. Oxford: Oxford University Press.

Dostoyevsky, Fyodor. 1991. *Crime and Punishment*. Translated by David McDuff. London: Penguin.
Forster, John. 1874. *The Life of Charles Dickens*. 3 vols. London: Chapman and Hall.
Shakespeare, William. 2008. *The Norton Shakespeare*. Edited by Stephen Greenblatt. London and New York: W. W. Norton.
Shelley, Mary. 2008. *Frankenstein: Or The Modern Prometheus: The 1818 Text*. Edited by Marilyn Butler. Oxford: Oxford University Press.

Primary Psychoanalytic Texts

Abraham, Nicolas and Maria Torok. 1994. '"The Lost Object—Me: Notes on Endocryptic Identification"'. In Nicholas Abraham and Maria Torok, *The Shell and the Kernel: Renewals of Psychoanalysis*. Edited and translated by Nicholas Rand, 139–156. Chicago: University of Chicago Press.
Freud, Sigmund. 'Childhood Memories and Screen Memories'. In *The Psychopathology of Everyday Life*. *SE* 6:43–52.
———. 'Mourning and Melancholia'. *SE* 14:237–260.
———. 'A Project for a Scientific Psychology'. *SE* 1:283–397.
Laplanche, Jean. 2011. *Freud and the Sexual*. Edited by John Fletcher. Translated by John Fletcher, Jonathan House, and Nicholas Ray. London: International Psychoanalytic Books.

Secondary Texts

Ackroyd, Peter. 1994. *Dickens: A Memoir of Middle Age*. Abridged edition. London: Mandarin.
Althusser, Louis. 1971. 'Ideology and Ideological State Apparatuses'. In *Lenin and Philosophy, and Other Essays*. Translated by Ben Brewster. London: New Left Books.
Barker, Juliet. 2010 [1994]. *The Brontës*. London: Abacus.
Berry, Laura. 1999. *The Child, the State and the Victorian Novel*. Charlottesville: University of Virginia Press.
Bodenheimer, Rosemarie. 2001. 'Knowing and Telling in Dickens's Retrospects'. In *Knowing the Past: Victorian Literature and Culture*, edited by Suzy Anger, 215–233. Ithaca: Cornell University Press.
———. 2007. *Knowing Dickens*. Ithaca: Cornell University Press.
Brooks, Peter. 1992. *Reading for the Plot: Design and Intention in Narrative*. Cambridge, MA: Harvard University Press.
Cain, Lynn. 2008. *Dickens, Family, Authorship: Psychoanalytic Perspectives on Kinship and Creativity*. Aldershot: Ashgate.

Caruth, Cathy. 1996b. *Unclaimed Experience: Trauma, Narrative, History.* Baltimore: Johns Hopkins University Press.

Collins, Philip. 'Dickens's Autobiographical Fragment and David Copperfield'. *Cahiers Victoriens et Edouardiens* 20 (1984): 87–96.

Douglas-Fairhurst, Robert. 2011. *Becoming Dickens.* Cambridge, MA: The Belknap Press of Harvard University Press.

Furneaux, Holly. 2009. *Queer Dickens: Erotics, Families, Masculinities.* Oxford: Oxford University Press.

Greenberg, Judith. 1998. 'The Echo of Trauma and the Trauma of Echo'. *American Imago* 55, no. 3: 319–47.

Ikonen, P. and E. Rechardt. 1984. 'On the Universal Nature of Primal Scene Fantasies'. *International Journal of Psychoanalysis* 65, no. 1: 63–72.

Jordan, John O. 1983. 'The Medium of Great Expectations'. *Dickens Studies Annual* 11: 73–88.

———. 2011. *Supposing Bleak House.* Virginia: Virginia University Press.

Kaplan, Fred. 1988. *Dickens: A Biography.* London: Hodder and Stoughton.

Klimazewski, Melisa. 2006. 'The Contested Site of Maternity in Dombey and Son'. In *The Literary Mother: Essays on Representation, Maternity and Childcare*, edited by Susan Staub, 138–158. Jefferson, NC: McFarland.

van der Kolk, Bessel A. ed. 1987. *Psychological Trauma.* Arlington, VA: American Psychiatric Press.

LaCapra, Dominick. 2001. *Writing History, Writing Trauma.* Baltimore: Johns Hopkins University Press.

Leys, Ruth. 2007. *From Guilt to Shame: Auschwitz and After.* Princeton: Princeton University Press.

Marcus, Steven. 1985. *Dickens, From Pickwick to Dombey.* London: W. W. Norton.

Newsom, Robert. 1983. 'The Hero's Shame'. *Dickens Studies Annual* 11: 1–24.

Pykett, Lyn. 2002. *Charles Dickens: Critical Issues.* Basingstoke: Palgrave Macmillan.

Rose, Jacqueline. 1991. *The Haunting of Sylvia Plath.* London: Virago.

Slater, Michael. 2009. *Charles Dickens.* New Haven: Yale University Press.

Weeks, Jeffrey. 2008. 'The Sphere of the Intimate and the Values of Everyday Life'. In *Modern Criticism and Theory: A Reader*, 3rd ed. Edited by David Lodge and Nigel Wood, 641–664. Harlow: Pearson Longman.

Welsh, Alexander. 1987. *From Copyright to Copperfield.* Cambridge, MA: Harvard University Press.

Wiley, Margaret. 1996. 'Mother's Milk and Dombey's Son'. *Dickens Quarterly* 13, no. 4: 217–228.

Wilson. Edmund. 1941. *The Wound and the Bow: Seven Studies in Literature.* Boston: Houghton Mifflin.

CHAPTER 5

Wilkie Collins—Vampiric Inheritances: *No Name* and *Armadale*

Throughout his mid-period novels, Wilkie Collins poses the dilemma of modern property ownership, in Richard Wilson's words, '*how far* we recognise [our relatives] and how far this recognition is represented socially' (1993, 187). However, for Collins, the recognition of relatives is not only an economic issue, it is also a literal problem; at times, the characters cannot be safely identified as being themselves. Collins's novels are occupied by characters in disguise or doubling one another, showing the fragility of the modern subject, in physical, psychological and economic terms. Further, his novels are defined by the intrusive, and seductive, intrusion of exiled or rejected family members, such as Anne Catherick, Captain Wragge and Lydia Gwilt. Collins's representation of family is made more specific through his reliance on the Gothicised theme: the 'sins of the fathers' are visited upon the children (see Walpole 1968, 41).

This familiar idea becomes increasingly sophisticated in Collins's mid-period novels, as the author presents complex transgenerational psycho-genealogies (see Schützenberger 1998, 62): the elder generation, notably the Father, transmits a persecutory or destabilising inheritance to the younger. These inheritances can render the second generation less recognisable—Laura Fairlie's plight in *The Woman in White* (1860)—or alternatively mark the body, as with Magdalen Vanstone in *No Name* (1862): in either case, the subject's ability to assume their economic inheritance is compromised. In both *No Name* and *Armadale*, this is persistently gendered, with Collins presenting, in John Fletcher's (2013) terms,

M. Wood, *Parents and Children in the Mid-Victorian Novel*,
https://doi.org/10.1007/978-3-030-45469-2_5

competing 'scenographies' relating to maternal and paternal inheritances. Collins portrays the name-of-the-father as an unstable and dubious presence: instead of providing the child with a secure origin, the name splits and divides personal identity, becoming the source of a compulsion to repeat. Patriarchal Victorian society appears in Collins's hands to be, by definition, traumatic.

There was increasing pressure throughout the 1860s and 1870s for legal change following the failure of the 1857 Matrimonial Causes Act to improve the position of married women significantly, and in *The Woman in White* and *No Name*, Collins enters the debate. The titles of the novels *No Name* and *Armadale* demonstrate a fundamental concern with the name-of-the-father, each interrogating the legitimising father-function. Trev Lynn Broughton and Helen Rogers (2007) argue that the 'Empire of the father was assailed in the nineteenth-century, as the home and family were, to a significant extent, annexed to the moral domination of the mother' (1). However, this statement requires qualification: maternal power operated on a moral and symbolic level and was not legally recognised. These ideological conflicts are consistently at work in mid-Victorian fiction, whether explicitly addressed by authors or not. Collins's novels do not obliterate the primacy of the father as man or the Father as God; however, they precipitate this primacy into crisis. Most significantly for us here, this crisis is represented in traumatic terms.[1]

By presenting the gendered transmission of property as overtly traumatic, Collins stresses the compromised position women and illegitimate children occupied in mid-nineteenth-century Britain. These concerns did not emerge suddenly; Collins's earlier, lesser known, novels also demonstrate his interest in cross-generational conflict. His first published novel, *Antonina* (1850), explores the clash between old and new religions in Classical Rome: this is a micro- and macrocosmic concern as the imaginative heroine, Antonina, is set in opposition to her stern father. Collins returned to a similar conflict in *Hide and Seek* (1854), in which, through a complex set of events, the deaf and dumb Mary is revealed

[1] Collins's concern for women's economic position was reflected in his own Will: not only did he protect his illegitimate children by naming them for the first time as his own, but he also inserted a clause to prevent his daughters from losing their money to their husbands when they married (the Last Will and Testament of William Wilkie Collins is held in the Public Record Office). The introduction of this clause had been made possible due to the introduction of the 1882 Married Women's Property Act which gave married women the same rights over their inherited property as unmarried women.

to be the daughter of the overbearing evangelical Mr. Thorpe. Collins became increasingly interested in the relationship between textuality and the compulsion to repeat: the circulation of narrative becomes symptomatic; in *The Dead Secret* (1857), Sarah Leeson's concealment of Mrs. Treverton's deathbed confession generates the novel's narrative pulse and Sarah's nervous sensibility.

Collins uses the narrative potential of 'trauma'—defined in terms of physiological disorder, belatedness and the inherited parental message—in order to interrogate the parameters of novelistic discourse; while earlier novels, such as *Basil* (1852), show the younger author's heavy debt to both melodrama and Dickens, by *No Name*, Collins had developed a recognisable voice. Irony is central to this newly confident style; Collins's third-person narrators slyly watch from the periphery, frequently allowing outsider characters such as Miss Garth and Captain Wragge to focalise the course of the events. Collins draws the reader's attention to the ideological fantasies propping up and sustaining the bourgeois home; in *No Name*, the mischievous narrator repeatedly informs us that Captain Wragge has no place in the family system: he is Mrs. Vanstone's mother's stepson, but apparently 'not *even* the *widest* stretch of courtesy could have included him *at any time* in the list of Mrs. Vanstone's *most distant* relations' ([my emphases] I.3, 30). The bombastic language of space and place protests too much. Wragge's connection to the family is real, and his exclusion reveals the tendentious manner in which the bourgeois family replicates itself through exclusion. Mrs Lecount's tank of grotesque amphibians appears to symbolise both the family and the novel itself—ostensibly shut in, a spectacle for outsider's gaze and above all a curiosity. It is telling that Wragge and Lecount, the two figures most responsible for the active progression of plot in the middle of the narrative, are figured as reptilian, inhabitants of the tank: Collins gently reminding us that they are an inescapable part of the family topography—or, in this case, ecology.

Collins has rightly been recognised as a sophisticated writer of 'trauma'. As D. A. Miller (1988) observes, Walter Hartright's meeting with Ann Catherick on the road to London is the 'primal scene' that drives *The Woman in White* (152). This scene haunts Walter and provides the dynamism for his desire for Laura. The scene engenders a symptomatic narrative in which the reader is actively encouraged to share in physiological and psychological disorder. However, at the same time, Collins complicates the idea of a single origin; the opening scene spirals back into the prehistory of the novel, to Glyde's forgery of his parents' marriage; their failure (and inability) to marry; and Philip Fairlie's dalliance with the future Mrs. Catherick. The circumstances surrounding Sir Percival's forgery suggest that society must be held to account. Mrs. Catherick informs Walter that Sir Percival's parents could not marry because his mother had been trapped in an abusive marriage; the failure to marry is not, then, the problem: it is the lack of legal recognition for illegitimate children which is the focus for criticism. Reading *The Woman in White* alongside *No Name*, a new vision of Glyde appears, possessed by a sense of his own non-belonging: 'Who could wonder, now, at the brute-restlessness of the wretch's life?' (471). Glyde is possessed by his secret: it grounds his subjectivity. By representing a parental secret (and in the case of Glyde a *non*-event) as the basis for the adult child's identity, Collins anticipates the concerns of Freudian psychoanalysis and twentieth- and twenty-first-century trauma theory.

Anticipating Anne Ancelin Schützenberger's model of genealogical inevitability, Collins's protagonists pay off 'debts of the past' and are governed by 'invisible' loyalties (Schützenberger, xii). Collins's grown-up child protagonists work through the traumas of the *previous* generation. In *No Name* (1862) and *Armadale* (1866), Collins brings this idea to the fore: the father emerges as a vampiric presence, determining the child's actions and desires from the grave, exercising, in Éric Toubiana's terms, a destructive *emprise*—a masterly influence or hold. The vampiric father is a symptom of patriarchy, as well as a neurosis experienced by the (adult) child. In their assessment of the Wolf Man's case, Nicolas Abraham and Maria Torok (1976) argue that an efficient therapeutic intervention would have needed to address Sergei's complex genealogy, and 'challenge the juridical code that permitted the nurse's blackmail', the latter responding to the primal scene of sexual abuse between Sergei's father and sister Anna (76). This hypothesis resonates powerfully with Collins's concerns. However, the extent to which his protagonists can appropriate or exorcise their genealogical narratives remains uncertain.

No Name: Sensation, Inheritance and Female Properties

Wilkie Collins structures *No Name* through a series of events which each replays the initial breach in Chapter 1 caused by the arrival of the letter from New Orleans telling of the first Mrs. Vanstone's death (for a plot summary of the novel, please consult the endnote).[i] As a result of this primal scene, the passing and receiving of texts represent the passage of familial desires and fantasies throughout the novel. The narrative is split into eight 'Scenes' (in different locations) each interspersed with letters comprising the action 'Between the Scenes': the 'progress of the story through the post'. Each scene stages Magdalen's assumption of a different identity, identities which are acted upon and compromised through the interchange of letters. This structure establishes the asymmetrical opposition between acting and writing in the novel: the crisis of individual agency—engendered by the inequities of Victorian society—located in the interruption found between the writ and the act. In *No Name*, Collins creates three characters who knowingly play on this idea: Magdalen, Captain Wragge and Mr. Clare.

Collins's emphasis on property and paternal responsibility implies that Mr. Vanstone's lack of legal knowledge is as equally problematic as his foolish first marriage, and potentially even more so: a heavier weighting is given to the father's sins, although both parents generate repetitive images and symbols. Pendril reveals *No Name*'s sensational 'secret' in Chapter 12, only a sixth of the way through the book; the rest of the novel documents Magdalen's progress in the light of her parental inheritance. The extended family topography constructs an originary doubling of desire and conflicts that become formative for both the narrative and Magdalen herself. As in Sigmund Freud's case of Lucy R. (discussed in Chapter 2), there are overlapping, but competing, scenographies referring to maternal and paternal influences. Magdalen's subjectivity is produced in relation to a sequence of identifications emerging from the cross-generational structure, which are alternately liberating, creative, oppressive and compulsive.

Magdalen takes on a dazzlingly decentred-centrality throughout the novel, symbolised by the monologic performance she creates in the north of England with Captain Wragge acting as impresario: 'conducted from beginning to end by the unaided exertions of a young lady, roused the public curiosity' ('Between the Scenes', 241). This statement can be read as a description of the novel as our interest is shifted from the father's will onto the daughter's actions: but from the very first scene, Magdalen *is* the sensation.

Collins explores the manner in which property is overwritten by conscious and unconscious processes of symbolisation. Éric Toubiana analyses the French Civil Code to reveal that the logic of bourgeois possession and inheritance presupposes and is reversed by an anterior, archaic logic: '*Le mort saisit le vif*' (98), or 'the dead seizes the living'. Toubiana delineates two processes: on the one hand, 'the dead seizes the living', but on the other, the subject assimilates, not just one, but a collection of properties and characteristics of the deceased, *taking in* the other (104). Magdalen fails to receive her expected inheritance, but she is caught in a double bind where both the property and the lack of it are equally compromising: she is seized by her dead father's thwarted desires. The absence of the property is overwritten by his narrative, his fundamental failure to act, and becomes persecutory as a consequence. Andrew Vanstone's assertion that he will not rest in his grave if his daughters are disinherited transmits an uncanny threat, which takes possession of Magdalen. The patriarchal function of paternity, the passing on of property, emerges as a dangerous fixation. Vanstone establishes a 'juridical code', attempting to right the family wrongs posthumously (Abraham and Torok 1976, 76), and this is defined, a priori, by failure.

Dead Inheritance

The reading of the letter is preceded by a detailed description of the Vanstone household. A sense of anticipation is created as we await the primary players to make their entrance:

> Who were the sleepers hidden in the upper regions? Let the house reveal its own secrets; and, one by one, as they descend the stairs from their beds, let the sleepers disclose themselves. (I.1, 7)

These opening passages demonstrate the playfulness and parodic tone of Collins's third-person narrator: we can be in little doubt that we are being teased. This opening scene introduces the novel's emphasis on processes of disclosure and revelation, the detached tone also establishing a sense of striptease. The narrator implies that omniscient narration must by necessity be meta-narrative: a deliberate discourse on the act of novel writing.

Andrew Vanstone's imprudent first marriage is hidden from view, but the reader is provoked by sensational clues, presented in a wry knowing tone. In a serious moment, we are told that Mrs. Vanstone has been aged by the loss 'of more than one of her children' but 'she still preserved the fair proportion and subtle delicacy of feature, once associated with the all-adorning brightness and freshness of beauty, which had left her never to return' (11). But an unspoken mystery resonates even before the arrival of the letter. The elder daughter, Norah, is 'dark' and 'majestic', the 'mirror in which [her mother] could look back' (11), but nevertheless a faded image:

> there was less interest, less refinement and depth of feeling in her expression: it was gentle and feminine, but clouded by a certain quiet reserve, from which her mother's face was free. (11)

Collins (in the recent wake of *On the Origin of Species* [1859]) raises the spectre of degeneration: evolution gone backwards. Inheritance is questioned in physical, psychological and moral terms:

> If we dare to look closely enough, may we not observe, that the moral force of character and the higher intellectual capacities in parents seem often to wear out mysteriously in the course of transmission to children? (11)

There is a kind of ethical joke being played here: the novel raises and then challenges the inverse teleology of degeneration. Throughout the opening chapters, there are hints that it is not 'degeneration' but an unconscious identification with an unknown secret that restricts Norah. Norah is the embodiment of her mother's guilt or unease: guilt that we never see Mrs. Vanstone experience herself.[2] In Jean Laplanche's terms, the transmission of the parental 'enigma'—or the compromised message—provides the dynamism for Norah's subjectivity. While this could seem a purely speculative point, we can remember that when her parents' secret is revealed, Norah becomes increasingly liberated: the 'certain quiet reserve' is replaced with a confiding and emotional tone. Collins handles this changing nuance through the increasing use of free indirect discourse: following the receipt of the letter, the narrative is increasingly focalised through Miss Garth, whose previous preference for Magdalen is repeatedly challenged after the death of Mr. and Mrs. Vanstone.

When Magdalen makes her first entrance, she 'dashed' in last 'with the suddenness of a flash of light', and her position in the family is immediately interrogated (13). She is presented as a sensual 'cat'-like

[2] Although we see its effect, we see how important marriage is to her in the opening chapter when the letter is received.

figure, physically unlike either of her parents, having 'overflowing physical health which strengthened every muscle, braced every nerve, and set the warm young blood tingling through her veins, like the blood of a growing child' (14). The narrator implants doubts regarding origins and causes: 'How had she come by her hair? how had she come by her eyes? Even her father and mother had asked themselves those questions, as she grew up to girlhood, and had been solely perplexed to answer them' (13). Magdalen's 'seductive, serpentine' (14) body is mapped by a sexual enigma, which encrypts, even falsifies, the real parental secret. Pondering the lack of resemblance to her parents, the spectre of illegitimacy appears. Magdalen's countenance is 'remarkable in its strongly-opposed characteristics', combining (like Marian Halcombe in *The Woman in White*) both masculine and feminine features (14). Her appearance is transformative, characterised by her 'plastic, ever-changing face' (14), her eyes expressing the 'subtle transparency of expression which no darker eyes can rival' (13).

The inflammatory narrator moves on to question her name:

> Magdalen! It was a strange name to have given her? Strange, indeed; and yet, chosen under no extraordinary circumstances. The name had been borne by one of Mr. Vanstone's sisters, who had died in early youth; and, in affectionate remembrance of her, he had called his second daughter by it – just as he had called his eldest daughter Norah, for his wife's sake. (15)

In the nineteenth century, the name 'Magdalen' evoked female sexual transgression and its possible redemption and therefore foreshadows the heroine's progress. The narrator highlights the disjuncture between the name's association with 'sad and sombre dignity' and Magdalen's own exuberance (15), Collins subtly reminding us that repentance has to come *after* something else. Cutting across the timescale of the narrative, the name Magdalen is not inherited from the mother's family, but from the father's; however, by referring to sexual transgression, the name refers back both to the family secret *and* to Andrew's first wife. The production of identity, through and within the unconscious and conscious processes at work across the family system, is implied.

Despite the narrator's mischievous protestations, naming is clearly significant. Schützenberger quotes Freud's remark regarding his own children's naming: "I had insisted on their names being chosen, not according to the fashion of the moment, but in memory of people I have been fond of. Their names made the children into 'revenants'" (Schützenberger 1998, 141). The fact that Magdalen is named after Andrew Vanstone's young sister alerts us to the paternal fantasies determining the novel. This sister is an innocent figure within an otherwise strife-ridden family. When Vanstone senior secretly disinherited his elder son Michael in favour of Andrew, their mother supported Michael and the family was sundered. Miss Garth describes Magdalen's behaviour towards her father: 'Exactly what I have said myself, till I am tired of repeating it', remarked Miss Garth. 'She treats Mr. Vanstone as if he was a kind of younger brother of hers' (I.1, 17). There is a subtle link created between the dead sister and Magdalen. Magdalen has evaded paternal strictures and authority, but is closely associated with her father's history. These subtleties undermine readings of the Victorian novel that simply equate fathers with paternity and paternity with patriarchy. Magdalen's association with the dead child not only determines her relationship with her father, but also suggests a blank at the centre of her familial and social identity: a blank with which she creatively *plays* prior to the trauma caused by her parents' death.

Magdalen is represented as both erotic adult and inquisitive growing child as she exclaims joyously, 'how I do like pleasure!' (I.1, 15): she wishes to make herself a spectacle illuminated with 'plenty of light' (16). Magdalen achieves her chance to shine in the Marrable's amateur production of *The Rivals*. Her theatrical debut is linked to family role-playing: she differentiates her two roles, Julia and Lucy, by impersonating her sister with a 'cool appropriation of [her] identity' (I.6, 62–63). The instability of identity is hinted at as Magdalen ventriloquises her sister: watching Magdalen perform, Norah can only watch 'startled' and disorientated, 'as if she was speaking herself, with an echo on the stage' (62). This kind of creative play is denied to Norah herself. Magdalen's desirousness and desirability are affirmed repeatedly; she takes a sensual pleasure in having her magnificent hair brushed for hours on end by the servant, in a 'luxury of sensation' (I.5, 52). Magdalen could not be further from being a subdued Florence Dombey, Amy Dorrit or even a tormented Tattycoram. Collins takes an obvious delight in creating his attractive heroine. There is a lurking feeling, however, that Magdalen's exuberance will be inevitably chastened: Vanstone's description of her as an 'unbroken filly' implies that the reality of womanhood, whether it be marriage or childbirth, will inevitably 'break' her in some way: as he says, 'Time enough to break her to harness, when she gets a little older' (I.1, 18).

In Chapter 2, Collins creates a parodic echo of the primary melodramatic encounter between Walter Hartright and Anne Catherick in *The Woman in White* when Captain Wragge approaches Miss Garth, Norah and Magdalen on the road. The female figure is once more the stimulating enigma; while Wragge has initially been drawn to Norah because of her resemblance to her mother, it is Magdalen's face that penetrates him:

> 'The younger lady,' he proceeded, 'takes after her father, I presume? I assure you, her face struck me. Looking at it with my friendly interest in the family, I thought it very remarkable. I said to myself – Charming, Characteristic, Memorable. Not like her sister, not like her mother. No doubt, the image of her father?' (I.2, 26)

His pause after 'No doubt' reinforces the emphasis on the phrase 'image of her father', but it is critical that her features, while bearing this strange 'non'-connection to her father, are marked by their absolute individuality. The father and daughter are linked via the father's desire rather than by a family resemblance. When we discover later in the first scene that Andrew Vanstone has been married to a 'fallen woman' (or 'Magdalen') in Canada, the question of paternal inheritance becomes further complicated. Magdalen is the focus for all the family's desires, the undeniable favourite, who has made her father 'her grown-up playfellow' (I.9, 88). She has a playful mastery over him, and this is clearly eroticised when she asks for his permission to marry Frank Clare, the 'convalescent Apollo' (I.8, 78), who is figured as Vanstone's adopted son. Sitting on her father's knee to discuss her 'business', he realises at this moment that she is no longer a child:

> He felt it in the trouble of her bosom pressed against his; in the nervous thrill of her arms clasped around his neck. The Magdalen of his innocent experience, a woman – with the master passion of her sex in possession of her heart already! (I.9, 88)

She persuades him to accept her engagement by appealing to the memory of his supposed marriage to her mother: Magdalen notices that he 'spoke to her with a forbearing gentleness, which was more like his manner to her mother, than his ordinary manner to herself' (89).[3] However, as we later discover from Pendril, by referring to his 'early life', Magdalen unknowingly reminds him of his American wife (I.13, 135). Magdalen's identity is closely connected to her father's past and to the dead American woman whose crime is inscribed in the name 'Magdalen'. These two factors provide the basis for her subjectivity, crossed over by her progressively obsessive attitude towards her inheritance.

Collins complicates the question of indirect and direct inheritance; identification can be a liberating space, as in the case of Magdalen and her dead child-aunt, or an inhibiting obsession. These variants can be compared to Laplanche's distinction between 'hollowed-out' and 'filled-in' transference discussed in Chapter 2: the paternal obsession appears 'filled-in' and immobile, while the relation to the dead child-aunt appears 'hollowed-out'.[4] Magdalen's coded connection to the American wife, the woman who had 'great personal attractions' and an 'immediate influence' over Andrew Vanstone (Ch. 13, 124–125), exists in a liminal space between these two poles. Although Magdalen's bewitching influence over others empowers her, it also contributes to her vulnerability prior to her first despised marriage, since she cannot escape the fact of her own desirability. These are not simply character-based phenomena, since they form a central component of the text's dialogue with socio-cultural norms: the transmission of affect and property. As we see in the fourth scene, Magdalen is at risk of becoming commodified within the patrilinear economy.

Letters

No Name plays with varying modes of inheritance; the heaviness of the paternal story is leavened by the excessiveness of Collins's treatment of the theme as a whole. The symbolic absent-presence of Andrew's first wife, the death of his younger sister, Mrs. Vanstone's loving salvation, all

[3] The shifting of subject positions—through unconscious identification—is key to Freud's conceptualisation of primal phantasy, as we saw in 'A Case of Paranoia', discussed in Chapter 2.

[4] As I outlined in Chapter 2, 'filled-in' transference involves translations of the parental message made in childhood. These are immobile representations, imagos, scenarios and repetitions that the analysand projects onto the analyst. 'Hollowed-out' transference instead maintains the open relation to the enigmatic other we bear in very early infanthood (see Laplanche, 'Transference: Its Provocation by the Analyst' [1999]).

these threads complicate and act upon the traumatic story grounded in paternal texts.

The receipt of the letter from New Orleans intrudes into the Vanstone family, interrupting them with a trauma that comes from the other, while being located firmly within. Reading and delivering letters become increasingly significant throughout *No Name*. Every letter implicates both writer and recipient, adding a codicil, or condition, which transforms the family story. In this opening scene, Collins underlines the connection between the father's history and Magdalen: she plays the role of post-master, sorting the letters with 'business-like rapidity' (I.1, 18): the story literally passes through her hands. The narrator constructs this scene as a founding moment of separation: looking away from Magdalen's face, Vanstone then looks at the letter in his hand:

> His face changed colour the instant he read the first lines; his cheeks fading to a dull, yellow-brown hue, which would have been ashy paleness in a less florid man; and his expression becoming saddened and overclouded in a moment. Norah and Magdalen, watching anxiously, saw nothing but the change that passed over their father. (19)

Vanstone becomes an unwitting actor on the family stage, his daughters' eyes fixed firmly on his face. Mr. and Mrs. Vanstone are set at odds for the first time, the family lawyer, Pendril saying in retrospect that 'From that day forth – when a past which *he* abhorred was forced back to his memory; when a future which *she* had never dared to anticipate was placed within her reach […] they both betrayed themselves, time after time' (I.13, 132). Although Pendril translates Vanstone's sadness, it is in fact irresolvable: we cannot be sure that he does not mourn his first wife. It is only Miss Garth who perceives the change that Mrs. Vanstone undergoes:

> Mrs. Vanstone looked excited rather than alarmed. A faint flush rose on her cheeks – her eyes brightened – she stirred the tea round and round in her cup in a restless impatient manner which was not natural to her. (I.1, 19)

Mrs. Vanstone's excitement refracts back onto our understanding of her profound social sacrifice. Sitting in 'painful silence', the previously unified family is divided (19), and it is of course Magdalen 'in her capacity as spoiled child' who breaks the silence.

This primal scene initiates the crisis of sight and knowledge perpetuated by the novel as a whole. The desire to penetrate the secret becomes Magdalen's overriding sensation: 'I have no secrets from papa – what business has papa to have secrets from me! I consider myself insulted' (20). The receipt of the letter leads the parents to make 'sudden resolutions' and give 'unexpected orders' (21): the normal routine of the house is disrupted as they secretly plan their forthcoming marriage:

> the sisters looked one another in the face; each feeling, and each betraying in her own way, the dreary sense that she was openly excluded, for the first time, from the confidence of her parents. (I.2, 22–23)

From the receipt of the letter, the narrator uses the word 'first' numerous times (there are two uses on page 19 and then once each on page 22 and 23), repeatedly stressing the scene's significance to the reader. In comparable fashion to Freud's primal phantasy, events propel the family into an Oedipal structure in which Magdalen's relationship with her father is complicated by their conflicting desires for the first time. Magdalen's desire to know is met by Andrew Vanstone's equally strong desire to conceal: she wants what he cannot and will not give her.[5] The letter causes Vanstone to differentiate himself from his children and assume paternal authority: 'When an easy-tempered man does assert himself in his family, the rarity of the demonstration invariably has its effect; and the will of that easy-tempered man is Law' (I.1, 20). The letter has a doubling force: it is the cause of a paternal mastery that is already dislocated and compromised by the father's history. After all, the story is engendered precisely because Vanstone's will is *not* law. The Law itself, as the impersonal sign of male mastery rather than the figure of the lawyer, is under consistent attack throughout. The narrative implies that Andrew Vanstone dies, not because of his imprudent first marriage, but because of his legal obligations within a system that will not 'naturally' provide for his children.

The arrival of the letter operates as a stimulating intrusion into the family, leading to the hasty marriage of Mr. and Mrs. Vanstone, and to Magdalen's first meeting with Wragge. Miss Garth attempts to bind events within a coherent framework, finding her 'memory [reverting]

[5] Comparable to Laplanche's account of female castration, '*il a cela, et moi je ne l'ai pas*' (*Problématiques II*: *Castration et symbolisations* 1980, 80).

oftener and oftener, to the March morning' when the couple departed for London (I.9, 80). The narrator intensifies the sensational anticipation, assuring us that 'Nothing in this world is hidden forever':

> Sand turns traitor, and betrays the footstep that has passed over it; water gives back to the tell-tale surface the body has been drowned [...] Look where we will, the inevitable law of revelation is one of the laws of nature: the lasting preservation of a secret is a miracle the world has never yet seen. (I.4, 34)

This is an eloquent description of inheritance in the novel: the imprint of the elder generation is unavoidably stamped upon the younger, and parental secrets can be read upon the body of the child. This passage also demonstrates that a secret, by its very nature, must be articulated or acted upon in some way; it must be kept secret. Pendril later tells us that it was only Mrs. Vanstone's meticulous efforts and 'safeguards' that prevented the secret from being betrayed through the carelessness of her gregarious partner, saying (with prophetic significance) that 'The women are few indeed, who cannot resolve firmly, scheme patiently, and act promptly, where the dearest interests of their lives are concerned' (I.13, 131).

In the largely monologic Chapter 13 Pendril narrates the Vanstone family history to Miss Garth, who has remained in ignorance throughout her twelve-year service with the family.[6] Pendril clarifies the daughters' position: as illegitimate children of a man who married after their birth, and died intestate, the daughters cannot inherit their father's estate:

> [...] a man's marriage is, legally, as well as socially considered to be the most important event in his life; that it destroys the validity of any will which he may have made as a single man; and that it renders absolutely necessary the entire reassertion of his testamentary intentions in the character of a husband. The statement of this plain fact appeared to overwhelm Mr. Vanstone. (I.13, 136)

The fortune reverts to the father's family, to Andrew's elder brother and his 'bitterest enemy' (133), Michael Vanstone, who (as we have noted)

[6] Collins reasserts the potency of female influence when we are told that the 'generous' and 'impulsive' Norah Blake 'saved' Andrew Vanstone by agreeing to live with him as his wife (I.13, 128–129)—this could be read as a corrective to Jane Eyre's decision to leave Rochester.

was disinherited by *their* father many years before. Pendril makes it clear that it is the 'vindictive will' (127) that Vanstone senior made in secret to disinherit his first-born son that was the cause of the tragic events which follow; describing the 'implacable father' (126), 'The harm done by that vindictive will is, I greatly fear, not over yet' (127). Degeneration is hinted at once again as we are told that 'Michael had inherited his father's temper, unredeemed by his father's better qualities' (127). *No Name* turns upon the accidental disinheritance of the two daughters, and this operates, not as an isolated event, but as a family myth: we are informed that Vanstone senior had disinherited Michael through a *secret* will, establishing the ghostliness of paternal legacies and their uncanny emergence after death. While all the novel's secrets are revealed in Chapters 12 and 13, the historical family story creates a psychological subtext that is never drawn fully into the plot, but becomes the suppressed dynamism for Magdalen's own struggle between 'good' and 'evil' (Collins, Preface, 5).

Andrew Vanstone's incompetent lack of knowledge regarding the legal ramifications of his second marriage means that he inadvertently replays his father's act of disinheritance, while enabling Michael Vanstone's negation of the two girls. Vanstone Sr. exercised a despotic control over his fortune, but, as a consequence, in the second generation paternity becomes correlated with a failure to pass on wealth effectively, and with the problems of property ownership. Vanstone's shrewd investments successfully safeguard the property during his lifetime (I.12, 121), Pendril telling us carefully that 'The fortune which Mr. Vanstone possessed [...] was part, and part only, of the inheritance which fell to him on his father's death' (I.13, 124); but despite this, the fortune is troubled at the point of his death by conflicting family obligations. Michael Vanstone bears an inverse mirror-image relation to property: as Magdalen finds out from Wragge, his two weak points are a passion for speculation, and a refusal to make his will.

Wilson (1993) observes that 'the question posed by modern property ownership has been *how far* we recognise [our relatives] and how far this recognition is represented socially' (187). In the novel, these alliances are in crisis: Andrew Vanstone alienated himself from his mother and brother by attempting to resolve the family conflict (I.13, 127), and Michael Vanstone's subsequent accusations make Andrew's proposition to share the paternal inheritance untenable. Andrew's property is overwritten by two conflicting narratives or fantasies, which involve reparation to his brother *and* responsibility for his children. Michael Vanstone reinforces the idea that Vanstone inadvertently pays off family debts through this contradictory logic, deeming it 'a Providential interposition' that the property comes to him rather than the two daughters (I.15, 155). Working on Schützenberger's model of genealogical inevitability, the grandfather's irascible act of disinheritance would be replayed indefinitely until it was worked through. This hypothesis is supported by the plot of *No Name:* the first traumatic disinheritance creates generational echoes, a paralysis of will as Michael himself dies intestate and his feminised son can only perform under dictation from Magdalen and Mrs. Lecount. The two women attempt to suture the wound caused by the failure of male 'will-power'.

The prehistory of the novel is reactivated through the narrative's careful traumatic structure; the primal scene in Chapter 1 cannot, of course, make psychological or literary sense without the accumulation of scenes that follow (as well as the scenes that lie hidden behind it), as we also saw in Freud's cases of Frau Emmy von N. and Lucy R. discussed in Chapter 2. The opening scene is replayed and significantly transformed following the deaths of the two parents when Michael's letter, relating his feelings towards the destitute daughters, operates as the exciting cause. Magdalen's insistence on seeing the letter is a bid for power: she may insist on hurting herself, but her hurt is a necessary consequence of reaching her goal. Her words to her sister after she has read the letter are characterised by a cold resolution, saying, 'Norah [...] if both of us live to grow old, and if you ever forget all that we owe to Michael Vanstone – come to me, and I will remind you' (I.15, 157). Magdalen's original desire to see the letter from New Orleans is violently transposed onto seeing this later document. Andrew's failure to provide for his daughters is transformed into Michael's self-righteous repudiation of them:

> I will not invite retribution on my own head, by assisting those children to continue the imposition their parents practised, and by helping them to take a place in the world to which they are not entitled. (155)

The relationship created between the two scenes of reading found in Chapter 1 and Chapter 15 engenders the phantasmatic structure that determines Magdalen's actions and the text's strategies as a whole. The letter appears perverse as Magdalen takes hold of it: 'She held out her hand [for the letter] – the soft, white, virgin hand that had touched nothing to soil it or harden it yet' (153). For the other participants in the scene, the letter represents a forbidden, dangerous knowledge: Pendril does not want Magdalen to read it, and Miss Garth and Norah are horrified that she wishes to. It is only Mr. Clare who defends Magdalen's inalienable right to do so.[7] Magdalen appropriates a form of male mastery, questioning Pendril as if she were the lawyer (157). She is transformed by her reading, and this directly parallels the way in which Vanstone's reading of the American letter led to the family's irretrievable division in the opening chapter: 'Something in her expression had altered, subtly and silently; something which made the familiar features look strange, even to her sister and Miss Garth' (156). There is a clear although ambiguous change engendered by the act of reading. The paternal enigma is reinscribed on Magdalen's face: an 'unfathomable mystery' (159), which is 'too deep for [...] sounding' (168). Magdalen tries to 'fasten' the contents of Michael Vanstone's letter in her mind (157). Despite their previous disgust, Miss Garth, Norah and Pendril watch 'eagerly' as Magdalen reads, with her bosom heaving with emotion, 'rising and falling faster and faster' (155). Her rising bosom refers us back to the scene in which she asked her father for permission to marry (I.9, 88); there is a coming of age here, intimately related to the father's history. Magdalen's assumption of authority becomes an eroticised spectacle for the other characters and the reader.

In 'traumatic' terms, Collins is doing something quite complex here. Although Magdalen's spectators observe her apparent alteration, as readers we are not granted any degree of intimacy with Magdalen herself at this point. She remains aloof from us. It is Miss Garth and Norah who feel the physical shock of this scene, not Magdalen. An indescribable 'something' penetrates them: 'something, through all after years, never to be forgotten in connection with that day – and never to be described' (I.15, 156). This failure of language—the indescribable 'something'—alerts us to the haunting echoes that reverberate through the novel (and seemingly beyond).

The traumatic structure is complicated by the impact of Andrew Vanstone's written legacies. Paternity becomes a kind of linguistic fetish for Magdalen; her father's failure is overwritten (and overdetermined) by

[7] Mr. Clare's loyalty to Magdalen, demonstrated by his final letter to her, clearly sets him apart from Pendril. The novel grants Mr. Clare moral authority, and he is justified in all his beliefs, if not in his parenting skills.

the two 'relics' Vanstone leaves the girls: his last letter to Pendril telling of his second marriage, and the words inscribed in his first 'useless' (139) will, making amends for their dubious birth:

> They may think bitterly of their birth […] but they shall never feel bitterly of *me*. I will cross them in nothing: they shall never know a sorrow I can spare them, or a want which I will not satisfy. (I.13, 140)

Magdalen places copies of the two documents in a silken purse around her neck, alongside the hair of her fiancé, Frank Clare. The disjunction between Vanstone's words and his failure of will is the stimulating force for Magdalen's actions throughout the novel. She attempts to fulfil her father's desire, saying that the documents tell 'me in his own words what his last wishes were for both of us' ('Between the Scenes', 174). Vanstone can speak to Magdalen 'from his grave' (I.14, 145): in his letter, Vanstone writes, 'If anything happened to me, and if my desire to do their mother justice, ended (through my miserable ignorance of the law) in leaving Norah and Magdalen disinherited, I should not rest in my grave!' (I.13, 136–137).

In analysing the political implications of the daughters' disinheritance, it is important to note that it is a direct consequence not of their illegitimacy but of the parents' belated marriage and Magdalen's engagement to Frank Clare. Collins's social criticism is directed at the problematic relation the father bears to the law, rather than the parents' 'sinful' relationship, and marriage as an institution is criticised by the novel. The juxtaposition of the brothers' letters means that paternal *failure* becomes implicitly confused with paternal *negation*. This failure takes on a 'thing-like' quality which Magdalen obsessively seeks to readdress, but only succeeds in reaffirming. Magdalen travels in a dangerous liminal state by her father's grave as her actions become more desperate. Before leaving Combe-Raven the two daughters visit the graveyard where their parents are buried, Norah writes to Miss Garth:

> 'We went together to the grave; we knelt down, side by side, in silence, and kissed the sacred ground […] Before we were out of the churchyard, she broke from me, and ran back. She dropped on her knees at the grave; tore up from it passionately a handful of grass; and said something to herself […] I asked what those words were, which she had spoken at the grave. "A promise to our dead father", she answered'. ('Between the Scenes', 177)

This 'promise' becomes the capitalised 'Purpose' (II.3, 222) that acts as the vampiric other within Magdalen.

Importantly, however, it is not until the loss of her parents and wealth is combined with the loss of her repellent lover, Frank Clare, that Magdalen suffers overwhelming physical and psychological shock. Afterwardsness defines Magdalen's traumatisation. Her doctor writes to Wragge from Vauxhall Walk:

> She sits, as I am informed, perfectly silent, and perfectly unconscious of what goes on about her, for hours together, with a letter in her hand, which she will allow no-one to take from her. ('Between the Scenes', 315)

Mrs. Wragge's unpunctuated letter adds pathos to this description: 'she sits and looks dreadful and wont speak a word her eyes frighten me' (315). The loss of Frank's love plays back retrospectively onto the loss of her parents, plunging Magdalen into melancholia:

> The woman never lived yet who could cast a true love out of her heart, because the object of that love was unworthy of her. All she can do is to struggle against it in secret – to sink in the contest, if she is weak; to win her way through it, if she is strong, by a process of self-laceration, which is of all moral remedies applied to a woman's nature, the most dangerous and the most desperate; of all moral changes the change that is surest to mark her for life. (IV.3, 354)

Magdalen is deadened physically and psychologically when she receives Frank's letter—a letter representing yet another act of masculine negation.[8] When she recovers she tells Norah, 'The shock I have suffered has left a strange quietness in me. I feel as if I had parted from my former self' ('Between the Scenes', 316). Later, when Magdalen casts the lock of Frank's hair in the sea, Wragge notes that 'There was a settled composure on her face which, except when she spoke, made it look as still and cold as marble' (IV.1, 327). It is as if she is becoming her father's living epitaph.

Magdalen has an increasingly difficult relationship with the inherited paternal narrative. Her determination to repossess the paternal property leads her inwards into the family and to a fraudulent marriage to her

[8] It is a cruel irony that Frank's letter claims that Magdalen had 'acted weakly under my father's influence' ('Between the Scenes', 314).

cousin. She is haunted by two significant absences: the property and the name. The property's association with Vanstone's failure to transform his will into an act, and the subsequent loss of her own named identity, means that it becomes a fetish incapable of transformation or speculation, and this is reflected in its destination: the miser Noel who is incapable of spending money. The money stands in for the paternal absence, as does Noel himself, who asserts himself with the repetitive phrase, 'I am my father's son!' (III.4, 300). When Magdalen sets out the terms of Noel's will, she demands the exact sum 'to the last farthing' that he has inherited from her father's estate (V.2, 554). Mrs Lecount is so impressed by this that she likewise dictates to Noel her own legacy: tellingly, the precise sum *his father* promised her (562). Neither Magdalen nor Mrs. Lecount are concerned with financial speculation or accumulation, but only with the acquisition of their rights: the fulfilment of dead promises and the laying of paternal ghosts.

Bygrave

Magdalen's alliance with Wragge is the cornerstone of her quest. He undertakes an investigation into Michael Vanstone's household for her in the Second Scene and protects her from Mrs. Lecount in the Fourth. But aside from his obvious role in the plot, Wragge operates as an ironic counterpoint in the novel's dialogue with inheritance. He asks to be present at the reading of Vanstone's non-existent will ('Between the Scenes', 174) and self-consciously intervenes in the family tradition with a comically inaccurate statement: 'The family spirit, Miss Vanstone. We all inherit our hot blood from my maternal grandfather' (II.1, 196). Magdalen and Wragge are not of course blood relations, but the latter's progress throughout the narrative radically undermines the insular family structure as he is repositioned centre stage. Wragge is the repudiated family member, 'the son of [Mrs. Vanstone's] mother's first husband' (I.3, 30).

This association with a negated first marriage creates a parallel between Wragge and Vanstone's American wife, and he displaces her by staging the seductive return of the (familial) repressed. His insistence on the (non-existent) blood relation between himself and Magdalen frames her within this same 'genealogical' context. Wragge plays a prosthetic role in the family constellation, constantly in the process of substituting himself for, and attaching himself to, different family members. His sardonic reference to his mother's father routes him through a specifically female genealogical line, emphasising the disrupted relationship Wragge has with patriarchal law, while setting him apart from the genealogical ripples caused by Magdalen's paternal grandfather, Vanstone Sr. The final irony is that the parodic identity Wragge assumes at the end of the novel is his own: his 'moral agriculture' is transformed into a 'legitimate' medical enterprise through the sale of his cure-all purgative pill (VIII.2, 710). This magical transformation is located solely within the public gaze: it is not the actor but the audience that has to change to legitimise Wragge's social identity. He begins and ends as an exuberant fraudster and as an effective capitalist. Collins creates a moral aporia and leaves us in radical doubt whether we should applaud or condemn Wragge; what is left is entirely pragmatic: Wragge charms us, and so we applaud, if he ceased to charm, we would condemn.

At Aldborough, Magdalen, Wragge and his wife assume the pseudonym 'Bygrave', Magdalen taking the role of Wragge's niece. Throughout the scene, Wragge engages in a series of interceptions and forgeries to distract Mrs. Lecount before the wedding takes place. The pseudonym 'Bygrave' itself is taken from Wragge's '*Skins To Jump Into*': these Skins are 'a list of individuals retired from this mortal scene' ('Between the Scenes', 322) and an account of their histories and circumstances. Wragge is an early proponent of the very modern crime of identity theft. Wragge resurrects and possesses dead bodies, going 'by-the-grave', and the assumption of different Skins becomes parodic of family inheritance. When he briefs Magdalen about her new persona, he focuses on the image of her father's grave in Belize, which is supposedly marked by 'a neat monument of native wood, carved by a self-taught negro artist' (322). This strange detail refracts back onto Magdalen's own story, but in a bathetic and playful manner.

Magdalen assumes the discarded textual Skin of Vanstone's first wife in her pursuit of Noel. Pendril's earlier description of the American fortune hunter anticipates the relationship between Magdalen and Noel[9]:

> He was just twenty-one: he was blindly devoted to a worthless woman; and she led him on, with merciless cunning, till it was too late to draw back. In one word, he committed the fatal error of his life: he married her. (Ch. 13, 125)

[9] Bearing in mind that Magdalen is listening, would it be going too far to suggest that she is inspired by this story in her pursuit of Noel?

The American wife is doubled: she does not just return, but returns twice through the figures of Magdalen and Wragge. Collins constructs this signifying sequence through the concept of influence (or *emprise* in Toubiana's terms). As we saw in the First Scene, Magdalen's eroticised mastery over her father was subtly correlated with the influence of his dead American wife, and in the Fourth Scene, the concept of influence recurs repeatedly. Wragge claims that Magdalen has 'laid a hold on me that I don't quite understand (IV.14, 506); Captain Kirke is 'bewitched' by seeing her once (IV.2, 346); and the unfortunate Noel is 'enchanted' in an 'intoxication of enjoyment' (IV.9, 445). Even the town of Aldborough itself is subject to the ever-encroaching influence of the sea's 'advancing waves' (IV.1, 325). It is telling that in her 'Bygrave' Skin Magdalen is described by Wragge as the 'living image' of her imaginary dead mother ('Between the Scenes', 323): it reminds us that while Norah *is* the living image of her mother, Magdalen does not resemble either of her parents.

There is a disrupted symbolic connection between the *first* Mrs. Vanstone and Magdalen, which is never explained or even necessitated by the plot. In this context, it is interesting that Magdalen's skill in mimicry is both heightened and coarsened in the fourth scene: impersonating Mrs. Lecount for Noel Vanstone's amusement, she creates an 'overcharged resemblance to the original' (IV.9, 445). The spectre of prostitution is raised as the narrator tells us that 'miser as he was, he would have paid, at that moment, five golden sovereigns out of his pocket, for five golden minutes more, passed in her society' (445).

Wragge's presence creates a reflective surface for the reader in the fourth scene:[10] his fear about what will happen following Magdalen's marriage becomes our fear as he raises the spectre of Noel Vanstone's possible murder:

> If Magdalen could have seen his face, in the dying light, his face would have startled her. For the first time, probably, since his boyhood, Captain Wragge had changed colour. He was deadly pale. (IV.1, 339)

For much of the scene, the reader is not given access to Magdalen directly: she is constituted via the relationship with Wragge. Wragge becomes

[10] This parallels how Collins mobilises Miss Garth in the First Scene—(likeable) familial outsiders are permitted to focalise the third-person narrative.

our interpreter, reflecting that 'the sense of [the familial] wrong haunts her, like a possession of the devil' (III.3, 291). Throughout the Fourth Scene, Magdalen appears increasingly deadened or zombified; the adverb 'mechanically' is applied to her actions several times (355; 370; 493). Most tellingly, directly after her marriage to Noel, *Wragge's* actions are figured in this way for the first time (IV.14, 513), implying the contagious operation of the trauma, and its power to reify. The references to the mechanisation of the self remind us that *No Name* is a story of the industrialised modern age, and it is worth remembering that Andrew Vanstone dies in a railway accident.[11]

Images of death imply the slippage between Magdalen and her dead father. When she reveals her plan to marry Noel Vanstone at Aldborough, the landscape she and Wragge are walking in appears disturbed and violent:

> Westward, a lurid streak of sunset glowed red in the dreary heaven – blackened the fringing trees on the far borders of the great inland marsh – and turned its little gleaming water-pools to pools of blood. (IV.1, 332)

She tears up tufts of grass (333), as she did by Vanstone's grave ('Between the Scenes', 177) the casual movement directly correlating these two decisive (and deciding) moments. Magdalen's strong identification with her father is petrified by her fixation on 'the purpose' (II.3, 221) she first formulated at his grave: the 'promise to [her] dead father' (177). The novel consistently addresses the difficulty of converting intention into action.

Before Magdalen's marriage, she walks on the beach at night and speculates if she could turn back from her crime:

> The backward path had closed behind her. Time that no wish could change, Time that no prayers could recall, had made her purpose a part of herself: once she had governed it; now it governed her. The more she

[11] As we see through Wragge's trajectory in the narrative, he moves from the shabby comfort he inhabits at the point he first meets Magdalen, to the aftermath of the railway crash in his second meeting with her (II.1, 186), moving onto crime, and finally capitalist success and supposed authenticity. The descriptions of London also question the state of modernity: the narrator questions 'modern progress' (III.1, 260) following on from his description, 'miserable women, whose faces never smile, haunt the butchers' shops' (259).

> shrank, the harder she struggled, the more mercilessly it drove her on. (IV.13, 484–485)

The 'Purpose' (II.3, 222) takes on independent existence as an obsessive, mystified, ritual that Magdalen feels compelled to enact. Magdalen's assumption of the name Bygrave (determined by the family outsider Wragge) implies a perilous proximity to the open mouth of the grave itself. She does not just travel by her father's grave but by her own, torn between her promise and her desire for death: 'Sleep that had come treacherously before, came mercifully now; came deep and dreamless, the image of her last waking thought – the image of Death' (IV.13, 486). Magdalen's will fails her when she attempts to commit suicide; she resolves 'to end the struggle, by setting her life or death on the hazard of a chance'. She counts the passing boats: 'If, in that time, an even number passed her – the sign given, should be a sign to live. If the uneven number prevailed – the end should be Death' (IV.13, 499). When 'providence' or 'chance' ensures that she will live, Magdalen's mental anguish is briefly lessened; sleeping like a helpless 'new-born child' (500), she temporarily evades responsibility for her illegitimate marriage. We should note here that the ships she counts, and which save her from suicide, almost certainly include Captain Kirke's ship *Deliverance:* in a foreshadowing of the end of the novel, he unknowingly contributes to Magdalen's salvation, just as his father, Major Kirke actively intervened when Andrew Vanstone wanted to kill himself (I.13, 125). In the wedding ceremony itself, Magdalen stands 'as if all the sources of human emotion were frozen up within her' (IV.14, 511). She mirrors the paternal death that is inscribed in her Purpose, reflecting back a corpse's unseeing gaze.

Trust

The crisis in Magdalen's physical identity is fundamental to the plot, separate parts of Magdalen's body or bodily image taking on monumental narrative importance. In attempting to unmask Magdalen, Mrs. Lecount asks Noel to read the sealed description to her when they are next alone, but instead Noel reveals it to Wragge, giving the latter time to paint out the moles on Magdalen's neck before she is examined. Her body lacks wholeness, increasingly fragmented, a 'body in pieces' (Laplanche and Pontalis 1988, 251–252), and static rather than plastic. These divided fragments are eroticised, becoming the reader's focal point for narrative resolution: it is of course the presence of the moles that finally convinces Noel of his wife's true identity.

Magdalen's body becomes contested: her flesh is impregnated with words and conflicting desires. The family enigma plotted upon her body in the First Scene is progressively stripped, violently clarified in a series of crises. Before she sets out to meet Noel Vanstone for the first time Magdalen is incapable of looking in the mirror: 'For the first time in her life, she shrank from meeting the reflection of herself' (IV.3, 355). Her narcissistic construction of self is disrupted; she is no longer in possession of her own body. In the final four scenes, inheritance develops into a labyrinth of winding paths, secrets and interrupted relationships, and Magdalen's identity becomes progressively complex. In a powerful letter, sent to Miss Garth 'between the scenes', Magdalen takes back her paternal name by simply assuming her marital name—Vanstone: 'You forget what wonders my wickedness has done for me. It has made Nobody's Child, Somebody's Wife' ('Between the Scenes', 590).

The Fifth Scene opens with the image of the now married Noel standing by a breakfast table in 'a state of transition' (V.1, 535) following Magdalen's hasty departure to London:

> Although his predecessor may have been the wife of his bosom or the child of his loins, no man can find himself confronted at table by the traces of a vanished eater, without a passing sense of injury in connection with the idea of his own meal. (535)

In an evocative and clever image, Collins uses the breakfast table with 'the battered egg-shell, the fish half-stripped to a skeleton' to represent Noel's mental state and the fragments of his marital illusions (535). Marriage ages the sickly Noel, and he gazes round the cottage with a 'pining discontent' (536). There is a notable pathos to the opening of the scene. Noel is a feeble shadow of the elder male Vanstones; an 'abject, miserable little man!' (V.3, 580). In language reminiscent of *Macbeth*,[12] 'The coat was a large one (it had belonged to his father); the hat was a large one (it was a misfit purchased as a bargain by himself). He was submerged in his hat and coat' (V.1, 538).

With Magdalen absent in London, Mrs. Lecount arrives, appearing as a 'withered and old' emanation. The use of free indirect discourse merges

[12] '[...] a dwarfish thief' wearing 'a giant's robe' (5.2.21–22),

Noel's shock with the narrator's and readers': 'Was it the spectre of the woman? or the woman herself?' (538). In a dramatic and protracted scene, described by Noel as being 'like a scene in a novel' (545), Mrs. Lecount exposes Magdalen's true identity. Once again referring Noel to the moles on Magdalen's neck, she tells him to approach Louisa and asks her if she has noticed them when dressing his wife's hair. The answer is, of course, in the affirmative and takes a 'paralyzing hold' on Noel (545). Mrs. Lecount reinforces her proof by showing Noel how the segment of Alpaca dress she cut from the unknown visitor in Vauxhall gardens perfectly fits the flounce of Magdalen's own gown. The shock of these multiple proofs strikes Noel with an immediate attack of illness, the result of which is Mrs. Lecount's discovery of the bottle of laudanum with which Magdalen intended to take her own life in the fourth scene:

> She instantly laid the other bottle aside on the table without looking at it. The other bottle lay there, waiting its turn. It held a dark liquid, and it was labelled – POISON. (V.2, 548)

The spectre of Noel Vanstone's murder which haunted Wragge prior to the wedding is raised again: it is critical, however, that this murder exists only as a textual possibility. Magdalen never had any intention of poisoning Noel as the narrator reminds us; the bottle is 'a false witness of treason' (549). Within *No Name*, there is a darker story waiting to be told, a story which Collins tackles openly in *Armadale*. The non-event that is Noel's murder is critical to the dynamism of the novel; as readers, we remain unsure at Aldborough quite what Magdalen's intentions are. In a novel so concerned with actions that are *not* performed (such as the Vanstones' presumed marriage and the father's failure to make a new will), Magdalen's crime participates in this pattern of negation.

Noel Vanstone dies directly after making his unusual will under Mrs. Lecount's direction. In inverse fashion to Andrew Vanstone (who leaves an eloquent letter but no will), Noel fails to express himself in writing. He dies with his pen in his hand, trying to write Magdalen a scathing letter which will 'brand her with [...] infamy' (581). Following Noel's death, his money passes to Admiral Bartram as planned. However, the irregularity of the phrasing of Noel's will means that Magdalen's lawyer, Mr. Loscombe, guesses that there is a 'secret trust' in operation. Disinherited, Magdalen swaps identities with Louisa and takes up residence at St. Crux-in-the-Marsh, the Admiral's macabre residence, to find the trust for herself.

The convoluted nature of Noel Vanstone's legacy suggests a desperate crisis in the concept of inheritance itself as the paternal legacy is reframed within a Gothic narrative. The past and present collide: St. Crux is built on the site of an ancient church and monastery, and the Admiral hides the secret trust in his medieval banqueting hall, named 'Freeze-your-Bones' by old Mazey because of its 'arctic' cold (VII.1, 630). The house is located at 'Ossory' in Essex, a name that conjures up images of skeletons and bones. There is a sense that the Admiral has been washed up here: the house abounds with seafaring imagery and grotesquery, epitomised by the presence of his leering, alcoholic, but ultimately harmless old coxswain, and the tidal streams which wind their way around the house and gardens (631). The 'bewildering' house (VIII.4, 733) is representative of history: a palimpsest in which old structures provide foundations for the present. The Admiral himself is clearly a figure of the pre-industrial past; chastising George for not marrying quickly, he says, 'Men were made of flesh and blood [...] They're made of machinery now' (VII.3, 646); Collins reminds us of the reifying effect of the trauma. Sitting in the garden, Magdalen imagines the flow of stories and desires that have passed through the building and grounds: 'the stream of human sin and human suffering had flowed, day after day, to the confessional, over the place where she now sat' (VII.4, 654).

Nowhere else in the novel does Collins make the persecutory nature of family secrets so clear: the Admiral is 'fretful', 'impatient' and 'fidgety' (VII.2, 638–639). The secret is buried, the Admiral changing its hiding place unconsciously while sleepwalking. He speaks to the internal spectre of Noel Vanstone: 'My good fellow, Noel, take it back again! It worries me day and night. I don't know where it's safe; I don't know where to put it. Take it back, Noel – take it back!' (VII.4, 667). The secret trust is constantly 'acted upon' by its neurotic keeper, and much like the sleepwalking Admiral Bartram himself, the secret has a 'death-in-life' existence (668): living on as a ghost-like, vampiric, form of paternal authority.

The property brings with it the inherited narrative, overwritten by each of its owners, and Admiral Bertram is overtly traumatised by his inheritance. Following Magdalen's expulsion from St. Crux and the Admiral's death (directly caused by his sleepwalking in 'Freeze-your-Bones'), the transmission of the paternal property is further complicated. The secret trust is lost, and the property passes to George Bartram, who has now married Norah Vanstone. The paternal legacy is halted, but has not left the bloodline. George Bartram is set in opposition to his sickly cousin, Noel; a jolly, healthy and bland narrative presence (a precursor to the younger Allan in *Armadale*), George is chiefly characterised by his uncanny resemblance to Andrew Vanstone as a young man. When she first meets him, Norah remarks on George's resemblance to the portrait of her father at Combe-Raven ('Between the Scenes', 520); Magdalen also notes this (VII.3, 644). By coming to George and Norah, the property figuratively returns to the source: in looks and personalities, George and Norah directly replace Mr. and Mrs. Vanstone. There is a lurking sense of incest created by all of this, naturally.

In a crucial scene, Magdalen distinguishes between different modes of inheritance. Repudiating her right to the fortune as a part of her husband's estate (which would, after all, be haunted by Noel's impotent *emprise*), she rips up the secret trust, which Norah has found at St. Crux. Instead, she proposes receiving her share of the family fortune from her sister:

> I will take from *you*, what I would never have taken, if that letter had given it to me. The end I dreamed of has come. Nothing is changed, but the position I once thought we might hold towards each other. Better as it is, my love – far, far better as it is! (VIII.4, 737)

At no point does Magdalen repudiate her right to the property. Her redemption does not involve self-condemnation of that kind. Magdalen's symbolic tearing of the letter, the final paternal secret, implies the necessity of a new kind of trust, dissociated from the Law and the persecutory inheritance.[13] The money is a reciprocal gift passed between the sisters. However, George Bartram's startling resemblance to Andrew Vanstone also implies that Magdalen will receive the money from her father's symbolic substitute, from the wearer of his Skin. Female agency is again formulated in relation to the paternal ideal. Despite this, moral redemption and patriarchal closure are both reinforced and undercut by the fact that Norah retrieves the family fortune by marrying George. Norah and George's first meeting at Aldborough occurs as a direct consequence of *Magdalen's* fraudulent marriage to Noel Vanstone. Since Norah meets George as a result of Magdalen's crimes, it could be argued that Magdalen indirectly gives her sister George, just as Norah will give Magdalen the

[13] It is telling that both lawyers—Pendril and Loscombe—ignominiously disappear from the narrative after dismissing Magdalen.

money. Norah writes, 'When we look back to our first impressions of each other, we look back to *you*' (VIII.3, 724). Norah goes onto say that she did not marry George until 'I had taught him to think of you as I think – to wish with my wishes, and to hope with my hopes' (724). The conservatively Oedipal courtship between Norah and George becomes a way of covertly legitimising Magdalen's crimes. Bearing in mind the bourgeois culture for and in which Collins wrote and published, surely this was as close as he could get to sanctioning Magdalen's rebellion.

In the Last Scene at Aaron's Buildings, the question of trust becomes increasingly significant as a mode of reconfiguring the family relationships and creating a new set of alliances. Following Old Mazey's discovery of Magdalen reading the secret trust, she is expelled from the wreck of St Crux (without the knowledge of the Admiral) and is struck down with illness in a seedy back street of London. Captain Kirke arrives in London, disembarking from his aptly named ship, *Deliverance*, with the memory of Magdalen possessing him:

> The spell so strangely laid on him, in that past time, had kept its hold through all after-events. The face that had haunted him on the lonely road, had haunted him again on the lonely sea. The woman who had followed him, as in a dream, to his sister's door, had followed him – thought of his thought, and spirit of his spirit – to the deck of his ship. (VIII.1, 696)

Magdalen's relationship with Captain Kirke recreates the association with her father-as-subject that we saw in the first sene. When Kirke finds Magdalen dangerously ill on the brink of being sent to the workhouse, he tells Mr. Merrick, the surgeon, that he will take 'sole charge of her':

> I see my position here surprises you [...] Will you consider it the position of a relation – the position of her brother or her father – until her friends can be found? [...] *I have taken this trust on myself* [...] and as God shall judge me, I will not be unworthy of it! (703) [my emphasis]

It is impossible that Collins's use of the word 'trust' is accidental considering the pivotal role Noel Vanstone's secret trust plays in the plot. The woman whom Mr. Merrick chooses to nurse Magdalen is also known to be a 'trustworthy' person (706). Even more significantly, Wragge is drawn back into the plot through 'trust'. In the absence of any other relative, the surgeon asks him to explain to Magdalen what happened when she fell ill and the presence of the unknown Kirke: ‘the captain was now seated at Magdalen’s bed-side in discharge of the trust confided in him’ (VIII.2, 713).

The giving and receiving of trust are intimately connected to Andrew Vanstone’s history. After Major Kirke saved him, he insisted on Vanstone’s marriage being hidden, preventing him from writing a letter of confession to his own father. Captain Kirke inherits this narrative of trust. He refuses to share the paternal narrative with the landlord at Aldborough, saying ‘I hardly think I should be doing right to tell it [...] it is not a story they might like strangers to know’ (IV.2, 344). As Wragge says, Kirke has the ‘hereditary right to help and protect [Magdalen] as his father’s son’ (VIII.2, 713). The relationship between Kirke and Magdalen is gently Oedipal: delirious she looks up at in his face believing him to be her father: ‘Why do you look so sorry? Poor papa!’ (VIII.1, 699). Kirke is neurotically obsessed with the difference between their ages, as if there was something potentially obscene in their connection:

> That terrible sum in subtraction, which had first presented itself on the day when she told him her age, began to trouble him again, as he left the house. He took twenty from forty-one at intervals, all the way back to the shipowners’ office in Cornhill. (VIII.3, 729)

Despite this subtext, Collins frames their relationship by the reciprocal sharing of their pasts: their stories and words: ‘Her questions were endless. Everything that he could tell her of himself and his life, she drew from him delicately and insensibly’ (VIII.2, 719). His story revivifies her. Kirke later becomes the recipient of Magdalen’s own written story, communicated via letter; this redefines her artistic identity and exposes her right and ability to structure her narrative and to possess a story of her own. When Magdalen asks him to return to London to tell her what he thinks of her story, she asks him, ‘Is it a promise between us?’, and he replies, ‘It is a promise’ (VIII.3, 729). This promise replaces the paternal Purpose. It is significant that she does not allow Kirke to write to her (728): the female text is accorded the higher status here.

Collins overdetermines the transmission of inheritance in *No Name*. The progress of the plot, so often relying on the non-event, participates in the negation that lies at the heart of the family. Despite Magdalen’s dangerous obsession with the paternal Purpose, she operates as the text’s moral arbiter, ending the novel by defending her moral and emotional right to marry Kirke, and be happy (VIII.4, 740). The disruption of will is finally healed: we are told that 'As he would have kept a pledged engagement with her, so she had kept her pledged engagement with him' (739). The primacy which Collins accords to the father's story is not a reassertion of the Law of the Father, but instead reveals the manner in which the Law is divorced from the very subjects who (supposedly) enunciate it. Andrew Vanstone's narrative is dislocated from his paternal function and reveals the problematic relation he bears to patriarchal law.

Will and trust are reconfigured as ethical values rather than legalistic discourse. At the end of the novel, Magdalen's identity, which has been defined and barred by the paternal letter, is freed of its persecutory burden, but has an indissoluble bond with the narrative her father has transmitted to her and its attendant fantasies. Andrew Vanstone's 'Skin' is never absent from the text; however, his story operates in conjunction with the ambivalent absent-presence of his first wife and the transgressive excess of Wragge. The question of degeneration, which recurs through the representation of Norah, Frank and Noel, is complicated by the vibrancy of Magdalen herself, and Collins refuses to impose a conventionally redemptive moral onto *No Name*. Female subjectivity, even when defined through Magdalen's transgressive actions, is accorded a significantly high status, coming to represent all of those who have felt and suffered (740).

Armadale: Sacred Confidence

Armadale begins in a style that was, by November 1864,[14] typical of Wilkie Collins, with a melodramatic and originary scene emerging from a compromised family system (please see the endnote for the novel's plot summary).[ii] In *Armadale*, the dramatic tension is created by the fact that the reader discovers the truth prior to its recipient: the little Allan Armadale, later Ozias Midwinter, happily plays on his father's deathbed as the latter dictates his murderous confession. The inscription of the letter refers back to the primal scene of the novel, the murder of Allan Armadale by another Allan Armadale. The writing of the letter indicates the text's engagement with the question of conscious and unconscious knowledge,

[14] The date of *Armadale*'s first instalment in the *Cornhill*.

and subjective authenticity.[15] While the moral and psychological ramifications of the paternal murder are always at the heart of the narrative, it would be incorrect to read *Armadale* purely as a re-enactment of the Gothic theme that the sins of the fathers are visited upon the sons. There is more than one crime at stake; Jane Blanchard's duplicity towards her own father is key to the development of the plot. Armadale Sr. is characterised by his attempt to exercise his posthumous *emprise*; emptied of all other qualities, he represents the compromised nature of paternal power, articulated in the act of inheritance.

The letter is persistently compromised: Armadale's prophecy that Ozias and Allan's encounter will prove deadly is both right and wrong. Significantly, the male suffering caused by this initial encounter becomes the means by which Lydia Gwilt can be redeemed and—more problematically—sacrificed. It is telling that Ozias's ongoing silence to Allan regarding their fathers' histories is a consequence of his desire to preserve Allan's sacred memories of his mother. The maternal figure is protected by a displaced filial sacrifice. As in *No Name*, a heavier weighting is given to the paternal, rather than maternal, crime. A bitter division between father and son—the original Allan Armadale and his son, Ingleby—lies at the apex of the family drama. Once again, we see the consequences of a (grand)father's implacable resentment.

Prehistories

If we interpret the writing of the letter as a secondary traumatic scene, relating back to the deadly male encounter, then it is significant that the wife—the beautiful, dark and unloved Mrs. Armadale—is excluded. She is relegated to the position of an eavesdropper—her ear to the keyhole as her husband dictates the letter to the Scotchman Mr. Neal, in the presence of the German doctor. As in *Dombey and Son*, the doting father looks forward to the establishing of a bond between father and son as two adults: a bond in which the mother is irrelevant. This is more sinister in Collins's novel—Armadale endows his letter with a posthumous paternal presence. The letter is loaded with a kind of magical significance as a consequence of this, foreshadowing the prophetic nature of Allan's

[15] Catherine Peters (1991) points out that in later years, probably induced through his constant use of opium, Collins frequently imagined a second shadow self present just on the verge of sight and perception (1).

dream. Letters and writing become invested material objects in the novel: talismans.

Armadale appears as a 'corpse', with the child's 'shrivelled', 'grim', 'old' and 'silent' black nurse standing at the bedhead like the figure of death (I.3, 23). The nurse is later associated with secret, even transgressive, cultural knowledge when Armadale recounts how she saved his life with a 'negro-antidote' when Ingleby poisoned him (31). The small child plays between his father's 'helpless' hands, indicating Ozias's predicament throughout the novel: trapped by his father's story. The child plays with his toy, a 'soldier on horseback', sending it over his father's hands and breast. Armadale watches the toy with sinister and 'ceaseless vigilance – a vigilance as of a wild animal, terrible to see' (23), policing the toy soldier's erratic journey. Mrs. Armadale can only watch with jealousy as her son plays contentedly on his father (25). There is an ironic disjunction created between the child's happiness and the content of the letter. The fact that Ozias speaks out in his 'fresh voice' (25) implies that he is old enough to understand at least some of what he hears. The child unwittingly receives his father's narrative. Ozias's childhood is compromised as a result of this first hearing and his mother's covert listening (she is sent out of the room before Neal reads the confession of the crime itself). Ozias's receipt of the letter is split across two time frames, the unconscious hearing of a child and the conscious reading of an adult. This sense of belatedness can connect Collins's temporalising of 'trauma' to Freud's concept of afterwardsness, *Nachträglichkeit*. Like Freud, Collins is interested in the symptomatic jarring between past and present.

This unconscious listening is complicated by the relationship between his father and mother. Ozias's mother is a tragic and passionate presence, mourning her husband's lack of love for her. She tells the doctor that Jane Blanchard is 'the shadow and the poison' of her life (I.2, 17), and the narrator echoes this a few pages later (I.3, 25). These two words anticipate the characteristics that define *Lydia* in Allan's prophetic dream: she is the shadow woman, who gives Allan the poison. While Collins's use of repetitive motifs could be seen as reductive, these differential repetitions create psychological richness. This image of the 'shadow' and 'poison' cuts in several directions. It immediately demonstrates the danger of women towards women throughout the novel: in startling contrast to *No Name*, *Armadale* rejects the possibility of female friendship. Secondly, it places the origins of trauma in a different psychological space. It is not the primal male conflict that is most potent here, but *Mrs. Armadale's* sense of cultural and emotional loss. This is demonstrated in Chapter 3; listening to Neal read the first part of the letter, she interjects:

> 'Was she a fair woman?' asked the voice, 'or dark, like me?'
>
> [...] The hot African blood burnt red in her dusky cheeks as she obstinately repeated the question, 'Was she a fair woman – or, dark, like me?'
>
> 'Fair,' said her husband, without looking at her.
>
> Her hands, lying clasped together in her lap, wrung each other hard – she said no more. (31)

We never learn anything about Ozias's mother, except that she is from Trinidad, beautiful, mixed-race and hopelessly devoted to her husband. Her use of the fatalistic terms, 'shadow' and 'poison', reminds us that there are many stories remaining to be told in *Armadale*. One of these stories is a colonial one.[16] This sad little moment demonstrates the intersection between cultural and personal guilt: Armadale says, 'It was my duty to spare her [his wife] the hopeless sacrifice of her freedom and her happiness to such an existence as mine – and I did her the injury of marrying her' (45). Here, her loveless marriage is figured as slavery: gendered and racial oppression, despite the imminent emancipation of the slaves (the novel opens in 1832, one year before this). Ozias inherits this composite history: as he tells Mr. Brock, 'there was I, an ill-conditioned brat, with my mother's negro blood in my face, and my murdering father's passions in my heart, inheritor of their secret in spite of them!' (II.2, 89).

Armadale first enters the novel as a disjointed series of eight letters when the landlord of Wildbad's inn spells out the outlandish English name (I.1, 10). The excited waiting of the German townsfolk builds anticipation, and the reader joins the crowd awaiting the arrival of the Armadale family, Collins constructing a theatrical *mise-en-scène* in which their arrival becomes a dramatic entrance. But when Armadale does appear, his face and figure offer a profound blank:

> The leaden blank of his face met every question as to his age, his rank, his temper, and his looks which that face might once have answered, in

[16] Caroline Reitz (2000) argues that the novel enacts a process of almost-guilt, or 'gwilt', regarding English colonial expansion (95).

> impenetrable silence. Nothing spoke for him now but the shock that had struck him with the death-in-life of Paralysis. The doctor's eye questioned his lower limbs, and Death-in-life answered, *I am here*. (13)

The paralysis, it is hinted, is connected to Armadale's 'wild' and 'vicious life' (I.2, 15), and bears the hidden taint of venereal disease such as syphilis. Collins references *The Rime of the Ancient Mariner* in the phrase 'Death-in-Life' (originally 'Life-in-death' in Samuel Taylor Coleridge's poem). This reinforces the novel's traumatic structure; Coleridge's poem also relies on an original crime: the shooting of the albatross. Following his inexplicable crime, the Mariner, like Armadale, is doomed to tell his story. Unlike the Mariner, however, Armadale cannot expiate his crime through his confession as he dies once it is completed. Chapter 2 underlines the sense of urgency and compulsion connected to the confession. The doctor repeats Mrs. Armadale's account of the letter's initial conception in Switzerland. She posits it as a gendered conflict between herself and the 'cruel pen':

> I heard his pen scrape, scrape, scrape over the paper – I heard him groaning and sobbing as he wrote – I implored him for God's sake to let me in. The cruel pen went scrape, scrape, scrape; the cruel pen was all the answer he gave me. I waited at the door – hours – I don't know how long [...] Over that fatal letter, the stroke had struck him – over that fatal letter, we found him, paralysed as you see him now. (17–18)

Armadale empties himself into the letter, and it takes on vampiric power, while he is rendered a 'leaden blank' (13). He insists on the ghostly nature of the letter in its opening clauses, saying he wishes 'to warn my son of a danger that lies in wait for him – a danger that will rise from his father's grave, when the earth has closed over his father's ashes' (I.3, 27). At this point, before the entrance of Lydia Gwilt, the pen appears as a powerful male tool, but one loaded with danger. The letter Armadale produces takes his life through a strange act of literary transference.

Throughout the novel, writing is coloured by a sense of danger and characterised by a radical questioning of authenticity. These questions are brought together in Lydia's first crime: her forgery of Mrs. Wrentmore's handwriting was a capital offence in the 1820s until the 1832 Forgery, Abolition of Punishment of Death Act (the exceptions were removed in the later act of 1837). Collins plays with two concepts; on the one hand, the letter is all too authentic, bound to its author and origin, binding the reader with words and images. On the other, writing consistently fails to provide the secure presence it promises: slippages of interpretation riddle the seemingly monolithic paternal narrative. In this opening scene neither the letter's origin nor its destination are certain, Ozias's mother listens outside the door to the end of the story she was not supposed to hear, leading to her cruel rejection of her son after her first husband's death. The letter is further displaced through Neal: the dour Scot retains his rights *as a reader*:

> […] I must ask you to excuse me, if I reserve my own entire freedom of action, when your wishes in relation to the writing and the posting of the letter have been fulfilled. (24–25)

Neal subsequently voices the wife's wishes when he asks to read the letter aloud. His desire for the woman interrupts the linear process of the male plot: he is a 'conquered man' (21). This model of female intervention is consistent throughout the novel and is first shown in the prehistory recounted by Armadale.

Mrs. Wrentmore, Armadale's mother, initiates the pattern of female intervention by refusing to name her son after his father, having 'a woman's romantic objection to [his] homely Christian name' Matthew (28). This becomes more interesting when Armadale later tells us that 'loving mothers' always name their sons after their husbands (45). Allan Wrentmore is instead named after his wealthy godfather, the original Allan Armadale. Later, Allan Wrentmore has only to assume the *nom du père* to become heir of both name and property. However, female desire appears to pre-empt the event. These details imply a powerful female agency at the heart of the narrative: the naming of an eldest son would conventionally fall to the father rather than the mother. By naming her son after his godfather, Mrs. Wrentmore reveals her wish to placate the wealthier man, at the expense of her husband. Her desire for social mobility, via her son, is clear.

The surname 'Wrentmore' has connotations of exploitation or manipulation, a 'wringing out' of the highest possible profit, while also implying that a rent is created in the family fabric. In the case of Allan Armadale and his son Ingleby, we see a primal, almost archetypal, conflict between father and son: predictable, Oedipal, resulting in disinheritance, an outcome typical of the Victorian novel. But set against this is a complex web of female plotting. Mid-Victorian novels, despite their structural differences, function in a similar way to Greek tragedy since the main source of action spirals out from the family history. We begin *in medias res*; there is no one origin or cause, since each event can be traced back further.

Mapping out the complexities of *Armadale*'s prehistory, two characteristics emerge which become formative for the novel. First, the woman is a dangerous catalyst for male agency: while this is initially only a small motif in the case of Mrs. Wrentmore's naming of her son, it becomes obvious in the arranged marriage between her son and Miss Blanchard. Second, we see the significance of intense male bonds. It is Armadale's excessive love for his servant Ingleby that leads to his downfall, and this love is set in opposition to maternal power:

> My impulses governed me in everything; I knew no law but the law of my own caprice, and I took a fancy to the stranger the moment I set eyes on him [...] I [...] insisted that he should have the place. My will was law, and he had it.
>
> My mother disliked and distrusted Ingleby from the first [...] she made effort after effort to part us, and failed in one and all. (28–29)

This passage is significant in grounding the generational trauma in terms of will. In *No Name*, Andrew Vanstone's vampiric presence emerged from the failure of his will (in literal and symbolic terms); *Armadale's* plot instead relies on an excess of will: 'My will was law, and he had it'. This reads like an erotic seduction.[17] Through Armadale and Ingleby, a dialectical play is established: intense love between men destabilises female power, while female figures destabilise the bonds between men. In the elder generations, Mrs. Wrentmore and Jane Blanchard play this role; in the younger generation, it is Lydia. This is complicated by the fact that Lydia transgresses generational boundaries by marrying the twenty-one-year-old Ozias. Significantly, Jane Blanchard and Lydia Gwilt further Ingleby's revenge. Lydia, at the tender age of twelve, forges a letter from Mrs. Wrentmore to be given to Mr. Blanchard ensuring that the marriage can take place: her 'wicked dexterity' (34) is the final act of deception required. In both *No Name* and *Armadale*, revenge appears as the dark

[17] Maria Bachman and Don Richard Cox (2003) argue that homosexuality is the 'unspeakable truth' of *Armadale*. However, homoeroticism (if not homosexuality) is anything but unspeakable in the novel: it provides the dynamism for the male story in the elder and younger generations.

shadow of justice. Ingleby's decision to usurp Armadale's intended bride can be justified within the context of his own disinheritance: a strange kind of equilibrium is sustained by his actions. This establishes the process of displacement characterising the relationship between Allan and Ozias: a process that begins in revenge and violence is transformed into a loving force.

Armadale's pursuit of Ingleby results in their encounter on the sinking *La Grâce de Dieu*. On board, Armadale locates the cabin to find Ingleby already half-submerged, attempting to rescue the proceeds of his deceit, his wife's jewels. 'The devil at [Armadale's] elbow whispered':

> Don't shoot him like a man: drown him like a dog!' He was under water when I bolted the scuttle. But his head rose to the surface before I could close the cabin door. I looked at him, and he looked at me – and I locked the door in his face. (44)

This is the 'sacred confidence' Armadale bequeaths to his son (45). The look between the two men is penetrative, lending violence to a murder that would otherwise appear quite passive—helping Ingleby to his death, rather than tearing his life away. The look replaces the physical act of violence that Armadale had anticipated. The way in which Collins frames this sentence means that the two men appear as mirror images; Armadale looks at Ingleby looking back at him. There is a struggle for identity between the two, which began with Allan Armadale's disinheritance of his son, and ends in this murderous exchange. Lying on his deathbed, listening to Neal recounting his confession, Armadale is unknowingly brought back to the ship: 'His helpless body was back on the wreck, and the ghost of his lifeless hand was turning the lock of the cabin door' (42).

Armadale has not won the struggle for identity—he simply passes it onto his son. But the very fact that Ozias receives this traumatic inheritance, this enigmatic 'noise' (Laplanche 2011, 21) means that he exists in the novel with a form of self-consciousness denied to the vacuous Allan. The latter is likewise the inheritor of this self-constituting, self-destructive, encounter between the two fathers, but unlike Ozias he remains in ignorance. For Allan, there is no enigma to be translated, and yet it is there on the level of *plot*, consistently determining his actions. Allan never recognises the encounter he has inherited from his father; he is blind.[18]

The fact that Ingleby is already half-drowned before Armadale locks the cabin door upon him complicates the question of agency: Is it God's will, or '*grâce*', which causes his death, or does the sinking of the ship reveal the failure of grace? The murder of Ingleby raises the question of whether there is room in the novel for two Armadales—or whether one must necessarily die to make way for the other. Armadale undoubtedly believes the latter:

> I see danger in the future, begotten of the danger in the past – treachery that is the offspring of *his* treachery, and crime that is the child of *my* crime [...] Never let the two Allan Armadales meet in this world: never, never, never! (47–48)

The trochaic phrase, 'never, never, never', echoes Lear's words following Cordelia's death and numerous moments in Dickens's writing. Collins emphasises the deadliness of Armadale's predictions, as well as the grand and intimate tragedies underpinning the novel. Armadale is convinced that the sins of the fathers will be visited upon the sons. Like Mr. Vanstone, he conceives of himself as a ghostly presence, writing 'My son! I have pursued you from my grave with a confession which my love might have spared you' (44). He dies with his hands gently placed on his son's head (50). But Armadale's belief that he can police his son's story from the grave—just as he policed Ozias's toy on the bed—ignores two key aspects of his own history: not only do female desires intervene in paternal narratives (a lesson he could have learnt from *King Lear*), but the trauma is also split across two consciousnesses, and therefore two sources of transmission—the letter and the dream.

A Dream

Self-consciously appropriating Sophocles, Collins interrogates parent-child relationships, and how religion, providence or fate, intervenes in

[18] Much, indeed, like his well-meaning maternal grandfather, Mr. Blanchard. This model is complicated by the fact that Allan's blindness is perpetuated by Ozias and Brock who collude to protect Allan from the past: as a consequence of this "good will" Allan can never act, he is acted upon.

these relationships. *Armadale* implies that familial narratives take the place of religious meta-narrative; families are constructed through myth-making, on the level of both plot and character. Mr. Brock's intervention in the paternal narrative addresses the issue of how the familial and the religious could be conceived of together, although it remains uncertain to what extent the text resolves this issue (or indeed whether Collins wished to resolve it).

Collins constructs the traumatic male narrative in scenographic terms and with a self-consciously theatrical eye. In 'The Shadow of the Past', Ozias and Allan find themselves on the ship where the infamous murder took place over twenty years before:

> Here, where the deed had been done, the fatal parallel between past and present was complete. What the cabin had been in the time of the fathers, that the cabin was now in the time of the sons. (II.4, 125)

Ozias has by this time read his father's letter and is penetrated with dread while Allan roams unconcerned over the ship. The encounter is placed dramatically at the beginning of a new monthly number, and Collins opens it with an intense look passed between the two young men, interrupted by Allan's boisterous laugh: 'the two friends turned face to face on the deck of the timber-ship, and looked at each other in silence' (123). This emphasis on the look creates an uneasy parallel with the primal scene in which the look was the carrier of violence and hatred, undermining the solidity of personal identity. As the bearer of seemingly dangerous and transgressive knowledge, Ozias's self is undermined. He appears dissociated: the ghost of his father, or of himself. As the deathbed scene implied, Armadale Sr. never really left *La Grâce de Dieu*. The phrasing of the paragraph in which Ozias 'reels giddily' (123) across the deck negates him as a solid presence. A lengthy description starts with the phrase, 'the other followed', while the rest of the passage compulsively follows the intricacies of Ozias's movements using 'he' and 'his' in monotonous procession (123). Collins uses this anonymising to greater dramatic effect when Allan teases Ozias over his seriousness:

> 'What is there to scare you in that rotten old cabin? What are you shaking and shivering about? Any company of the supernatural sort on board? Mercy preserve us! [...] do you see a ghost?'

> '*I see two!*' answered the other [...] 'The ghost of a man like you, drowning in the cabin! And the ghost of a man like me, turning the lock of the door on him!' (124–125)

The avoidance of Ozias's assumed name here is dramatically resonant. Ozias believes he hears 'footsteps' 'following him in the dark' (123), echoing Armadale's earlier prophecies. Ozias is a virtual non-presence throughout this scene, 'stealthy', 'furtive', bearing the guilt of his father's murder. The slippage between father and son is apparent throughout: 'So, like a noisome exhalation from the father's grave, the father's influence rose and poisoned the mind of the son' (130). Ozias cannot translate his father's message—he is possessed by it. Collins predicates this moment as a conflict between Ozias's adherence to his father and his love for his friend:

> The struggle between the hereditary superstition that was driving him on, and the unconquerable affection for Allan that was holding him back, suspended the next words on his lips. (131)

Once again, as we saw in the prehistory of the novel, homosocial desire subverts parental authority. Male-male relations undermine the overwhelming parental demand for loyalty and the father's *emprise*. It is only Ozias's immense love for Allan that prevents him from fulfilling his father's demands.

Collins disrupts the linearity of the paternal narrative when Allan receives the prophetic dream on *La Grâce de Dieu*. The dream presents Allan with a series of scenes, beginning with Ingleby taking him by his hand and leading him into the ship's cabin: 'Water rose slowly over us in the cabin; and I and my father sank through the water together' (II.5, 141). Darkness and oblivion follow, and a series of scenes appear in which a 'Shadow of a Man' and a 'Shadow of a Woman' ultimately appear to collude in his falling down with a 'deadly faintness' as he is poisoned (142). This follows a montage in which these same shadowy characters are seen in distinctive locations, including a room with long windows and a view of flower gardens which we later discover is the library at Thorpe-Ambrose: Allan's mother's favourite room.

Collins emphasises the tortuous nature of the story as Allan writhes on the deck of the ship. However, we hear the contents of the dream from the document which Ozias has constructed based on Allan's unheard verbatim report; Allan saying that it is 'exactly what I should have written myself, if I had thought the thing worth putting down on paper, and if I had had the knack of writing' (141). In a heated debate with Ozias, Hawbury succeeds in relating each of the dream's images to events of the previous day, which, he claims, Allan's subconscious has merged together in a kind of dream soup: notably this includes the appearance of the miniature of Allan's father, which Ozias examined. Ozias maintains that the dream has a prophetic message: a completely reasonable mystic belief bearing in mind his knowledge of Armadale's crime. Although we are not told at this point, Ozias relates the two 'shadows' to himself and Lydia, and to the warning in his father's confession that the three surviving figures connected to the crime (Allan, Ozias and Lydia) should never meet.[19]

Significantly, the dream is really the first and only moment in the novel when Allan is granted any kind of interiority. The primal loss of the father, and Allan's wish for his return, is implied. Allan is never represented as a grieving son, but through the dream an unknowing wish for his father's presence could be read. Condensed within this, however, is the significance of the maternal figure, and her absence and loss. Allan treasures the portrait of Ingleby primarily because it was precious to his mother (II.3, 109), and his first tears are shed on the death of his mother (II.1, 73). The father and mother are therefore conflated in the dream. The fact that Jane raised Allan means that, despite his total ignorance regarding his father's history, he has received a significant void. Looking at the dream through a Freudian lens, the dark moments in the dream could refer to the passing over of time and the lack of conjunctions in the dreamwork. Allan's prophetic visions of the shadow man and woman could represent unacknowledged fears regarding his mother's silences. But, unlike Ozias's interpretation, which immediately places himself and Lydia in the starring roles, the dream censors the identity of the man and woman. These sources of fear and desire are obscured and can relate to figures from the past (his dead parents) and to future events: perhaps to an anticipated conflict between his homoerotic love for Ozias and his desire for a female lover: a conflict realised through the introduction of Lydia. Ultimately,

[19] The dream, which Jenny Bourne Taylor (1988) analyses in depth, traverses questions of determinism and free will, and engages with contemporary Victorian theories. Taylor addresses this through a sustained close reading of the argument between Mr. Hawbury, 'the voice of medical authority', and Ozias concerning the nature of the dream (138).

however, a Freudian reading is limited by the fact that Allan's dream is genuinely prophetic: the dream thought *is* also the dream content. The dream is central to the novel's dialogue with fate and chance: it is mythic as well as psychological.

The way in which the dream is constructed as a written presence is critical. Ozias has by this point burnt his father's letter with its grim predictions in the presence of Mr. Brock, but his copy of Allan's dream takes its place. The burning of the father's letter is tantamount to a betrayal, even a murder. Armadale repeatedly emphasises the posthumous paternal presence with which he endows his letter, the inscription of which seemingly led to the stroke that killed him. The burning of the letter can be seen as symbolic patricide:

> 'For God's sake, let me burn it!' he exclaimed. 'As long as there is a page left, I shall read it. And, as long as I read it, my father gets the better of me, in spite of myself!' (II.2, 107)

Ozias repudiates the direct expression of the story, the vampiric object that seemingly killed his father, but his inscription of the dream involves a new act of appropriation. Allan's story is mediated through Ozias, who takes the story as his own. Just like an oracle's, the dream's prediction is inescapable; by struggling to free himself, Ozias enmeshes himself still further. Ozias's intimate relationship with the contents of Allan's dream strengthens the doubling created between them; the fact that Allan unconsciously inherits the knowledge of the murder reinforces this once more. *Armadale* operates as a direct address to, even rewriting of, *Oedipus Tyrannus* with its interrogation of fate, agency and the paternal demand for loyalty,[20] and in case we were in any danger of missing the point, the narrator tells us that Ozias carries a copy of Sophocles's plays (II.1, 60).

Ozias Midwinter becomes an inverse Oedipus. While the latter unconsciously worked to his own destruction by becoming the detective of his own crimes—Franklin Blake's role in *The Moonstone*—Ozias is prematurely convinced of his own guilt and attempts to exile himself. Ozias does not just play detective, he plays his own judge, jury and executioner. Oedipus is at the mercy of unconscious forces over which he has no control; Ozias is more like the obsessional neurotic, panicking over

[20]Collins had a copy of Aeschylus's *Tragedies* translated by T. W. A. Buckley in his library at the time of his death: this was his only classical text (Baker 2002, 16).

crimes he has no intention of committing, but whose images are burnt symbolically upon his eye. The son is perhaps all too conscious of his *textual* Oedipal crime, and his refusal to renounce the dream-text can be seen as a reparative act towards his father, although one in which the homosocial bond between the two young men is placed at the centre of the narrative.[21]

In his letter to Ozias, Mr. Brock reframes the supernatural aspects of the dream within a biblical context:

> The great sacrifice of the Atonement – I say it reverently – has its mortal reflections, even in this world. If danger ever threatens Allan, you, whose father took his father's life – YOU, and no other, may be the man whom the providence of God has appointed to save him' (III.14, 514).[22]

Ozias creates an ongoing dialogue between the text of the dream and this letter from Brock. Much later, in Naples, Lydia finds him asleep clutching both manuscripts, torn between two interpretations of the dream-text: his own (coloured by his father's fears) and the clergyman's:

> Part of the open manuscript, however, was not covered by his hand. I looked at it to see what he had secretly stolen away to read, besides Mr. Brock's letter – and made out enough to tell me it was the Narrative of Armadale's Dream. (V.1, 554)

Letters are ghosts, testifying to a longed-for presence, but equally failing to provide this presence. In this context, Brock's reassertion of Christian values, and of the omnipotent presence of an all-mighty God, is undercut. His promise of God's presence can only be represented within the drastic instability of the text. If we think about the way in which Brock's letter structurally counterpoints Armadale's, then we can interpret God as another parent making an overwhelming demand for loyalty.

[21] Ozias's relationships with a whole series of father figures are textually mediated. Mr. Neal inscribes the letter his father dictates, Ozias Midwinter the elder gives him his gipsy name, the bookshop keeper allows Ozias to educate himself in the works of Sophocles and Goethe (while he dreams away life in an opium trance), and finally, Mr. Brock provides the counterpoint to the first paternal letter.

[22] Reading Brock's letter leaves Lydia 'trembling' and doubting her criminal path. She echoes Armadale Sr. and Lear, speaking of Ozias before their wedding: 'I have never loved him yet, never, never, never as I love him now' (514).

In both Armadale's and Brock's accounts, Ozias is at the mercy of his *inherited* sin. This irony would not have been lost on the unconventional Collins, who 'was never a church-goer [...] and had no belief in the after-life' (Peters 1991, 108); he loved his parents, but resisted their religious rigidity (ibid., 38). Collins's subtle irony, that God (in Brock's account) is also a pushy father, undercuts *Armadale*'s redemptive narrative. Simply put, God's paternal narrative wins out over Armadale's. Ozias's attempt to follow Brock's faith demonstrates not only an adherence to a Christian discourse, but also reconciliation with the figure of the father: both the father as man and the Father as God.

The novel's series of written legacies testifies to a danger encrypted within the process of writing. This danger is twofold and is appropriately split across the figures of Ozias and Allan, whose blithe confidence in his own atrocious letter writing reveals the perils of linguistic failure: 'People make a fuss about letter-writing', Allan remarked, when he had done. '*I* find it easy enough' (II.3, 113). Allan repeatedly influences the progress of the plot by simply writing bad letters. In 'Day and Night', Allan must choose between two prospective tenants for the Steward's cottage on the Thorpe-Ambrose Estate: the family solicitor, Mr. Darch, and the unknown Major Milroy. In a breach of etiquette, Allan chooses the Major because he has a young daughter. He spins a coin to confirm his half-made decision. His absurdly brief letter to Mr. Darch subsequently contributes to his isolation in the neighbourhood and his vulnerability to Lydia's plotting. Through the spinning of the coin, and the intervention of chance, Collins implies a fundamental paradox: fate and agency are inextricably bound together since Allan is fated to make his decision. Writing is shown to be a heavy responsibility throughout *Armadale*; starting as a 'sacred confidence' (I.3, 45), language never entirely shakes off this supernatural quality. Not only does language fail Allan, but also (like Andrew Vanstone in *No Name*) *Allan* fails language. As Jenny Bourne Taylor (1988) argues, Ozias has the opposite problem: his physiology is tied into his writing (202). While Ozias is travelling through France, a doctor advises him: 'When you find your nerves playing you strange tricks, don't neglect the warning – drop your pen' (V.1, 554).

By making Ozias a professional writer (with his health at the mercy of his writing), Collins creates an uncanny repetition: writing accelerated Armadale's death. This problem is reformulated through the intervention of female voices; writing is not only a physiological or genealogical battle, but also a battle between the sexes. This takes us back to the beginning of the novel and the scene of inscription, in which the beautiful Mrs. Armadale was excluded from the room, secretly listening at the door while her unloving husband dictated his confession. The compulsion to repeat is emphatically gendered throughout the novel.

From One Lady to Another

In the prehistory of the novel, as recounted by the dying Armadale Sr., female plotting is initially dominant. The three key figures, Mrs. Wrentmore, Jane Blanchard and Lydia Gwilt, play determining roles in the conflict between the two Allan Armadales. Like the three fates, or three witches, they have a formative impact on everything that follows. Lydia herself is both a blank and a blazing narrative presence. She denies knowledge to the other protagonists, but she speaks to us in her diary. Through Lydia, female inheritance becomes a disturbing void and as readers we must follow James Bashwood's advice to 'Fancy anything you like' about her origins (IV.15, 521). In Book Three, the female narrative interrupts the male as Mother Oldershaw's bathetic letter follows an anxious missive from Ozias to Brock. Lydia's entrance in the narrative reminds us that there are several genealogical crimes at stake in *Armadale*: Jane Blanchard's deceit towards her father is also primal, leading to the uncanny reappearance of Lydia in the story. Female transgression leads to female retribution. Collins's traumatic narrative structure is self-consciously imploded by the introduction of female voices.

Narrative is gendered throughout *Armadale*: while the confession passed from father and son is described as a 'sacred confidence' (I.3, 45), female narratives are shown to adhere to Mrs. Milroy's description of a 'sealed communication' (IV.3, 332). The differing connotations are telling; the male narrative implies a sanctified act, similar to the Catholic confessional. 'Communication' instead implies a form of openness, a passage of information represented by the 'letter', but a *sealed* communication calls that passage into question. The communication is encrypted, hidden. Throughout the novel, female communication relies on this paradox. By withholding her father's letter from Mrs. Wrentmore, Jane Blanchard initiates this pattern of female secrecy. There is something inherently manipulative about the female narratives: the women deceive each other, while Armadale's letter is a revelation of a primal truth. That is not to say that men do not deceive each other, because they clearly do, beginning with Ingleby's seduction of Armadale and ending with Ozias's ongoing silence towards Allan. Female deception, though, is intimately related to textuality. Female narratives are bound up with written forgeries and shrouded in mystery. The female narrative becomes parodic of the male trauma and crucially, brings the seriousness of the latter into question.

On a superficial level, the homosocial love triangle created by Lydia's entrance at Thorpe-Ambrose appears to conform to René Girard's idea of 'mimetic desire' in erotic triangles, Girard suggesting that it is the love rival who confers value upon the woman (Sedgwick 1985, 20). In *Between Men: English Literature and Male Homosocial Desire* (1985), Eve Kosofsky Sedgwick appropriates Girard's reading of the triangulation of desire to theorise 'a continuum between homosexual and homosocial –a continuum whose visibility, for men, in our society is radically disrupted' (1–2). In *Armadale*, the two men's love for Lydia briefly transforms their loving friendship into an intense rivalry. However, since the relationship between Ozias and Allan is *already* the primary invested relation, things are more complicated. The two young men do not need Lydia to act as the mediating object for feeling to pass between them, as they gained this inherited right from their fathers. As with Cathy and Heathcliff in *Wuthering Heights*, the men's love is indexed by trauma: the trauma, even in silence, operates as the mediating object between them. Lydia is, in this perspective, simply the embodiment of the crime, and it is within this context that Ozias falls in love with her. The narrator carefully tells us that Ozias would have recognised Lydia's true identity 'instinctively' on first sight, if it had not been for Brock's recent failed adventure in London (III.10, 280). This strange almost-knowing provokes Ozias's desire. Under the influence of his attraction for Lydia, Ozias is left enacting 'glaring self-contradictions' (III.12, 293): 'in accepting the Dream as the revelation of a fatality, and in attempting to escape that fatality by an exercise of free will' (293). Allan's love for Lydia is, on the other hand, of the most superficial kind and is easily forgotten in his renewed relations with Miss Milroy. This superficiality can be linked back to Allan's ignorance of the primal trauma—he lacks the negative internal spaces in which Collins shows desire can flourish.

Ozias is undeniably seduced by Lydia. But between the two men, Lydia operates as a representative of a maternal prohibition, rather than as an erotic object. As we saw in the prehistory of the novel, Mrs. Wrentmore attempted to prevent the intimacy between Armadale and Ingleby, and Jane Armadale likewise attempted to prevent Allan meeting his namesake. Lydia's most significant action is to persuade Ozias that Allan has misjudged her and set spies on her trail; it is this action that precipitates Ozias's departure from Thorpe-Ambrose. The breach between Ozias and Allan is therefore caused by their varying treatments of Lydia's (and therefore their own) history, rather than by erotic competition. Lydia's generational offence in marrying a man fifteen years younger than herself, and lying about her age, strengthens the sense that Lydia is symbolically connected with *Armadale*'s maternal discourse.

Lydia undoubtedly comes to represent 'destiny' as it is she who fulfils Armadale's predictions by posing a murderous threat to Allan and Ozias. But she is far from being a passive instrument of fate. Instead, Lydia comes to represent the idea of Fate itself. As we have seen in relation to *Armadale*'s paternal narratives, Collins plays with the ideas of fate and chance he found in Greek tragedy. Lydia's association with fate becomes apparent when we consider her second act within the novel's timeframe: her attempted suicide following Manuel's desertion. Hugely improbably, the current heir to Thorpe-Ambrose, Arthur Blanchard, is at the scene and jumps into the river to save her; this action, through a bizarre sequence of events, leads to the death of all possible heirs to the property save Allan himself. Through this plot device, Collins shows that Lydia's fateful role is first an unconscious one before she self-consciously plots around the new developments in Book Three. From representing Fate in the abstract, Lydia subsequently takes control of the narrative's fate. The primal murder represented a violent confrontation with the self, as well as an ambivalent and eroticised encounter with the male other. While this was initially a male problem passed from father to son, through Lydia, female identity becomes ascendant.

The trauma begins with the primal scene of murder and moves through the inscription of the father's letter, and onto the second scene on *La Grâce de Dieu* where Allan receives his prophetic dream. The violent and penetrative look that characterises the primal murder is transformed into this penetrative gaze into the future. But from Book Three onwards, agency is removed from Ozias and Allan and resited within Lydia. The question of how Ozias will respond to the overwhelming parental demand for loyalty becomes somewhat effaced, even irrelevant. The confrontation with personal identity becomes Lydia's concern: she gazes at herself in her diary, and we gaze with her. The thematic reconciliation of selfhood can only be achieved through her. But this self is already complicated; by telling Lydia his story, Ozias transfers the narrative responsibility for it onto Lydia herself:

> 'Sit down,' he said. 'You have given me back my courage – you shall know who I am.'
>
> In the silence and the darkness all round us, I obeyed him, and sat down.
>
> In the silence and the darkness all round us, he took me in his arms again, and told me who he was. [*Followed by a space equivalent to three lines of text*] (IV.9, 423)

The story is invested with a curious, possessive power. Collins stresses the possessive power of the story through the repetitive and portentous language Lydia uses in this scene, as well as the empty space in the text. This latter would have been Collins's own; throughout the publication of *Armadale*, he made typesetting decisions himself (see Sutherland, introduction, xxxiv).

In Book Four, Chapter 9, Lydia returns to the diary to judge how much of its contents she wishes to share with Mrs. Oldershaw, and as readers, we are privy to the process as we read the diary with her (423). Lydia eventually refuses Mrs. Oldershaw's demand for information and continues to write purely for herself. Ozias's narrative possesses her:

> Let me think. What *haunts* me, to begin with?
>
> The Names haunt me. I keep saying and saying to myself: Both alike! – Christian name and surname, both alike! (424)

She continues shortly after, 'When I am not thinking of him or of his story, my mind feels quite stupefied. I who have always known what to do on other occasions, don't know what to do now' (433). She sets out the novel's prehistory in her diary and returns to her letters from Manuel for casual inspiration, from which she forms her plan.

Collins associates feminine writings with a flirtatious process of revelation-concealment, and the diary becomes a veritable narrative striptease. When Lydia places a dose of arsenic in Allan's lemonade in Naples (directly fulfilling the predictions of his dream), she initially refuses to impart the incident to her diary, saying, 'I won't put down what I said to him – or what I did, afterwards. I'm sick of Armadale!' (V.2, 559). She subsequently reveals it, displacing the story from herself, by transcribing a conversation between herself and Ozias. Ozias recounts the scene between Lydia and Allan, and Lydia betrays herself by crying out to him, '*Do you think I tried to poison him*?' (562). She never directly admits, even to the reader, what has been placed in his glass:

> I *was* innocent – so far as the brandy was concerned. I had put it into the lemonade, in pure ignorance of Armadale's nervous peculiarity, to disguise the taste of – never mind what! (563)

Lydia is split between self and written-self, and the diary-self begins to take on a transgressive resonance; it becomes her confessor, the partner in her crimes: the 'secret friend of my wretchedest and wickedest hours' (V.1, 545). Through the splitting engendered by writing, Lydia shifts identity in the transition from Book Four to Book Five: the first woman is incapable of murder and unwilling to write, the second is an author and a murderer. She describes her diary as her 'second self' (545). It is the rereading of her own salacious diary which provokes her to take up her murderous cause once more:

> I think I shall look back through these pages, and live my life over again when I was plotting and planning, and finding a new excitement to occupy me in every new hour of the day. (547)

In her first re-entry into the diary, she makes it clear that it is a replacement for both friend and lover:

> My misery is a woman's misery, and it *will* speak – here, rather than nowhere; to my second self, in this book, if I have no-one else to hear me [...] I cannot even lay my finger on the day when the cloud first rose between us [...] Day after day, the hours that he gives to his hateful writing grow longer and longer; day after day, he becomes more and more silent, in the hours that he gives to Me. (545)

As this passage shows, the diary takes the place of the male lover, while also becoming the *only* feminine exchange possible in the novel. It is telling that Lydia perceives Ozias's writing as a competitor for his affections, and looking at the dynamics of the text as a whole, this is not so strange. For Ozias, writing is associated with paternal narratives and with adherence to the word of the Father, whether this is his own father, Brock or God. Lydia correctly feels that there is something in the male written word which conflicts with her own interests. Feeling this, she takes up *her* pen once more.

Following her failure to poison Allan, Lydia conspires with Manuel to recreate the primal scene between the two fathers, resulting in Allan disappearing at sea on a yacht. As we later find out in Allan's lengthy letter to Bashwood, this murderous plan fails: instead of being locked into the cabin to drown, Allan is saved by the English mate. Allan's poor narrative technique is vastly (and amusingly) improved by his near-death experience: 'You will agree with me that it is a terribly long letter'; 'I seem to have lost my old knack at putting things short, and finishing on the first page' (V.3, 604). It is as if Allan's unconscious encounter with his father's fate endows him with a depth of character, interiority and pathos new to the novel, simultaneously developing his narrative skill. Collins reinforces the *narrative power* of the paternal trauma. On the back foot, Lydia is forced into fashioning another plot, this time with the help of the sinister Dr. Downward. The scene of murder moves from the vast immensity of the ocean to the enclosed, modern space of the private asylum located in the newly suburban area of Hampstead. The quasi-magical power of the written word resonates through this portion of Lydia's narrative. Writing names becomes akin to a summoning spell, bringing the bearer of the name to consciousness, a ghost. As the time when she will have to repudiate Ozias (in order to pose as Allan's widow) draws closer, Lydia superstitiously avoids written encounters with her husband and vows that she will never write his name again:

> Was there ever such an infatuated fool as I am, to be writing of him at all, when writing only encourages me to think of him? I will make a new resolution. From this time forth his name shall appear no more in these pages. (599)

The haunting, vampiric, presence of Armadale is transformed: here it is his son who emerges as the ghostly influence. The diary breaks off following the conversation between Lydia and the doctor that confirms Allan will meet his death in the Sanatorium (607). The breaking off of the narrative is directly correlated with Lydia's impending death: she feels a 'foreshadowing of disaster' approaching its final page (611):

> I might be in a humour to sit here for some time longer, thinking thoughts like these, and letting them find their way into words at their own will and

> pleasure – if my Diary would only let me. But my idle pen has been busy enough to make its way to the end of the volume. I have reached the last morsel of space left on the last page [...]
>
> Good-by, my old friend and companion of many a miserable day!
>
> Having nothing else to be fond of, I half suspect myself of having been unreasonably fond of *you*. (611–612)

This implies that if Lydia had had the luxury of more space, she might have been able to retreat from her murderous and suicidal course. The end of the diary signals an end to her plotting role; events are unavoidably set in motion and will take their course. Lydia has assumed her silent fate: death. This impression is reinforced by the fact that it is Dr. Downward, via the third-person narrator, who describes the form the murder will take to Lydia, while conducting a tour of the sanatorium to a group of interested female visitors. The gauze-like veil Collins places between the reader, Lydia and the murder heightens suspense while exposing the sinister narrative presence of the doctor.

By saving Ozias, and taking his place in the gas-filled chamber, Lydia usurps the reparative act intended for the 'son' of the guilty father (VI.3, 666). Lydia intervenes in the paternal story once more, and the final written legacy left to Ozias is her own, written on the back of Brock's letter no less, just before she steps into the gas-filled room. The paternal legacy is transformed:

> The one atonement I can make for all the wrong I have done you is the atonement of my death. It is not hard for me to die, now I know you will live. Even my wickedness has one merit – it has not prospered. I have never been a happy woman. (666)

Lydia dies to save Ozias from her 'poisonous' presence: standing over his unconscious body, she murmurs, 'All your life is before you – a happy life, and an honoured life, if you are freed from *me*' (666). Her fated role, in the end, is her own death. Atonement, previously correlated with Christ in Brock's letter, becomes a feminised concern: it is female *desire* that leads to reparation.

Ozias and Allan's friendship undermines the persecutory primal narrative passed down from Armadale, while also destabilising, rather than destroying, Lydia's potent narrative power. The homoerotic, the source of violence in the elder generation, is transformed into a homely friendship that has the power to stop narrative itself. Silence becomes the wished-for end: Ozias never tells Allan the truth about their fathers or even his own identity. He becomes the keeper of all the novel's secrets. Lydia's grave is marked with a simple 'L', her story, and her name, curtailed. The isolated but overwhelming presence of Lydia's diary demonstrates the extent to which female homosociality is problematised throughout the novel. Nowhere do we see a female relationship that can parallel the bonds between Allan, Ozias and Brock. On the contrary, women are extremely dangerous to one another. On both the male and female sides of the narrative, we see the impact of wilful same-sex desire: Armadale's account of his meeting with Ingleby reads like a seduction, and the teenage Jane Blanchard likewise takes a strong fancy to the twelve-year-old Lydia. These 'likings' are subversive and dangerous. But despite this, male bonds become idealised: at the end of the story, it is the pairing of Allan and Ozias which remains dominant (despite Allan and Miss Milroy's marriage): the subversive female element is eradicated through Lydia's death.

As Pedgift tells us in a letter to his son, it is Ozias who insists on silence concerning events in the sanatorium. Although he is denied the grandeur of dying to save Allan, Ozias performs a symbolic self-sacrifice by denying his own identity to the last. Significantly, however, this also protects two guilty women, Lydia and Jane:

> 'I entreat you to believe that the reasons I have for leaving it unexplained, are reasons which, if Mr Brock was living, Mr Brock himself would approve.'
>
> In those words, he kept the secret of the two names – and left the memory of Allan's mother, what he had found it, a sacred memory in the heart of her son. ('Epilogue', 676–677)

Throughout the novel, legacies—and therefore traumas—are displaced, and here Ozias appropriates the feminised legacies of silence and forgery. While the narrative appears to endorse Ozias's decision to protect the maternal figure, the wording of the passage above complicates this by reminding us that the first 'sacred' act in the novel was the writing of the letter which confessed hatred and murder: the 'sacred confidence between father and son' (I.3, 45). By protecting Jane, Ozias serves his own interests by protecting Allan's memory of Lydia, another murderer. In this final chapter, God is seemingly given the final word. But, if we consider the talismanic nature of texts in *Armadale*, then Ozias's final eulogising of Brock's letter places a profound question mark over the end of the novel. He may be quoting directly from Brock's letter, but it is *Lydia's* words blessing Ozias's future which are on the final page. Unquoted, they blaze across it nevertheless.

Notes

i. ***No Name* plot summary**

As we discover, at the age of twenty-one Andrew Vanstone had married a debauched fortune hunter in Canada. Following his discovery of her unexplained (but undoubtedly sexual) crimes, he leaves her in despair and is saved from committing suicide by his friend Major Kirke. Back in England, the young orphaned Norah Blake agrees to live with him as his wife, and they have two children: Norah and Magdalen. 'Mrs.' Vanstone is subsequently blackmailed by her mother's stepson, Captain Wragge: 'not even the widest stretch of courtesy could have included him at any time in the list of Mrs. Vanstone's most distant relations' (I.3, 30).

When Andrew Vanstone receives news that his American wife is dead and he is free to marry, he and his partner leave for London and wed in secret without the knowledge of their children, Miss Garth, their lawyer, or the reader. This situation is further complicated by the fact that Mrs. Vanstone is now dangerously pregnant at the age of forty-four. Vanstone's failure to apprehend the legal ramifications of his own marriage forms the primary trauma and motivates Magdalen's later search for revenge and justice.

When Andrew Vanstone inadvertently invalidates his previous will by marrying his daughters' mother, he rushes to rectify his mistake but is killed in a railway accident before the new will can be drawn. The fortune is automatically passed to Mrs. Vanstone and her newborn child: however, they both die in the shock of the father's death before the fortune can be reassigned to the daughters. Norah and Magdalen are illegitimate and therefore 'nobody's children'.

Magdalen makes a promise to her dead father that she will regain the family fortune, first from Michael Vanstone and then from his sickly son, Noel. With the assistance of Wragge, at Aldborough Magdalen engages on a pursuit of Noel. Noel's cunning housekeeper, Mrs. Lecount, plans to expose Magdalen through her sister, claiming in a letter to Norah that a description of Magdalen is necessary to protect her from legal action, and that family considerations would prevent Noel Vanstone from pressing charges if the adventuress Miss 'Bygrave' is proved to be his cousin (IV.6, 392). Noel, of course, knows nothing of this. Miss Garth answers for Norah with a full description of Magdalen's appearance, which rivals the narrator's own in its precision. This breach of trust is a direct repetition of an earlier moment: in the Second Scene, Magdalen's discovery of the lawyer's handbill attempting to trace her spurs her on, as she reflects broodingly that it was 'like the description of a strayed dog' (II.1, 195). However, Wragge capsizes Mrs. Lecount's plans, and Magdalen successfully marries Noel under her assumed name.

Following the covert marriage, Mrs. Lecount is struck down with brain fever and recuperates at St. Crux-in-the-Marsh; with her beauty irretrievably lost through illness, she subsequently tracks down her 'miserable' (V.2, 549) and abject employer hiding at Baliol Cottage in Dumfries. Revealing his wife's true identity, Mrs. Lecount constructs a new will for Noel. The will she dictates is designed to be accompanied by a letter to Noel's legatee, Admiral Bartram, which tells the admiral exactly what he wishes to be done with the money: this is the 'secret trust'. The letter reveals that the legacy is to be given to George Bartram on the condition that he marries within six months of Noel Vanstone's death, a clause designed to prevent Magdalen trying to marry her cousin George for the Combe-Raven money (V.3, 567).

Magdalen subsequently swaps identities with her maid, Louisa, and takes up residence at St. Crux-in-the-Marsh; however, she is not successful in her quest to steal the trust. With a sharp twist, typical of sensation fiction, Norah later finds the trust at St. Crux in the dead ashes of the fire in the 'gaunt ancient tripod' (VII.1, 630), where the sleepwalking Admiral placed it before his death. The fortune reverts to Noel Vanstone's estate, and Magdalen is again eligible to inherit the property.

ii. ***Armadale* plot summary**

Armadale has an immensely convoluted plot, even by comparison with other Victorian novels. The novel is driven by a murder, which occurs in the pre-history of the novel. One man named Allan Armadale murders another man named Allan Armadale; they are not related (excepting a very distant cousinship), but are drawn together through the disrupted process of paternal inheritance. Briefly, the original Allan Armadale, later known as Fergus Ingleby, is disinherited and the second Allan Armadale (né Allan Wrentmore) becomes Ingleby's father's heir. Mrs. Wrentmore then arranges an advantageous marriage for her son with the daughter of her past beau, Mr. Blanchard. Ingleby takes his revenge on Armadale by marrying the latter's intended bride (Jane Blanchard) through an act of forgery, perpetrated by Jane's 12-year-old maid, Lydia Gwilt, with Jane's knowledge and blessing. Jane is complicit in the deception, withholding the letter her father dictates to be sent to Mrs. Wrentmore: 'with the daughter's privity and consent, the father's confidence was abused to the very last' (I.3, 34). Armadale belatedly arrives in Madeira to find Ingleby married to his intended bride.

Neglecting all established rules of duelling, Armadale proposes meeting with Ingleby: 'I will take a pistol in my right hand [...] and he shall take a pistol in his: I will take one end of a handkerchief in my left hand, and he shall take the other end in his, and across that handkerchief the duel shall be fought' (35). This disturbing 'murder' and 'suicide' (35) is avoided when Ingleby—sensibly—flees from Madeira. Armadale's bizarre proposition stresses the doubling between the two men; even in conflict, they are conjoined.

Armadale subsequently murders Ingleby by locking him inside the cabin on a sinking ship, *La Grâce de Dieu*. This is, then, the situation before the novel's opening. In the opening chapters, the dying Armadale writes a letter confessing his crime to his son, who assumes the pseudonym Ozias Midwinter following his father's death (although his name is also legally Allan Armadale). Meanwhile, Jane Blanchard has given birth to a son, fathered by Fergus Ingleby, and this child is also Allan Armadale.

The two sons meet and become friends, and Ozias becomes aware that Allan is the son of the man his father murdered. Driven by a compulsion, Ozias confesses everything to Allan's friend, the Reverend Brock, who, in a key letter, convinces him that he can play a part for good in his friend's life. For the first two Books of the novel, the narrative charts the relationship between the two young men, posing the question of whether the sins of the fathers will be visited upon the sons, or if Ozias can make reparation for his father's crime. The first two Books are structured around three key texts (embedded within the third-person omniscient narration): Armadale Senior's confession to Ozias; the letter from Reverend Brock; and the transcription of the younger Allan's prophetic dream. Allan has this dream when the two young men find themselves—against all probabilities—on the stranded *La Grâce de Dieu*, where the murder happened years before. The dream is proved to be accurate on all counts as the novel progresses, and depicts Allan at the mercy of a mysterious woman, later revealed to be Lydia Gwilt.

Lydia plots for her own advantage. She sets out the novel's prehistory in her diary and returns to her letters from her lover Manuel for casual inspiration. It is this deadly combination of texts that inspires her audacious and murderous plan that could settle twelve hundred pounds on her for life. She will marry Ozias, murder Allan and then pose as Allan's widow at Thorpe-Ambrose in order to receive the generous inheritance granted to females marrying into the family. When it comes to the final scenes, though, it is Ozias who is asleep in the sealed room into which Lydia passes the poisonous gas intended to kill Allan. The terms of Brock's paternal invention are very nearly fulfilled here; Ozias will unconsciously take Allan's place, saving him from the deadly legacy inherited from his father, Ingleby. However, the Christian narrative is disrupted and Ozias is denied his sacrificial role.

Works Cited

Literary Texts

Brontë, Emily. 2008. *Wuthering Heights*. Edited by Ian Jack. Oxford: Oxford University Press.

Coleridge, Samuel Taylor. 2002. *Coleridge's Poetry and Prose*. Edited by Nicholas Halmi, Paul Magnuson and Raimonda Mondiano. New York: W. W. Norton.

Collins, Wilkie. 1850. *Antonina*. London: Richard Bentley.

———. 1973. *The Woman in White*. Edited by Harvey Peter Sucksmith. Oxford: Oxford University Press.

———. 1982. *The Moonstone*. Edited by Anthea Trodd. Oxford: Oxford University Press.

———. 1986. *No Name*. Edited by Virginia Blain. Oxford: Oxford University Press.

———. 1990. *Basil*. Edited by Dorothy Goldman. Oxford: Oxford University Press.

———. 1993. *Hide and Seek*. Edited by Catherine Peters. Oxford: Oxford University Press.

———. 1995. *Armadale*. Edited by John Sutherland. London: Penguin.

———. 1997. *The Dead Secret*. Edited by Ira B. Nadel. Oxford: Oxford University Press.

Dickens, Charles. 1974. *Dombey and Son*. Edited by Alan Horsman. Oxford: Clarendon Press.

Sophocles. 1984. *The Three Theban Plays*. Translated by Robert Fagles. Rev. ed. London: Penguin.

Walpole, Horace. 1968. *The Castle of Otranto*, in *Three Gothic Novels*, edited by Peter Fairclough, 87–148. London: Penguin.

Primary Psychoanalytic Texts

Abraham, Nicolas and Maria Torok. 1976. *The Wolf Man's Magic Word: A Cryptonymy*. Translated by Nicholas Rand. Minneapolis: University of Minnesota Press.

Breuer, Josef and Sigmund Freud. 2001. *Studies on Hysteria*. *SE* 2.

Freud, Sigmund. 'A Case of Paranoia Running Counter to the Psychoanalytic Theory of the Disease'. *SE* 14:261–272.

Laplanche, Jean. 1980. *La Castration*. In *Problématiques II: Castration—Symbolisation*, 6–161. Paris: Presses Universitaires de France.

———. 1999. 'Transference: Its Provocation by the Analyst'. In *Essays on Otherness*, 214–233.

———. 2011. *Freud and the Sexual*. Edited by John Fletcher. Translated by John Fletcher, Jonathan House, and Nicholas Ray. London: International Psychoanalytic Books.

Laplanche, Jean and Jean Bertrand Pontalis. 1988. *The Language of Psychoanalysis*. Translated by Donald Nicholson Smith. London: Karnac.

Schützenberger, Anne Ancelin. 1998. *The Ancestor Syndrome: Transgenerational Psychotherapy and Hidden Links in the Family Tree*. Translated by Anne Trager. London: Routledge.

Toubiana, Éric. 1988. *L'Héritage et sa Psychopathologie*. Paris: Presses Universitaires de France.

Secondary Texts

Bachman, Maria K. and Don Richard Cox. 2003. 'Wilkie Collins' Villainous Miss Gwilt, Criminality and the Unspeakable Truth'. *Dickens Studies Annual* 32: 319–337.

Baker, William. 2002. *Wilkie Collins and His Library*. London: Greenwood.

Broughton, Trev Lynn and Helen Rogers, eds. 2007. *Gender and Fatherhood in the Nineteenth Century*. Basingstoke: Palgrave Macmillan.

Darwin, Charles. 1985. *On the Origin of Species by Means of Natural Selection: Or, the Preservation of Favoured Races in the Struggle for Life*. Edited by J. W. Burrow. London: Penguin.

Fletcher, John. 2013. *Freud and the Scene of Trauma*. New York: Fordham University Press.

Miller, D. A. 1988. *The Novel and the Police*. Berkeley: University of California Press.

Peters, Catherine. 1991. *The King of Inventors: A Life of Wilkie Collins*. London: Minerva.

Reitz, Caroline. 2000. 'Colonial "Gwilt" in and Around *Armadale*'. *Victorian Periodicals Review* 33, no. 1: 92–103.

Sedgwick, Eve Kosofsky. 1985. *Between Men: English Literature and Male Homosocial Desire*. New York: Columbia University Press.

Taylor, Jenny Bourne. 1988. *In the Secret Theatre of Home: Wilkie Collins, Sensation Narrative, and Nineteenth-Century Psychology*. London: Routledge.

Wilson, Richard. 1993. *Will Power: Essays on Shakespearean Authority*. London: Harvester Wheatsheaf.

CHAPTER 6

Elizabeth Gaskell and George Eliot—Mourning and Elegy: *North and South* and *The Mill on the Floss*

By drawing together Elizabeth Gaskell and George Eliot in this final chapter, I do not imply that their writings can be conflated. Rather, I explore the treatment of mourning in these female-authored texts and relate this back to the mid-Victorian literary moment investigated in this study. Gaskell and Eliot construct social and personal ethics in relation to mourning: a negotiation between past and present circumstances—memory and present-tense reality. In so doing, the influence of Charles Dickens can be felt. However, for both Gaskell and Eliot, mourning cannot take place within the enclosed domestic scene, but requires movement out into new social and communal spaces. Both novels addressed in this chapter ultimately resist the sewing-up of family, albeit in different ways.

Gaskell directly addresses this outward motion in the Preface to *Mary Barton* (1848). Hinting towards the death of her infant son, she writes:

> Three years ago I became anxious (from circumstances that need not be more fully alluded to) to employ myself in writing a work of fiction. Living in Manchester, but with a deep relish and fond admiration for the country, my first thought was to find a frame-work for my story in some rural scene; and I had already made a little progress in a tale, the period of which was more than a century ago, and the place on the borders of Yorkshire, when I bethought me how deep might be the romance in the lives of some of those who elbowed me daily in the busy streets of the town in which I resided. (3)

M. Wood, *Parents and Children in the Mid-Victorian Novel*,
https://doi.org/10.1007/978-3-030-45469-2_6

This passage is critical for our understanding of Gaskell's fiction. Rates of infant mortality were extremely high in the period, but this did not make the death of a baby any less shocking or painful for the parents—as we see through both Gaskell and Dickens (Uglow 1993, 127, 152–153; Slater 2009, 327–328, 345). Gaskell's pain on losing her son, Willie, is presented as the motive force for her authorship. Her movement from the loss of her baby, to her fiction, and outwards into the working-class crowd, becomes a way of mourning. Gaskell occupies an essential place in *Traumatic Encounters*, since she, like Dickens, self-consciously formulates literary realism in relation to parent-child trauma: in this case, the tragic loss of her own son. Vision and proximity are central to how she conceives her writing. The female novelist must be close to her subjects: 'some of those who elbowed me daily in the busy streets of the town'; this insistence on her own nearness works to legitimise her authorial enterprise. Bearing witness to social injustice is repeatedly foregrounded in her novels and short stories. While the self-conscious narrator of *Mary Barton* tries hard not to offend her middle-class readership, John Barton's cry—'Han they ever seen a child o' their'n die for want o' food?' (Ch. 6, 66)—remains unanswerable, reverberating throughout the novel. He is a witness and must be heard. The death of a baby emotionally draws together the fictional working-class family and the middle-class female author and subtly undermines the narrator's economic platitudes. In *North and South*, Mrs. Hale is physically and emotionally broken by the separation from her son. In a moment laden with symbolic importance, she turns her face to the wall rather than questioning Frederick's integrity in the mutiny. If it is not pushing the idea too far, Gaskell seems to imply that her authorship is bound up in a specifically parental 'sympathy' (*Mary Barton*, 3) and gaze: her refusal to turn away.[1]

In *Precarious Life* (2004), Judith Butler argues that ethics must be founded on our recognition of our shared vulnerability and the equal

[1] Gaskell first represented a character turning her face to the wall in 'The Old Nurse's Story' (*Household Words*, Christmas 1852). The story is a potent example of the way in which mid-century authors formulated the 'traumatic' compulsion to repeat *avant la lettre*. In the prehistory of the novel, old Mr. Furnivall brutally strikes his young granddaughter and casts her and Miss Maude out into the frost-bound winter landscape. They die and haunt the manor house's grounds. Miss Grace watches her father's criminal actions and fails to intervene. In the final dramatic scene, the trauma is re-enacted in front of the elderly Miss Grace by the ghosts, including the ghost of herself as a young woman. She is 'stricken down by the palsy' ('Old Nurse's Story' *Gothic Tales*, 31) and the story ends:

right to mourn our losses. Gaskell works on an equivalent premise: the apparent gulf between working-class man and middle-class woman is bridged through a shared recognition of loss. As we see in *North and South*, mourning for the self means becoming open to the trauma of the other. This proposition is equally applicable to Eliot. Despite their manifest differences, Eliot's view of authorship is comparable to Gaskell's. In her biography of Gaskell, Jenny Uglow (1993) provides a fascinating account of Eliot's admiration for Gaskell, and Gaskell's gradual apprecia-tion of Eliot, framing this in terms of their shared realist ethic (464–465). In January 1858, Eliot reflected upon the positive reception of *Scenes of Clerical Life*:

> I wonder how I shall feel about these little details ten years hence, if I am alive. At present I value them as grounds for hoping that my writing may succeed, and so give value to my life; as indications that I can touch the hearts of my fellow-men, and so sprinkle some precious grain as the result of the long years in which I have been inert and suffering. But at present fear and trembling still predominate over hope. (Cross 1885, II.1, 2)

Eliot's language resonates with Gaskell's. Writing is presented as a way out of 'inert' 'suffering', and outwards towards others, to 'fellow-men'. In *Silas Marner: The Weaver of Raveloe* (1861), Silas's love for Eppie

> She lay with her face to the wall, muttering low, but muttering always: 'Alas! alas! what is done in youth can never be undone in age! What is done in youth can never be undone in age!' (32)

Gaskell shows the devastating ramifications of refusing to bear witness to the trauma of the other. This refusal becomes, in its turn, a wound to the self. Miss Grace has been frozen at the moment of her first refusal: in Hester's words, she is 'cold and gray and stony' (15), a clear precursor to Mrs. Clennam in *Little Dorrit*. She is painfully written over by time, with 'fine wrinkles as if they had been drawn all over with a needle's point' (15). This wound turned back upon the self can be related to the model that Gaskell establishes in the Preface to *Mary Barton*. Prior to Rosamund's arrival, Miss Grace observes the house's phantoms without speaking. At eighty, she is deaf, but not blind. She never ceases to 'see' what happened in the past and continues to be complicit in her father's actions, condemning the phantom child as 'evil' (23). This only changes in the final denouement, when she calls out 'Oh father! father! spare the innocent child!' (31). By finally turning her face to the wall, she resists and repeats her younger self's refusal to intervene, and it is only the working-class nurse Hester who can tell this aristocratic criminal story. The surrogate parent is granted authorial authority.

means he can relinquish his resentment at his past treatment. The child—a figure of future hope—heals the psychological wounds of the past. In *Romola* (1863), the historical drama is driven by familial restitution: the novel concludes with Tito's death and the two wives, Romola and Tessa, creating a new family unit without him.

With the exception of *Romola*, Eliot's novels set out to chart the passage of Victorian modernity. The troubled relationship between the elder and younger generation is therefore key to each of her novels. Despite the seeming lack of Gothic spectrality, *Middlemarch* (1872) provides us with a potent example of *emprise* carried through from the grave. Riddled with jealousy, anger and selfishness, the dying Edward Casaubon adds a codicil to his will stipulating that Dorothea will lose all rights to his property after his death if she marries Will Ladislaw. Dorothea eventually repudiates this legal *emprise* by forfeiting her property in favour of her love, Eliot subtly implying that the malicious codicil exacerbates the already potent attraction between Dorothea and Will. Mr. Brooke makes the surprisingly perspicacious observation that 'it was the sort of will to make things worse' (Ch. 84, 815), Mrs. Cadwallader adding, 'Mr. Casaubon had prepared all this as beautifully as possible' (816). Casaubon's influence works in exactly the opposite fashion to the manner in which he willed, but he is the determining force nevertheless. Toubiana's theory of vampiric influence posits a similar active agency after death. In repudiating this heavily laden legacy, Dorothea forfeits her social position and enters a new kind of middle-class future. If found in a novel by Wilkie Collins, this would probably comprise the major plot line; however, in *Middlemarch*, it forms part of the 'web'[2] of interlinking stories, in which troubled generational relations are repeatedly inscribed.

Eliot formulates a realist mode adequate to her expansive vision, while simultaneously calling this mode and vision into question. The narrator of *The Mill on the Floss* is self-conscious about the layering of concepts,[3] and this connects to Eliot's representation of history, the passing of time and the relationship between temporal and spatial awareness. While Eliot does not generate the polyphonic tonality found in *North and South*,

[2] J. Hillis Miller explores the 'web' in his classic reading of science and vision, 'The Optic and Semiotic of *Middlemarch*' (1975).

[3] In a letter to Sara Hennell, dated 16 October 1855, Eliot writes 'Herbert Spencer's views, like every other man's views, could not have existed without the substratum laid by his predecessors' (Cross 1885, I, 387).

her intellectual heterodoxy serves a similar purpose. She functions as the bridge between two literary moments: the mid-century period dominated by Dickens and the late-nineteenth-century realist moment, in which she, Thomas Hardy and Henry James were the key figures. Eliot increasingly employed a wider sociological perspective.[4] The familial *mise-en-scène*, foregrounded in *Adam Bede, The Mill on the Floss* and *Silas Marner*, remained a determining force, but was decentred in *Middlemarch* and *Daniel Deronda* (1876). In the latter, Daniel's questions of identity cannot be healed or solved within the confines of the novel, since they open up a much larger question concerning Zionism: the establishment of a Jewish state or homeland. Eliot's approach therefore differs substantively from the authors addressed in my previous chapters. Dickens was consistently alert to the way in which the home is constructed through economic forces; however, despite this awareness, his novels redefine the home's territorial boundaries through sentiment. The conscious failure of this is clearly felt at the end of *Little Dorrit* and *Great Expectations*. For both Gaskell and Eliot, the home cannot heal the wounds caused by the historical process that defines it, and this profoundly affects their deployment of familial trauma.

North and South: Mourning and Community

In a letter to Charles Dickens written during the serial publication of *North and South* in *Household Words*, Gaskell humorously remarked that a 'better title than N. & S. would have been "Death & Variations". There are 5 deaths, each beautifully suited to the character of the individual' (Gaskell 1997, 324). Mourning is placed at the heart of the novel—it is the prism through which Gaskell explores the nature of social change. The act of mourning is formulated as the route to an ethical realisation that is communal, social and therefore political.

North and South's third-person narrator is positioned nearer to the characters than the narrator of *Mary Barton*, or indeed *Wives and Daughters*. The comparative lack of direct narratorial interjection in *North and South* cuts into two directions. First, the 'now-ness' of the novel's concerns is emphasised: we are placed closely within the drama. Second, the narrator does not resolve the social or emotional complexities that

[4] Shuttleworth (1984) explores the influence of Auguste Comte upon Eliot.

she presents: the novel presents a *provisional* vision on the world. This contrasts with *Mary Barton*, in which Gaskell's narrator reaches out to a specifically middle-class reader by countering the interpretations offered by the working-class protagonists; however, this should not be read as simply reflecting the author's own perspective: the narrative voice is a construct, designed to mediate between two different spheres of experience. In *North and South*, the use of free indirect speech engenders a series of subtle effects, without requiring the overt intrusion of the third-person narrative persona. In *Wives and Daughters* and Eliot's *The Mill on the Floss*, narrative intervention is used to negotiate history: the self-conscious writing of old-fashioned stories. *North and South*, despite the title, undoes binaries and opens a conversation concerning personal and social loss, the nature of change and the ethics of authority: 'variations' upon a theme. Gaskell's use of the musical term in her letter to Dickens is significant. Polyphony, felt but not wholly permitted in *Mary Barton*, is allowed to a greater extent here. *North and South*, through Margaret and Thornton, and their interlocutors, is multi-vocal. These voices are heard in the context of snowballing familial and social trauma, and are provoked *by* such trauma. The coming-to-terms with irrevocable change provides the dynamism of the novel as a whole.

Crisis, Dissent, Representation

North and South begins in a seemingly trite moment of change: Edith's marriage to the handsome and vacuous Captain Lennox. This is rapidly shown to be less trite than it first appears. Margaret is introduced in the context of her displacement: her return to Helstone is no homecoming, but only the precursor to a more profound problem: the defection of her father from the Church of England and the family's move to Milton-Northern. The impending loss of Edith is a sparkling refraction of the darker, more tragic, events that are to come. Edith, at this moment, becomes a source of nostalgia for Margaret: her impending absence, 'seemed to give force to every sweet quality and charm which Edith possessed' (I.1, 5); she is already a figure of the past, gaining importance through afterwardsness. The novel opens with Margaret attempting to wake Edith; addressing her listener, who sleeps on calmly: 'But in default of a listener, she had to brood over the change in her life silently as heretofore. It was a happy brooding, although tinged with regret at being separated for an indefinite time from her gentle aunt and dear cousin' (6). The novel begins, then, with the failure of communication. It is a gentle, subtle symbolism: Margaret's life in Milton is redefined through cross-class and cross-gender communication. Throughout the novel, when dealing with her loss, Margaret must negotiate the move from silence to articulation. Margaret's departure from her London home operates as an iteration of her previous displacement; looking at the nursery, she remembers being first taken there as a little girl of nine:

> Oh! well did the tall stately girl of eighteen remember the tears shed with such wild passion of grief by the little girl of nine, as she hid her face under the bed-clothes, in that first night; and how she was bidden not to cry by her nurse, because it would disturb Miss Edith; and how she had cried as bitterly, but more quietly, till her newly-seen, grand, pretty aunt had come softly upstairs with Mr. Hale to show him his little sleeping daughter. Then the little Margaret had hushed her sobs, and tried to lie quiet as if asleep, for fear of making her father unhappy by her grief [...] (8)

Looking at the novel in scenographic terms, this moment is critical. It provides a prototype for a series of scenes enacted between father and daughter, and provides the clue to their relationship. The emotion felt by the little girl is performed through the sentence structure. The pacing evokes the rush of the child's thought processes. We feel her anxiety. The narrator moves into the little girl's consciousness; the reference to 'papa' later in the paragraph alerts us to the free indirect speech being employed. This first displacement foreshadows Margaret's departure from Helstone, just as the loss of Frederick is hidden behind the happier separation from Edith.

When the time of homecoming arrives, Margaret finds that her feelings have reversed: 'Margaret's heart felt more heavy than she could ever have thought it possible in going to her own dear home, the place and the life she had longed for for years – at that time of all times for yearning and longing, just before the sharp sense lose their outlines in sleep' (I.2, 16). Helstone is a picture in her head, idealised but without being clearly defined. When she attempts to describe the hamlet to Henry Lennox, he mocks her seemingly hackneyed image of the 'cottages [...] with roses growing all over them' (I.1, 12): she replies, 'Helstone is like a village in a poem – in one of Tennyson's poems' (12). Tennyson's poems from the 1830s present numerous elegiac and haunting rural scenes; further, as the author of *In Memoriam* (1850), no other poet could be connected quite so closely with the act of mourning. However, when we return to Helstone with Margaret and Mr. Bell at the end of the novel, the hamlet bears no resemblance to one of Tennyson's early poems, and all sense of elegy is lost. The idealisation of Helstone occurs at distance. Margaret regrets whatever is past and gone: when Edith marries, it is London not Helstone which is the source of nostalgic, even melancholic, longing. Margaret, even before her father's defection, appears mournful.

The family's traumas are inseparable from the wider questions of social change posed through Helstone. Margaret's consciousness takes us back to a happier era, in which she was 'all untamed from the forest' (I.1, 8) and 'her mother's dressing-room had been her nursery' (8). Margaret's early childhood is presented here in prelapsarian terms; however, the narrator's account of Mrs. Hale's marriage calls into question the accuracy of this memory: we are told that because of the lack of shared interests between husband and wife, Mr. Hale 'withdrew, while the children were yet young, into his library' (19). As the novel progresses, we see that the family is subtly split into two, with Mrs. Hale and Frederick constituting one pairing, and Mr. Hale and Margaret the other. Dixon sees her mistress's marriage to Mr. Hale as a fall from grace. When Margaret is reunited with her father, she is struck by his 'worn, anxious expression' (I.2, 16), and she reflects internally on the family's primary trauma: 'Oh! if Frederick had but been a clergyman, instead of going into the navy, and being lost to us all! I wish I knew all about it. I never understood it from Aunt Shaw' (16). The dramatic irony is potent: becoming a clergyman does not prevent Mr. Hale's rebellion. At the same time, this passage ensures that the mutiny and defection are formulated in relation to one another. Mr. Hale's revelation that he plans to leave the Church of England echoes Frederick Hale's mutiny onboard ship, which led to the latter's permanent exile from his family and country; both are rebellions against professional authority. The loss of Frederick is revealed to the reader in the wider context of the parents' disunity. Before his religious dissent is revealed, Margaret believes that her father's unhappiness is caused by Frederick's exile: she 'could not help believing that there had been some late intelligence of Frederick, unknown to her mother, which was making her father anxious and uneasy' (I.2, 21). However, while her supposition is incorrect, the link is an important one. There is a traumatic repetition at work here: the father and son are inverse mirror images. There is a sense of genealogical inevitability, but more than that, Gaskell poses a question concerning professional life and the psychological effects of existing within masculine institutions.

When Margaret is reunited with her father, Mr. Hale's face shows his 'habitual anxiety' and he has an 'undecided expression' (16). Sadness concealed, 'She was ready with a bright smile' (16); Margaret suppresses her emotions, Gaskell subtly reminding us of the nine-year-old girl stifling her sobs to protect her father. As the novel progresses, it becomes clear that Margaret's difficulty in mourning the past, and reconciling herself to the reality of change, is connected to her desire to protect her parents. Her own sadness is 'stuffed away into a dark cupboard' (II.16, 344). Margaret's hidden sadness therefore results from a self-enforced, but *parentally* induced, silence, and this can be traced back to her move to London at the age of nine. This move also speaks, in some way, to her parents' failure to provide for her: she was brought to share 'the home, the play, and the lessons of her cousin Edith' (I.1, 8). The loss of closeness between Margaret and Mrs. Hale is a painful consequence of this decision. There is nothing melodramatic about the Hale family at Helstone; however, Gaskell hints at the conflicts and divisions which define the family, in spite—because—of their love for one another.

The focalisation of the narrative through Margaret in Chapter 2 manoeuvres the reader through her thought and memory, rather than positioning us so we 'see' the house or landscape directly. In returning home, Margaret's vision of Helstone gives the reader emotional insight: 'With the healthy shame of a child, she blamed herself for her keenness of sight, in perceiving that all was not as it should be there' (17). This is a *feeling* sight: 'This marring of the peace of home, by long hours of discontent, was what Margaret was unprepared for' (18). Frederick's exile is everywhere felt, but nowhere spoken of:

> But a consciousness that her mother's delicate health, and positive dislike to Helstone, all dated from the time of the mutiny in which Frederick had been engaged, – the full account of which Margaret had never heard, and which now seemed doomed to be buried in sad oblivion, – made her pause and turn away from the subject each time she approached it. (20)

The Hale family is characterised by silence and melancholy; while Frederick's mutiny is undoubtedly placed at the apex of this, the parents' disunity predates their son's rebellion. Gaskell's representation of traumatisation therefore implies that a marriage based in love, but not in shared interest, is damaging to the younger generation. This connects to a wider failure of communal engagement addressed by the novel. While considering his resignation from the Church, Margaret observes that her father 'did not go out among his parishioners as much as usual; he was more shut up in his study' (21). At Milton, Mr. Hale fails to become part of any community. The problem, which Gaskell explores through Mr. Hale, is not that of dissent per se, but dissent without decision or recuperative action. Frederick's mutiny is represented later in comparable terms.

The reader's view of Helstone is enabled by the focalisation of the narrative through Henry Lennox's 'scrutinising way' (II.3, 25). This is significant. 'Home' is displaced—not 'itself'—and this can also be said of the Hale family. Both Lennox and Margaret possess discriminating 'eyes'; they watch and judge, as the scene in which they sketch the cottage shows. Sketching side by side, Margaret blushes to realise that Henry has included her within his own composition (25). This moment reminds us of their earlier debate about Helstone, as either a 'painting' or a poem by Tennyson. Rachel Bowlby (2007) writes, 'realism can never be simply codeless in its claimed replication of reality' (xv). To stake such a claim involves annexing territory and creating an interpretative frame through which the reader engages with the world of the novel. In comparing Helstone to Tennyson's poetry, Margaret deploys a pre-existing code from the foremost poet of the period; this is, however, shown to be inadequate. Gaskell creates a metatextual discourse on the nature of authorship and realist representation. In Chapter 3, there is a moment of conflict, gentle as it may be, between incompatible visions of the world: until Henry's entrance to Helstone, Margaret focalises the narrative; in 'The More Haste the Worse Speed', Lennox's 'scrutinising way' dominates. The question of who can write of—and upon—the world is raised. Female understanding is positioned alongside male professional authority. Margaret's perspective is driven by a pre-existing system of signification: her family and their story. Henry's vision of Helstone is propelled by his desire for Margaret and his desire to succeed professionally. Neither perspective is complete: there is something lacking.

The manner in which the younger generation responds to the elder is placed within this representational discourse. As I argue throughout this study, parents are read or deciphered. When returning to the parsonage after the sketching scene, we are once more placed with Margaret: 'her quick eye sought over his [Mr. Hale's] face and found there traces of some unusual disturbance, which was only put aside, not cleared away'

(I.3, 26). Margaret, like the children found throughout the mid-Victorian moment, has to translate a parental enigma. Gaskell places this in the context of a social problematic: the appropriate parameters of political and authorial authority, and the difficulty of locating an ideological foundation for such authority. Henry Lennox relates the ability to paint the world, or taking likenesses, to willpower: responding to Margaret's comment regarding her own artistic limitations, he says, 'I should say that a likeness you very much wish to take you would always succeed in [...] I have great faith in the power of will. I think myself I have succeeded pretty well in yours' (26). This comment on painting is noteworthy. First, voiced by Henry, it obviously links the ability to paint the world with an erotic and masculine gaze. Second, the statement reflects back upon Gaskell's own authorship; she considers the moral basis and the authority of her novel writing. Henry pauses before handing his sketch to Mr. Hale for inspection: it was 'withheld from him one moment, no more' (26). In *Can the Subaltern Speak* (2010), Gayatri Chakravorty Spivak reminds us that aesthetic representation—who is representing whom—is inextricable from political representation. Lennox's attempt to keep hold of the sketch, rather than passing it willingly to the elder man for judgement, indicates his desire for power: it is a brief, but unfulfilled, mutiny. Margaret's dream, in which Henry falls from the tree, reinforces this reading.

Jill Matus (2009) persuasively argues that the prevalence of dreams and trance-like states in *North and South* demonstrates Gaskell's awareness of the connection between nervous shock and psychological dissociation. Psychological disorder is not presented as simply medical. It is never neutral: 'the novel's crises of inner life and consciousness are an integral part of Gaskell's attempts to chart the social transformations of mid-century England and understand the forces of feeling and unconscious life that jolt the individual into self-scrutiny and renewed engagement with the outside world' (Matus 2009, 82). Matus's reading does not, however, explore this renewed engagement in detail. Reading Margaret's dream, Matus highlights the manner in which the memory of Henry's proposal is pushed out of consciousness. She argues that Gaskell's presentation of the dream supports the physiological theories of William Carpenter, 'who argued that dreams do replay experiences of the recent past, and "transform immediate physical sensations into vivid dramas which are ultimately determined by the character of the dreamer"' (72). However, this interpretation, taken in isolation, elides the wider structure of the novel: the repetition of a *mise-en-scène*.

Margaret's dream of Henry Lennox moves between past, present and future. It is not simply a transformation of 'immediate physical sensations' or the 'recent past'. Margaret's memories of the day blur into the consciousness of Frederick's experiences and her father's defection: when she awakes she is 'conscious of some reality worse even than her feverish dreams' (I.5, 43). As we have seen, the focalisation of the narrative through Margaret means that Mr. Hale's defection is always placed within the context of Frederick's mutiny: the mutiny is defined by afterwardsness. Henry can be read as a composite figure in the dream:

> Mr. Lennox – his visit, his proposal – the remembrance of which had been so rudely pushed aside by the subsequent events of the day – haunted her dreams that night. He was climbing up some tree of fabulous height to reach the branch whereon was slung her bonnet: he was falling, and she was struggling to save him, but held back by some invisible powerful hand. He was dead. And yet, with a shifting of the scene, she was once more in the Harley Street drawing-room, talking to him as of old, and still with a consciousness all the time that she had seen him killed by that terrible fall. (43)

The fall of the male figure is literal and symbolic. The dream is key to the novel's scenography: it lies at the heart of Gaskell's ethical exegesis. As we—and Margaret—later discover, in leading his men to mutiny, Frederick revenged the death of a sailor who fell from the rigging, fearful of Captain Reid's threats. The dream captures the novel's hidden primal scene: a man falling. The tree is not just the mast; it is also the gibbet that waits for Frederick. This scene is not restricted to the Hale family. Thornton's father hangs himself: 'His father speculated wildly, failed, and then killed himself, because he could not bear the disgrace' (I.11, 87). There is a pattern of male overreaching—played out here in the dream—which is potentially deadly and self-destructive. At the same time, the scene onboard ship complicates the concept of free will: did the sailor fall or was he pushed? Whose authority should be respected? Looking at the manifest content, the dream encodes Margaret's loss of respect for Henry in the wake of the proposal. For Margaret, overreaching is about the male's overreaching *for her*. Until she recognises her own love for Thornton, she sees men's desire as an insult. The dream, then, has two interwoven narratives: the male and the female. The novel as a whole works to bridge these: male rebellion, and the problematisation of authority, is worked through in the context of growing female self-recognition and a shared mourning for the past. The dream is highly literary but not unrealistic: it creates a fantasy structure that dominates the novel.

Mr. Hale's defection is presented as shocking in the medical and common sense. When he finally confesses his secret to Margaret, it wounds her. Gaskell uses free indirect discourse throughout this scene: Margaret 'suddenly bursting into tears. The one staid foundation of her home, of her idea of her beloved father, seemed reeling and rocking. What she could she say? What was to be done?' (I.4, 34). Home reels and rocks like a ship. When she hears a poacher outside the garden, for the first time Margaret is terrified and rushes inside to the cheerless house (I.6, 54). Mr. Hale connects his defection to the long-standing dissension between him and his wife: 'Your poor mother's fond wish, gratified at last in the mocking way in which over-fond wishes are too often fulfilled – Sodom apples as they are – has brought on this crisis' (I.4, 36). The lack of unity between the parents is patent throughout: it is Margaret who breaks the news to her mother, while Mr. Hale retreats from the house. She is in a 'stunned and dizzy state' (I.4, 40):

> [...] too full of sorrow to cry, but with a dull cold pain, which seemed to have pressed the youth and buoyancy out of her heart, never to return. Mr. Henry Lennox's visit – his offer – was like a dream, a thing beside her actual life. The hard reality was, that her father had so admitted tempting doubts into his mind as to become a schismatic – an outcast; all the changes consequent upon this grouped themselves around that one blighting fact. (I.5, 42)

The shock is a moral one. Her father's defection links back to the older family trauma: Frederick's rebellion and exile. Frederick rebels, Mr. Hale dissents, and Lennox presumes; their 'crimes' are drawn together through Margaret's consciousness and her dream: all are exiled. Home is represented as a ship losing 'buoyancy', with dubious captaincy. Mr. Hale's insistence that 'I can always decide better by myself, and not influenced by those whom I love' (I.4, 38) alerts us to the problem that underpins the novel: the proper exercise of authority and the need for community engagement and dialogue. After telling her mother, Margaret cries 'as if her heart would break' (I.5, 47), shortly afterwards, 'sobbing away as if her heart would break' (I.6, 55). Looking out into the night sky, she feels that there is 'yet no sign of God!' (I.5, 42):

> It seemed to her at the moment, as if the earth was more utterly desolate than if girt in by an iron dome, behind which there might be the ineffaceable peace and glory of the Almighty: those never-ending depths of space, in their still serenity, were more mocking to her than any material bounds could be – shutting in the cries of earth's sufferers, which now might ascend into that infinite splendour of vastness and be lost – lost forever, before they reached His throne. (42)

There is a crisis of faith—and more specifically loss of faith in the efficacy of articulation. The impossibility of ever coming nearer to God is hinted at it, directly contradicting the first Epistle of John, 'And this is the confidence that we have in him, that, if we ask anything according to his will, he heareth us' (1 John 5:14), and Hebrews: 'Let us therefore come boldly unto the throne of grace, that we may obtain mercy, and find grace to help in time of need' (4:16). She is, like her father, a 'heretic' in this moment and 'a far more utter sceptic' (I.5, 43). It is only at Milton that this scepticism, which is familial, social and religious, can be worked through: by listening and by speech.

'Death and Variations'

The move to Milton refigures these problems of authority and the exercise of power within a larger social context. The narrative becomes increasingly polyphonic, and the focalisation is widened; the play of voices drives the mourning represented and performed by the novel. The five deaths are woven together, part of a larger social tragedy. At the same time, these deaths bring the issue of bearing witness to the fore.

Milton is presented as noisy, bustling and physically intimate compared to the alternating expansiveness and claustrophobia of Helstone. Margaret's internal description of Milton as 'strange, desolate, noisy, busy' (I.13, 104) demonstrates her urban alienation. She walks closely alongside the mill workers, in a scene which echoes Gaskell's preface to *Mary Barton*: 'The tones of their unrestrained voices, and their carelessness of all common rules of street politeness, frightened Margaret a little at first' (I.8, 71). The third-person narrator corrects Margaret's perception: 'the very out-spokenness marked their innocence of any intention to hurt her delicacy, as she would have perceived if she had been less frightened by the disorderly tumult' (71–72). Working-class outspokenness contrasts favourably with the secrecy and silence of Helstone. It is this context that Margaret meets Higgins: standing absorbed in her own thoughts, he addresses her: 'You may well smile, my lass; many a one would smile to have such a bonny face' (72). It is significant that it is he who initiates the friendship. From this point onwards, a 'silent recognition' is established between them (72), becoming dialogue through Margaret's friendship with Bessy. Higgins's religious doubt, expressed in front of his dying daughter, 'shocked but not repelled' Margaret. Higgins and Bessy represent a 'human interest' and Milton becomes 'brighter' (74).

Bessy and Higgins are interlocutors: their entrance into the novel is central to the plot and the dialectical play of ideas. In Margaret and Bessy's first conversation, Margaret is able to articulate her love for Helstone, and Bessy shares her own pain: 'and my mother gone, and I never able to tell her again how I loved her' (I.13, 101). The loss of her mother signalled Bessy's decline, as it was at this point that she entered the carding room and the 'fluff' 'poisoned' her lungs (102). There is a trauma here too: a working-class social determinism. The two young women approach one another through speech, and in so doing, Margaret reaffirms her faith in God: 'Bessy – we have a Father in Heaven' (101). Bessy's illness parallels Mrs. Hale's: there is an abrupt shift from the young women's conversation to the narrator's brusque statement: 'From that day forwards Mrs. Hale became more and more of a suffering invalid' (103). Margaret's insight into Frederick's rebellion, granted by her mother, is simultaneous with her exposure to working-class rebellion through Higgins. This does not create a simple equivalence: rather, it reposes the question concerning the parameters and exercise of authority. This question is repeatedly figured in terms of familial traumatisation—through 'Death & Variations'.

Margaret and her mother are brought closer through the latter's illness and decline: she 'was getting to understand' her mother (II.5, 249). When Mrs. Hale recounts Frederick's story to Margaret using her son's 'yellow, sea-stained letters', Mrs. Hale dominates the narrative for the first time, directing Margaret's reading with 'hurried, anxious remarks' 'almost before her daughter could have understood what they were' (I.14, 106). Mrs. Hale attempts to control Margaret's interpretation; however, the extracts we hear subtly undermine the view of Frederick as a hero:

> [...] my father may rely upon me, that I will bear with all proper patience everything that one officer and gentleman can take from another. But from

> my former knowledge of my present captain, I confess I look forward to a long course of tyranny on board the Russell. (107)

The 'But' invalidates Frederick's promise. His mother's claim that 'he was the sweetest-tempered boy, when he was not vexed' would be comic, if it were not for the reality of the mutiny and his exile. Margaret's reading, rendered through free indirect speech, is more measured: 'It might be – it probably was – a statement of Captain Reid's imperiousness in trifles, very much exaggerated by the narrator' (107). The use of free indirect discourse creates an interpretative ambiguity: we are not sure whether we are hearing Margaret, Margaret and the narrator, or only the narrator. It is here that we learn the tragic story which led to the mutiny:

> Some sailors being aloft in the main-topsail rigging, the captain had ordered them to race down, threatening the hindmost with the cat-of-nine-tails. He who was the farthest on the spar, feeling the impossibility of passing his companions, and yet passionately dreading the disgrace of the flogging, threw himself desperately down to catch a rope considerably lower, failed, and fell senseless on the deck. (107)

It is important that it is the shame of the flogging that the sailor fears. This links his fall with Frederick, who will not accept the degradation of Captain Russell's oppression; Thornton Sr., committing suicide after the spectacular failure of his business; Mr. Hale, whose defection from the Church is interpreted as a shameful act by Margaret; Henry, whose proposal is seen as shameful by Margaret; and finally Margaret herself, who is shamed by her behaviour at the riot and by lying to the policeman after Frederick's departure. Shame, in a slightly different manner to guilt, is a *social* feeling: it anticipates how others look and judge us. Shame was central to Freud's reading of Emma's trauma ('A Project for a Scientific Psychology'): at twelve, Emma belatedly feels the shame of being sexually abused as a little girl. This is about visibility—her uncanny fear that the shopkeepers can see something about her. Gaskell's representation of shame as a recurring 'trauma' not only indicates a concern with the parameters of public and private action, but also with the physiology of society itself: the physical impact of social relationships.

Gaskell reformulates the idea of the social body found in Thomas Carlyle's *Past and Present*. This does not negate her psychological insight: shame involves a psychological agency, the internalisation of the social gaze. The ethics of shame—the moral 'rightness' of feeling shamed—is explored in detail through these differential repetitions. When Margaret finally speaks she defends Frederick's actions, saying to her mother, 'it is still finer to defy arbitrary power, unjustly and cruelly used – not on behalf of ourselves, but on behalf of others more helpless' (I.14, 109). However, the subsequent execution of Frederick's fellow mutineers calls into question the altruism of his actions (109). The shame bound up in the first scene—the sailor falling from the rigging—remains unresolved, and this lack of resolution drives the repetition of feeling and nervous sensibility throughout *North and South*.

Mrs. Hale remembers Mr. Hale bowed down when he heard of Frederick's involvement in the mutiny: 'his head sunk' 'as if every step was a labour and a trouble' (108); she continues, 'I could hardly lift myself up to go and meet him – everything seemed so to reel around me all at once' (108). This directly echoes the language Gaskell uses when Margaret hears her father's confession at Helstone. Frederick's actions lead to the mother's trauma, and the father's dissent leads to Margaret's. Mrs. Hale remembers reading the account of her son in the newspaper, 'I took the paper in my hands as soon as I had read it – I tore it up to little bits – I tore it – oh! I believe Margaret, I tore it with my teeth. I did not cry. I could not. My cheeks were as hot as fire and my very eyes burnt in my head. I saw your father looking grave at me' (109). Her subsequent depression at Helstone pushes this agony out of sight. Mrs. Hale's confirmation that Frederick's crime is a capital one reminds us of the falling man, first hinted at in Margaret's dream.

Parents do not simply author their children; children write upon their parents: the yellowed letters and the torn newspaper stand in for Frederick himself. It is critical, however, that the texts are shown in a state of decay or disintegration. There is a problem of representation bound up in Frederick. Concluding her confession, 'Mrs. Hale turned her face to the wall, and lay perfectly still in her mother's despair' (109). This gesture represents a failure or unwillingness to bear witness to Frederick's actions: a figure of melancholy, her gesture enacts the solipsism which has previously defined her. It is clearly not enough for her to express her grief; she must become emotionally invested in Margaret. In being the means through which mother and daughter are brought closer together, Mrs. Hale's illness has a redemptive quality, but it is partial. Her death is undoubtedly hastened by Milton's environment; however, Gaskell represents it as the culmination of a much longer process of dying, which began with Frederick's revolt. In so doing, Gaskell draws together physiological and psychological symptomologies:

> At the mention of that one word, she suddenly cried out loud, as in some sharp agony. It seemed as if the thought of him upset all her composure, destroyed the calm, overcame the exhaustion. Wild passionate cry succeeded to cry – 'Frederick! Frederick! Come to me. I am dying. Little first-born child, come to me once again!'
>
> She was in violent hysterics. (I.16, 129)

We get a sense of afterwardsness: the 'sharp agony' is the agony provoked by Frederick's mutiny and reactivated by the family's move to Milton-Northern. Moving closer to death, Mrs. Hale remembers the physical bond of motherhood: she had, 'Fred in my arms every minute of the day, and his cot was close by my bed and now, now – Margaret – I don't know where my boy is, and sometimes I think I shall never see him again' (I.25, 203). Comforted by her daughter, 'Mrs. Hale cried without restraint'.

Mrs. Hale's deathbed scene reverses the position of mother and son: 'She sate with his hand in hers; she would not part with it even while she slept; and Margaret had to feed him like a baby, rather than he should disturb her mother by removing a finger' (248). When she dies, it is in his arms (II.5, 250). This mother-son romance cannot heal the world of the novel: after Mrs. Hale's death, Frederick can no longer act. Conversely, Margaret 'could not think of her own loss in thinking of her father' (251). In losing his mother, Frederick is cast adrift:

> For Frederick had broken down now, and all his theories were of no use to him. He cried so violently when shut up alone in his little room at night, that Margaret and Dixon came down in affright to warn him to be quiet: for the house partitions were but thin, and the next door neighbours might easily hear his youthful passionate sobs, so different from the slower trembling agony of after-life, when we become inured to grief, and dare not be rebellious against the inexorable doom, knowing who it is that decrees. (251)

Despite his heartbreak upon his mother's death, Frederick cannot perform a work of mourning; the narrator tells us carefully: 'though his sorrow for the loss of his mother was a deep real feeling, and would last out his life, it was never to be spoken of again' (II.7, 261). Frederick's perpetual exile is commensurate with his incapacity or inability to mourn communally: his ideology shifts between individualism—'I will bear with all proper patience everything that one officer and gentleman can take from another' (I.14, 107)—and a too-easy adherence to authority (represented in Gaskell's terms by his conversion to Catholicism). Gaskell precisely formulates melancholia in opposition to mourning. When Mr. Hale leaves for Oxford, Margaret reflects on her psychological condition:

> For months past, all of her personal cares and trouble had had to be stuffed away into a dark cupboard; but now she had leisure to take them out, and mourn over them, and study their nature, and seek the true method of subduing them into the elements of peace. All these weeks she had been conscious of their existence in a dull kind of way, though were hidden out of sight. Now, once for all she would consider them, and appoint to each of them its right work in her life. So she sat motionless for hours in the drawing room, going over the bitterness of every remembrance with an unwincing resolution. (II.16, 344–345)

This passage summarises a process of working-through: it is condensed, but nevertheless operates in a comparable fashion to Freud's model. Margaret performs a self-analysis, purposefully testing her reality against her feelings. She reaches out into the community directly after this moment, speaking to Martha and visiting Boucher's children. However, Freud's theory of melancholia involves more than unresolved or hidden pain. Melancholia involves a regressive identification with the lost object. During Mrs. Hale's illness, Margaret is opened to her mother's trauma concerning Frederick; after her death, she takes on, or inherits, this trauma. For Gaskell, mourning also means giving an account of oneself, as Margaret eventually does: 'her plans for Frederick had all failed, and the temptation lay there a dead mockery, – a mockery which had never had life in it; the lie had been so despicably foolish, seen by the light of ensuing events, and faith in the power of truth so infinitely the greater wisdom' (II.16, 345).

'Faith in the power of truth' is a religious rather than legal prospect in *North and South.* The mutiny and the sailor's death that led to it are the prehistorical scenes that drive the novel. But we cannot bear witness to them, nor hear an adequate array of witnesses in order to make a judgement. This problem is not only the reader's, but also Frederick's. Explaining his predicament to his sister, he criticises the court martial describing it as a 'court where authority weighs nine-tenths in the balance, and evidence forms only the other tenth. In such cases, evidence itself can hardly escape being influenced by the prestige of authority'. He goes on to add, 'No one would read a pamphlet of self-justification so long after the deed, even if I put one out' (II.6, 259). His legal predicament—and permanent exile from Britain—is a problem of *representation*: evidence is inseparable from the operation of authority. Spivak (2010) analyses the female predicament within discourses surrounding *Sati* in which the sacrificial woman is trapped between two opposing discourses: 'One never encounters the testimony of the women's voice-consciousness' (50), trapped in an 'ideological battleground' elided by both Imperial and Indian accounts (54, 57). Frederick is also trapped within a semantic binary: condemned by the Navy as a traitor and elevated by his mother to a hero. Gaskell does not resolve this impasse: we are never sure how to respond to Frederick's mutiny. However, she presents the traumatic echoes that occur as a result. At the railway station, the reader's relationship to Frederick is complicated again:

> In an instant – how, Margaret did not see, for everything danced before her eyes – but by some sleight of wrestling, Frederick had tripped him up, and he fell from the height of three or four feet, which the platform was elevated above the space of soft ground, by the side of the railroad. There he lay. (II.7, 264)

The blurring of Margaret's sight means that neither she, nor the reader, can assess the justness of Frederick's action. This reproduces the impossibility of the reader judging the mutiny and the death which precedes it. Gaskell's formulation of mourning as a source of ethics is sophisticated. Mourning involves opening oneself up to the other, which means—in its turn—being able to see, hear and respond to others. Frederick may remember, but he cannot bear witness to the mutiny, because—as we also see in relation to his mother—he cannot perform the work of mourning it requires. As he says to Margaret, 'Thinking has, many a time, made me sad, darling; but doing never did in all my life' (II.5, 250). His letter, written directly after the sailor's death, is 'half illegible through the fading of the ink' (I.14, 107). His inability to testify is social, forced upon him because it would lead inevitably to the gibbet, and personal. It is the result of his failure to mourn or come to terms with the past. The narrator carefully gestures towards this failing when Margaret reads one of his letters:

'Frederick spoke so joyfully of the future that he had no thought for the past' (II.16, 343).

Margaret's reunion with Frederick highlights the difficulty of her prior position within the family: 'She knew then how much responsibility she had had to bear, from the exquisite sensation of relief which she felt in Frederick's presence' (II.5, 248). Margaret's recognition is driven by afterwardsness, it comes after the event: 'she knew *then*'. She only feels the separation from Frederick when he leaves the family for the second time. Having opened herself to her mother's agony, Margaret inherits her pain and the problem of bearing witness. Margaret falls ethically by lying to the policeman in order to protect Frederick from discovery when they are seen at the railway station. After this key moment, 'she lay with her face to the wall, shaking with her sobs' (II.10, 286), replaying her *mother's* earlier gesture of refusal. Gaskell establishes the novel's *mise-en-scène* in Margaret's earlier dream; the recurring image of a fallen man is bound up with Margaret's own fallen state: 'he was falling, and she was struggling to save him, but held back by some invisible powerful hand. He was dead' (I.5, 43). After the policeman leaves: Margaret 'went into the study, paused – tottered forward – paused again – swayed for an instant where she stood, and fell prone of the floor in a dead swoon' (II.9, 275). Cast down—potentially cast out—she symbolically suffers the punishment correlated with Frederick's crime. She acts it out. However, the ambivalence of the image remains: on the one hand, it evokes male rebellion; on the other, we are reminded of the innocent man, falling to his death in fear of shame and degradation. The image recurs; considering her lie, Thornton's 'trust dropped down dead and powerless' (II.8, 270). Margaret's fallenness relates directly to her relationship with Thornton. When the protesting mill workers close in on the mill, Margaret rushes to protect him, only to be injured herself, shamed in her own eyes and Mrs. Thornton's. Margaret's actions, like Frederick's, raise questions concerning the appropriate parameters of personal and public action. The siblings are driven by a desire for justice: by a sense of what one person owes to another person. However, Gaskell demonstrates the difficulty (if not the wrongness) of translating this *intimate* concept of justice into the public sphere.

Communal Voices

In *Giving an Account of Oneself* (2005), Judith Butler (by way of thinkers such as Michel Foucault, Jean Laplanche and Friedrich Nietzsche) explores the difference between ethics and morality: 'The capacity to make and justify moral judgements does not exhaust the sphere of ethics and is not coextensive with ethical obligation or ethical relationality' (45). I would suggest, bearing this in mind, that to judge we must be at distance, whereas ethical obligation involves proximity. This distinction is at work everywhere in *North and South*: not only do Gaskell's characters have to learn how to approach one another, but the narrative discourse itself also creates 'ethical relationality'. The shifting focalisation ensures that the reader is proximate to the changing world of the novel, rather than occupying a static space of judgement. The impossibility of moral or legalistic judgement opens up a new kind of conversation about ethics, mourning and bearing witness.

Throughout Mrs. Hale's illness, Margaret cushions her father from reality, repeating the problem set up in the London nursery. His childlike inability to recognise his wife's condition directly contrasts with Higgins and Bessy's ability to communicate with one another. Mr. Hale's inability to engage with the reality of his wife's illness is a continuation of his inability to create a new foundation for community engagement once he leaves the Church. Margaret's increasing openness to the world is juxtaposed against her father's enclosure within the domestic sphere:

> Margaret went out heavily and unwillingly enough. But the length of a street – yes, the air of a Milton Street – cheered her young blood before she reached her first turning. Her step grew lighter, her lip redder. She began to take notice, instead of having her thoughts turned so exclusively inward. (I.17, 131)

Speaking to Bessy, she reinforces the imperative of taking notice, 'I came here very sad, and rather too apt to think my own cause for grief was the only one in the world' (I.17, 138). Her watchful eye, so critical to the narrative at Helstone, is refocused. However, at the same time, the narrative increasingly presents a play of voice and perspective. Margaret's exposure to the realities of working-class life in Milton is simultaneous with her nursing of her mother and thematically inseparable from it. Both indicate her openness to the *other's* trauma. This openness connects Margaret and Thornton. His attendance on Mrs. Hale parallels Margaret's upon Bessy. However, his *laissez-faire* Malthusianism contrasts with the kindness and delicacy with which he treats Mrs. Hale. Margaret cannot reconcile this:

> What business had he to be the only person, except Dr. Donaldson and Dixon, admitted to the awful secret, which she held shut up in the most dark and sacred recess of her heart – not daring to look at it, unless she invoked heavenly strength to bear the sight – that, some day soon, she should cry aloud for her mother, and no answer would come out of the blank, dumb darkness. Yet he knew it all. She saw it in his pitying eyes. She heard it in his grave and tremulous voice. How reconcile those eyes, that voice, with the hard-reasoning, dry, merciless way in which he laid down axioms of trade, and serenely followed them out to their full consequences? The discord jarred upon her inexpressibly. (I.19, 153)

Gaskell's polyphonies do not ever coalesce in a monotone; however, competing voices harmonise more successfully as the narrative progresses. The 'discord' becomes less. Thornton's 'tremulous voice' hints at his capacity to establish a new mode of communication with his workers at the end of the novel. Through the entwining of optical and aural functions in this paragraph, Gaskell points towards the difficulty of bearing witness to one's own loss. Thornton is the keeper of a grief that Margaret cannot yet look at, paralleling the role which Margaret plays for her mother.

Margaret's openness to the pain of others is not enough to mourn her own losses; Thornton and Higgins also, very literally, mourn *for her*. Both men attend Mrs. Hale's funeral (II.8, 269), although 'Margaret never heard that [Thornton] had attended her poor mother's funeral' (270). Thornton brings the family's suffering into focus for the reader: 'he turned to Margaret. Not "better than likely" did she look. Her stately beauty was dimmed with much watching and with many tears' (II.9, 271). Thornton speaks his condolences in 'so tender a voice' that Margaret is overwhelmed and she 'turned away to hide her emotion' (271). As before, sight and hearing are drawn together. Gaskell conceives the act of bearing witness in terms of vision and articulation: who sees and who can speak are not identical, but cross over. When Mr. Hale articulates his pain to Thornton, his 'frost-bound' 'fancies and fears' are relieved for the first time:

> Mr. Thornton said very little; but every sentence he uttered added to Mr. Hale's reliance and regard for him. Was it that he paused in the expression of some remembered agony, Mr. Thornton's two or three words would complete the sentence, and show how deeply its meaning was entered into. (II.10, 276)

Thornton performs a therapeutic, even analytic, role here. He does not speak for Mr. Hale, but elicits his speech.

This kind of speech becomes associated with maternity. *North and South* presents motherly (although not necessarily the mother's) care as having social impact. After the collapse of his business, Thornton pleads with his mother to speak to him again, as she did after his father's suicide:

> 'Mother', he went on, seeing that she would not speak, 'I, too, have been rebellious; but I am striving to be so no longer. Help me, as you helped me when I was a child. Then you said many good words – when my father died, and we were sometimes sorely short of comforts – which we shall never be now; you said brave, noble, trustful words then, mother, which I have never forgotten, though they may have lain dormant. Speak to me again in the old way, mother. Do not let us have to think that the world has too much hardened our hearts. If you would say the old good words, it would make me feel something of the pious simplicity of my childhood. I say them to myself, but they would come differently from you, remembering all the cares and trials you have had to bear.' (II.25, 425)

The mother-child bond is represented as healing and redemptive. But it would be wrong to interpret the novel as simply affirming the power of the maternal blessing. Mrs. Hale cannot mourn the loss of her son without her daughter; Mr. Hale cannot mourn without Thornton. The intimacy of the mother-child bond provides a basis for a wider model of shared feeling and responsibility: if Mrs. Thornton speaks, then her son can feel, and yet his speech precipitates hers. This scene encapsulates the ethical basis of *North and South*. Ethical realisation occurs via the working-through of loss.

Children are, in Butler's terms, the source of 'ethical relationality', providing the basis for communication and truthful testimony. Boucher's children, for example, operate as the focal point for reparation in the wake of the strike. When Margaret speaks to them, we learn 'Daddy had been a kind daddy to them; each could tell, in their eager stammering way, of some tenderness shown, some indulgence granted by the lost father' (II.12, 300). Boucher's inability to operate in line with the Union does not condemn him morally, as Thornton and Higgins are brought together through their mutual concern for the children. Higgins, making 'the greatest concession he could persuade himself to make', asks for work from Thornton (II.13, 319). Higgins's sacrifice for Boucher's children forces Thornton to reassess and offer it to him: 'I could not have taken care of another man's children myself, if he had acted towards me as I hear Boucher did towards you. But I know now that you spoke the truth' (II.14, 326). The bond between the men, established here, leads to the creation of the dinner club at the mill. This project is grounded in sound market principles—Thornton proposes buying food in bulk because it is cheaper—but is also a tacit acknowledgement that the workers do not earn enough to compete in the marketplace as individuals. Collectivity endows them with purchasing power. But the dinner club is also a leveller, as Bell remarks (II.17, 362). Thornton tells Mr. Bell, 'I saw that the men would be hurt if, after making the advance, I didn't meet them half-way, so I went in, and I never made a better dinner in my life'; the men 'talk pretty freely before' him (II.17, 362). Thornton's initiative draws together two principles: the first belonging to the marketplace; the second belonging to the private sphere, and translated into a community setting. The proximity of Thornton and his workers engenders a new, and potentially radical, mode of communication between them, which—when Thornton's business collapses—ensures their loyalty. Through the dinner club, Gaskell shows how capitalist enterprise could operate with shared interest. How this model could be translated into the wider global market remains, self-consciously and necessarily, unanswered by Gaskell. However, bearing in mind that the novel's primary traumas are male and professional, this form of working-through is deeply politicised.

This form of ethical relationality is inextricable from Margaret herself. Thornton and Higgins are brought together through their response to Margaret's losses, as well as their own and Boucher's. Mourning in the mid-Victorian novel is heavily gendered. Thornton must work through his father's breakdown and suicide, and reformulate his agency in the light of Margaret's losses, and *her* integration with the working-class community of Milton. Thornton's business is finally given a new economic foundation through Margaret's intervention. Gaskell shows the importance of men and women, middle and working class, taking shared social responsibility, which consequently produces truthful testimony in the wake of trauma. Despite the collective action, the Union is flawed because, in Higgins's account, it silences and alienates working people who do not adhere to its authority. Middle-class protection is no longer couched as paternal protection as it was in *Mary Barton*: the only surviving father amongst the main actors, Higgins, is working class. Therefore, a new contract for communication has to be established.

As Freud, Jean Laplanche and Éric Toubiana recognise, to mourn is to negotiate the limits of our own agency, but this is also a wider concern. We are at the mercy of the 'invisible powerful hand' felt in Margaret's dream, whether we see that as God, or the fluctuations of the global marketplace. Both are central to the novel. *North and South* is a novel of capitalist modernity: the power of God is reconceptualised in relation to the arbitrary power of *laissez-faire* capitalism. Mr. Hale's dissent recognises the inadequacy of the Anglican Liturgy to express his belief, but he has nothing to put in its place. He is a liminal but not a transitional figure: Higgins and Thornton take this latter role. Gaskell's radicalism is not only a result of her clear sympathy and respect for the working classes (the respect apparent through her drawing of Higgins), but also at work in the play of voice: the central section of the novel in Milton is orchestrated like a symphony. Each death is interwoven with the other. Radically, suicide draws together the mill-owner Thornton Sr. with Boucher. Thornton's harshness towards his workers is shown to be a result of his father's painful legacy: this harshness impacts on his workers and leads, in combination with the Union's dictates, to Boucher's death. Trauma repeats across social class, and therefore cross-class communication is the means by which it can be worked through. These traumas are the result of industrialisation, but that is not to claim that Gaskell looks back nostalgically to a prelapsarian, pre-industrial world. The untamed forest where Margaret and Frederick roamed as children remains intangible, and when Margaret and Mr. Bell visit the New Forest, change is felt everywhere. Gaskell implies that modernity itself entails a work of continual mourning, arguing through her novel that a shared recognition of suffering could lead to a more ethical form of capitalist enterprise *and* a new foundation for family and gender.

The Mill on the Floss: Elegy, Memory and Desire

The Mill on the Floss is built upon layers of intellectual and literary strata: through her network of literary and non-literary intertextualities, Eliot offers up an intellectual hermeneutic to the reader, though this is not prescriptive. It is critical to my argument that despite this Eliot bases her novel in cross-generational trauma. The damaging effects of Mr. Tulliver's contestations *in law* alert us to the danger of asserting a single vision. Like Mr. Vanstone in *No Name* and Sir Percival Glyde in *The Woman in White*, Mr. Tulliver's patriarchal power is necessarily incomplete: the more he attempts to control his world, the more desperately he becomes entangled. Moreover, he passes this problem on to his two children.

The conjuration with which the narrator of *Adam Bede* opens the novel reminds us that realist narrative is a trick. Reading means submitting ourselves to someone else's vision; however, the metafictional elements within Eliot's novels ensure that we remain alert to our predicament. Eliot's self-consciousness in *Adam Bede* prefigures the narrator's famous comments in *Middlemarch* concerning the ordering of personal experience: 'It is demonstrable that the scratches are going everywhere impartially, and it is only your candle which produces the flattering illusion of a concentric arrangement, its light falling with an exclusive optical selection' (Ch. 27, 264). Traumatic return in *The Mill on the Floss* is inseparable from Eliot's ongoing discourse concerning realism and the self. Mr. Tulliver's tragic legacy functions as the candle that orders his children's consciousness, as well as the novel itself. But to say this is not to grant it hermeneutic legitimacy. His fall, undeniably tragic, is based on an interpretative mistake: 'water's water'. But of course it isn't. The novel's waters are inseparable from Eliot's representation of the eddying waves of consciousness and desire.

Tragedy

Tragedy is both individual and communal in *The Mill on the Floss*; social 'downfall' is shown to be shocking, in the medical sense of the term: 'filing of bills in Chancery, decrees of sale, are legal chain-shot or bombshells that can never hit a solitary mark, but must fall with widespread shattering' (III.7, 243). The law is formulated as technological or war trauma, and Eliot formulates male shock in terms of an attempted rebellion against the conditions of professional life. Mr. Tulliver's illness falls within the category of brain fever analysed by Jill Matus (2009) in relation to 'The Lifted Veil' (1859) and *Daniel Deronda* but not *The Mill on the Floss*. Mr. Tulliver's memory is directly impacted, and he suffers a recurring dissociation: 'The full sense of the present could only be imparted gradually by new experience – not by mere words, which must remain weaker than the impressions left by the *old* experience' (*Mill on the Floss*, II.8, 254).

Mr. Tulliver's early decision not to educate Tom in his business is decisive. Like Laius and Oedipus, it leads, through a series of seemingly fateful events, to his premature death and Tom's eventual possession of the mill: 'Nay, nay, I've seen enough o' that wi' sons. I'll never pull my coat off before I go to bed [...]; Pretty well if he gets it when I'm dead an' gone. I shan't be put off wi' spoon-meat afore I've lost my teeth' (I.3, 16). Maggie overhears Mr. Tulliver's conversation with Riley concerning Tom, and like all the children addressed in this study, has to decode a parental message:

> These angry symptoms were keenly observed by Maggie, and cut her to the quick. Tom, it appeared, was supposed capable of turning his father out of doors, and of making the future in some way tragic by his wickedness. (17)

Tom is innocent of this crime; however, he undoubtedly makes *Maggie's* future 'tragic' by turning her out of doors after she rejects Stephen. There is a tragic reversal. Mr. Tulliver's casual suspicion of his son strikes at the core of Maggie's being: 'Tom's name served as well as the shrillest whistle: in an instant she was on the watch, with gleaming eyes, like a Skye terrier suspecting mischief, or at all events determined to fly at any one who threatened it towards Tom' (16). The metaphor is significant. Eliot presents the mind's territory in aural terms.

Mr. Tulliver—like Mr. Vanstone—fails to maintain his position as patriarch, and this has a damaging impact upon his children, who must somehow make reparation for his failure. Eliot's treatment of the theme differs substantively (and indeed predates *No Name*). Mr. Tulliver becomes embroiled in the legalities of capitalist enterprise without having the wherewithal to deal with them. His claim that 'water's water' is increasingly unconvincing: the disputed water powers the area's developing prosperity. Mr Tulliver and Wakem are set in opposition in ideological terms, and this is formulated in relation to historical process.

Wakem is the professional man of business: his home is strictly separated not only from his work, but also from the adulterous affairs he conducts, and his 'chiaroscuro parentage', or illegitimate children (III.7, 253). The Tullivers' mill encompasses home, business and kinship: it *is* the family. There is a decisive historical change at work. The 'old-fashioned' (III.9, 263) Mr. Tulliver is all-adrift in this changing state of affairs. Until his downfall, he engages in legal action as if it were a dual: two adversaries facing one another. He does not understand, until later, that the law is a system in which the dice are loaded in favour of those who can afford to push their suit (a fact to which Dickens, of all the authors addressed in this study, is most alert), and in which a whole series of vested interests are staked. When Mr. Tulliver borrows five hundred pounds from a client of Wakem's to pay back Mrs. Glegg, the narrator reminds us this decision will be fateful: he 'had a destiny as well as Œdipus, and in this case, he might plead, like Œdipus, that his deed was inflicted on him rather than committed by him' (I.13, 130). But it is critical that this is not fated; it is his choice and clearly a foolish one. Eliot is alert to the nexus of factors which link cause and effect, creating a sense of necessity (discussed more fully in the following section) because of the seeming impossibility of unravelling, in Mr. Tulliver's words, this 'puzzling world' (III.1, 196). Despite this, she does not exclude the possibility of free will: the narrator's caveat in the quotation above, 'he might plead', undercuts the determinism. Mr. Tulliver frames himself as Oedipus, but he cannot solve the riddle of the sphinx pertaining to the span of human life: at his death, his 'dimly-lighted soul had for ever ceased to be vexed with the painful riddle of this world' (V.7, 359).

In a key passage, Eliot reaffirms the tragic force of Mr. Tulliver's story:

> The pride and obstinacy of millers, and other insignificant people, whom you pass unnoticingly on the road every day, have their tragedy too; but it is of that unwept hidden sort, that goes on from generation to generation, and leaves no record [...] where the unexpectant discontent of worn and disappointed parents weighs on the children like a damp, thick air, in which all the functions of life are depressed; (III.1, 197)

Eliot insists on the validity of our notice and our tears. If we find *The Mill on the Floss* heartbreakingly sad, it is not because Eliot's narrator encourages us in unthinking sentiment, but rather because she directs our eyes so effectively and nurtures our analytic powers.[5] The fact that she formulates tragedy in relation to parents and children is critical. Eliot, like Shakespeare, Thomas Carlyle, the Brontës, Dickens, Wilkie Collins and Freud, follows in the best Greek tradition. Tragedy is *by definition* generational. The 'time is out of joint', and the past somehow makes a demand on the present. The traumatisation of children within this process becomes a matter of psychological and literary realism in the mid-Victorian period. Eliot reinforces this later in further reflection on the nature of tragedy: 'For the tragedy of our lives is not created entirely from within. "Character," says Novalis, in one of his questionable aphorisms – "character is destiny." But not the whole of our destiny. Hamlet, Prince of Denmark, was speculative and irresolute, and we have a great tragedy in consequence. But if his father had lived to a good old age, and his uncle had died an early death, we can conceive Hamlet's having married Ophelia, and got through life with a reputation of sanity, notwithstanding many soliloquies' (VI.6, 401–402). The narrator refutes the determinism of *hamartia,* interpreted as either tragic flaw or error, and instead reminds us of the primacy of cross-generational inheritance or traumatisation: the *otherness* of tragedy.

Eliot's subtle references to Alfred Tennyson's dramatic monologue, *Maud* (1855), ensure that we remember *The Mill on the Floss* is a tragedy of the modern age. Tennyson's poem opens *in medias res*, in the wake of a family trauma: the suicide of the speaker's father in the 'dreadful hollow behind the little wood' (1.1) following the failure of his financial speculation. The unnamed speaker is caught between two different worlds, in psychological and social terms, and cannot reconcile himself to present-tense reality. Tennyson depicts the modern self as haunted, sublimating itself in war and death, and this view resonates powerfully in *The Mill on the Floss*. Eliot presents Mr. Tulliver's fall as symptomatic of an encroaching modernity and traumatic for the younger generation. The primal conflict between the two fathers in Tennyson's poem anticipates the conflict between Mr. Tulliver and Wakem; the Red Deeps echo Tennyson's 'dreadful hollow' (1.1) 'dabbled with blood-red heath' (1.2). The subtle reference to Tennyson ensures that Mr. Tulliver's foolish and irresponsible actions (in the strict legal sense of the term) haunt the

[5] In Book IV, the narrator discusses the ineffectiveness of deductive—or top-down—reasoning. She therefore advocates an analytic—bottom-up—approach. This is a scientific and sociological statement, as well as a literary one (IV.1, 273).

Red Deeps and Maggie's own struggles with selfhood. Eliot's exploration of tragedy raises questions concerning the reader's relationship with the text—are we reading in order to experience catharsis? Is catharsis approximate to mourning?

Mr. Tulliver binds his children within a destructive narrative. After his financial downfall, and Wakem's purchase of the mill, Mr. Tulliver orders Tom to write a curse in the family bible: 'and then write, as I don't forgive Wakem, for all that; and for all I'll serve him honest, I wish evil may befall him. Write that. [...] Now write – write as you'll remember what Wakem's done to your father, and you'll make him and his feel it, if ever the day comes. And sign your name Thomas Tulliver' (III.9, 267). This moment is decisive; it dramatically ends Book III and leads to the reflective and transitional Book IV. Mr. Tulliver attempts to author his children's history—and this pushes the novel, through a complex network of cause and effect, to its tragic conclusion. Thinking back to Chapter 2, this is a clear example of a parental message that is not enigmatic *enough*. Maggie's subsequent attempts at self-abnegation are inconceivable without this originary moment. Later, when Tom discovers Maggie has been meeting Philip in the Red Deeps, he forces her to promise 'not to meet him or write to him again without [Tom's] knowledge' on this same bible (V.5, 343). Mr. Tulliver's curse becomes Tom's own motive force and the foundation for a continuing conflict with Maggie. Eliot self-consciously echoes *Hamlet*: the father's vengeful demand persists after death. For Tom, hatred towards Wakem and Philip is an inherited duty; it is what he owes to his father's memory. It becomes an act of memorialisation.

Eliot reconsiders the binding of the children from a historical perspective in Book IV:

> I share with you this sense of oppressive narrowness; but it is necessary that we should feel it, if we care to understand how it has acted on the lives of Tom and Maggie – how it acted on young natures in many generations, that in the onward tendency of human things have risen above the mental level of the generation before them, to which they have been nevertheless tied by the strongest fibres of their hearts. The suffering, whether of martyr or victim, which belongs to every historical advance of mankind, is represented in this way in every town, and by hundreds of obscure hearths; (IV.1, 272–273)

Historical progress is reformulated in terms of evolution *and* cross-generational trauma. There is a 'struggle for existence' (in Charles Darwin's terms) played out across generations, and the younger generation's 'fibres' are directly affected by the elder generation. Eliot's representation of consciousness and unconsciousness is more profoundly physiological than in any of the other authors addressed in this study: the 'fibres' of the self are defined by cross-generational relationships, which are biological and affective. When Mr. Tulliver is caught in his first 'living death', the narrator considers Maggie and Mr. Tulliver's relationship: 'Her father had always defended and excused her, and her loving remembrance of his tenderness was a force within her that would enable her to do or bear anything for his sake' (III.2, 205). Her 'remembrance' operates through afterwardsness: her childhood memory is a present-day force.

As adults, Tom and Maggie's love is inextricable from the events that divide them from one another. After Mr. Tulliver attacks Wakem, Eliot reflects on the interfusion of happiness and pain: 'mingled seed must bear a mingled crop'; 'Apparently the mingled thread in the web of their life was so curiously twisted together, that there could be no joy without a sorrow coming close upon it' (V.7, 357). In this sense, we could compare *The Mill in the Floss* to *Wuthering Heights*; Cathy and Heathcliff's love also emerges in relation to primal traumatisation. Eliot's novel differs, however, in tentatively positing a "before". Maggie's subjectivity is bound up in Tom's, and this is increasingly damaging in the context of the parental trauma because they cannot respond to it in the same way. While Paul and Florence Dombey are brought together through their shared loss, Maggie and Tom are divided. This is a matter of character and gender. As we see in 'The Valley of Humiliation' and 'Wheat and Tares', Tom sublimates his suffering in work while Maggie must stay at home. Their difference, though, is established in childhood. Maggie's early years are presented as a series of frustrated longings and small daily tragedies: tragic because of the child's inability to place their pain within a wider history: 'These bitter sorrows of childhood! when sorrow is all new and strange' (I.5, 37); 'that bitter sense of the irrevocable which was almost an everyday experience of her small soul' (I.7, 65). Tom operates as a force of prohibition, and this is inseparable from an ethics of memory. His first role in the novel is to berate Maggie for forgetting to feed the 'nash' lop-eared rabbits (I.2, 13). By establishing the siblings' difference in these terms, Eliot sets the foundation for what follows:

> 'O, Tom, it's very cruel,' sobbed Maggie. 'I'd forgive you, if *you* forgot anything – I wouldn't mind what you did – I'd forgive you and love you.'
> 'Yes, you're a silly – but I never *do* forget things – *I* don't.'
> 'O, please forgive me, Tom; my heart will break.' (I.5, 36)

In this key scene, the siblings' difference is established by their polarised attitudes towards the past. Maggie cannot share her father and brother's implacable resentment towards Philip—she forgets it in her care for him—and Tom cannot forgive her for it. Reflecting on his actions after the argument with Bob, Tom 'would have said "I'd do just the same again." That was his usual mode of viewing his past actions; whereas Maggie was always wishing she had done something different' (I.6, 53). When unhappy, Maggie 'took her opium' by 'refashioning her little world into just what she would like it to be' (I.6, 48). Maggie attempts to rewrite the conditions of family. To use Eliot's own metaphor and physiological terminology, Tom's view of life runs in a pre-given channel: a result of his inflexible character and his paternal inheritance.

Maggie's tremulous sensibility is incompatible with Tom's plotting. As a boy, he considers his future with Maggie, he 'meant always to take care of her, make her his housekeeper, and punish her when she did wrong' (I.5, 40); as a man, he 'wished my sister to be a lady, and I would always have taken care of you, as my father desired, until you were well married. But your ideas and mine never accord, and you will not give way' (V.4, 392). Brother and sister struggle to recognise each other's difference; for Tom, this leads to a sense of disappointment and frustration; for Maggie a soul-wrenching sense of desertion. Later, considering Tom's silence towards his father, the narrator reflects on concealment within families: 'partly it was that disinclination to confidence which is seen between near kindred – that family repulsion which spoils the most sacred relations of our lives' (V.2, 324). This 'family repulsion' is at work in Greek and Shakespearean tragedy, and throughout the mid-Victorian novel. As Eliot's narrator argues, tragedy comes from the outside, as well as from within: it is the 'otherness' of the family that operates with such force in the genre—something that is, and is not, of the self.

Elegy

The Mill on the Floss opens with a dream. The narrator, dozing in her chair, talks to herself[6] in her sleep, remembering the rural scene in the present tense: 'How lovely the little river is, with its dark, changing wavelets! It seems to me like a living companion while I wander along the bank and listen to its low placid voice, as to the voice of one who is deaf and loving. I remember those large dipping willows. I remember the stone bridge' (I.1, 7). The repetition of 'remember' creates an emotional anatomy; each object is examined and placed. The landscape is body and soundscape; deploying Eliot's own terminology, it is woven into the fibre of the narrating self. William Wordsworth's description of the mind in *The Prelude* (1805) directly prefigures *The Mill on the Floss*:

> The mind of man is framed even like the breath
> And harmony of music; there is a dark
> Invisible workmanship that reconciles
> Discordant elements, and makes them move
> In one society. (ll.351–355)

This description creates a productive ambiguity: although Wordsworth refers to a process of emotional reconciliation, or psychological harmonisation, the discordant elements are not necessarily negated, but are the foundation for the mental symphony. As Wordsworth goes on to show in *The Prelude*'s sublime boat scene, terrifying childhood experiences are formative of the self. Eliot's narrator is comparable to Wordsworth's poetic speaker: she speaks to the past from a distant present moment and discusses the production of mental harmony. However, through Maggie's story, Eliot simultaneously interrogates the mind's ability to reconcile 'Discordant elements'. The novel performs a work of mourning; but the characters are unable to do so. To perform a work of mourning means putting things in place: it is temporal and spatial. In 'Time and the Other', Jean Laplanche writes, 'mourning is a kind of *work*, the work of memory [...]; and it is an affect with a *duration*' (242–243).

The moment of reverie that opens the novel reminds us that everything we read is mediated via someone else's consciousness. In line with George

[6] The narrator's gender is undefined; although at one point she *seems* to identify as male (66), this is far too ambiguous to justify the conclusion that the narrator is a male persona. I use the female pronoun in the place of the neuter throughout.

Lewes's idea that dreams carry out intentions formed when awake,[7] the narrator begins her planned storytelling in her sleep; in so doing, Eliot alerts us to the distortions of consciousness involved in giving testimony. The resonating sound of the river is felt in memory, bringing a 'dreamy deafness': 'a great curtain of sound, shutting one out from the world beyond' (I.1, 8). In synaesthetic fashion, sight and sound blur; sound blocks vision—it 'curtains' off the world. This landscape is embodied, not only the passive object of the narrator's sensibility but endowed with sensibility. The work of mourning carried out by the narrator over the course of the novel is inseparable from this moment of embodiment. In the conclusion, Eliot reframes the family tragedy: 'The desolation wrought by that flood, had left little visible trace on the face of the earth, five years after'; 'Nature repairs her ravages – but not all' (VII. 'Conclusion', 521). The novel's scenography operates on varying levels of narrative discourse: the Tullivers' story is not self-identical with *The Mill on the Floss*.

In my analysis of Dickens's 'autobiographical fragment', I argued that the distinction between 'memory writing' and 'trauma writing' is unsustainable because it implies that trauma cannot be the source of phantasmatic investment. This is pertinent again here. The opening to *The Mill on the Floss* draws together memorisation and traumatisation: the longed-for past scene is also the scene of Tom and Maggie's drowning. The present-tense reverie expresses the narrator's longing, the 'now-ness' of the writing only making it more apparent that this moment has been snatched: 'I must stand a minute or two here on the bridge and look at it, though the clouds are threatening' (I.1, 7). The ending of the novel is felt everywhere in this beginning—we are told the sea 'checks' the Floss with 'an impetuous embrace'; the 'clouds are threatening'; 'The stream is brimful'; it 'half drowns the grassy fringe of the croft in front of the house' (7). Maggie and Tom's final embrace is encoded in the landscape. The dream feels like a screen memory: in luminous form, it represents the novel. Looking at the ducks, the narrator remarks, 'I am in love with moistness'. This retrospectively hints at a danger; the immersion in desire; and subjection to embodied consciousness (8): the 'passion that expelled every other form of consciousness' (I.4, 8). Spinoza also explores this danger in *Ethics* (1677), which Eliot translated in the 1850s.

[7] Discussed by Shuttleworth in relation to Mr. Tulliver's attack on Wakem (1984, 73).

Spinoza's view of nature as the predicate of God means that he reads cause and effect as deterministic: the result of necessity, not free will. The human mind is an extension of nature and is therefore equally determined by necessity. This idea is at work in *The Mill on the Floss*, but is simultaneously critiqued. Spinoza's contention that 'Nature is always the same, and its virtue and power of acting are everywhere one and the same' (qtd. Nadler 2002, 384) is not simply contradicted by the novel's plotting, but it is undercut—in *feeling* terms—by the centrality of loss and all-pervading sense of elegy. It is through childhood that this is mobilised. At the same time, Spinoza's insistence on the way in which 'passions' are created resonates with later theories of trauma. Spinoza identifies 'passion' as an 'affect' which comes from outside, affecting our ability to 'strive' or to act (ibid., 235): human feelings are initiated by a primary openness (reminding us perhaps of Jean Laplanche's general theory of seduction). However, this idea differs substantively from a psychoanalytic model since Spinoza does not posit an unconscious psychological stratum. He argues that we can and should fight against these passions brought from the outside. This proposition resonates with William Carpenter's argument concerning the will discussed in Chapter 1: Eliot addresses and complicates these ideas.

Eliot's biographers, beginning with John W. Cross (1885), highlight the biographical source material in *The Mill on the Floss* and insist upon the authenticity of the childhood scenes in the novel. However, this insistence on biographical truth is problematic. Biography's appeal to authenticity must be approached cautiously; it is a heavily loaded concept and comes with numerous caveats. Like Dickens's 'autobiographical fragment', the opening chapter of *The Mill on the Floss* creates an uncanny encounter between adult narrator and longing child self, and this encounter brings the narrative into being, comparable to the loss that drives Gaskell's enterprise in *Mary Barton*. As the narrator of *The Mill on the Floss* leans on the 'cold stone of this bridge', looking at the 'unresting wheel', she notices 'That little girl is watching it too: she has been standing on just the same spot at the edge of the water ever since I paused on the bridge' (I.1, 8). Their two gazes meet on the wheel, but their meeting is asymmetrical: the narrator can see both wheel and girl, while the girl's vision is intangible.

Eliot's discourse on the writing of history has implications for our understanding of the present moment. The present interpellates the past; the adult interpellates the child—and vice versa. The novel is based on this—perhaps—impossible thought: a problem explored and enacted by Freud in his writing of the Wolf Man case. These ideas are presented in paradigmatic form in the opening chapter. In her dream, the narrator brings Maggie into the present moment—into the present tense—but this highlights her inaccessibility. It is significant that the narrator and Maggie are separated spatially. If we accept that Eliot uses memories of her own early life in her representation of Maggie, then this opening scene implies the difficulty of simply writing *oneself*. Eliot's narrator creates an ongoing discourse on the present-tense self and how that self is created by, and separated from, childhood. The fact that this discourse is placed within a plot dealing with childhood traumatisation is vital.

The rippling effects of Maggie's early experiences complicate the temporal and spatial division between adulthood and childhood. Maggie's subjectivity is inseparable from Tom's; as she later explains to Philip: 'the first thing I ever remember in my life is standing with Tom by the side of the Floss, while he held my hand: everything before that is dark to me' (V.1, 307). If we were to interpret this as the novel's primal scene, then it is interesting that the parents are absent or invisible. Childhood is presented as an Eden from which Tom and Maggie must depart. In *Paradise Lost*, Satan observes Adam and Eve walking hand in hand (IV.321); when they are led out of the garden by Michael: 'The world was all before them, where to choose / Their place of rest, and providence their guide: / They hand in hand with wandering steps and slow, / Through Eden took their solitary way' (XII.646–649). The narrator presents the past through elegy: a consciousness of loss pervades her voice, and she consistently draws attention to the distance from which she observes. Discussing Maggie's promise to kiss Philip, she writes:

> This promise was void, like so many other sweet, illusory promises of our childhood; void as promises made in Eden before the seasons were divided, and when the starry blossoms grew side by side with the ripening peach – impossible to be fulfilled when the golden gates had been passed. (II.7, 185–186)

Childhood is a lost realm—Eden—the source of nostalgic longing.[8] However, the novel undercuts this prelapsarian image. Maggie's impossible promise to Philip provides the foundation for her adult relationship with him. Her desire to make reparation—to offer him the love which she feels he deserves and which adulthood curtails—is inseparable from her own tragic conflict. It is not 'void', but determining. Philip's desire is likewise mobilised by this impossible childhood promise. Maggie's wistful attitude towards her childhood perpetuates a wider narrative strategy; the fact that her nostalgic view is represented as damaging is important. Eliot, like Freud in his two essays, 'Screen Memories' and 'Childhood Memories and Screen Memories', shows memory to be a negotiation between past and present time frames: Freud moves beyond the empiricist idea of memory; in his view, the trace cannot be identical to the perception that engendered it (Laplanche and Pontalis 1986, 248). Memory cannot be separated from fantasy production.

Eliot's narrator is not immune to the distorting effects of memory, and the fact that the novel opens the novel with a dream demonstrates how self-conscious a strategy this is. Maggie's first memory of herself and Tom holding hands, recounted to Philip after the Tullivers' downfall, is counterpoised and complicated by the narrator's dream in which Maggie stands alone on the bank, while the narrator watches her over the water from the bridge. The adult's gaze brings the child's story into the present moment, the childhood scene reactivated by the adult's investment in it. It is vital that it is as a young woman, not as a child, that Maggie identifies her 'first' memory, which draws together a series of childhood feelings. It encodes Maggie's *frustrated* longing to be understood by her brother and its power is defined by afterwardsness—speaking to the formative power of childhood scenes.

The inherited family trauma does not break the bond between Tom and Maggie; however, it reveals the pre-existing asymmetry between them. Maggie's 'first memory' is invoked throughout the novel, becoming inseparable from Mr. Tulliver's decline, dishonour and death. In another echo of *Paradise Lost*, Tom and Maggie leave Mr. Stelling's house 'together into their new life of sorrow' (II.7, 191). The irony, that Tom's time studying with Mr. Stelling has been anything but an Eden, is silenced. When Tom first sees his father after the financial collapse, the

[8] When Tom leaves school, she writes: '[…] the golden gates of their childhood had for ever closed behind them' (II.7, 191).

bond between the siblings is again reaffirmed: 'When Maggie saw how he was moved, she went to him and put her arm round his neck as he sat by the bed, and the two children forgot everything else in the sense that they had one father and one sorrow' (III.2, 205). After Mr. Tulliver's death, they are briefly reconciled: 'Their eyes turned to the same spot, and Maggie spoke: "Tom, forgive me – let us always love each other;" and they clung and wept together' (V.7, 359). Their embrace becomes symptomatic of their shared loss, and this is finally realised in the deaths: 'brother and sister had gone down in an embrace never to be parted: living through again in one supreme moment the days when they had clasped their little hands in love, and roamed the daisied fields together' (VII.5, 521). Eliot's handling of the pathos is masterful, but she is clearly unwilling for us to submerge ourselves in sentiment: in the Conclusion, we are told a tomb was built for 'for two bodies that were found in close embrace' (VII. 522). Her shift to the materiality of death prevents us from indulging in feeling without thought. It creates a doubled ending. The first is haunting, reminding us of Maggie's first memory and the prehistorical Eden which the novel invokes. The second reminds us of the social and communal dimensions of the tragedy: its otherness.

Memory and Desire

Maggie's adult conflict hinges upon a perceived dichotomy between memory—the primacy of that which is most familiar—and present desire. The latter is represented by the 'vibrating' (VI.10, 440) 'mutual consciousness' (VI.13, 461) of her and Stephen. The language of vibrations poses a question concerning the frequency at which experience resonates in physiological and psychological terms, and this reflects back onto the conflict between memory and desire. At what frequency does the past resonate? Is it felt or heard, or both?[9] Eliot presents the play of sound and voices across past and present time frames. Maggie resonates with shifting frequencies; like Samuel Taylor Coleridge's poetic speaker in 'The Eolian Harp', and Caroline in Charlotte Brontë's *Shirley*, she is played: nature's instrument. It is therefore unsurprising that for Eliot

[9] The term 'frequency' was first used in this manner in 1832 (*OED*). Eliot's use of the word 'vibration' also echoes Percy Shelley's (2002) prose piece, 'On Love', composed in July 1818 (503).

trauma is inseparable from the voice, breath and nerves. Traumatisation is dynamic—it moves—it is spoken—but it is also the vibrating pause beyond speech. Matus (2009) persuasively analyses Eliot in relation to 'Sound and Shock' (138), connecting this to Lewes's physiological theories and technological developments at the *fin de siècle* such as the telegraph and the phonograph. However, there is more at stake than shock; considering tragedy in *Middlemarch*, Eliot writes, 'If we had a keen vision and feeling of all ordinary human life, it would be like hearing the grass grow and the squirrel's heart beat, and we should die of that roar which lies on the other side of silence' (Ch. 20, 118). The near-synaesthesia, rendered through the simile, is important: 'keen vision' means 'hearing' more. Like Gaskell, Eliot posits an ethical foundation for her authorship through the concept of bearing witness: by not averting her gaze, she will make the silence speak. She will perform a work of mourning. In *Dombey and Son*, Dickens used the echoing voice of Florence to represent the family's tragic failure to mourn. Eliot also relies heavily on aural motifs, but this is part of a wider examination of the embodied mind and minded body. Eliot, unlike Dickens, is interested in the lived reality of female *sexual* desire; the language of vibrations is not just related to her representation of traumatic return, it is also the language of desire: the 'hunger of the heart' (*Mill on the Floss*, 38). This doubled usage means that traumatisation is presented as inseparable from desire: the form in which we desire is birthed in painful circumstances. Contemporary theories of memory, notably Thomas De Quincey's, use trace and legibility as a way of theorising memory. It is significant that Dickens and Eliot, while undoubtedly presenting memory in such terms, also present it in terms of sound. It is intimate and proximate. The inner voice of consciousness speaks the past: Dickens uses the word 'echo' to render this, the more scientific Eliot deploys a physiological lexis, hinging upon the word 'vibration'.

The narrator considers the relationship between memory and desire when formulating the primacy of childhood experience:

> And there is no better reason for preferring this elderberry bush than that it stirs an early memory – that it is no novelty in my life, speaking to me merely through my present sensibilities to form and colour, but the long companion of my existence, that wove itself into my joys when joys were vivid. (II.1, 152)

Eliot separates perception from memory: the 'present sensibilities', the senses, 'merely' speak to aesthetic issues of 'form and colour'. It is memory that makes the familiar sight desirable. The elderberry bush connects to a constellation of past feelings, which coalesce in the *remembrance* of the object and play into present-day perception. In this passage, Eliot conceptualises memory as a process rather than as the *mirror* of perception: it is 'woven' into the narrator's desire or 'joys'. Eliot's interest in the way in which memory is woven resonates with Freud's insistence on the multiple inscriptions of memory. Eliot herself was undoubtedly influenced by Herbert Spencer's theory of organic memory set out in *Principles of Psychology* (1855). Spencer discusses how memory is transformed into automatic reflex: 'It would be thought a misuse of language were any one to ask another whether he remembered that the sun shines, that fire burns, that iron is hard, and that ice is cold' (Spencer 1855, 561). He explains this process by reference to the musician: 'By long-continued practice, however, the series of psychical changes that occur between seeing the mark and striking the appropriate key, have coalesced into one almost automatic change' (562). However, Spencer is not overtly concerned with the way in which feeling or desire play into the consolidation of long-term memory. It is this lacuna that Eliot addresses.

Like Spencer, Eliot thinks about the memory in relation to learning. Her narrator rejects John Locke's empiricist model when critiquing Tom's education. Classicism cannot simply write itself upon Tom's empty mind; it gives him mental indigestion:

> It is astonishing what a different result one gets by changing the metaphor! Once call the brain an intellectual stomach, and one's ingenious conception of the classics and geometry as ploughs and harrows seems to settle nothing. But then it is open to someone else to follow great authorities, and call the mind a sheet of white paper or a mirror, in which case one's knowledge of the digestive process becomes quite irrelevant. (II.1, 139–140)

This witty passage is working hard conceptually. The mind is represented as taking in and devouring what it perceives. In so doing, external reality is transformed and metabolised. It is broken down: reallocated. Tom cannot translate Latin (literally and in Laplanchean terms): he cannot take it in and make it a part of himself. The unequal and uneven process of memory is hinted at; Eliot simultaneously makes a powerful point regarding educational practices and the damaging consequences of inflicting an inappropriate knowledge-set upon the child.[10] Latin is part of an adult discourse with which Tom wants nothing to do. Philip operates as a mediator or translator for Tom, turning the Classical cycles into more easily digested tales.[11] The impressionability of childhood is repeatedly represented through eating: Maggie's desire for love is described as 'hunger of the heart' (I.5, 38). The little scene in which Tom and Maggie share the cake gestures towards this: 'she put out her mouth for the cake and bit a piece: and then Tom bit a piece, just for company, and they ate together and rubbed each other's cheeks and brows and noses together, while they ate, with a humiliating resemblance to two friendly ponies' (39). Love is taken in: it sustains herself, but it is also metabolised, not simply placed in an a-temporal unconscious. Later, when they are grown up, the narrator reminds us of this moment: 'There was a little tremor in Tom's voice as he uttered the last words, and Maggie's ready affection came back with as sudden a glow as when they were children, and bit their cake together as a sacrament of conciliation' (VI.4, 394).

The narrator represents the longed-for past as an inalienable part of the self: 'Life did change for Tom and Maggie; and yet they were not wrong in believing that the thoughts and loves of these first years would always make part of their lives. We could never have loved the earth so well if we had had no childhood in it' (I.5, 41). She goes on to relate this primary knowledge to language:

> – such things as these are the mother tongue of our imagination, the language that is laden with all the subtle inextricable associations the fleeting hours of our childhood left behind them. Our delight in the sunshine on the deep-bladed grass to-day, might be no more than the faint perception of wearied souls, if it were not for the sunshine and the grass in the far-off years which still live in us, and transform our perception into love. (41–42)

This evocative passage echoes 'Ode: Intimations of Immortality' and *The Prelude*. Eliot insists upon the desirousness of language: the terms on

[10] This impropriety is not class-based, but personal. Tom has no predilection for this form of knowledge, and it runs counter to his skills.

[11] At the same time, Eliot's reference to the story of Philoctetes, marooned by his shipmates when his injured foot becomes putrid, alerts us to the fact that those who are wounded will be cast out.

which we first engage with the world continue to define perception and thought. But she performs a sleight of hand here. By offering up this seemingly nostalgic vision, we accept another. Childhood pains are woven within the fabric of the self:

> We have all of us sobbed so piteously, standing with tiny bare legs above our little socks, when we lost sight of our mother or nurse in some strange place; but we can no longer recall the poignancy of that moment and weep over it, as we do over the remembered sufferings of five or ten years ago. Every one of those keen moments has left its trace, and lives in us still, but such traces have blent themselves irrevocably with the firmer texture of our youth and manhood; and so it comes that we can look on at the troubles of our children with a smiling disbelief in the reality of their pain. Is there any one who can recover the experience of his childhood, not merely with a memory of what he did and what happened to him, of what he liked and disliked when he was in frock and trousers, but with an intimate penetration, a revived consciousness of what he felt then – when it was so long from one Midsummer to another? (I.7, 65–66)

The text shrewdly draws attention to its own skill. After presenting us with the pathetic, even twee, image of the 'tiny bare legs' and 'little socks', the narrator asks who is able to represent the sufferings of childhood: 'Its own creation is, as it were, admired for its poignancy' (Lesnik-Oberstein 2002, 93). However, this passage is more than metafictional self-congratulation. Like Freud in 'Childhood Memories and Screen Memories', Eliot suggests that we see ourselves in the third-person in early childhood memories; we recreate our child self with pathos: the 'tiny bare legs' and 'little socks'. Recent sufferings are more easily 'remembered' but are not necessarily more profound than these primary experiences. Eliot presents archaic childhood experience as the core of subjectivity. The narrator questions whether childhood traumatisation can be felt in adulthood; like Wordsworth in *The Prelude*, she suggests that 'Discordant elements' are brought into harmony: 'blent' 'irrevocably' with later experience. But this passage also represents childhood experience as necessarily traumatic: we are penetrated, wounded, by the complexity of our encounter with the adult world. This concept is fundamental to Laplanche's general theory of seduction and Emma's history (the latter from Freud's 'A Project for a Scientific Psychology'). The rhetorical question that ends the passage leaves open the possibility that adults *can* feel the 'intimate penetration' in 'revived consciousness'. In

Eliot's terms, this is also about the resonating timbre of past experience. At numerous points in the novel, we see past feeling vibrating in the present moment.

Throughout the novel, Maggie is defined by her complex and impassioned fantasy life. As a young child, she takes out her anger against her family upon the wooden Fetish kept in the attic, grinding its head against the wall, 'sobbing all the while with a passion that expelled every other form of consciousness – even the memory of the grievance that had caused it' (I.4, 28). Maggie, like an X-rated Ernst (the famous protagonist of Freud's *fort-da*), attempts to heal her traumatisation within the family through play: it is an act of mastery. At the same time, the gratuitously violent nature of this mastery seems to play out the damage and disenfranchisement she suffers within the family in hyperbolic and desperate form. This representation of childhood passion resonates forcefully with the Brontës' writings. Maggie is, like a less melodramatic Heathcliff, also placed at the heart of a gendered conflict as a child, beloved of her father, but despaired of by her mother and the Dodson clan. She is somehow anomalous or alien; her brother is not her second self, but rather her inverse mirror image (thus contrasting with Heathcliff and Cathy). Her impassioned childhood state prefigures her response to her father's fall:

> She rebelled against her lot, she fainted under its loneliness, and fits even of anger and hatred towards her father and mother, who were so unlike what she would have them to be – towards Tom, who checked her, and met her thought or feeling always be some thwarting difference – would flow out over her affections and conscience like a lava stream, and frighten her with a sense that it was not difficult for her to become a demon. (IV.3, 287)

As an adult, there is no 'Fetish' which can stand in for the family in fantasy or play. She cannot heal the world by brutally damaging the doll, and she cannot make herself forget or (in Freud's terms) *bind* her pain. Eliot again represents memory in terms of vibrating frequencies: 'Every affection, every delight the poor child had had, was like an aching nerve to her. There was no music for her any more – no piano, no harmonized voices, no delicious stringed instruments, with their passionate cries of imprisoned spirits sending a strange vibration through her frame' (IV.3, 285–286). This is a complex passage. Memory's incapacity to resonate at the same frequency as sensory and sensual experience is hinted at.

However, the *difference* between past and present—the loss of music—is a physically potent experience: like an 'aching nerve'. The *memory* of what she has lost creates a kind of psychological and physical neuralgia, comparable to Freud's concept of anxiety as unchannelled libido. When Maggie reads Thomas à Kempis, the little book seemingly gives her a mode through which she can sublimate her passion, counterbalancing the cacophony of voices which define the Tulliver and Dodson families: 'this voice out of the far-off middle ages was the direct communication of a human soul's belief and experience, and came to Maggie as an unquestioned message' (291). It gives her a fantasised mode through which she can bridge past, present and future: something both the Fetish and her father's destructive legacy fail to do. Eliot formulates this in physiological terms: 'Now and then, that sort of enthusiasm finds a far echoing voice that comes from an experience springing out of the deepest need. And it was by being brought within the long lingering vibrations of such a voice that Maggie, with her girl's face and unnoted sorrows, found an effort and a hope' (292).

Later, Maggie attempts to heal her world through Philip, as she did previously through the Fetish and à Kempis. However, their unequal relationship actually replays in inverse form the asymmetrical relation between herself and Tom. Philip operates as a metonym for a wider discourse on childhood traumatisation and its after-effects; his subjectivity is inseparable from his injury, for which it is hinted his father was to blame. His childhood wound is both physical and psychological: 'An anatomist – even a mere physiognomist – would have seen that the deformity of Philip's spine was not a congenital hump, but the result of an accident in infancy' (II.3, 161). When Philip asks Wakem for permission to marry Maggie, his words give his father a 'pang': 'they had stirred a feeling which had been a habit for a quarter of a century' (VI.8, 425). Philip has 'been marked from childhood for a peculiar kind of suffering' (V.4, 333). The intertwining of Maggie and Philip's stories constructs a proto-traumatic discourse by bridging physical and psychological damage. Their asymmetrical love for one another cannot be read outside of this childhood context. Maggie relates her desire for friendship with Philip to the family's troubles: 'I may not keep anything I used to love when I was little. The old books went; and Tom is different – and my father. It is like death. I must part with everything I cared for when I was a child' (V.1, 301). Philip stands in for everything Maggie has lost. When Maggie meets Philip at the Red Deeps, she feels an 'opening in the rocky wall [...] some of the memory-haunting earthly delights were no longer out of her reach' (V.3, 325).

In contrast to Maggie's response to Philip, Maggie and Stephen's desire for one another is presented in terms of a mutual vibration. The 'deep tone' (VI.13, 465) of his voice lowers the *frequency* of the past, including the message of renunciation which Maggie takes from à Kempis: 'the old voices' (VI.13, 458). The harmony created through Stephen and Maggie's mutual desire operates in the present tense; it jars with Maggie's loyalty towards Lucy and Philip, and is incompatible with her wider mourning process, in which Philip occupies a central place as a substitute for Tom. When they are on the boat, 'she felt nothing else. Memory was excluded' (464). It is a 'fatal intoxication' (465):

> Such things, uttered in low broken tones by the one voice that has first stirred the fibre of young passion, have only a feeble effect – on experienced minds at a distance from them. To poor Maggie they were very near: they were like nectar held close to thirsty lips: (469)

She loses consciousness in the eddying of her desire: 'But now nothing was distinct to her: she was being lulled to sleep with that soft stream still flowing over her, with those delicious visions melting and fading like a wondrous aërial land of the west' (470). Eliot's vibrations work on a similar premise to Freud's theory of traumatic excitation set out in *Beyond the Pleasure Principle*. Freud writes, 'another problem arises instead – the problem of mastering the amounts of stimulus which have broken in and of binding them, in the psychical sense, so that they can then be disposed of' (29–30). Unfortunately for Maggie, the only way she can bind these stimuli is through memory and therefore through the destructive family legacy, overseen by the shadowy figure of Tom: 'There are memories, and affections, and longings after perfect goodness, that have such a strong hold on me; they would never quit me for long' (VI.14, 476); 'it would rend me away from all that my past life has made dear and holy to me. I can't set out on a fresh life, and forget that' (478).

The Mill on the Floss does not present a work of mourning in the same way as *North and South*, or indeed Eliot's *Silas Marner*. Maggie is only able to reconcile past and present in death. However, the narrator, creating numerous prolepses for the final tragedy throughout, performs a work of mourning which the characters themselves are incapable of. She contextualises the trauma: she is the chorus, mediating the tragedy of the main actors. She writes, 'moral judgements must remain false and hollow, unless they are checked and enlightened by a perpetual reference to the special circumstances that mark the individual lot' (VII.2, 498). After Tom casts out Maggie, she adds, 'remember that the responsibility of tolerance lies with those who have the wider vision' (VII.3, 500). This is the implied author's function. Through her 'wider vision', she bears witness to the Tullivers' tragedy. As in the dream that opens the novel, the narrator situates herself at intimate distance from the Tullivers's story. In *The Mill on the Floss*, Eliot frequently reminds us of the temporal distance from which she writes. However, in the dream, she stands on the bridge, not on the other side of the riverbank. This 'bridge' between past and present, a bridge co-extensive with the act of mourning, does not enforce moral judgement, but 'the responsibility of tolerance': ethical obligation towards others.

Works Cited

Literary Texts

Brontë, Charlotte. 2008. *Shirley*. Edited by Herbert Rosengarten and Margaret Smith. Oxford: Oxford University Press.

Brontë, Emily. 2008. *Wuthering Heights*. Edited by Ian Jack. Oxford: Oxford University Press.

Carlyle, Thomas. 1971. *Past and Present*. In *Selected Writings*, edited by Alan Shelston, 257–312. Harmondsworth: Penguin.

Collins, Wilkie. 1973. *The Woman in White*. Edited by Harvey Peter Sucksmith. Oxford: Oxford University Press.

———. 1986. *No Name*. Edited by Virginia Blain. Oxford: Oxford University Press.

Cross, John W. 1885. *George Eliot's Life as Related in Her Letters and Journals*. 3 vols. Edinburgh: Blackwood.

Dickens, Charles. 1974. *Dombey and Son*. Edited by Alan Horsman. Oxford: Clarendon Press.

———. 1979. *Little Dorrit*. Edited by Harvey Peter Sucksmith. Oxford: Clarendon Press.

———. 1993. *Great Expectations*. Edited by Margaret Cardwell. Oxford: Clarendon Press.

Eliot, George.1981. *The Mill on the Floss*. Edited by George Haight. Oxford: Oxford University Press.

———. 1993. *Romola*. Edited by Andrew Brown. Oxford: University Press.

———. 1994. *Middlemarch*. Edited by Rosemary Ashton. London: Penguin.

———. 2008. *Adam Bede*. Edited by Carol A. Martin. Oxford: Oxford University Press.
———. 2008. *Silas Marner*. Edited by Terence Cave. Oxford: Oxford University Press.
———. 2009. *Scenes of Clerical Life*. Edited by Thomas A. Noble. Oxford: Oxford University Press.
———. 2009. *The Lifted Veil and Brother Jacob*. Edited by Helen Small. Oxford: Oxford University Press.
———. 2014. *Daniel Deronda*. Edited by Graham Handley and K. M. Newton. Oxford: Oxford University Press.
Gaskell, Elizabeth. 1969. *Wives and Daughters*. Edited by Frank Glover Smith. Harmondsworth: Penguin.
———. 1996. *Mary Barton*. Edited by Macdonald Daly. London: Penguin.
———. 1997. *The Letters of Elizabeth Gaskell*. Edited by J. A. V. Chapple and Arthur Pollard. Manchester: Manchester University Press.
———. 2000. 'The Old Nurse's Story'. In *Gothic Tales*, edited by Laura Kranzler, 11–32. London: Penguin.
———. 2008. *North and South*. Edited by Angus Easson. Oxford: Oxford University Press.
Milton, John. 1997. *Paradise Lost*. Edited by Alastair Fowler. 2nd ed. Edinburgh: Pearson.
Shelley, Percy. 2002. 'On Love'. In *Shelley's Poetry and Prose*, edited by Donald H. Reiman and Neil Fraistat, 503–504. New York: W. W. Norton.
Tennyson, Alfred. 2007. *In Memoriam A. H. H.* In *Selected Poems*, edited by Christopher Ricks, 96–198. London: Penguin.
———. 2007. *Maud: A Monodrama*. In *Selected Poems*, edited by Christopher Ricks, 217–265. London: Penguin.
Wordsworth, William. 1984. *The Major Works*, edited by Stephen Gill. Oxford: Oxford University Press.
———. 1995. *The Prelude: The Four Texts*. Edited by Jonathan Wordsworth. London: Penguin.

Primary Psychoanalytic Texts

Abbreviations

SE: *The Standard Edition of the Complete Psychological Works of Sigmund Freud*. 2001. Translated from the German under the general editorship of James Strachey, in collaboration with Anna Freud and assisted by Alix Strachey and Allan Tyson. London: Vintage.
Freud, Sigmund.
———. *Beyond the Pleasure Principle*. *SE* 18:3–64.

———. 'Childhood Memories and Screen Memories'. In *The Psychopathology of Everyday Life*. *SE* 6:43–52.
———. *From the History of an Infantile Neurosis*. *SE* 17:3–122.
———. 'Mourning and Melancholia'. *SE* 14:237–260.
———. 'A Project for a Scientific Psychology'. *SE* 1:283–397.
———. 'Screen Memories'. *SE* 3:301–322.
Laplanche, Jean. 1999. *Essays on Otherness.* Edited by John Fletcher. Translated by Luke Thurston, Philip Slotkin, and Leslie Hill. London: Routledge.
———. 1999. 'Time and the Other'. In *Essays on Otherness*, 238–263.
Laplanche, Jean and Jean Bertrand Pontalis. 1986. 'Fantasy and the Origins of Sexuality'. In *Formations of Fantasy*, edited by Victor Burgin, James Donald and Cora Kaplan, 5–34. London: Methuen.
Toubiana, Éric. 2014. 'The Ides of March: From Mastery to Vampirism'. In *Seduction and Enigmas: Laplanche, Theory, Culture*, edited by John Fletcher and Nicholas Ray, and translated by Nicholas Ray, 176–208. London: Laurence and Wishart.

Secondary Texts

Bowlby, Rachel. 2007. Foreword to *Adventures in Realism*. Edited by Matthew Beaumont, x–xviii. Oxford: Blackwell.
Butler, Judith. 2005. *Giving an Account of Oneself*. New York: Fordham University Press.
———. 2004. *Precarious Life: The Powers of Mourning and Violence*. London: Verso.
Darwin, Charles. 1985. *On the Origin of Species by Means of Natural Selection: Or, the Preservation of Favoured Races in the Struggle for Life*. Edited by J. W. Burrow. London: Penguin.
Hillis Miller. 1975. 'Optic and Semiotic in Middlemarch'. In *The Worlds of Victorian Fiction*, edited by Jerome H. Buckley, 125–143. Cambridge, MA: Harvard University Press.
Lesnik-Oberstein, Karin. 2002. '*Holiday House*: Grist to *The Mill on the Floss*, or Childhood as Text'. *The Yearbook of English Studies* 32: 77–94.
Matus, Jill. 2009. *Shock, Memory and the Unconscious in Victorian Fiction*. Cambridge: Cambridge University Press.
Nadler, Steven, ed. 2002. *A Companion to Early Modern Philosophy*. Oxford: Blackwell.
Shuttleworth, Sally. 1984. *George Eliot and Nineteenth-Century Science: The Make-Believe of a Beginning*. Cambridge: Cambridge University Press.
Slater, Michael. 2009. *Charles Dickens*. New Haven: Yale University Press.
Spencer, Herbert. 1855. *Principles of Psychology*. London: Longman, Brown, Green and Longmans.

Spivak, Gayatri Chakravorty. 2010. 'Can the Subaltern Speak?' In *Can the Subaltern Speak? Reflections on the History of an Idea*, edited by Rosalind Morris, Rev. ed., 21–78. New York: Columbia University Press.
Uglow, Jenny. 1993. *Elizabeth Gaskell*. London: Faber and Faber.

CHAPTER 7

Conclusion

George Eliot is a decisive author for *Traumatic Encounters*: her relentless intellectual engagement is key to my historical understanding and argument. The mid-Victorian novel does not anticipate Sigmund Freud because of a proleptic accident. The authors examined here, as has been established by historicist criticism, engage with contemporary psychological and physiological theories to greater or lesser extents. However, this is never in a single or straightforward manner. Eliot's synthesis of contemporary thought does not resolve the ambiguities within various theories (and neither is it intended to). The narrator's discourse openly poses questions that can be related back to contemporary theories; these questions are tackled in the Tullivers' story. The overall vision of selfhood supersedes the scientific and philosophical models on which it initially draws. By focalising psychological enquiries through the familial—the *mise-en-scène* of the home—the mid-Victorian novelists move beyond their medical contemporaries and anticipate Breuer and Freud's paradigmatic text, *Studies on Hysteria*.

Jill Matus (2009) shows the active manner in which literary texts, in conjunction with mid-Victorian physiological theories, constructed proto-traumatic models. However, discourses of shock cannot encompass the subtleties of the everyday traumatisation represented by the mid-Victorian novel. Elizabeth Gaskell's *Wives and Daughters* demonstrates this point eloquently. Gaskell resolutely avoids melodrama or the physiological palpitations of *North and South*; a theory of shock cannot account for

M. Wood, *Parents and Children in the Mid-Victorian Novel*,
https://doi.org/10.1007/978-3-030-45469-2_7

the beautifully understated handling of Molly's story. However, Molly's experience can be linked coherently to the melodramatic events found in other mid-Victorian novels. *Wives and Daughters*, like all the novels examined here, represents the interweaving of memory and fantasy: it relies on a scenography. Confronted with her father's newly decorated bedroom following his second marriage, Molly remembers a scene from when she was three years old:

> Molly could just remember, in faint clear lines of distinctness, the being taken into this very room to bid farewell to her dying mother. She could see the white linen, the white muslin, surrounding the pale, wan wistful face, with the large, longing, eyes, yearning for one more touch of the little soft warm child, whom she was too feeble to clasp in her arms, already growing numb in death. Many a time when Molly had been in this room since that sad day, had she seen in vivid fancy that same wan wistful face lying on the pillow, the outline of the form beneath the clothes; and the girl had not shrunk from such visions, but rather cherished them, as preserving to her the remembrance of her mother's outward semblance. Her eyes were full of tears [...]. (Ch. 13, 186)

Molly does not avoid this memory: rather, this scene of irrefutable maternal love guarantees her happy childhood with her father. Reading the passage above, we think back to another bedroom: the luxurious room where 'Clare' (as Mrs. Kirkpatrick is called by the Cumnors) forgets about Molly—allowing her to sleep alone and uncared for. Molly's memory is not disrupted, neither is she subject to dissociation, but her subjectivity is built up through a complex interweaving of memory, forgetfulness, love and loss.

Parent-child traumatisation does not disappear from the literature after the mid-Victorian period; on the contrary, the authors addressed in this study establish paradigms critical for later literature, psychological discourse and twentieth-century commonplaces. Henry James above all takes up the figure of the displaced child. However, there was a shift in literary focus after 1866 (the year of Gaskell's death), and at the *fin de siècle,* the mid-century literary family plot was taken up in Freud's psychological discourse. Eliot decentres the *mise-en-scène* of the home in *Middlemarch* (1872) and *Daniel Deronda* (1876). Her ethical sociological vision is positioned between two nineteenth-century realist extremes: Dickens's spectrality and Emile Zola's neo-Darwinian naturalism.

The literary shift after the mid-century was consolidated by Dickens's death, but was already at work in his final two novels. While cross-generational relationships remained critical for his structuring and plotting, Dickens did not exploit this in quite the same way. Bonds between young men, whether destructive or loving, are emphasised. As Hilary Schor (1999) notes, Jenny Wren and her father are a parodic version of Amy and William Dorrit (201), and through this strange pair, Dickens self-consciously flags up the grotesquery of his sentimental set-up in *Little Dorrit*. In *The Mystery of Edwin Drood*, youthful orphans are once more placed at the mercy of a persecutory adult force in the form of Jasper. However, as we might expect following the developments of *Our Mutual Friend*, the younger generation assumes a new kind of power and autonomy in this last novel. Even the beautiful, whimsical Rosa Budd is granted a determination, dignity and humour of her own, subtly different from Dickens's previous treatment of young blonde girls. But the sexualisation of Jasper's threat undoubtedly picks up where Miss Havisham and Bradley Headstone left off. Most interestingly, trauma in *The Mystery of Edwin Drood* is overtly represented as an internalised trauma of the self, in which subjective dissolution is divorced from empirical reality, and tied into a repetitive hallucinatory and erotic fantasy. The dislocated dreamlike atmosphere to the novel marks a subtle change in Dickens's writing tone, a proto-modernist feel which tragically was to remain in embryonic form. At the *fin de siècle*, in the context of Walter Pater's aestheticism and the later decadent movement, authors no longer prioritised the familial scene as a matter of course. *Fin-de-siècle* Gothic texts are frequently propelled by tension between public and private performances of self. This became increasingly potent in the wake of the 1885 Labouchere Amendment, which proscribed 'gross indecency'—all sexualised acts—between men. *Our Mutual Friend* and *Edwin Drood* presage the *fin-de-siècle's* heightening concern with relationships between men, in terms of both the homosocial and the homoerotic.

Evolutionary paradigms exist alongside the repetition compulsion of trauma in later mid-century texts, including *The Mill on the Floss*, *Great Expectations*, *Our Mutual Friend* and *No Name*. Gillian Beer (1983) and George Levine (1988) (amongst others) demonstrated the significance of evolutionary thinking to Victorian plots, and the shared *literary* history deployed by Darwin and contemporary writers, including Dickens, Eliot and Thomas Hardy. In *Death and the Mother* (1998), Carolyn Dever analyses the manner in which Darwin's *Autobiography* effaces the maternal in favour of paternal inheritance: 'This partheno-genetic phantasy, the phantasy of continuity from "Father" to son, produces the "origin of species", and arguably, *The Origin of Species*' (199). It is important to remember that Darwin did not create the first, or only, theory of evolution. In *Victorian Sensation* (2000), James Secord reveals the impact of Robert Chambers's anonymously published *Vestiges of the Natural History of Creation* in 1844. This brought an overarching theory of transmutation to a huge audience and undoubtedly played into our mid-Victorian moment by placing cosmic development centre stage. Human evolution was part of an interstellar and geological process, overseen by a benevolent 'Divine Author' (Chambers 1887, 150). It is notable, however, that the mid-Victorian novels examined here present something far more unsettling. Human development—the *Bildungsroman*—is not a divinely ordered progression, but haunted, possibly regressive and defined by the compulsion to repeat.

The use of trauma as a narrative mode was undoubtedly affected by the growing dominance of neo-Darwinian social thinking in the latter half of the century. Herbert Spencer's idea of the 'survival of the fittest' set out in *Principles of Biology* (1864) reformulated society in terms of a pseudo-Darwinian 'struggle for existence', very different from Chambers's more reassuring model of natural history. Thomas Hardy constructs experimental realisms by deploying deterministic evolutionary paradigms, which differ substantively from what we see in the mid-Victorian novel. Inheritance is critical to Hardy, but it is mobilised in newly biologised terms. This idea plays out in novels such as *Tess of the D'Urbervilles* (1892), in which Wessex emerges as the *mise-en-scène* of trauma. It is the landscape that is haunted; Hardy tends towards an epic phylogenetic and ancestral vision. Beer (1983) notes that, the 'awareness of an unfathomable past whose individualities are wholly lost, and rarely human, is one of the traits in Darwin's writing to which Hardy most sensitively responded' (41). But Hardy is concerned with both meta-narrative and its destabilisation, exploring the heightening tension between the material and the ideal in scientific and philosophical terms. In *The Well-Beloved* (1897), Jocelyn's strange obsession with the feminine ideal means that the female's material body becomes debased: 'Each shape, or embodiment, has been a temporary residence only, which she has entered, lived in a while, and made her exit from, leaving the substance, so far as I have been concerned, a corpse, worse luck!' (Ch. 7, 200). Jocelyn chases the well-beloved across three generations of the same family of women. His strange predicament shows the possible convergence between materialist and idealist modes of thought: his Neoplatonic desire is rooted in the anthropological reality of the Wessex Isle of Slingers.

A displaced New Englander, Henry James's understanding was undoubtedly influenced by his own history and in his case, the *mise-en-scène* of home was conceived as displacement. James did not simply reject mid-century realist forms; it is clear from both *What Maisie Knew* (1897), and *The Turn of the Screw* (1898), that he developed them. However, the replacement of sentiment with irony clearly demarcates James from his mid-century predecessors. James's account of meeting Dickens in 1867 is provocative:

> I saw the master – nothing could be more evident – in the light of an intense emotion, and I trembled, I remember, in every limb, while at the same time, by a blest fortune, emotion produced no luminous blur, but left him shining indeed, only shining with august particulars. […] but intense though the positive perception there was an immensity more left to understand – for the long aftersense, I mean; and one, or the chief, of these later things was that if our hero neither shook hands nor spoke, only meeting us by the barest act, so to say, of the trained eye, the penetration of which, to my sense, revealed again a world, there was a grim beauty, to one's subsequently panting imagination, in that very truth of his then so knowing himself (committed to his monstrous 'readings' and with the force required for them ominously ebbing) on the outer edge of his once magnificent margin. (*Notes of a Son and Brother*, 205–206)

This reads like a paternal seduction. The child—James—appears at the mercy of the powerful but declining father, Dickens, who is framed as a 'shining' idol, capable of penetrating James's nervous system. James's 'aftersense' is comparable to the concept of afterwardsness: the belated power of experience central to the mid-Victorian novel, to the emergence of trauma as a psychological category at the *fin de siècle*, and to psychoanalytic theory.[1]

[1] William James wrote on the belatedness of trauma in the 1890s (Matus 2009, 87); however, Henry James's reference to 'aftersense' predates William's first academic appointment in 1872 and first publication, 'Remarks on Spencer's Definition of the Mind as Correspondence' (1878).

In *The Turn of the Screw* (1898), James takes up the figure of the abandoned child in self-consciously unoriginal fashion, exploiting, developing *and* parodying the intensity and seriousness of the Brontës and Dickens: 'If the child gives the effect another turn of the screw, what do you say to *two* children –?' (115). The unnamed governess is a Jane Eyre type, without any of her predecessor's solidity. She is dislocated from her home and unable to place herself successfully in a romance plot. Unlike Jane, she does not have to contend with the haunting effects of her own childhood; instead she projects—or provokes—the ghostliness of the present moment. Unconsciousness is turned inside out. In *What Maisie Knew* (1897), James exploits the ironic epistemological disjunction between adult and child. As he explains in the preface, Maisie is the focal point for this irony—the apparently blank space necessary for signification. However, James is also concerned with the psychological dynamics of the adult-child relationship. Maisie is represented as a translator of the adult world: 'Her little world was phantasmagoric – strange shadows dancing on a sheet. It was as if the whole performance had been given for her – a mite of a half-scared infant in a great dim theatre' (Ch. 1, 39). Her consistent desire to give the adults what they want, to please whomever she is with by submitting herself to their vision, becomes increasingly tragic. Focalised largely through Maisie's consciousness, the novel constructs and deconstructs a series of primal phantasies: disquietingly, the adults' adulterous sexual relationships take on meaning *through* Maisie herself. At the heart of the novel is a maternal problematic: speaking to one of Ida's many lovers in the park, we glimpse Maisie's unhappiness clearly for the first—and perhaps only—time: 'She became on the spot indifferent to her usual fear of showing what in children was notoriously most offensive – presented to her companion, soundlessly but hideously, her wet, distorted face. She cried, with a pang, straight *at* him, cried as she had never cried at anyone in all her life. "Oh do you love her?" she brought out a gulp that was the effect of her trying not to make a noise' (Ch. 16, 130). The Captain's love for Ida gives Maisie a way in which to identify with her mother for the first time: Ida becomes briefly, and tantalising, real and Maisie—this once—has an authentic voice.

Reading *What Maisie Knew* and Freud's *Fragment of an Analysis of a Case of Hysteria*, Neil Hertz (1990) argues that the texts can be brought together through ideas of authorial identification and seduction. He argues that both authors not only recount, but also covertly identify with the young girls' stories. Dora's subjection to older men is read in conjunction with Freud's presentation of himself as the subordinate junior colleague in 'The History of the Psychoanalytic Movement' (237); interestingly, as we have seen, James represented himself in exactly these terms in relation to Dickens. In 'Female Narrative Energy', I interpret Freud's identification with Dora in more asymmetrical terms than Hertz, charting the irruption of Dora's *voice* in relation to Freud's failed attempt to control her *narrative* (Wood 2012, 20–21). Psychoanalysis cannot stand outside of questions concerning authorship, writing and textuality, but this does not negate the social import of Freud's propositions. In creating a framework through which to understand the vicissitudes of desire, and the problems bound up in the act of narration, Freud adopts a mid-Victorian form: trauma's compulsion to repeat is birthed within the familial *mise-en-scène* of the bourgeois home, resulting from the asymmetry of the extended parent-child relationship. Frau Emmy von N.'s case history in *Studies on Hysteria* reads like the gathering of ideas for a rather macabre and Dickensian novel. However, Freud does not successfully organise—or plot—the material; the text self-consciously hinges upon failure, and the majority of his analysis takes place in the footnotes. He apologises for, but defends the necessity of, 'becoming lost in the [...] maze of sign-reading' (Breuer and Freud 2001, 93*n*). By contrast, in the Wolf Man's history, Freud employs startling techniques for handling the complexity of the case; he constructs scenographies as a way of plotting the compulsion to repeat, and of ordering the clinical material. This links his narrative discourse back to the mid-Victorian moment examined in *Traumatic Encounters* (as well as the modernism which came afterwards) and the hidden compulsive logic that drives the novels. The mid-Victorian novelists and Freud were equally concerned with the problem of how to plot a life, pointing us towards the lived reality and dynamic force of the parent-child relationship, while remaining alert to their own textual production. The working-through of loss underpins both the mid-Victorian novel and Freudian psychoanalysis.

Works Cited

Literary Texts

Brontë, Charlotte. 2008. *Jane Eyre*. Edited by Margaret Smith. Oxford: Oxford University Press.

Collins, Wilkie. 1986. *No Name*. Edited by Virginia Blain. Oxford: Oxford University Press.

Dickens, Charles. 1972. *The Mystery of Edwin Drood*. Edited by Margaret Cardwell. Oxford: Oxford University Press.

———. 1979. *Little Dorrit*. Edited by Harvey Peter Sucksmith. Oxford: Clarendon Press.

———. 1993. *Great Expectations*. Edited by Margaret Cardwell. Oxford: Clarendon Press.

———. 2008. *Our Mutual Friend*. Edited by Michael Cotsell. Oxford: Oxford University Press.

Eliot, George. 1981. *The Mill on the Floss*. Edited by George Haight. Oxford: Oxford University Press.

———. 2014. *Daniel Deronda*. Edited by Graham Handley and K. M. Newton. Oxford: Oxford University Press.

———. 1994. *Middlemarch*. Edited by Rosemary Ashton. London: Penguin.

Gaskell, Elizabeth. 1969. *Wives and Daughters*. Edited by Frank Glover Smith. Harmondsworth: Penguin.

Hardy, Thomas. 1997. *The Pursuit of the Well-Beloved* and *The Well-Beloved*. Edited by Patricia Ingham. London: Penguin.

———. 2008. *Tess of the D'Urbervilles*. Edited by Simon Gatrell, Juliet Grindle, and Penny Boumelha. Oxford: Oxford University Press.

James, Henry. 1985. *What Maisie Knew*. Edited by Paul Theroux and Patricia Crick. London: Penguin.

———. 1992. *The Turn of the Screw and Other Stories*. Edited by T. J. Lustig. Oxford: Oxford University Press.

———. 2011. *Notes of a Son and a Brother* and *The Middle Years: A Critical Edition*. Edited by Peter Collister. Charlottesville: University of Virginia Press.

Primary Psychoanalytic Texts

Abbreviations

Breuer, Josef and Sigmund Freud. 2001. *Studies on Hysteria*. *SE* 2.

Freud, Sigmund. *Fragment of an Analysis of a Case of Hysteria*. *SE* 7:3–122.

———. *From the History of an Infantile Neurosis*. *SE* 17:3–122.

———. 'On the History of the Psychoanalytic Movement'. *SE* 14:7–66.

Secondary Texts

Beer, Gillian. 1983. *Darwin's Plots: Evolutionary Narrative in Darwin, George Eliot and Nineteenth-Century Fiction*. London: Routledge & Kegan & Paul.

Chambers, Robert. 1887. *Vestiges of the Natural History of Creation*. Glasgow: George Routledge and Sons.

Dever, Carolyn. 1998. *Death and the Mother from Dickens to Freud: Victorian Fictions and the Anxiety of Origins*. Cambridge: Cambridge University Press.

Hertz, Neil. 1990 [1985]. 'Dora's Secrets, Freud's Techniques'. In *In Dora's Case: Freud, Hysteria, Feminism*, edited by Charles Bernheimer and Claire Kahane, 221–242. 2nd ed. New York: Columbia University Press.

James, William. 1878. 'Remarks on Spencer's Definition of the Mind as Correspondence'. *The Journal of Speculative Philosophy* 12, no. 1 (January): 1–18.

Levine, George. 1988. *Darwin and the Novelists: Patterns of Science in Victorian Fiction*. Cambridge, MA: Harvard University Press.

Matus, Jill. 2009. *Shock, Memory and the Unconscious in Victorian Fiction*. Cambridge: Cambridge University Press.

Schor, Hilary. 1999. *Dickens and the Daughter of the House*. Cambridge: Cambridge University Press.

Secord, James. 2000. *Victorian Sensation: The Extraordinary Publication, Reception, and Secret Authorship of Vestiges of the Natural History of Creation*. Chicago: Chicago University Press.

Spencer, Herbert. 1864. *Principles of Biology*. London: William and Norgate.

Wood, Madeleine. 2012. 'Female Narrative Energy in the Writings of Dead White Males: Dickens, Collins and Freud'. In *Cross-Gendered Literary Voices: Appropriating, Resisting, Embracing*, edited by Rina Kim and Claire Westall, 15–35. Basingstoke: Palgrave Macmillan.

Works Cited

Literary Texts

Aeschylus. 1984. *The Oresteia: Agamemnon; The Libation Bearers; The Eumenides*. Translated by Robert Fagles. Edited by W. B. Stanford. London: Penguin.

Braddon, Mary Elizabeth. 1862. *Lady Audley's Secret*. 3 vols. London: Tinsley Bros.

Brontë, Anne. 2008. *Agnes Grey*. Edited by Robert Inglesfield and Hilda Marsden. Oxford: Oxford University Press.

———. 1996. *The Tenant of Wildfell Hall*. Edited by Stevie Davies. London: Penguin.

Brontë, Charlotte. 2008. *Jane Eyre*. Edited by Margaret Smith. Oxford: Oxford University Press.

———. 2008. *Shirley*. Edited by Herbert Rosengarten and Margaret Smith. Oxford: Oxford University Press.

———. 2008. *Villette*. Edited by Margaret Smith. Oxford: Oxford University Press.

———. 1916. 'The Violet'. London: Privately printed by Clement Shorter. http://contentdm.baylor.edu/cdm/ref/collection/ab-wpc/id/96789.

Brontë, Emily. 1992. *The Complete Poems*. Edited by Janet Gezari. London: Penguin.

———. 2008. *Wuthering Heights*. Edited by Ian Jack. Oxford: Oxford University Press.

Carlyle, Thomas. 1971. *Selected Writings*. Edited by Alan Shelston. Harmondsworth: Penguin.

M. Wood, *Parents and Children in the Mid-Victorian Novel*,
https://doi.org/10.1007/978-3-030-45469-2

———. 1971. 'Chartism'. In *Selected Writings*. Edited by Alan Shelston, 149–232. Harmondsworth: Penguin.

———. 1971. *Past and Present*. In *Selected Writings*. Edited by Alan Shelston, 257–312. Harmondsworth: Penguin.

———. 1971. *Signs of the Times*. In *Selected Writings*. Edited by Alan Shelston, 59–86. Harmondsworth: Penguin.

Chaucer, Geoffrey. 1872. 'The Parlement of Briddes, or the Assembly of Foules'. In *The Poetical Works of Geoffrey Chaucer*, edited by Richard Morris. Vol. 4, 51–74. London: Bell and Daldy.

Coleridge, Samuel Taylor and William Wordsworth. 2005. In *Lyrical Ballads*. Edited by R. L. Brett and A. R. Jones, 156–161. London: Routledge Classics.

Coleridge, Samuel Taylor. 2002. *Coleridge's Poetry and Prose*. Edited by Nicholas Halmi, Paul Magnuson and Raimonda Mondiano. New York: W. W. Norton.

Collins, Wilkie. 1850. *Antonina*. London: Richard Bentley.

———. 1973. *The Woman in White*. Edited by Harvey Peter Sucksmith. Oxford: Oxford University Press.

———. 1982. *The Moonstone*. Edited by Anthea Trodd. Oxford: Oxford University Press.

———. 1986. *No Name*. Edited by Virginia Blain. Oxford: Oxford University Press.

———. 1990. *Basil*. Edited by Dorothy Goldman. Oxford: Oxford University Press.

———. 1993. *Hide and Seek*. Edited by Catherine Peters. Oxford: Oxford University Press.

———. 1995. *Armadale*. Edited by John Sutherland. London: Penguin.

———. 1997. *The Dead Secret*. Edited by Ira B. Nadel. Oxford: Oxford University Press.

Cross, John W. 1885. *George Eliot's Life as Related in Her Letters and Journals*. 3 vols. Edinburgh: Blackwood.

De Quincey, Thomas. 1996. *Confessions of an English Opium Eater*. In *Confessions of an English Opium Eater and Other Writings*, edited by Grevel Lindop, 1–80. Oxford: Oxford University Press.

———. 1996. *Suspiria de Profundis*. In *Confessions of an English Opium Eater and Other Writings*, edited by Grevel Lindop, 87–182. Oxford: Oxford University Press.

Dickens, Charles. 1850. 'A Child's Dream of a Star'. *Household Words* 1, no. 2 (6 April): 25–26.

———. 2004. *American Notes*. Edited by Patricia Ingham. London: Penguin.

———. 2008. *Bleak House*. Edited by Stephen Gill. Oxford: Oxford University Press.

———. 1981. *David Copperfield*. Edited by Nina Burgis. Oxford: Clarendon Press.

———. 1974. *Dombey and Son*. Edited by Alan Horsman. Oxford: Clarendon Press.

———. 1974. 'The Number Plans'. Appendix to Dickens, *Dombey and Son*, 835–855. Oxford: Clarendon Press.

———. 1993. *Great Expectations*. Edited by Margaret Cardwell. Oxford: Clarendon Press.

———. 1998. *Hard Times*. Edited by Paul Schlicke. Oxford: Oxford University Press.

———. 1979. *Little Dorrit*. Edited by Harvey Peter Sucksmith. Oxford: Clarendon Press.

———. 1982. *Martin Chuzzlewit*. Edited by Margaret Cardwell. Oxford: Clarendon Press.

———. 1972. *The Mystery of Edwin Drood*. Edited by Margaret Cardwell. Oxford: Oxford University Press.

———. 2008. *Nicholas Nickleby*. Edited by Paul Schlicke. Oxford: Oxford University Press.

———. 1998. *The Old Curiosity Shop*. Edited by Elizabeth M. Brennan. Oxford: Oxford University Press.

———. 1966. *Oliver Twist: Or the Parish Boy's Progress*. Edited by Kathleen Tillotson. Oxford: Clarendon Press.

———. 2008. *Our Mutual Friend*. Edited by Michael Cotsell. Oxford: Oxford University Press.

———. 2012. *The Selected Letters of Charles Dickens*. Edited by Jenny Hartley. Oxford: Oxford University Press.

———. 2009. 'The Signalman'. In *Ghost Stories*, 303–320. London: CRW Publishers.

———. *Speeches: Literary and Social*.http://www.gutenberg.org/files/824/824-h/824-h.htm.

———. 2008. *A Tale of Two Cities*. Edited by Andrew Sanders. Oxford: Oxford University Press.

———. 1861. *The Uncommercial Traveller*. London: Chapman and Hall.

Dickens, Charles, ed. *The Household Narrative of Current Events (for the year 1850) Being a Monthly Supplement to Household Words, Conducted by Charles Dickens*. 27 March 1850; 30 March 1850; 28 July 1850. Dickens Journals Online. http://www.djo.org.uk/household-narrative-of-current-events/year-1850.

Dostoyevsky, Fyodor. 1991. *Crime and Punishment*. Translated by David McDuff. London: Penguin.

Eliot, George. 2008. *Adam Bede*. Edited by Carol A. Martin. Oxford: Oxford University Press.

———. 2014. *Daniel Deronda*. Edited by Graham Handley and K. M. Newton. Oxford: Oxford University Press.

———. 2009. *The Lifted Veil and Brother Jacob*. Edited by Helen Small. Oxford: Oxford University Press.

———. 1994. *Middlemarch*. Edited by Rosemary Ashton. London: Penguin.

———. 1981. *The Mill on the Floss*. Edited by George Haight. Oxford: Oxford University Press.

———. 1993. *Romola*. Edited by Andrew Brown. Oxford: University Press.

———. 2008. *Silas Marner*. Edited by Terence Cave. Oxford: Oxford University Press.

———. 2009. *Scenes of Clerical Life*. Edited by Thomas A. Noble. Oxford: Oxford University Press.

Forster, John. 1874. *The Life of Charles Dickens*. 3 vols. London: Chapman and Hall.

Gaskell, Elizabeth. 1997. *The Letters of Elizabeth Gaskell*. Edited by J. A. V. Chapple and Arthur Pollard. Manchester: Manchester University Press.

———. 1971. *The Life of Charlotte Brontë*. London: Everyman.

———. 1996. *Mary Barton*. Edited by Macdonald Daly. London: Penguin.

———. 2008. *North and South*. Edited by Angus Easson. Oxford: Oxford University Press.

———. 2000. 'The Old Nurse's Story'. In *Gothic Tales*, edited by Laura Kranzler, 11–32. London: Penguin.

———. 1969. *Wives and Daughters*. Edited by Frank Glover Smith. Harmondsworth: Penguin.

Hardy, Thomas. 1997. *The Pursuit of the Well-Beloved* and *The Well-Beloved*. Edited by Patricia Ingham. London: Penguin.

———. 2008. *Tess of the D'Urbervilles*. Edited by Simon Gatrell, Juliet Grindle, and Penny Boumelha. Oxford: Oxford University Press.

Hemans, Felicia. 1875. *The Poems of Felicia Hemans*. London and Edinburgh: William P. Nimmo.

Hogg, James. 2001. *Private Memoirs and Confessions of a Justified Sinner*. Edited by Adrian Hunter. Ontario: Broadview Literary Texts.

James, Henry. 2011. *Notes of a Son and a Brother* and *The Middle Years: A Critical Edition*. Edited by Peter Collister. Charlottesville: University of Virginia Press.

———. 1992. *The Turn of the Screw and Other Stories*. Edited by T. J. Lustig. Oxford: Oxford University Press.

———. 1985. *What Maisie Knew*. Edited by Paul Theroux and Patricia Crick. London: Penguin.

Milton, John. 1997. *Paradise Lost*. Edited by Alastair Fowler. 2nd ed. Edinburgh: Pearson.

Moodie, Susanna. 2005. *Roughing It in the Bush*. New York: Cosimo Classics.

Ovid. 2008. *Metamorphoses*. Translated by A. D. Melville, with an Introduction and Notes by E. J. Kenney. Oxford: Oxford University Press.

———. 1826. *Ovid's Metamorphoses: Translated by Various Authors*. Translated by John Dryden et al. London.

Pankeyev, Sergei. 1989a. *The Memoirs of the Wolf Man*. In *The Wolf-Man and Sigmund Freud*. Edited and translated by Muriel Gardiner, 3–132. London: Karnac Books.

———. 1989b. 'My Recollections of Sigmund Freud'. In *The Wolf-Man and Sigmund Freud*, edited and translated by Muriel Gardiner, 135–152. London: Karnac Books.

Richardson, Samuel. 2008. *Pamela*. Edited by Thomas Keymer and Alice Wakely. Oxford: Oxford University Press.

Sala, George. 1853. 'Little Children'. *Household Words* 8, no. 192 (26 November): 289–293.

Shakespeare, William. 2008. *The Norton Shakespeare*. Edited by Stephen Greenblatt. London and New York: W. W. Norton.

Shelley, Mary. 2008. *Frankenstein: Or the Modern Prometheus: The 1818 Text*. Edited by Marilyn Butler. Oxford: Oxford University Press.

Shelley, Percy. 2002. 'On Love'. In *Shelley's Poetry and Prose*, edited by Donald H. Reiman and Neil Fraistat, 503–504. New York: W. W. Norton.

Sophocles. 1984. *The Three Theban Plays*. Translated by Robert Fagles. Rev. ed. London: Penguin.

Tasso, Torquato. 1600. *Jerusalem Delivered*. Translated by Edward Fairfax. London. http://www.gutenberg.org/cache/epub/392/pg392.html.

Tennyson, Alfred. 2007. *In Memoriam A. H. H.* In *Selected Poems*, edited by Christopher Ricks, 96–198. London: Penguin.

———. 2007. *Maud: A Monodrama*. In *Selected Poems*, edited by Christopher Ricks, 217–265. London: Penguin.

Walpole, Horace. 1968. *The Castle of Otranto*, in *Three Gothic Novels*, edited by Peter Fairclough, 87–148. London: Penguin.

Wordsworth, William. 1984. *The Major Works*. Edited by Stephen Gill. Oxford: Oxford University Press.

———. 1995. *The Prelude: The Four Texts*. Edited by Jonathan Wordsworth. London: Penguin.

Primary Psychoanalytic Texts

Abbreviations

SE: *The Standard Edition of the Complete Psychological Works of Sigmund Freud*. 2001. Translated from the German under the general editorship of James Strachey, in collaboration with Anna Freud and assisted by Alix Strachey and Allan Tyson. London: Vintage.

Abraham, Nicolas. 1994. 'Notes on the Phantom: A Complement to Freud's Metapsychology'. In Nicholas Abraham and Maria Torok, *The Shell and the*

Kernel: Renewals of Psychoanalysis. Edited and translated by Nicholas Rand, 171–176. Chicago: University of Chicago Press.

———. 1994. 'The Phantom of Hamlet: Or the Sixth Act: Preceded by the Intromission of Truth'. In Nicholas Abraham and Maria Torok, *The Shell and the Kernel: Renewals of Psychoanalysis*. Edited and translated by Nicholas Rand, 187–205. Chicago: University of Chicago Press.

Abraham, Nicolas and Maria Torok. 1994. '"The Lost Object—Me: Notes on Endocryptic Identification"'. In Nicholas Abraham and Maria Torok, *The Shell and the Kernel: Renewals of Psychoanalysis*. Edited and translated by Nicholas Rand, 139–156. Chicago: University of Chicago Press.

———. 1994. 'The Topography of Reality: Sketching a Metapsychology of Secrets'. In Nicholas Abraham and Maria Torok, *The Shell and the Kernel: Renewals of Psychoanalysis*. Edited and translated by Nicholas Rand, 157–161. Chicago: University of Chicago Press.

———. 1976. *The Wolf Man's Magic Word: A Cryptonymy*. Translated by Nicholas Rand. Minneapolis: University of Minnesota Press.

Breuer, Josef and Sigmund Freud. 2001. *Studies on Hysteria*. *SE* 2.

Freud, Sigmund.

———. 'The Aetiology of Hysteria'. *SE* 3:191–221.

———. *Beyond the Pleasure Principle*. *SE* 18:3–64.

———. 'A Case of Paranoia Running Counter to the Psychoanalytic Theory of the Disease'. *SE* 14:261–272.

———. 'A Child is Being Beaten'. *SE* 17:175–204.

———. 'Childhood Memories and Screen Memories'. In *The Psychopathology of Everyday Life*. *SE* 6:43–52.

———. 'Creative Writers and Daydreaming'. *SE* 9:141–154.

———. 'Delusions and Dreams in Jensen's *Gradiva*'. *SE* 9:3–96.

———. *The Ego and the Id*. *SE* 19:3–63.

———. *Fragment of an Analysis of a Case of Hysteria*. *SE* 7:3–122.

———. *From the History of an Infantile Neurosis*. *SE* 17:3–122.

———. 'Heredity and the Aetiology of the Neuroses'. *SE 3*:141–156.

———. *The Interpretation of Dreams*. *SE* 4 and 5.

———. 'Leonardo da Vinci and a Memory of his Childhood'. *SE* 11:63–137.

———. 'Letter 52'. *SE* 1:233–239.

———. 'Letter 69'. *SE* 1:259–260.

———. 'Letter 75'. *SE* 1: 268.

———. 'Mourning and Melancholia'. *SE* 14:237–260.

———. 'The Neuro-Psychoses of Defence'. *SE 3*:43–61.

———. *Notes upon a Case of Obsessional Neurosis*. *SE* 10:153–320.

———. 'On Narcissism: an Introduction'. *SE* 14:67–104.

———. 'On the History of the Psychoanalytic Movement'. *SE* 14:7–66.

———. 'A Project for a Scientific Psychology'. *SE* 1:283–397.

———. 'Screen Memories'. *SE* 3:301–322.
———. 'A Special Type of Choice of Object Made by Men (Contributions to the Psychology of Love I)'. *SE* 11:163–176.
———. 'The Theme of the Three Caskets'. *SE* 12:289–301.
———. *Three Essays on the Theory of Sexuality. SE* 7:125–245.
———. 'The Uncanny'. *SE* 17:217–256.
———. 'The Unconscious'. *SE* 14:161–215.
Gardiner, Muriel, ed. 1989. *The Wolf-Man and Sigmund Freud*. London: Karnac.
James, William. 1878. 'Remarks on Spencer's Definition of the Mind as Correspondence'. *The Journal of Speculative Philosophy* 12, no. 1 (January): 1–18.
———. 1890. 'The Hidden Self'. *Scribner's Magazine*. Vol. 7: 361–373. Online at https://babel.hathitrust.org/cgi/pt?id=coo.31924097557262&view=1up&seq=369&q1=William%20James.
Kristeva, Julia. 1989. *Black Sun: Depression and Melancholia*. Translated by Leon S. Roudiez. New York: Columbia University Press.
———. 2002. *Revolution in Poetic Language*. In *The Portable Kristeva*, edited and translated by Kelly Oliver, 27–70. New York: Columbia University Press.
Laplanche, Jean. 1999. *Essays on Otherness*. Edited by John Fletcher. Translated by Luke Thurston, Philip Slotkin, and Leslie Hill. London: Routledge.
———. 1980. *La Castration*. In *Problématiques II: Castration—Symbolisation*, 6–161. Paris: Presses Universitaires de France.
———. 2011. *Freud and the Sexual*. Edited by John Fletcher. Translated by John Fletcher, Jonathan House, and Nicholas Ray. London: International Psychoanalytic Books.
———.1999. 'Implantation, Intromission'. In *Essays on Otherness*, 133–137.
———. 1999. 'Interpretation Between Hermeneutics and Determinism'. In *Essays on Otherness*, 138–165.
———. 1976. *Life and Death in Psychoanalysis*. Translated by Jeffrey Mehlman. Baltimore: Johns Hopkins University Press.
———. 1999. 'Notes on Afterwardsness'. In *Essays on Otherness*, 260–265.
———. 1999. 'Reference to the Unconscious'. In *The Unconscious and the Id*, translated by Luke Thurston and Lindsay Watson, 1–121. London: Rebus Press.
———. 1999. 'A Short Treatise on the Unconscious'. In *Essays on Otherness*, 84–116.
———. 1999. 'Time and the Other'. In *Essays on Otherness*, 238–263.
———. 1999. 'Transference: Its Provocation by the Analyst'. In *Essays on Otherness*, 214–233.
———. 1999. 'The Unfinished Copernican Revolution'. In *Essays on Otherness*, 52–83.

Laplanche, Jean and Jean Bertrand Pontalis. 1986. 'Fantasy and the Origins of Sexuality'. In *Formations of Fantasy*, edited by Victor Burgin, James Donald and Cora Kaplan, 5–34. London: Methuen.

———. 1988. *The Language of Psychoanalysis*. Translated by Donald Nicholson Smith. London: Karnac.

Scarfone, Dominique. 2003. '"It Was *Not* My Mother": From Seduction to Negation'. *New Formations* 48: 69–76.

Schützenberger, Anne Ancelin. 1998. *The Ancestor Syndrome: Transgenerational Psychotherapy and Hidden Links in the Family Tree*. Translated by Anne Trager. London: Routledge.

Toubiana, Éric. 1988. *L'Héritage et sa Psychopathologie*. Paris: Presses Universitaires de France.

———. 2014. 'The Ides of March: From Mastery to Vampirism'. In *Seduction and Enigmas: Laplanche, Theory, Culture*, edited by John Fletcher and Nicholas Ray, and translated by Nicholas Ray, 176–208. London: Laurence and Wishart.

Secondary Texts

Ackroyd, Peter. 1994. *Dickens: A Memoir of Middle Age*. Abridged Edition. London: Mandarin.

Allott, Miriam, ed. 1974. *The Brontës: The Critical Heritage*. London and New York: Routledge.

Althusser, Louis. 1971. 'Ideology and Ideological State Apparatuses'. In *Lenin and Philosophy, and Other Essays*. Translated by Ben Brewster. London: New Left Books.

Appignanesi, Lisa and John Forrester. 1994. *Freud's Women*. London: Phoenix.

Armstrong, Nancy. 1987. *Desire and Domestic Fiction: A Political History of the Novel*. New York and Oxford: Oxford University Press.

Auerhahn, Nanette and Dori Laub. 1998. 'The Primal Scene of Atrocity: The Dynamic Interplay Between Knowledge and Fantasy of the Holocaust in the Children of Survivors'. *Psychoanalytic Psychology* 15, no. 3: 360–377.

Bachman, Maria K. and Don Richard Cox. 2003. 'Wilkie Collins' Villainous Miss Gwilt, Criminality and the Unspeakable Truth'. *Dickens Studies Annual* 32: 319–337.

Baker, William. 2002. *Wilkie Collins and His Library*. London: Greenwood.

Barker, Juliet. 2010 [1994] *The Brontës*. London: Abacus.

Bateson, Gregory. 1972. *Steps to an Ecology of Mind*. Chicago and London: Chicago University Press.

Beer, Gillian. 1983. *Darwin's Plots: Evolutionary Narrative in Darwin, George Eliot and Nineteenth-Century Fiction*. London: Routledge & Kegan & Paul.

Berry, Laura. 1999. *The Child, the State and the Victorian Novel*. Charlottesville: University of Virginia Press.
Bodenheimer, Rosemarie. 2001. 'Knowing and Telling in Dickens's Retrospects'. In *Knowing the Past: Victorian Literature and Culture*, edited by Suzy Anger, 215–233. Ithaca: Cornell University Press.
———. 2007. *Knowing Dickens*. Ithaca: Cornell University Press.
Bowlby, Rachel. 2007a. *Freudian Mythologies: Greek Tragedy and Modern Identities*. Oxford: Oxford University Press.
———. 2007b. Foreword to *Adventures in Realism*. Edited by Matthew Beaumont, x–xviii. Oxford: Blackwell.
Brodie, Benjamin. 1834. *Pathological Diseases of the Joints*. 3rd ed. Washington: Duff Green.
Brooks, Peter. 1992. *Reading for the Plot: Design and Intention in Narrative*. Cambridge, MA: Harvard University Press.
Broughton, Trev Lynn and Helen Rogers, eds. 2007. *Gender and Fatherhood in the Nineteenth Century*. Basingstoke: Palgrave Macmillan.
Burke, Edmund. 1764. *A Philosophical Enquiry into the Origins of our Ideas of the Sublime and the Beautiful*. 4th ed. London.
Burnham, John. 1986. *Family Therapy*. London: Tavistock Publishing.
Butler, Judith. 1993. *Bodies That Matter: On the Discursive Limits of Sex*. New York and London: Routledge.
———. 2005. *Giving an Account of Oneself*. New York: Fordham University Press.
———. 2004. *Precarious Life: The Powers of Mourning and Violence*. London: Verso.
———. 2014. 'Seduction, Gender and the Drive'. In *Seduction and Enigmas: Laplanche, Theory, Culture*, edited by John Fletcher and Nicholas Ray, and translated by Nicholas Ray, 118–134. London: Laurence and Wishart.
Cain, Lynn. 2008. *Dickens, Family, Authorship: Psychoanalytic Perspectives on Kinship and Creativity*. Aldershot: Ashgate.
Carpenter, William. 1855. *Principles of Human Physiology: With Their Chief Applications to Psychology, Pathology, Therapeutics, Hygiene and Forensic Medicine*. 5th ed. London: John Churchill.
———. 1875 [1874]. *Principles of Mental Physiology: With Their Applications to the Training and Discipline of the Mind and the Study of Morbid Conditions*. New York: D. Appleton and Co.
Caruth, Cathy. 1995. Introduction to Part II, 'Recapturing the Past'. In *Trauma: Explorations in Memory*, 151–157. Baltimore: Johns Hopkins University Press.
———. 1996a. 'Traumatic Departures: Survival and History in Freud'. In *Trauma and Self*, edited by Charles B. Strozier and Michael Flynn, 29–44. London: Rowman and Littlefield.

———. 1996b. *Unclaimed Experience: Trauma, Narrative, History.* Baltimore: Johns Hopkins University Press.
Chambers, Robert. 1887. *Vestiges of the Natural History of Creation.* Glasgow: George Routledge and Sons.
Collins, Philip. 1984. 'Dickens's Autobiographical Fragment and David Copperfield'. *Cahiers Victoriens et Edouardiens* 20: 87–96.
Conolly, John. 1830. *An Inquiry Concerning the Indications of Insanity: With Suggestions for the Better Protection and Care of the Insane.* London: John Taylor.
Darwin, Charles. 1985. *On the Origin of Species by Means of Natural Selection: Or, the Preservation of Favoured Races in the Struggle for Life.* Edited by J. W. Burrow. London: Penguin.
Davidoff, Leonore and Catherine Hall. 2002. *Family Fortunes: Men and Women of the English Middle Class 1780–1850.* Rev. ed. London: Routledge.
Derrida, Jacques. 1976. Foreword: *Fors*: The Anglish Words of Nicholas Abraham and Maria Torok. In *The Wolf Man's Magic Word: A Cryptonymy*, translated by Nicholas Rand, xi–xlviii. Minneapolis: Minneapolis University Press.
Dever, Carolyn. 1998. *Death and the Mother from Dickens to Freud: Victorian Fictions and the Anxiety of Origins.* Cambridge: Cambridge University Press.
Douglas-Fairhurst, Robert. 2011. *Becoming Dickens.* Cambridge, MA: The Belknap Press of Harvard University Press.
Ellenberger, Henri. 1981. *The Discovery of the Unconscious: The History and Evolution of Dynamic Psychology.* New York: Basic Books.
Elliotson, John. 1846. 'Instances of Double States of Consciousness Independent of Mesmerism'. *The Zoist: A Journal of Cerebral Physiology & Mesmerism* 14 (July): 157–187.
Englander, David. 1998. *Poverty and Poor Law Reform in Nineteenth-Century Britain, 1834–1914: From Chadwick to Booth.* London: Longman.
Fletcher, John. 2013. *Freud and the Scene of Trauma.* New York: Fordham University Press.
———. 2002. 'Freud, Hoffmann and the Death-Work'. *Angelaki* 7, no. 2: 125–141.
———. 1999. 'Introduction: Psychoanalysis and the Question of the Other'. In *Essays on Otherness*, by Jean Laplanche, 1–51. London: Routledge.
Furneaux, Holly. 2009. *Queer Dickens: Erotics, Families, Masculinities.* Oxford: Oxford University Press.
Gallop, Jane. 1984. *Feminism and Psychoanalysis: The Daughter's Seduction.* Ithaca: Cornell University Press.
Gilchrist, Alexander. 1863. *Life of William Blake, 'Pictor Ignotus', with Selections from His Poems and Other Writings.* London and Cambridge: Macmillan.

Greenberg, Judith. 1998.'The Echo of Trauma and the Trauma of Echo'. *American Imago* 55, no. 3: 319–347.
Hamilton, William. 1998. 'Three Degrees of Mental Latency'. In *Embodied Selves: An Anthology of Psychological Texts 1830–1890*, edited by Sally Shuttleworth and Jenny Bourne Taylor, 80–82. Oxford: Oxford University Press.
Hartley, David. 1834. *Observations on Man: His Frame, His Duty and His Expectations*. 6th ed. London: Thomas Tegg and Son.
Hertz, Neil. 1990 [1985]. 'Dora's Secrets, Freud's Techniques'. In *In Dora's Case: Freud, Hysteria, Feminism*, edited by Charles Bernheimer and Claire Kahane, 2nd ed., 221–242. New York: Columbia University Press.
Hillis Miller, J. 1982. *Fiction and Repetition: Seven English Novels*. Cambridge, MA: Harvard University Press.
———. 1975. 'Optic and Semiotic in Middlemarch'. In *The Worlds of Victorian Fiction*, edited by Jerome H. Buckley, 125–143. Cambridge, MA: Harvard University Press.
Hume, David. 2007. *A Treatise of Human Nature*, edited by David Fate Norton and Mary J. Norton. The Clarendon Edition of the Works of David Hume. Vol. 1. Oxford: Clarendon Press.
Ikonen, P. and E. Rechardt. 1984. 'On the Universal Nature of Primal Scene Fantasies'. *International Journal of Psychoanalysis* 65, no. 1: 63–72.
Janet, Pierre. 1889. *L'Automatisme psychologique: Essai de psychologie expérimentale sur les formes inferieures de l'activité humaine*. Paris: Félix Alcan.
Jordan, John O. 1983. 'The Medium of Great Expectations'. *Dickens Studies Annual* 11: 73–88.
———. 2011. *Supposing Bleak House*. Virginia: Virginia University Press.
Kaplan, Fred. 1988. *Dickens: A Biography*. London: Hodder and Stoughton.
Klimazewski, Melisa. 2006. 'The Contested Site of Maternity in Dombey and Son'. In *The Literary Mother: Essays on Representation, Maternity and Childcare*, edited by Susan Staub, 138–158. Jefferson, NC: McFarland.
van der Kolk, Bessel A. 2005. 'Developmental Trauma: Toward a Rational Diagnosis for Children with Complex Trauma Histories'. *Psychiatric Annals* 35, no. 5: 402–408.
———. ed. 1987. *Psychological Trauma*. Arlington, VA: American Psychiatric Press.
van der Kolk, Bessel A. and Onno van der Hart. 1995. 'The Intrusive Past: The Flexibility of Memory and the Engraving of Trauma'. In *Trauma: Explorations in Memory*, edited by Cathy Caruth. Baltimore: John Hopkins University Press.
LaCapra, Dominick. 1985. *History and Psychoanalysis*. Minneapolis: Minnesota University Press.

———. 2001. *Writing History, Writing Trauma*. Baltimore: Johns Hopkins University Press.

Lerner, Paul. 2001. 'From Traumatic Neurosis to Male Hysteria: The Decline and Fall of Hermann Oppenheim, 1889–1919. In *Traumatic Pasts: History, Psychiatry, and Trauma in the Modern Age, 1870–1930*, edited by Paul Lerner and Mark S. Micale, 140–171. Cambridge: Cambridge University Press.

Lerner, Paul and Mark S. Micale, eds. 2001. *Traumatic Pasts: History, Psychiatry, and Trauma in the Modern Age, 1870–1930*. Cambridge: Cambridge University Press.

Lesnik-Oberstein, Karin. 2002. '*Holiday House*: Grist to *The Mill on the Floss*, or Childhood as Text'. *The Yearbook of English Studies* 32: 77–94.

Levine, George. 1988. *Darwin and the Novelists: Patterns of Science in Victorian Fiction*. Cambridge, MA: Harvard University Press.

———. 1973. 'Frankenstein and the Tradition of Realism'. *Novel: A Forum on Fiction* 7, no. 1: 14–30.

Leys, Ruth. 2007. *From Guilt to Shame: Auschwitz and After*. Princeton: Princeton University Press.

———. 2000. *Trauma: A Genealogy*. Chicago: University of Chicago Press.

Locke, John. 2014. *Essay Concerning Human Understanding*. Ware: Wordsworth Editions.

———. 2007. *Some Thoughts Concerning Education*. Edited by John William Adamson. Mineola, NY: Dover Publications, Inc.

Lukits, Steve. 2008. 'The Devastated Nest: Crises of Identity in *Wuthering Heights* and *Antigone*'. *Mosaic: A Journal for the Interdisciplinary Study of Literature* 41, no. 3 (September): 103–116.

Malthus, Thomas. 1809. *An Essay on the Principle of Population: Or, A View of Its Past and Present Effects on Human Happiness with an Inquiry into Our Prospects Respecting the Future Removal or Migration of the Evils Which It Occasions*. Vol. 1. Washington City: Roger Chew Wrightman.

Marcus, Steven. 1985. *Dickens, From Pickwick to Dombey*. London: W. W. Norton.

Marx, Karl. 1990. *Capital*. Vol. 1. Translated by Ben Fowks. London: Penguin.

Masson, J. M. 1984. *The Assault on Truth: Freud's Suppression of the Seduction Theory*. New York: Farrar, Straus and Giroux.

———. trans. and ed. 1985. *The Complete Letters of Sigmund Freud to Wilhelm Fliess, 1887–1904*. Cambridge MA: Harvard University Press.

Matus, Jill. 2009. *Shock, Memory and the Unconscious in Victorian Fiction*. Cambridge: Cambridge University Press.

McDonagh, Josephine. 1987. 'Writings on the Mind: Thomas De Quincey and the Importance of the Palimpsest in Nineteenth-Century Thought'. *Prose Studies* 10, no. 2 (September): 207–224.

———. 2013. 'Rethinking Provincialism in Mid-Nineteenth-Century Fiction: *Our Village* to *Villette*'. *Victorian Studies* 55, No. 3 (Spring): 399–424.

Miller, D. A. 1988. *The Novel and the Police*. Berkeley: University of California Press.

Miller, Lucasta. 2001. *The Brontë Myth*. London: Vintage.

Nadler, Steven, ed. 2002. *A Companion to Early Modern Philosophy*. Oxford: Blackwell.

Nares, Robert. 1825. *A Glossary or, Collection of Words, Phrase, Names, Allusions to Customs, Proverbs, etc. in the Works of English Authors, Particularly of Shakespeare and His Contemporaries*. Stralsund: Charles Loeffler.

Newsom, Robert. 1983. 'The Hero's Shame'. *Dickens Studies Annual* 11: 1–24.

Oppenheim, Hermann. 1892 [1889]. *Die traumatischen Neurosen nach den in der Nervenklinik der Charité in den letzten 5 Jahren gesammelten Beobachtungen*. Berlin: Hirschwald.

Peters, Catherine. 1991. *The King of Inventors: A Life of Wilkie Collins*. London: Minerva.

Poovey, Mary. 1989. *Uneven Development: The Ideological Work of Gender in Mid-Victorian England*. London: Virago.

Pykett, Lyn. 2002. *Charles Dickens: Critical Issues*. Basingstoke: Palgrave Macmillan.

Prichard, James. 1837 [1835]. *A Treatise on Insanity and Other Disorders Affecting the Mind*. Philadelphia: E. L. Carey & A. Hart.

Rand, Nicholas T. 'Editor's Note'. In Nicholas Abraham and Maria Torok, *The Shell and the Kernel: Renewals of Psychoanalysis*. Edited and translated by Nicholas Rand, 207–209. Chicago: University of Chicago Press.

Reitz, Caroline. 2000. 'Colonial "Gwilt" in and Around *Armadale*'. *Victorian Periodicals Review* 33, no. 1: 92–103.

Richardson, Alan. 1994. *Literature, Education, and Romanticism: Reading as Social Practice, 1780–1832*. Cambridge: Cambridge University Press.

Rose, Jacqueline. 1992 [1984]. *The Case of Peter Pan: Or the Impossibility of Children's Fiction*. Philadelphia: Pennsylvania University Press.

———. 1991. *The Haunting of Sylvia Plath*. London: Virago.

Rousseau, Jean Jacques. 1979. *Emile: On Education*. Translated by Allan Bloom. New York: Basic Books.

Schor, Hilary. 1999. *Dickens and the Daughter of the House*. Cambridge: Cambridge University Press.

Secord, James. 2000. *Victorian Sensation: The Extraordinary Publication, Reception, and Secret Authorship of Vestiges of the Natural History of Creation*. Chicago: Chicago University Press.

Sedgwick, Eve Kosofsky. 1985. *Between Men: English Literature and Male Homosocial Desire*. New York: Columbia University Press.

Shuttleworth, Sally. 1984. *George Eliot and Nineteenth-Century Science: The Make-Believe of a Beginning*. Cambridge: Cambridge University Press.

———. 2010. *The Mind of the Child: Child Development in Literature, Science and Medicine, 1840–1900*. Oxford: Oxford University Press.

Shuttleworth, Sally, and Jenny Bourne Taylor, eds. 1998. *Embodied Selves: An Anthology of Psychological Texts 1830–1890*. Oxford: Oxford University Press.

Slater, Michael. 2009. *Charles Dickens*. New Haven: Yale University Press.

Spencer, Herbert. 1864. *Principles of Biology*. London: William and Norgate.

———. 1855. *Principles of Psychology*. London: Longman, Brown, Green and Longmans.

Spivak, Gayatri Chakravorty. 2010. 'Can the Subaltern Speak?' In *Can the Subaltern Speak? Reflections on the History of an Idea*, edited by Rosalind Morris, Rev. ed., 21–78. New York: Columbia University Press.

Steedman, Carolyn. 1995. *Strange Dislocations: Childhood and the Idea of Human Interiority*. London: Virago.

Swinburne, Algernon. 1868. *William Blake: A Critical Essay*. London: John Camden Hotten. http://www.gutenberg.org/files/35995/35995-h/35995-h.htm.

Taylor, Jenny Bourne. 1988. *In the Secret Theatre of Home: Wilkie Collins, Sensation Narrative, and Nineteenth-Century Psychology*. London: Routledge.

Thormählen, Marianne. 2014. *The Brontës in Context*. Cambridge: Cambridge University Press.

Uglow, Jenny. 1993. *Elizabeth Gaskell*. London: Faber and Faber.

Vine, Steve. 1999. 'Crypts of Identity: The Refusal of Mourning in *Wuthering Heights*'. *English* 48, no. 192 (Autumn): 169–186.

Webb, Nancy Boyd. 2015. 'Family and Community Contexts of Children and Adolescents Facing Crisis or Trauma. In *Play Therapy with Children and Adolescents in Crisis*, edited by Nancy Boyd, 4th ed., 3–21. New York, NY: The Guildford Press.

Weeks, Jeffrey. 2008. 'The Sphere of the Intimate and the Values of Everyday Life'. In *Modern Criticism and Theory: A Reader*, edited by David Lodge and Nigel Wood, 3rd ed., 641–664. Harlow: Pearson Longman.

Welsh, Alexander. 1987. *From Copyright to Copperfield*. Cambridge, MA: Harvard University Press.

Wiley, Margaret. 1996. 'Mother's Milk and Dombey's Son'. *Dickens Quarterly* 13, no. 4: 217–228.

Wilson, Edmund. 1941. *The Wound and the Bow: Seven Studies in Literature*. Boston: Houghton Mifflin.

Wilson, Richard. 1993. *Will Power: Essays on Shakespearean Authority*. London: Harvester Wheatsheaf.

Wood, Madeleine. 2012. 'Female Narrative Energy in the Writings of Dead White Males: Dickens, Collins and Freud'. In *Cross-Gendered Literary Voices:*

Appropriating, Resisting, Embracing, edited by Rina Kim and Claire Westall, 15–35. Basingstoke: Palgrave Macmillan.
Young, Robert. 2007. *The Idea of English Ethnicity*. Oxford: Wiley Blackwell.
Žižek, Slavoj. 1989. *The Sublime Object of Ideology*. London: Verso.

Index

M. Wood, *Parents and Children in the Mid-Victorian Novel*,
https://doi.org/10.1007/978-3-030-45469-2

G

Printed in Great Britain
by Amazon

43611017R00205